The History of Clinical Psychology in Autobiography

Volume I

Edited by

C. Eugene Walker

University of Oklahoma Health Sciences Center

Brooks/Cole Publishing Company
Pacific Grove, California

To James D. Linden,
Professor, Mentor, Friend

Consulting Editor: *C. Eugene Walker*
Brooks/Cole Publishing Company
A Division of Wadsworth, Inc.

Printed in the United States of America
10 9 8 7 6 5 4 3 2 1

Library of Congress Cataloging-in-Publication Data
The History of clinical psychology in autobiography/edited by C.
Eugene Walker.
       p.   cm. — (Brooks/Cole professional books)
    Includes bibliographical references.
    ISBN 0-534-14436-5 (v. 1)
    1. Clinical psychology—Biography.   2. Clinical psychology-
-History.   I. Walker, C. Eugene (Clarence Eugene), [date].
II. Series.
    [DNLM: 1. Psychology, Clinical—biography.   2. Psychology,
Clinical—history.   WZ 112.5.P6 H673]
RC466.8.H57   1990
616.89′0092′2—dc20
DNLM/DLC
for Library of Congress   90-2241
                                                            CIP

Sponsoring Editor: *Claire Verduin*
Editorial Assistant: *Gay C. Bond*
Production Editor: *Marjorie Z. Sanders*
Manuscript Editor: *Jessie Wood*
Permissions Editor: *Marie DuBois*
Interior and Cover Design: *Katherine Minerva*
Art Coordinator: *Lisa Torri*
Typesetting: *BookPrep*
Printing and Binding: *Arcata Graphics/Fairfield*

Preface

◆

The modern era of clinical psychology spans a scant 45 or 50 years, having grown largely from the impetus of the need for mental health services for military personnel during World War II and for veterans after the conflict. Thus the individuals who pioneered the field and shaped the current course of the discipline are still very much with us. Many are still professionally active, while others are enjoying active retirement. With this in mind, the present editor determined to begin a series of volumes of autobiographical essays by these founders of the field. New volumes will appear periodically, as new contributors are identified.

Numerous individual works and series of autobiographical essays have already been published in the field of psychology. These have proved to be worthwhile and significant contributions. The present series, concentrating on the field of clinical psychology, is presented with the hope that it will be similarly valuable and yet unique. Although this series will attempt to present a history of clinical psychology in autobiography, it is not merely a history of clinical psychologists. We intend to include in this series many individuals who were primarily researchers but whose work greatly influenced the thinking and work of clinical psychologists. We will also include representatives from other fields such as psychiatry, sociology, and education who have had a major impact on the field of clinical psychology.

My sincere appreciation is expressed to Division 12 of the American Psychological Association and its advisory board: Charles D. Spielberger, Chair, and board members Theodora M. Abel, Norman Abeles, Roderick W. Pugh, Jerome Resnick, Donald Routh, and Rogers Wright. I am greatly impressed with the willingness of the authors of the essays included in the present volume to share their experiences and their thoughts with us. These authors tell us of their successes and their failures, their friends and their enemies, their contributions and their mistakes. It is my hope that those who are pursuing a career in clinical psychology, or who are simply interested in the field, will find these essays exciting and valuable.

C. Eugene Walker
Oklahoma City, 1990

Brooks/Cole Professional Books

◆

Consulting Editor: C. Eugene Walker

*Family Therapy and Beyond: A Multisystemic Approach to Treating the
Behavior Problems of Children and Adolescents*
Scott W. Henggeler and Charles M. Borduin

Changing Expectations: A Key to Effective Psychotherapy
Irving Kirsch

Panic Disorders and Agoraphobia: A Comprehensive Guide for the Practitioner
John R. Walker, G. Ron Norton, and Colin A. Ross, Editors

The History of Clinical Psychology in Autobiography, Volumes I and II
C. Eugene Walker, Editor

Contents

◆

Albert Ellis, Ph.D.

President, Institute for Rational-Emotive Therapy
New York, New York

◆

My Life in Clinical Psychology

Birth, Family Background, Early Years[1]

I do not believe that the events of my childhood greatly influenced my becoming a psychotherapist, nor oriented me to becoming the kind of individual and the type of therapist that I now am. That notion is the "psychoanalytic bag," and fortunately I am no longer suffocating in that particular bag. Having nicely survived my own psychoanalysis, and having achieved a reasonable degree of self-realization in spite of my early devotion to the psychoanalytic *mishigas* (with which I not only afflicted myself but also, alas, helped inflict on a good many poor innocent analysands whom I treated when I first became a therapist), I now believe that children bring to their early environments (and to their benighted and entrapped parents) their own powerful innate predispositions to act in highly individualized ways. Consequently, I hypothesize, I was almost as instrumental in raising my mother (and, to an even greater degree, my younger brother and sister) as she was in raising me. But since the editor of

---

[1]This section is adapted from A. Ellis, "Psychotherapy Without Tears," in Arthur Burton (Ed.), *Twelve Therapists.* San Francisco: Jossey-Bass, 1971. Used with permission.

this volume has asked for some material on my early life, and since many readers are likely to be plain damned curious about what happened to me before I began sprinting along psychotherapeutic pathways, let me begin with some of my beginnings.

In many ways, my early life was replete with poor circumstances. For one thing, I was always a semiorphan. My father, a traveling salesman and a promoter at that time, was frequently away from home for weeks or months on end. When he was living with us, he was so busy with his daytime business activities and his nighttime pinochle games (or running around with attractive women, or whatever the hell else he did) that my younger brother and sister and I literally spent about five minutes a day with him, kissing him goodbye in the morning, just before we scooted off to school. Saturday and Sunday were again (as far as I could tell) mainly card-playing days for him, and only occasionally did he take an hour or two for a drive with us, in our chauffeur-driven electric Cadillac. When he finally was divorced from my mother (I was 12, my brother 10, and my sister 8), he was so devoted to our welfare that he came around to visit us less than once a year—even though most of the time he lived only a few miles away in Manhattan, while we were being raised on the streets of the Bronx.

As for my nice Jewish mother, a hell of a lot of help she was! Born at least 20 years before her time, thrown out of school in the sixth grade for compulsive talking, and quite unequipped to deal adequately with either marriage or child-rearing, she was much more immersed in her own pleasures and her own ego-aggrandizing activities than she was in understanding and taking care of her children. Her typical day: she arose about eight forty-five (after her 8-year-old son, Albert, had already awakened himself with the alarm clock, dressed, made his own breakfast, and started for school, crossing three of the busiest and most dangerous streets in the Bronx). She sloppily and desultorily did a minimum of cleaning, shopping, and child-tending. She spent most afternoons at her temple sisterhood functions or playing bridge or mah-jongg with some of her woman friends. She returned home around five or six (long after her son Albert had come home from school, made himself a snack, and helped take care of his younger brother and sister). She cooked or brought from the delicatessen very simple, ill-prepared meals that required a minimum of effort. And she spent most nights with her friends (most of them 15 or more years younger than she and from a lower socioeconomic stratum), quite unrelated to her children (and often out of the house, leaving them unattended, in the charge of brother Albert).

As if all this parental neglect were not enough, I had a few other problems as a child. When I was 5, I almost died of tonsillitis and suffered, as a sequel, acute nephritis or nephrosis (the doctors never did decide the differential diagnosis). During the next few years, I went into Presbyterian Hospital about eight times, once for a period of ten months. As a result of this hospitalization and my convalescence from it, I was forbidden to take active part in any of the usual childhood games for months on end. Sportswise, I developed into something of a sissy; soon my brother was easily able to surpass me in every conceivable athletic respect. He was also a courageous, happy-go-lucky extrovert, while I was unusually shy and introverted, and particularly afraid of any kind of public presentation during my childhood and adolescence. Finally, to augment these hassles (and many more like them), my solidly middle-class family was soundly whacked by the Great Depression of 1929 (when I was 17), and when my mother's savings were completely wiped out and my father (who was still living fairly comfortably) refused to pay her a cent of the tens of thousands of dollars of alimony he owed her, our family came within a hair of going on welfare.

Despite all this, I somehow refused to be miserable. I took my father's absence and my mother's neglect in stride—and even felt good about being allowed so much autonomy and independence. I ignored my physical disabilities and determined to take care of my health in a rigorous manner so that I would no longer be subject to the frequent headaches and other pains I then had. I decided not to hate my mother for her ineptness and used it instead to twist her around my little finger, and even in some ways to exploit her. I allowed—in fact, almost encouraged—my brother to get into one scrape after another (while I played the nice-boy role) and my sister to whine about her sorry lot (while I a little chivalrously protected her from my brother, who could not stand her whinyness and often tried to beat her to a pulp).

I beautifully protected my shyness by refusing to participate in any public performances, even minor classroom plays, and by refraining from risking overtures to any of the female neighors and classmates with whom I kept serially falling madly in love from the age of 5 onward. Not that I didn't suffer at all: I sometimes had to recite a poem in class or ascend the auditorium podium to accept an award, and at those times I sweated and sizzled with anxiety and desperately looked for (and sometimes managed to cleverly find) some way out. And I never did make it, sexually or otherwise, with any of those girls of whom I was enamored until my early twenties, because I wouldn't even risk dating, much less pulling up the skirts of any of them.

So I suffered more by omission than by commission, and for all my neurotic tendencies, I cannot say that I led anything but a pretty happy childhood. Which, come to think of it, is interesting. For I am reminded that my mother, too, for all her blabber-mouthness, her feelings of inadequacy, and her inability to achieve anything significant in life and work at a level anywhere near her potential (she was always a talented actress-singer-comedienne, as well as a real beauty, and might have gotten somewhere in the theatrical world had she ever really tried), was rarely really unhappy, in spite of troubles and traumas that would have knocked the average woman of her day into severe states of depression. My father and brother, too—each of whom has had his share of worldly troubles, and perhaps a bit more—have seldom been depressed. Only my sister, the most pampered and least put-upon of my immediate family, suffered fairly continuously from anxiety, self-hatred, and depression. Which leads me to wonder, once again, about the genetic rather than the psychologically overemphasized environmental sources of emotional disturbance.

Anyway, my difficult childhood helped me do one important thing: become a stubborn and pronounced problem solver. If life, I said to myself, is going to be so damned rough and hassle-filled, what the devil can I do to live successfully and happily nevertheless? I soon found the answer: use my head! So I figured out how to become my nutty mother's favorite child, how to get along with both my brother and sister in the spite of their continual warring with each other, and how to live fairly happily without giving up my shyness.

Does this mean that the difficulties I encountered *caused* me to become unusually rational during my childhood? Not that I can see. For my sister had her own share of problems. She was the only female child; she had almost every possible manifestation of allergy, as well as a host of other physical afflictions; she had closer contact with and was treated more inconsistently by my mother than the rest of us; she was somewhat persecuted by my brother; she was the youngest child and, although bright, was not able to compete with her two unusually clever brothers; and she had various other handicaps. Why, then, didn't she, like me, develop more problem-solving skills?

My answer is partly that she was born with a whiny, demanding, injustice-collecting temperament and that consequently she *chose* to make the worst of her childhood conditions. Later on, as she entered the second 50 years of her life, she worked very hard against her temperamental handicaps, used rational-emotive therapy (RET) to achieve a saner way of living, and began to be much happier. I, fortunately, was never quite *that* crazy; and in spite of my natural predisposition toward anxiety, shyness, and inhibition, I seemed to have a biological tendency toward objectively perceiving, scientifically assessing, and often energetically correcting my own irrational behavior.

I was also innately inclined to build some consummately clever defenses. My mother busied herself so much with avocational and entertainment pursuits that she left herself little time for overt self-hatred. My brother acted out so many of his frustrations and hostilities—by refusing to do his homework, for example, and by sassing his teachers when they got after him about it—that he became a notorious rebel and achieved a villainous kind of acclaim. My sister whined so much about my mother's favoring "the boys" (a favoring that was almost completely a figment of her imagination since, by her whimpering, she actually managed to get most of the favors) that some people actually took pity on her. But I did even better: I did so well in my schoolwork, in being tractable and kind with practically everyone, in mastering the art of understanding others, in developing interesting hobbies (especially voracious reading), and in various other constructive pursuits that I could genuinely like myself for my accomplishments.

In other words, I built a whale of a lot of false self-esteem. So what if I was fairly lousy at sports, in manly aggressiveness, and in asserting myself with any of the girls with whom I was madly (and completely silently!) in love? So what if my brother and most of my close friends were better than I was in these respects? Who was better at English, math, history, and ten other subjects than I? Who would all my friends and classmates come to for practical advice? Who was more favored by practically every adult woman? Who better figured out (until, at the age of 12, he became an unregenerate atheist) what God really wanted people to do to get in His good graces? And who best (albeit with a little backsliding) stuck to this kind of heaven-promulgated conduct?

In sum, the conditions of my childhood were in many ways worse than those of most of my contemporaries. But I basically liked myself for the wrong reasons: I took these conditions as problems to be surmounted and I rather cleverly, and with deliberately arranged-for social approval, surmounted them. I based my worth as a human being—which I now realize is quite an error—on my achievements and my popularity; but I did such a good job of using this wrong method that I had a fairly happy, productive childhood (Ellis, 1962b, 1973c, 1988b; Ellis & Harper, 1975).

College and Graduate Education

I went to the High School of Commerce in New York, mainly because I had decided to be a writer who could write anything he wanted without having to depend on how well it sold. So I decided in 1927 to be an accountant, make a lot of money, and retire around 30, free to write anything I wanted.

Unfortunately, between 1927 and 1930, when I graduated from high school, the stock market crashed and we were in the midst of the Great Depression. There went my resolve to be a young millionaire! Nonetheless, I decided to take a B.B.A. degree at the Baruch School of Business and Civic Administration of City College and to do as much writing as I could right then and there. I also found accounting, my major, too easy and boring, and began to write comic verses and song lyrics in class, to make life more interesting. I did well in college, as I had always done in high school, with a minimum of work, but I did work hard at becoming the school poet and the main columnist for the school paper. I specialized in writing comic triolets, such as these:

Triolet on Love

I love a lass,
I love a miss,
You can't surpass.
I love a lass
Who's of the class
That will not kiss.
I love—alas!
I love amiss!

Triolet on Head Gear

I told her that
She had a fit
In her new hat.
I told her that,
With head so fat,
She fitted it.
I told her *that*
She had a fit!

Triolet on Dough

"You love me, dear."
She said: "I? No!"
"Ah, have no fear:
You love me, dear—
For I have here
A lot of dough.
You love me, dear."
She said: "I know."

Triolet on a Bored Lover

"I
Go."
"Why?"
"I
Sigh—"
"Oh?"
"I"—
"Go!"

In college, I took a bare minimum of accounting courses and really, without the school authorities realizing it, majored in English. I would have taken several psychology courses, too, but then we only had general psychology (which I didn't like) and applied psychology (which I did) with Alexander Mintz, who *was* the psychology department at Baruch at that time. I did well in his classes and became friendly with him, partly because we were both nonbusiness people and were mutually interested in socialist philosophy. Oh, yes, he was also impressed by my scoring in the 99th percentile on the Army Alpha Intelligence Test. I thought at that time of becoming a psychologist but decided that I would write psychological novels instead.

Since the Depression was on, I would have been wise to study to be a teacher of accounting in the New York City high schools by taking a few extra courses in education before I graduated from college. But I was still phobic about public speaking, as I had been since childhood. I got myself over this phobia a little later by using in vivo desensitization, which I learned from reading about John B. Watson's experiments with little children. So instead of teaching, I got a variety of small and unimportant jobs to keep from starving to death while I kept writing, writing, writing.

While I was still in college, I wrote a 500,000-word autobiographical novel; and between the ages of 19 and 28 I finished no fewer than 20 full-length manuscripts, including several novels, plays, books of poems, and nonfiction volumes. At first I intended to be the Great American Novelist, but after writing six novels, with no takers, I realized that was not meant to be. So I decided to concentrate on nonfiction instead. I almost had some books published, especially my simplified, question-and-answer version of the three volumes of Marx's *Das Kapital,* which I wrote to show socialist revolutionaries that Marx was really wrong about his theory of surplus value and that if they wanted to get on more efficiently with the revolution, they had better forget him and get a better theory.

I was never sympathetic to the Communist party, because of its dogma and its dedication to a dictatorship in the Soviet Union, and I became disillusioned with socialism, too, as I observed its economic failings. So I decided to start my own kind of revolution by collecting an immense amount of data and writing another 500,000-word book entitled *A History of the Dark Ages: The Twentieth Century.* Its main theme was that the Middle Ages were dark indeed, but mainly because of ignorance, while in the twentieth century we have dispelled much of that ignorance but still behave incredibly stupidly in almost all important areas, such as politics, economics, religion, and health. I received many fine rejection letters on this book, but nothing close to an acceptance.

Nothing daunted, I started still another potential masterpiece, *The Case for Sexual Promiscuity.* Five hundred thousand words later, it too was finished—to no avail. I received another batch of great rejection letters, but no publication offer until almost 20 years later, when the first—and only—volume of it was published by Rey Anthony, the infamous author of *The Housewife's Handbook on Selective Promiscuity,* as *The Case for Sexual Liberty* (Ellis, 1965a).

Sex, however, finally paid off and catapulted me into the field of clinical psychology. In order to write so authoritatively on promiscuity, and especially to pursue my long-time interest in romantic love, I read hundreds of books and thousands of articles on sex, love, and marriage and became something of a walking encyclopedia of erotic fiction and nonfiction. My friends started asking me to help solve their personal sexuo-amative problems, and somewhat to my surprise I found that I was able to be of considerable help to them. What is more, I greatly enjoyed counseling them. Since my writing was still getting me nowhere financially, and since I had done very well in several business jobs over the years but had no real liking for commercial ventures, I decided that it was time to get a real profession and some status as a counselor, so I began graduate training in psychology.

I thought that Columbia University had the best psychology department at that time, so I applied there, but ran into serious trouble with the head of the department, the well-known psychologist and psychometrician, Henry Garrett. Although he had a clinical psychology program, Garrett was personally opposed to psychologists doing clinical work, and was most unenthusiastic about the Love and Marriage Problems (LAMP) Institute, which I had already set up as a pioneering couples-therapy organization. He literally shuddered when he interviewed me and spoke to me about it. To make matters worse, he thought that my B.B.A. degree from City College—a really good degree at that time, since it involved two full years of regular academic work before students were allowed to major in business subjects—was worthless because it included only one year of science (in my case, physics). "We don't care if you have no psychology in your undergraduate work," said Garrett. "We'll teach you that. But we insist that our students have a good science background. Yes, I understand that you've read hundreds of books on biology, psychology, astronomy, sociology, and political science. But that doesn't count, because it's not really academic training."

I saw that I was getting nowhere with Garrett and was about to give up on Columbia (and formally apply to New York University, which had already tentatively accepted me in its psychology program), when I suggested a deal that I challenged him to accept. I would take two courses in psychology during the summer term, which was just about to start, and if I did well in them, he would let me matriculate in his goddamned department. To my surprise, he agreed to this bargain— probably because he thought that anyone who was obsessed with clinical work in the area of love, sex, and marriage could not possibly do well academically.

Well, I fooled him. I took two of Garrett's courses that summer—one in statistics and one in psychometric measurement—and got "A's" in both. In fact, in the statistics midterm exam I achieved a record-breaking 100%. Garrett enthusiastically accepted me in his clinical program, although I still refused to take his advice and become a teacher of psychology, for which the program was mainly designed.

Fortunately, however, I had in the meantime become aware that Teachers College at Columbia had a rival clinical psychology program, which was staffed by several outstanding people including Irving Lorge, Goodwin Watson, Bruno Klopfer, Arthur Jersild, Percival Symonds, Esther Lloyd-Jones, Rollo May, and Robert Thorndike, and that Teachers College didn't give a damn about my undergraduate work in business administration and would not require me to take any additional science courses, as Garrett wanted me to do. So I went across the street and matriculated in September of 1942 in the Psychological Services Department, which soon became the Department of Clinical Psychology after Garrett abandoned his own clinical department.

I lied to the people at Teachers College when I told them that I was working part-time, instead of admitting my full-time job as personnel manager of a gift and novelty concern, Distinctive Creations. They therefore let me take a full 32-unit program for my M.A. degree the very first year; and I got the degree with honors. I enjoyed most of my courses, but was amazed that they often had more than a hundred students in a class, while dear old City College would close out practically all its classes after 30 students had registered. So, apart from the testing and therapy practicum courses, the level of teaching was often not very high. Also, although I was mainly psychoanalytically oriented at that time and definitely not Rogerian (as the Guidance Laboratory at Teachers College then was), I was by no means an orthodox Freudian, as several of my teachers (especially Dr. Robert Challman and Dr. Percival Symonds) were.

So I was something of a dissenter at Teachers College and not too popular with either the Freudians or the Rogerians. I also thought that the Rorschachers, led by the redoubtable Bruno Klopfer (a Jungian!) were dedicated to projective methods of psychological testing but hardly to science; and that not being bright or labile enough to do good psychotherapy, they compulsively stuck to "brilliant" test interpretations which, as far as I could see, were only vaguely related to reality. I was delighted when Klopfer once did a brilliant blind Rorschach analysis of a student's client and proved himself almost 100% wrong.

I also took full advantage of the courses in the psychology department of Columbia

University, because of some of the outstanding people there, including Carney Landis, Joseph Zubin, Abram Kardiner, and Otto Klineberg. Landis was particularly nice to me when I talked to him about the study of the love emotions of college women, the subject on which I was preparing to write my Ph.D. thesis. To my surprise, he told me about the as yet unpublished work of Alfred C. Kinsey, which he had helped sponsor through the National Research Council. Before hearing about Kinsey's work, which began in 1938 (my own sex researches started in 1939), I had intended to do a huge study of sex, such as the Kinsey Report turned out to be. But since Kinsey had definitely got a jump on me, and since he largely neglected the feeling and practice of love, I decided to concentrate instead on those areas of human behavior.

I met Kinsey and his associates, Wardell Pomeroy and Clyde Martin, and was delighted with his interviewing me for his study because, although he was a zoologist and a nonclinician, he purveyed, throughout his questioning, a thoroughly accepting, nondamning attitude that would put virtually any person at ease—yes, even the worst kind of "deviant." Kinsey was interested in my study of love, wanted copies of my questionnaire, and kept in touch with me over the years. He particularly liked my long review of *Sexual Behavior in the Human Male*, which appeared in the *Journal of General Psychology* (Ellis, 1948b). When my woman friend Ruth and I visited him at Indiana University in 1952, he spent the entire day with us, from 8:30 A.M. to 11:00 P.M. He was eager to have another long visit, and to take films of me and my incredibly orgasmic wife, Rhoda, on our honeymoon trip in 1956; unfortunately, he had a sudden heart attack and died. A few years later, Paul Gebhard, Kinsey's successor at the Institute for Sex Research, invited me to Indiana University again to confer on the Kinsey research project on sex offenders.

Back to Columbia University! After I received my M.A. degree, I had to take a six-hour qualifying exam to matriculate for my Ph.D. I had no trouble with the essay part, but almost got into serious trouble on the part with 200 objective questions covering the whole field of psychology. I thought it was a silly test to give graduate students, as it asked for specific rote information on famous psychologists' dates of birth and death, titles of obscure books they had written, how popular they were with their students, and similar unimportant issues. Feeling somewhat pissed off about this kind of exam, I foolishly wrote a note on it questioning the advisability of giving graduate psychology students tests of rote learning while at the same time teaching them that such learning was useless compared to contextual and meaningful learning. I thought my comments on the test were quite relevant and clever—until I discovered from my faculty advisor, Percival Symonds, that one of the leading psychology professors, Arthur Gates, took one look at them and commented to the other professors, "Who is this guy Ellis? A Communist? I think we should refuse to matriculate him."

Fortunately, I received the highest score on the objective part of the exam that any Teachers College student had ever received. So Gates very reluctantly withdrew his objections to my matriculation for the Ph.D. degree.

The next grim thing that happened was the interruption of my Ph.D. thesis on love. Knowing that objections would be made to any dissertation on sex, I stuck to questions about love, easily passed my thesis seminars, gathered all the data for and was about to write up my thesis, when suddenly all hell broke loose. Some people at Teachers College, seeing that I was about to finish my project, thought that the New York *Journal-American,* a lurid Hearst paper, might publish a sensational article headlined "Columbia University Student Writes Erotic Thesis for Clinical Psychology Department." Several prudes in the department were so horrified by this possibility that a special seminar was called to include all 12 professors in the department as well as the provost of the university, who normally had nothing to do with academic affairs.

As the *pièce de résistance* at this unusual seminar, I presented my hypotheses about love, my methods of gathering and analyzing the data, the observed data, and my tentative conclusions. Everyone seemed entranced, and I expected and got a favorable decision. Because my main thesis advisor, Percival Symonds, was on leave from the university to serve as a consultant for the army in Washington, Goodwin Watson was my acting advisor and he informed me that the vote was 11 to 2 in my favor. They thought my topic on love was fine, my methodology was great, and that I was marvelously equipped to do this thesis for good old Columbia's glory, as well as my own. Great! But, Goodwin added, the two voting against me were so adamant that it was clear that they would block *any* thesis that I (or any other Teachers College student) wrote on sex, love, marriage, or any derivative thereof.

Since part of the objection to my study was the fact that I had the gall—the *chutzpah*!—to actually ask young women about the details of their amative lives, I suggested to Goodwin that perhaps I could do a much more conservative study, such as comparing the love feelings of characters in novels of the 1890s to the feelings of characters in novels of the 1940s. No go, he said. My two opponents were so fiercely determined to scotch anything—yes, anything—I might do that was even vaguely related to love that they would sabotage me to the bitter end and make sure that I failed at the final oral defense of my thesis. So that, Goodwin sadly said, was that. And I sorrowfully had to agree with him.

Goodwin never did tell me who the two firm dissidents were, but I could easily guess. First, there was Arthur Gates, an arrant prude and no fan of mine. Second, there was Professor Ruth Strang, a woman who was never known to have any sex or love relationship in her 55 years of life and who said, when I first came to discuss my thesis topic with her, "I think, Mr. Ellis, that you have outlined a good study, and I quite approve of your methodology. But do you think that any number of people are really interested in this subject of love?" Well!

Seeing that I would get nowhere at Teachers College with this topic, I decided to finish my study and publish it in various psychological and sociological journals (Ellis, 1949a, 1949b, 1950b). Alas, my pioneering studies in this important area were only mildly recognized, and are often ignored today by researchers who followed me in this field.

Much better received was my study "The Psychology of Human Hermaphrodites," (Ellis, 1945) which was published in *Psychosomatic Medicine* while I was still in graduate school. While doing a long term paper on the causes of homosexuality for Symonds, I noted that practically all hermaphrodites were heterosexual in accordance with their upbringing, no matter what their physiological and hormonal makeup. So I collected data on all the cases of hermaphroditism in which the direction of the libido was known and discovered that if pseudohermaphrodites or true hermaphrodites were reared as males, they almost always desired and tried to have sex with women, while if they were reared as females, they almost always tried to mate with men. I concluded that although the power or intensity of the human sex drive is largely innate, the direction that it takes depends mainly on familial and cultural upbringing. This first study of mine on sex has been cited hundreds of times in the literature and importantly influenced John Momey, among others, to become sex researchers and clinicians. I soon followed it with many other professional and popular articles and books on sex (Ellis, 1948b, 1950c, 1951a, 1951b, 1953, 1954a, 1954b, 1958; Ellis & Brancale, 1956; Pillay & Ellis, 1953), and by the time the 1960s arrived, I had become one of the main instigators of the modern sex revolution.

Back to my censored thesis on love! Abandoning it as a dissertation, I deliberately selected an innocuous topic, *A Comparison of the Use of Direct and Indirect Phrasing with Personality Questionnaires* (Ellis, 1947a), and proceeded to rush it quickly through the academic mill. I first did a thorough background review of the literature, "The Validity of Personality Questionnaires" (Ellis, 1946), which was published in the influential *Psychological Bulletin* (then the official journal of the American Psychological Association, sent to all APA members). This long review, which concluded that contemporary paper-and-pencil personality tests, except possibly the MMPI, had dubious reliability and very little validity, created quite a stir and made me one of the world's leading authorities on personality tests. I was thereupon asked, while still in graduate school, to do a number of other reviews in this area, and consequently enhanced my reputation as a psychologist (Ellis, 1947b; Ellis & Conrad, 1948). I could have remained in this area forever, but found personality tests relatively boring, refused to do further writing on the subject, and returned to my main interests, psychotherapy, sex therapy, and marriage and family therapy.

Meanwhile I finished my thesis on personality questionnaires in record time (a few months), confidently went for my orals, and met a serious snag. At that time, all Ph.D. dissertations of Teachers College students had to be defended before a committee of professors from both Teachers College and the Columbia Department of Psychology, and the latter always did their best to give Teachers College students a hard time. This was especially true of Henry Garrett, who still hated clinicians and was determined to see that they did not pass the oral defense.

Fortunately for me, Garrett couldn't come to my orals and sent, in his stead, Carl Warden, the famous comparative psychologist, who (alas!) knew virtually no statistics and frankly said that he didn't understand analysis of variance, which in 1947 was little understood and rarely used. But one of our own Teachers College professors, Robert Thorndike, who was an outstanding statistician, checked my statistical analysis with a computer, and found that I had added one column in my tables vertically instead of horizontally, and that therefore one of my main conclusions was exaggerated. Joe Zubin, ostensibly a friend of mine, said that he had also checked my computations (which I suspected he had not), and he agreed with Thorndike that I was in serious trouble. Also, as a defender of Columbia versus

Teachers College, he gave me a hard time by asking picayune questions, such as "Who was the first creator of paper-and-pencil personality tests, and what year did he create the first one?" I knew it was Robert Woodworth and guessed that he did so in 1918, which seemed to shut Zubin up.

Anyway, I quickly saw that Thorndike and Zubin were right about my mathematical error and was about to say so, when the main statistical genius of the university, Irving Lorge, rose to a brilliant—and illegitimate—defense of my procedures. I was very friendly with Lorge, because after my statistical advisor, Helen Walker, then president of the American Statistical Association, went to Europe on a sabbatical, I went to Lorge for advice. He was the person who urged me to pioneer the use of the analysis of variance (ANOVA) technique. He not only agreed with everything I did, he often took advantage of our sessions to consult with me about his marital, sex and other personal problems.

Nonetheless, he was deliberately vicious to me in the seminars on my thesis, to make sure that I did everything right and fully satisfied those "bastards" in the Columbia Psychology Department at the final orals. Symonds, who had returned from the army and resumed being my main thesis advisor, once asked me, "How come you don't seem to get upset when Lorge keeps viciously assailing you?" I replied, "I follow my own rational philosophy and simply refuse to upset myself about anything like his criticism." You see, I was already on my way to discovering and using RET!

In any event, Lorge jumped both Thorndike (our Teachers College boy) and Zubin (Columbia's bad boy) and gave a long peroration on how analysis of variance was a new statistical procedure, how no one really knew anything much about it yet, how I was most probably right about my data and interpretations of it, and how therefore they should definitely award me the Ph.D degree. No one, including Thorndike and Zubin, had the temerity to challenge Lorge. Symonds (who had previously been a math teacher), Laurence Shaffer (the head of the new Clinical Psychology Department at Teachers College), and Warden all admitted that they really didn't know a damned thing about analysis of variance, and Lorge persuaded them to award me the degree, providing I later checked with him and corrected any possible statistical errors in it. I breathed a sigh of relief.

I then went to see Lorge, showed him that Thorndike and Zubin had been right about my mistakes, corrected them and made some new interpretations, and published my dissertation in the prestigious *Psychological Monographs* (Ellis, 1947a). I was the first Teachers College student to achieve this honor.

Everyone seemed to be happy, including Thorndike and Zubin, and that ended my formal training at Teachers College. Several other interesting incidents happened later, however. First, when I submitted a paper on psychological tests to the *Journal of Consulting Psychology* a few years later and the editor was skeptical that I had really read the scores of studies I cited and questioned Laurence Shaffer about this, he replied unequivocally, "If Ellis cites these studies, he has definitely read them. No one surveys the literature more thoroughly than he does!" So my article was accepted, albeit in a highly summarized form.

Second, when I ran into Henry Garrett at an Eastern Psychological Association convention a few years after I got my Ph.D. from Columbia, and he asked me what I was then doing, I informed him that in record time (two years) I had risen from the rank of senior clinical psychologist of the New Jersey Northern Mental Hygiene Clinic to become chief psychologist of the entire state of New Jersey. Garrett sneered and said, "Oh, clinical!"

Third, although along with Rollo May and Carl Rogers, I soon became one of the most distinguished psychological alumni of Teachers College, because of my writings on sex and love I was for several years *persona non grata* there, was refused a teaching job when I resigned from the state of New Jersey, and was not invited to lecture there, even though many less known alumni were cordially welcomed. Not until 1988, 41 years after I received my Ph.D., did Teachers College Columbia grant me its Distinguished Alumni award.

Nonetheless, I gained appreciably from my graduate work at Columbia, in spite of its Rogerian and Freudian orientations, and got along well with several of my professors—especially Symonds, Watson, Landis, and Zubin—for many years afterward.

Career: The Early Years

As I described in the section on graduate training, my career as a well-known psychologist began with my work on sex and personality testing. I soon discontinued the latter but went on actively with the former. In the late 1940s and the 1950s I continued to write professional articles on sex, love, and marriage (Ellis, 1945, 1948b, 1949a, 1949b, 1950b, 1951a, 1951b, 1954a, 1954b, 1958; Pillay & Ellis, 1953). In 1949, I was asked to write my first published book, *The Folklore of Sex* (Ellis, 1951a), and soon after I published *Sex, Society and the Individual* (Pillay & Ellis, 1953) and *The American Sexual Tragedy* (Ellis, 1954a). I became a pioneering sex therapist and marriage and family therapist, as well as a member of the Executive Committee of the American Association of Marital and Family Therapy and one of the founders and the first president of the Society for the Scientific Study of Sex. I fought for the rights of homosexuals and was awarded honorary membership in the Mattachine Society in the 1950s. I also became an authority on sex offenders (Ellis & Brancale, 1956).

My books on sex, love, and marriage began to become best-sellers, starting with *Sex Without Guilt* (Ellis, 1958) and *The Art and Science of Love* (Ellis, 1960). Many of my sex books sold widely in paperback, including the *Encyclopedia of Sexual Behavior* (Ellis & Abarbanel, 1961), *Sex and the Single Man* (Ellis, 1963b), *The Intelligent Woman's Guide to Manhunting* (Ellis, 1963a), *Nymphomania* (Ellis & Sagarin, 1964), and *The Art of Erotic Seduction* (Ellis & Conway, 1967).

Why did I write so many popular sex books? Because (1) publishers asked for them; (2) they sold well and helped support the nonprofit Institute for Rational-Emotive Therapy, to which all the royalties on my writings go; and (3) I always used them as a vehicle to slip in a good deal of RET, for I started to do RET early in 1955, after giving up psychoanalysis two years before that and after experimenting with several therapy methods and seeking for those that were more efficient than I found analysis to be.

I was never an orthodox Freudian because from my first avid reading of all Freud's major works at the ages of 16 and 17, I could see that he was a brilliant theoretician—an honest-to-goodness genius at theorizing—but was also (like Marx) an arrant overgeneralizer, a devout and rigid believer in many of his own dubious theories (especially his sex theories), and an antiscientist who continually claimed to be very scientific. I read later that Karl Popper (1985) also held that Freud and Marx were largely nonscientific, but long before I heard of Popper I had figured this out for myself. Also, as a well-informed sexologist, I (along with Havelock Ellis) easily saw that Freud really knew very little about sex, asininely invented rigid oral, anal, and phallic stages of sexual development, and foolishly blew up the existence of an occasional Oedipus complex into a universal law of human disturbance. As for his notion of the primacy of the vaginal orgasm for "healthy" female sex relations, I saw that this was pernicious garbage, and several years before the findings of Kinsey (Kinsey, Pomeroy, & Martin, 1948; Kinsey et al., 1953), Masters and Johnson (1960, 1970), and Hite (1976) appeared, I began to actively disabuse my male and female clients of this iatrogenic idea. As a result, my success rate after a few sessions of active-directive sex therapy was phenomenally high (Ellis, 1953, 1954a, 1954b, 1958, 1960, 1961, 1963b; Ellis & Harper, 1961b).

In spite of my non-Freudian early sex therapy, I was still a neoanalyst and largely followed the teachings of Alfred Adler, Erich Fromm, Karen Horney, and Harry Stack Sullivan. So to become a more kosher analyst, I spent six years, from 1947 to 1953, being analyzed, getting psychoanalytic supervision from a training analyst at the Horney Institute for Psychoanalysis, and doing classical analysis and psycho-analytically oriented psychotherapy with virtually all my institutional and private practice clients. I thereby enjoyed the "detecting" I did as an analyst, got as good results as other analysts did, and by 1953 was building a very popular practice. I also worked from 1948 to 1952 for the New Jersey Mental Hygiene Clinic, as chief psychologist of the New Jersey State Diagnostic Center and as chief psychologist of the entire state of New Jersey. From 1947 to 1948, I taught general psychology at Rutgers University; and from 1949 to 1950, I taught mental hygiene at New York University.

In all these positions, I upheld a liberal psychoanalytic view; and I continually tried to revise psychoanalysis and make it more scientific by publishing critical papers (Ellis, 1948c, 1949c); a monograph "An Introduction to the Scientific Principles of Psychoanalysis" (Ellis, 1950a); and finally "An Operational Reformulation of Some of the Basic Principles of Psychoanalysis" (Ellis, 1956), based on my 1953 presentation at the University of Minnesota's conference on psychoanalysis and the philosophy of science. I was delighted to meet the arrangers of this conference, Herbert Feigl and Michael Scriven, as well as two of the main participants, Starke Hathaway and Paul Meehl. All of them, particularly Hathaway and Meehl, became very favorable to the developing theory and practice of RET and I continued to be friendly with them. Paul Meehl, in fact, became probably the first practitioner of RET (combined with liberal psychoanalysis) in the Midwest, and still employs it to this day. At that same conference I also met Daniel Wiener and became quite friendly with him, sent him my first publications on RET, and soon found him incorporating a good deal of my theory in his teaching and practice. A number of years later, he wrote the first biography of me, *Albert Ellis: Passionate Skeptic* (Wiener, 1989), which has some limitations but nicely shows my development as a sexual and psychotherapeutic rebel.

Between 1953 and 1955, I rebelled so much against psychoanalysis, and especially Freudian analysis, that I began to call myself a "psychotherapist" rather than a "psychoanalyst." I completed a monograph, "New Approaches to Psychotherapy Techniques" (Ellis, 1955a), and also wrote "Psychotherapy Techniques for Use With Psychotics" (Ellis, 1955b), which outlined many behavioral, cognitive, and emotive methods. After experimenting for two years with these methods (and discovering that some of them—like Ferenczi's (1952) "let's-give-our-clients-real-love technique"—were often iatrogenic), I finally wound up, at the beginning of 1955, with RET.

Rational-emotive therapy, as I very often have written about and taught (to more than 10,000 clients, to over 200,000 professionals and paraprofessionals, to about 1500 supervisees, and to millions of readers, listeners, and viewers) is easily the first of the major cognitive-behavioral therapies, preceding the therapies of Glasser (1965), Beck (1967), and Bandura (1969) by about 10 years; those of Lazarus (1971), Maultsby (1971), Mahoney (1974), and Meichenbaum (Meichenbaum & Goodman, 1971) by about 15 years; and those of Raimy (1975), Guidano and Liotti (1983), Greenberg & Safran (1984), and Wessler (1984) by 20 to 30 years. Most of these cognitive-behavioral therapists, and perhaps all of them, might never have become the pioneers and innovators they are without the great influence of RET— and without my beating the drum strongly since 1955 for rational-emotive methods. I am, therefore, happy to be known as the father of RET and the grandfather of cognitive-behavioral therapy (CBT).

My career as a practicing psychologist began very auspiciously. As described earlier, I became an authority on sex and on personality tests while still in graduate school, and by the time I received my doctorate in 1947 I had already published or had in press a dozen articles and reviews. I was soon making regular presentations to the APA, to the Eastern Psychological Association, and at sociological association conventions, and also became an associate editor of *The International Journal of Sexology* and of *Marriage and Family Living.*

Although I began a small private practice in 1943, after I received my M.A. in clinical psychology, I did not begin my first regular job as a clinical psychologist until a year after I received my Ph.D. I was offered several jobs in places, such as San Diego, where there were no training analysts, so I declined these jobs. New York had very few psychological positions at that time; but fortunately New Jersey had some positions within commuting distance of New York. So I accepted a job as senior clinical psychologist at the Northern New Jersey Mental Hygiene Clinic, which was based at the New Jersey State Hospital at Greystone Park, near Morristown. Because travel time from my apartment and office in the Bronx to Greystone Park was a full two hours, I arranged to live at the hospital and to go in to New York City two or three times a week for my private practice and analytic training.

I was very interested in psychological research and had the full use of the clinic files for the previous 20 years. So I immediately started doing research papers, and finished no fewer than 12 of them during the first year I was at the clinic. Of course, I sent reprints to all my bosses and to high officials all over the state. Because I was the first state psychologist in many years to publish *any* research papers, I soon became the fair-haired boy of the State Department of Institutes and Agencies—an immense department that included all the state hospitals, clinics, mental deficiency institutions, and other social service facilities.

As a result of my numerous publications, when the innovative New Jersey State Diagnostic Center opened in 1949 I was selected as its chief psychologist, although I was the newest clinician in the system and other psychologists had served it well for 25 or 30 years. But none of them had recently published any studies!

I learned a great deal and gained experience with a large number of clients in the year I spent at the Northern New Jersey Mental Hygiene Clinic. This badly run clinic arranged to see clients only once every three months in order to pad the number of people serviced annually. Consequently, although I did little therapy and much testing, I saw scores of child and adult clients, from lower- to middle-class status, and became, if I say so, an excellent diagnostician. Meanwhile, mostly on weekends, I continued my private practice of therapy in New York, especially with people who had sexual and marital problems.

When I started at the diagnostic center in 1949, I continued to gain a great deal of clinical experience. Although I was chief psychologist, the highest position in the state except for the chief psychologist of the entire Department of Institutions and Agencies, I had only a few professionals under me. So I continued to diagnose many sex offenders, criminals, seriously disturbed children, and other individuals; and since the center kept children and adolescents up to 90 days, and since I instituted a therapy program for them during their stay, I also did a considerable amount of individual and group therapy with these residents.

While I was at the diagnostic center I commuted each day to Manhattan, where I lived, and began to have a thriving psychoanalytic practice in the evenings and on weekends. As my writings and talks on sex became popular, I saw many more people with sex problems than, I am sure, did the average analyst.

In 1950, because of the department officials' discontent with the acting chief psychologist of the state of New Jersey, they made him head of another department and appointed me chief psychologist of the entire Department of Institutions and Agencies. Thus, after only two years of working for a governmental agency I became one of the highest psychological officials in the United States. My talent as a clinician and administrator and my tactful handling of New Jersey politicians of course had something to do with my rapid rise to power. But my continuous research and writing—by the end of 1950 I had published 46 articles and reviews and had a book in press—were my main achievements, which the state of New Jersey had the good taste to acknowledge.

So far, so good. But not entirely. The same writings that spurred my remarkable upward mobility as a psychologist also got me in trouble with certain prudes in the New Jersey state system, particularly Sanford Bates, Commissioner of the Department of Institutions and Agencies. Noted for his record in prison reform, he was hardly a liberal. When my first book, *The Folklore of Sex* (Ellis, 1951a) appeared, he said nothing bad to me about it but told several other people in the department that he was shocked by its sexual liberalism. He also insisted that my book in progress—*The Psychology of Sex Offenders* (Ellis & Brancale, 1956)— have my co-author, Dr. Ralph Brancale (a psychiatrist and the director of the diagnostic center) appear as the first and main author of the book. Actually, Ralph gave me a few ideas, but I alone did the research study on which the book was based, and I did all of the writing.

So I resisted Sanford Bates, forcefully told him that the American Psychological Association considers it unethical to put the name of a minor author before that of the major author of a study, and insisted that the book would be published with my name first.

To complicate matters, although Ralph was willing to go along with me in this respect, he was silently hating my guts because both of us were in love with the same psychologist, Ruth, and I was actively having a torrid affair with her while she was firmly resisting him. So when Ruth and I drove to Chicago together in August of 1951 to attend the APA convention—and to do a study there of the sexual preferences of psychologists—Bates and Brancale got together behind our backs and had a decree ready for me when I returned, stating that I was illegally serving as chief psychologist of the state of New Jersey because I was residing in New York instead of New Jersey, and I was conducting a private practice as well as working for the state.

When I read Bates's decree I laughed at these charges, because I saw that they were illegitimate and of course did not mention my real offenses—writing liberal books on sex and having a hot affair with Ruth. It was true that New Jersey government employees were not supposed to live in another state, but almost half the government officials in Trenton, including some high ones, lived in Philadelphia or other parts of Pennsylvania and a number, like myself, lived in New York.

Second, the civil service rules did state that psychiatrists and other physicians who worked for New Jersey hospitals were not permitted to have a private practice too. But they said nothing, absolutely nothing, about psychologists! The rules had been made many years ago, when the state of New Jersey hired virtually no psychologists.

I could easily have appealed my "dismissal" by Bates to the Civil Service Commission, and almost certainly would have won my case. I thought of doing so, and entertained making the real issue, free speech, a *cause célèbre*. I would have enjoyed pleading before the commission and would also have enjoyed the subsequent publicity. I realized, however, that even if I won my case and continued as chief psychologist, I would get no cooperation from Bates or from any of the other commissioners who normally helped me revise and develop the state psychological system, and that the great advances in the system that I had gained over the past two years would soon be impeded and lost.

Also, I had already planned that a year after the time of my "dismissal," when my private practice in New York would be even more developed, I would quit the state job anyway, so that I could take on more clients and also do more research and writing. Commuting to New Jersey and building its psychological resources was quite time-consuming, and I could think of better things to do with my life.

So for a number of reasons I negotiated with Sanford Bates to stay on as chief psychologist until the beginning of 1952 and then to leave my post on amicable terms rather than tell the Civil Service Commission what bastards certain high officers were. So I left New Jersey in 1952, but continued my public service by acting as a consultant in psychology to the New York City Board of Education and to the Veterans Administration. I also began to give scores of talks, workshops, seminars, and other presentations each year, for both the profession and the public, in New York and other parts of the country. Additionally, in the early 1950s I began to make numerous radio and television presentations and to be interviewed by leading newspapers and magazines.

As a result of all this publicity, and of my popular and professional writings, my psychoanalytic and sex therapy practice grew rapidly, and I soon became one of the few psychologists in New York who was in full-time practice and who mde a good living at it. I read and wrote almost every night until 1:00 or 2:00 A.M., then saw my first client at 10:00 A.M. and worked steadily until 11:00 P.M., seeing about 16 clients for 45-minute sessions each day. I tried to teach some clinical psychology classes, too. But because of my growing reputation in the field of sex, and my consequent designation as "controversial," none of the New York universities would allow me in their sacred classrooms except for occasional talks or workshops. As far as New York academia was concerned, my public notoriety outweighed my growing professional reputation.

Disappointed but not at all depressed, I continued to build my practice and to write, write, write, write, write. In the 1950s I published six sex books—*The Folklore of Sex* (Ellis, 1951a), *Sex, Society and the Individual* (Pillay & Ellis, 1953), *The American Sexual Tragedy* (Ellis, 1954a), *Sex Life of the American Woman and the Kinsey Report* (Ellis, 1954b), *The Psychology of Sex Offenders* (Ellis & Brancale, 1956), and *Sex Without Guilt* (Ellis, 1958).

In the 1950s I also published five books and monographs on psychotherapy—"An Introduction to the Principles of Scientific Psychoanalysis" (Ellis, 1950a),"New Approaches to Psychotherapy Techniques" (Ellis, 1955a), *How To Live with a "Neurotic"* (Ellis, 1957a), *What Is Psychotherapy* (Ellis, 1959b), and *The Place of Value in the Practice of Psychotherapy* (Ellis, 1959a)—as well as scores of professional and popular articles, reviews, and book chapters.

In the 1950s, I helped found and was very active in the Society for the Scientific Study of Sex and the American Academy of Psychotherapists, and served as a member of the executive committees of these organizations, as well as of the American

Association of Marital and Family Therapy, the New York Society of Clinical Psychologists, the New York Association of Psychologists in Private Practice, and the New York Joint Council of Psychologists on Legislation. I also served on the Committee on Private Practice of the Division of Clinical Psychology of the APA and on the ethics committees of the New York State Psychological Association and the APA.

By the time the 1960s arrived, I was easily one of the best-known clinical psychologists, as well as one of the most famous sexologists, in the United States and in the world. My 13 years of steady research, writing, and speaking, ever since I had obtained my Ph.D. in 1947, had indeed paid off!

Most important in the 1950s, however, was not my development as a leading sexologist, but my creation of rational-emotive therapy in 1955, two years after I had abandoned psychoanalysis and become an eclectic therapist. RET not only radically changed my practice, it gave me an incentive to give many talks and to write a number of books and articles on this new form of therapy. In 1959 I founded the nonprofit Institute for Rational-Emotive Therapy, and even before that I had begun to train therapists all over the country in RET. I recorded hundreds of RET sessions with my clients and sent tapes of many of these sessions to other therapists. Some of my leading trainees in RET were Bob Harper, Dave Kahn, Penelope Russianoff, Paul Hauck, Al Freeman, Henry Guze, Paul Meehl, Starke Hathaway, Haim Ginott, and Leonard and Merry Haber.

The two people who were most supportive of RET, right from the start, were Robert A. Harper, a well-known psychologist and marriage and family counselor, whom I had known since 1949, and Edward Sagarin, a sociologist whom I had known since 1950. Bob and I have always closely agreed on martial, sex, and general therapy, and he became my first collaborator in developing RET. As a leading psychologist and RET practitioner, as president or officer of many important professional organizations, as the main reviewer for the *Journal of Rational-Emotive and Cognitive-Behavioral Therapy,* and as the designer and chairperson of many APA symposia, he has been incredibly helpful in spreading the influence of RET.

Ed Sagarin, an outstanding sociologist and a leader in the field of sex liberalism who was devoted to RET from its inception in 1955, helped me with some of its early formulations, and greatly helped spread its influence until his death in 1987. Without Bob and Ed, and later the immense help of Janet L. Wolfe, my mate and collaborator since 1965, RET would never have prospered to the extent that it has over the years, in spite of its many detractors.

My first and best friend at Teachers College, Gordon Derner, also appreciably fostered the growth of RET, although he remained basically psychoanalytical. He was so enthralled by my early taped RET sessions that he played them to his classes at Adelphi University and to his workshops and courses all over the world. He served as one of the best early propagandists for this new form of therapy and helped get me scores of speaking engagements.

By the end of the 1950s, therefore, not only was I very well known, but RET was also acknowledged to be one of the most popular of the new therapies, along with

Gestalt therapy, Reichian therapy, and some of the neo-Freudian and neo-Adlerian therapies, such as those of Harry Stack Sullivan, Erich Fromm, and Karen Horney. The later cognitive-behavioral therapies of William Glasser, Aaron Beck, Albert Bandura, Donald Meichenbaum, Michael Mahoney, and others were as yet nonexistent; and some of the leading behavior therapists, especially Hans Eysenck, began to see that cognition, too, was an aspect of behavior, and had better be dealt with in psychotherapy.

My career forged ahead during the 1960s, partly because my sex books began to become best sellers in paperback, including *Sex Without Guilt* (Ellis, 1958), *The Art and Science of Love* (Ellis, 1960), *Sex and the Single Man* (Ellis, 1963b), *The Intelligent Woman's Guide to Manhunting* (Ellis, 1963a), *Nymphomania* (Ellis & Sagarin, 1964), and *The Art of Erotic Seduction* (Ellis & Conway, 1967). Although these were very liberal and very sexy books, and although they made me one of the main fathers of the sex revolution that hit America in the 1960s, they actually included a good deal of material on RET—as, of course, the other popular sex books did not. Along with the revised edition of *The American Sexual Tragedy* (Ellis, 1962a), and a number of professional articles, they set the stage for the sex therapy revolution of Masters and Johnson (1970) and other sex therapists in the 1970s. So my reputation as a chief promulgator of both the public and the professional sex revolution was fairly solid by the end of the 1960s.

RET also began to make great strides at the same time. *How To Live with a "Neurotic"* (Ellis, 1957a) went into several reprint editions, and other RET books for the public—especially *A Guide to Rational Living* (Ellis & Harper, 1961a) and *A Guide to Successful Marriage* (Ellis & Harper, 1961b)—brought much American and foreign acclaim and were soon recommended as bibliotherapy by a large number of therapists. I started to give scores of well-attended talks and workshops, for the public and for professionals, in the United States, Canada, Puerto Rico, Guatemala, West Germany, Belgium, and other parts of the world. I also appeared on a great many radio and television shows, especially talk shows, during which I used RET and sex therapy to tell radio and television listeners how to help themselves. In doing so, I pioneered the application of clinical psychology to radio and television therapy presentations. Although I was often criticized by other professionals for doing this, my appearances helped establish the rights of reputable psychologists to do this kind of work in a big way in the 1970s and 1980s.

Most notable of all, however, in 1964 the Institute for Rational-Emotive Therapy bought its own large New York townhouse, at 45 East 65th Street, where it is still headquartered. The building was bought for $250,000 with some of the royalties of *The Art and Science of Love.* (The royalties on all my writings have gone to the institute since its founding in 1959.)

Since it opened in the spring of 1965, the institute's fine building has been used for hundreds of thousands of RET individual and group sessions, for thousands of RET lectures and workshops, for the training of over 1500 RET therapists, for about 200 marathons and intensives, and for numerous other RET activities. It is particularly noted for the Friday Night Workshops that I have been giving since 1965, in the course of which I give live demonstrations of RET therapy to volunteers from the audience, and then throw the discussion open to the audience members, many of whom interact with me and the volunteers. Without this stately headquarters building, which is now worth millions of dollars, the institute and RET would never have thrived so well over the years. Nor would they have thrived without the enormous help of its board of directors, originally Manny Birnbaum, Mike Feinstein, and myself, all still functioning; then Janet Wolfe, Eddie Cohen, and Paul Ellis, the last two now unfortunately deceased; and finally Jill Steinberg and Rory Stuart. They, along with several dedicated directors of training and research—especially Bill Knaus, Ed Garcia, Ray DiGiuseppe, and Dom DiMattia—have beautifully helped to preserve the institute and its stately building.

Anyway, by the end of the 1960s RET was firmly established as the leading form of cognitive-behavioral therapy, and several studies of its clinical effectiveness had already appeared. Its own journal, *Rational Living,* later called the *Journal of Rational-Emotive and Cognitive-Behavior Therapy,* was started under the able editorship of Paul A. Hauck in 1966. Still going strong under the editorship of Paul Woods and Russell Grieger, the journal too has promoted important RET articles and research studies.

I was briefly married in 1939 to Karyl Corper, a beautiful, charming, but disturbed woman, lived with her for a year after our annulment, and have remained friendly with her and her family ever since we ended our relationship in 1940. After having a number of other affairs, I married Rhoda Winter in 1956 and for two and a half years had a very sexy and loving partnership with her. But when she got less involved with modern dancing and wanted to spend much more time with me and our friends, we became less compatible and got divorced.

Since 1965 I have lived with Janet L. Wolfe, without legal sanctions, and have found this 25-year relationship by far the most fulfilling one of my entire life. Janet, a fine clinical psychologist in her own right, a leading feminist psychotherapist, and now executive director of the Institute for Rational-Emotive Therapy in New York, is the only woman I have ever found who easily puts up with my incredible busyness, who is independent enough to maintain her own happy and very productive life, and who finds sufficient time to live, laugh, and love with me on a high affectional plane. It is a wonder how she manages to let me sandwich my time with her in between the scores of other things I do. But she is remarkably rational and creative in that respect and is therefore one of the few women in the world that I could comfortably live with. Thank goodness for that!

Janet and I have mutually chosen to have no children. For my part, I would make a lousy father, since I have little interest in taking kids to ball games or picnics and frankly enjoy the various things that I do, especially "therapizing," lecturing, giving workshops, and writing, distinctly more than I would enjoy cavorting with children. I would have liked to have the experience of trying to rear a "rational" child; but I am skeptical that the child himself or herself would have enjoyed it that much. So my sense of ethics has kept me away from the responsibility of being a full-time father. I nurture, in my own way, my many clients; and that makes up for my lack of being a conventional family man.

Career: The Later Years

By the beginning of the 1970s, several well-known therapists began to do cognitive-behavioral therapy and to carry out important studies that supported the basic RET hypotheses and practices. These therapists included Bandura (1969), Beck (1967), Glasser (1965), Goldfried and Davison (1976), Lazarus (1971), Mahoney (1974), Maultsby (1971), and Meichenbaum (Meichenbaum & Goodman, 1971). By the mid-1970s, the cognitive-behavioral revolution was in full swing; literally scores of research papers were published supporting its main tenets; and the entire world of therapy was radically changed. Other schools of therapy still flourished—including those inspired by Sigmund Freud, Alfred Adler, Carl Jung, Wilhelm Reich, Karen Horney, Fritz Perls, Melanie Klein, Eric Berne, B. F. Skinner, and Rollo May—but most of them tended to utilize, or to sneak in, many important RET and cognitive-behavioral concepts and practices. It is probably safe to say, in this connection, that since the introduction of RET in 1955, the field of psychotherapy has never been the same!

While most creators of "new" schools of cognitive-behavior therapy were using the original ABCs of RET and were teaching their clients that Activiating Events (As) significantly contribute to people's emotional Consequences (Cs), but that the more important and more direct "cause" of these Cs stems from their Beliefs (Bs) and particularly from their irrational Beliefs (iBs) (Ellis, 1957a, 1957b, 1958, 1962b), I started reconstructing RET in the late 1960s and early 1970s, making it both simpler and more complex. Some of the main innovations that I added to "mature" RET were these:

1. Where I originally proposed 11 main irrational ideas and later added another dozen or so (Ellis, 1962b; Ellis & Grieger, 1977; Ellis & Whiteley, 1979), I realized that they could all be subsumed under three major headings: (a) *I* must perform well and/or be approved by significant others, else *I* am an incompetent, unlovable person! (b) *You* must treat me kindly and fairly, else *you* are a rotten, damnable individual! (c) *Conditions* must be favorable and fortunate, and bring me much gain and little pain, else life is terrible, I can't stand it, and life is hardly worth living! (Bernard, 1986; Ellis, 1973b, 1977d, 1988b; Ellis & Becker, 1982; Ellis & Harper, 1975; Ellis & Knaus, 1977.)
2. I clearly saw that all three of these grandiose irrational Beliefs could be logically and empirically held as strong *preferences* and *wishes,* but that when we change them into absolutist, dogmatic, unconditional *musts* and *commands,* we usually make ourselves—yes, *make* ourselves—"emotionally" disturbed. I realized, more fully than I previously had, that scientific thinking—empiricism, logic, probability-seeking, flexibility, pluralism, and alternative-seeking—is probably the essence of "sanity," and that absolutism and dogma are its chief saboteurs (Ellis, 1962b, 1973b, 1977d, 1983a, 1987b, 1987d, 1988b; Ellis & Becker, 1982; Ellis & Harper, 1975; Ellis & Whiteley, 1979).
3. I realized that the main other irrational Beliefs and inferences that I had orginally posited (Ellis, 1957a, 1957b, 1962b, 1971; Ellis & Harper, 1961a, 1961b), and

that Beck (1976), Burns (1980), and other cognitive-behavioral therapists later emphasized, were usually *derived* from conscious or tacit absolutist musts, shoulds, and oughts. Thus, if we start with only strong preferences—such as "I'd *like* to perform well and to be loved"—we strongly imply or infer "*but* I never *have to.* Too bad if I don't!" While if we start with an unconditional must—such as "No matter what happens, I absolutely *must* achieve well and be loved!"—we almost always unrealistically infer and conclude "it's *awful,* I *can't stand* it, I'm *no damned good,* and I will *always* fail if I don't achieve and be loved well enough!"

4. Because of my discovery, in the 1970s, that absolutist musts almost always seem to underlie many other kinds of irrational Beliefs and inferences, RET came to emphasize, as one of its cardinal rules, *"Cherchez les shoulds, cherchez les musts,* look for the *shoulds,* look for the *musts!"* As an active-directive RET practitioner and supervisor, I now assume that neurotics and other disturbed individuals almost always have underlying demands and insistences, and that these had better be clearly revealed and vigorously and repetitively disputed. I also assume that people easily and "naturally" derive several antiempirical, overgeneralized misperceptions and inferences from their profound masturbatory thinking. So I teach them how to discover and attack both of these major forms of self-defeating thinking. But particularly their *musts*!

5. I realized in the 1960s that people's self-sabotaging philosophies were to some degree learned from their families and their culture but were also biologically based, largely stemming from a powerful innate tendency to think crookedly (Ellis, 1962b, 1965c). In the 1970s and 1980s, I found more clinical and other evidence than ever to bolster this conclusion. This does not mean that people cannot think more sanely and cannot significantly lessen their disturbances. But it does mean that they usually have to work very hard to do so (Ellis, 1962b, 1973c, 1985b, 1987a, 1987b, 1988b, 1989b).

6. The theory that people often *strongly* and *rigidly* construct and hold on to their neurotic and other disturbances led to the RET use of powerful, emotive, evocative, dramatic techniques to *forcefully* help people to help themselves to surrender their irrational Beliefs (Ellis, 1969, 1971, 1972a, 1973d). Since the 1960s, therefore, RET has been very *emotive,* while most of the other cognitive-behavioral therapies have only recently employed these effective methods (Greenberg & Safran, 1984). Through the years, as a result of clinical and research findings, RET has become even more emotive in its theory and practices (Dryden, 1984; Ellis, 1985a, 1985b, 1987a, 1987c, 1988d; Ellis & Dryden, 1987, 1989).

7. RET originally accepted the philosophy of science of logical positivism; but when that was shown to have serious limitations (Bartley, 1962), it largely adopted the open society views of Karl Popper (1985).

8. RET was partly "rationalist" in that it assumed that people largely learned irrational behaviors, ideas, and feelings and almost by rote tended to maintain them. But in the 1960s, I strongly realized that people mainly *originate* and

construct their self-defeating musts and that they *constructively* defend and hang on to them. Unlike some other cognitive-behavioral therapies that teach clients coping statements by rote, RET uses many cognitive, emotive, and behavioral methods to encourage clients to creatively *rethink* and *reconstruct* their habitual irrational thinking. It also pushes them to be constructively self-actualizing and growth-oriented, in addition to making themselves less disturbable (Ellis, 1973a, 1973b, 1983b, 1989b; Ellis, Young, & Lockwood, 1987).

9. Like most other cognitive and noncognitive therapies, RET at first largely emphasized ego or self problems, especially feelings of personal worthlessness, and it still does (Ellis, 1968, 1972c, 1976b, 1988b; Ellis & Harper, 1975). But it now almost equally stresses discomfort, anxiety, or low frustration tolerance (Ellis, 1971, 1976a, 1977d, 1988a, 1988b, 1989a; Ellis & Becker, 1982; Ellis & Dryden, 1987; Ellis & Knaus, 1977).

10. I always used a great deal of humor in ripping up my clients' irrational Beliefs (Ellis, 1962b, 1971; Ellis & Harper, 1961b). But in giving a presentation on fun in psychotherapy at the APA annual conference in Washington in 1976, for the first time I presented some of my rational humorous songs (Ellis, 1977a, 1977b, 1987e). These went over so well that I and many other therapists started to use them as part of the regular RET armamentarium. In some circles, I am now better known for my song lyrics than for my therapy innovations!

In the 1970s I continued my devotion to RET and, with the start of my sixth decade, my labors in its behalf became, if anything, greater. At the institute's clinic, I saw from 75 to 100 clients in individual sessions each week and led six group therapy sessions. I did my regular Friday Night Workshop and a number of other talks and workshops each year. I also supervised about ten Fellows in individual and group therapy. One or two days a week I went out of town (or out of the country), usually to give all-day workshops on RET. I participated in about ten three- or five-day training practica in New York or elsewhere. I supervised 20 or more recorded sessions by would-be RETers. I wrote about 20 articles and book chapters and one or two full-length books every year. Well, you can see that I was hardly idle!

I wrote a number of books on sex in the 1970s, especially *Sex and the Liberated Man* (Ellis, 1976c) and the revised edition of the *Intelligent Woman's Guide to Dating & Mating* (Ellis, 1979). Once again, I put a great deal of RET into these books. As for pure RET, my most important books included *Growth Through Reason* (Ellis, 1971), *How To Master Your Fear of Flying* (Ellis, 1972a), *Humanistic Psychotherapy: The Rational-Emotive Approach* (Ellis, 1973b), *A New Guide to Rational Living* (Ellis & Harper, 1975), *Handbook of Rational-Emotive Therapy*, Vol. 1 (Ellis & Grieger, 1977), and *Brief Psychotherapy in Medical and Health Practice* (Ellis & Abrahms, 1978).

Also in the 1970s, the institute began to record some of my main talks and therapy sessions and to issue them as audio cassettes. Some of them became very popular and spread RET to many people who did little or no reading. Cassettes like *Twenty-One Ways to Stop Worrying* (Ellis, 1973d), *How to Stubbornly Refuse to Be Ashamed of Anything* (Ellis, 1973a), *Rational Living in an Irrational World* (Ellis, 1974), and *RET and Assertiveness Training* (Ellis, 1975b) were especially popular. At the Institute for Rational-Emotive Therapy in New York, we also found that our clients often seemed to benefit considerably, and to speed up their therapy, when they read some of my books and pamphlets and when they listened to some of my cassettes.

In 1978 I reached the "retirement" age of 65, but I had no intention of retiring. My father had just about died in the saddle when he was 80, and had worked until the day of his death at the large insurance agency he had founded a quarter of a century before. My mother lived to be 93 and enjoyed herself, dancing and singing until the day she died. Practically all of my uncles and aunts, on both sides of the family, were hale and hearty in their 90s. Having fortunately arranged to have such long-lived ancestors, I approached the 1980s with the full intention of continuing to actively push my ass for another few decades.

So far, I have partly made it. At 75, I am still going strong and have, in fact, broken several of my own records. In the course of my 75th year, between September 27, 1988 and September 27, 1989, I have had over 3000 half-hour and 700 hour-long sessions with clients at the psychological clinic of the Institute for Rational-Emotive Therapy in New York. I have led my regular weekly therapy groups throughout the year. I have conducted about 50 talks and workshops for the public at the institute, especially my regular famous Friday Night Workshop, where I interview volunteer clients about typical emotional and behavioral problems in public. I have steadily supervised the individual and group therapy of 12 Fellows and interns of the institute. And I have helped lead four 9-hour RET intensives.

The thousands of therapy sessions, talks, workshops, and supervision sessions that I have given at the institute during my 75th year are par for the course, continuing a pattern very similar to the one I have been following there for almost 25 years.

This last year I have also been busier than ever with outside American presentations. I have been the keynote speaker at eight state, national, and international psychology conventions, and have also conducted 35 RET workshops and other presentations, most of them full-day affairs, in many parts of the United States. Foreign sites for my lectures and workshops have included Canada, Israel, England, Germany, Puerto Rico, Australia, and—oh, yes!—Brooklyn. How many hundreds of thousands of miles I have flown during this year is hard to compute; but my Frequent Flyer totals are very high!

Just to polish off my doings during my 75th year, let me record that I have read (quickly, I admit!) scores of professional books and hundreds of journals. Without taking an exact count, I have published 12 articles and book chapters (and have about 10 more in press); and have published three books (Ellis & Dryden, 1989; Ellis, Sichel, Yeager, DiMattia, & DiGiuseppe, 1989; Ellis & Yeager, 1989), with two more in progress.

During my 75th year I also got myself into another major controversy, thereby living up to my reputation of being a passionate skeptic (Wiener, 1989). In the 1930s I rebelled against both capitalism and the Communist party. In the 1940s, 1950s, and 1960s I rebelled against conventional sexual "morality." In the 1950s I rebelled against psychoanalysis and most other forms of psychotherapy and started the cognitive-behavioral revolution. In the 1960s and 1970s I started to write and speak skeptically about dogmatic religion and transpersonal psychology (Ellis, 1972b, 1973c, 1975a, 1977c). In the 1980s I continued my efforts to fight against mysticism, occultism, and transpersonal psychology (Ellis, 1980, 1983a, 1985b, 1986c; Ellis & Yeager, 1989). Finally, I aroused the verbal wrath of some of the big guns of the now very popular transpersonal and New Age psychology movements, several of whom were irate and mystical enough to confuse my skepticism with dogmatism and to lambaste me savagely (Walsh, 1989; Wilber, 1989). Good! I still enjoy a fine bout with antiscientists, hope that they will always keep after me, and hope that our ensuing discussions will encourage therapists and counselors to discover for themselves some of the more dangerous sides of devout religiosity and occultism.

My "old age," during the 1980s, has seen my professional and public popularity, as well as that of rational-emotive therapy and cognitive-behavior therapy steadily progress. Almost innumerable professional books have appeared during the last decade, including my own *Rational-Emotive Therapy Approaches to the Problems of Childhood* (Ellis & Bernard, 1983), *Clinical Applications of Rational-Emotive Therapy* (Ellis & Bernard, 1985), *Handbook of Rational-Emotive Therapy,* Vol. 2 (Ellis & Grieger, 1986), *The Practice of Rational-Emotive Therapy* (Ellis & Dryden, 1987), *Rational-Emotive Therapy with Alcoholics and Substance Abusers* (Ellis, McInerney, DiGiuseppe, & Yeager, 1988), *Rational-Emotive Couples Therapy* (Ellis, Sichel, Yeager, DiMattia, & DiGiuseppe, 1989), and *The Essential Albert Ellis* (Ellis & Dryden, 1989).

During the 1980s a score of other professional books on RET were also published, including outstanding texts by Bard (1980), Walen, DiGiuseppe, and Wessler (1980), Grieger and Boyd (1980), Wessler and Wessler (1980), Grieger and Grieger (1982), Bernard and Joyce (1984), Dryden (1984), Dryden and Trower (1986), and Bernard and DiGiuseppe (1989).

In the popular field, RET and CBT books were practically flooding the self-help market. Best-selling publications included books by Beck (1988), Bernard (1986), Burns (1980, 1989), Ellis (1988b), Ellis and Becker (1982), Emery (1982), Hauck (1973, 1974, 1986), and Maultsby (1986).

Also in the 1980s, innumerable audio and video cassettes spread the RET message to millions of people throughout the world. Out of 11 best-selling *Psychology Today* audio tapes in May, 1989, 5 were cassettes that I made for the series (Ellis, 1985a, 1986a, 1986b, 1987a, 1988c), and 4 others were CBT tapes. Other recent popular RET tapes published by the Institute for Rational-Emotive Therapy include *Solving Emotional Problems* (Ellis, 1982b), *How to Be Happy Though Human* (Ellis, 1984), and *Briefer and Better Ways of Helping Yourself Emotionally* (Ellis, 1988d).

In the 1980s, RET was also recognized in several interviews and films and in one full-length biography. The interviews included those by Weinrach (1980) and Dryden (Dryden & Ellis, 1989). A film featuring me and RET (Ellis, 1982a) was produced by Research Press, and a biography, *Albert Ellis: Passionate Skeptic* (Wiener, 1989), was published by Praeger.

What do I consider my main contributions to the fields of sex-love relations, to cognitive-behavior therapy, and to general psychotherapy? Let me make a prejudicial selection.

In the area of sex-love relations, I have been a pioneering sex therapist since 1943, and was one of the very first psychologists to integrate sex therapy with general psychotherapy. I published a seminal paper, "The Sexual Psychology of Human Hermaphrodites" (Ellis, 1945). I was the main clinical psychologist to vigorously support Alfred Kinsey (Ellis, 1948b, 1954b). I became the American editor of the first scientific sex journal, *The International Journal of Sexology,* in 1947. I became the main popularizer of the myth of the vaginal orgasm and of the value of noncoital sex relations (Ellis, 1953, 1954a). I started a campaign to found the Society for the Scientific Study of Sex in 1949, and when I finally succeeded in getting it started became its first president. I began to use four-letter words in my public talks on sex and psychotherapy in the 1940s and was the first psychologist to use them at APA conventions and other professional meetings before 1950.

I began to give public talks and to write popular articles espousing very liberal sex views in the 1940s, became the most popular clinical psychologist in this respect in the 1950s and 1960s, and am often credited, along with Kinsey, with being the "father" of the modern sex revolution (Ellis, 1951a, 1951b, 1953, 1954a, 1954b, 1960, 1963a, 1963b, 1965a, 1965b; Ellis & Conway, 1967; Ellis & Sagarin, 1964). I have been one of the chief architects of gay liberation, and have often been wrongly accused of homosexuality because of my advocacy of gay rights and my frequent court appearances defending homosexuals. As a testifier in sex cases in the 1950s, I also helped O. John Rogge, the famous lawyer, obtain a Supreme Court decision allowing nudist magazines to be sold on newsstands. I was one of the few male supporters of women's liberation in the 1940s and 1950s (Ellis, 1954b, 1958), and my book, *The Intelligent Woman's Guide to Dating and Mating* (1963a, 1979) was in press when Betty Friedan published her landmark book, *The Feminine Mystique,* in 1963. My *Guide* was, I think, the first book to urge women to take up equal rights with men in regard to approaching suitable partners for dating, for sex, and for love relationships.

My professional and popular writings on sex therapy (Ellis, 1954a, 1958, 1960, 1961, 1963a, 1963b) helped inspire Masters and Johnson (1970) and others to start the revolution in that area in the 1970s. Along with Patricia Schiller and Warren Johnson, I was also one of the founders and chief architects of the American Association of Sex Education, Counselors and Therapists, and wrote its original standards for certifying sex therapists.

As a result of my sex-love liberalism, I have been censured and censored on many occasions. My books, such as *Sex Without Guilt,* have been banned in several American countries and in foreign countries. "Respectable" publications like *Playboy* and *The New York Times* have refused to carry ads for *The Art and Science of Love* and several of my other books. Several of my scheduled talks at universities have been canceled, even though the talks themselves were on RET and not on sexual topics. Some leading television and radio shows—such as the Johnny Carson show— have booked me and then canceled me at the last minute because I was "too controversial." Innumerable psychologists and psychiatrists who largely agree with me about therapy have defamed me for writing about sex and for using four-letter words in public. Antiabortion groups have picketed me at professional conferences where I talked about sex. Professional groups and journals have stopped publication of some of my presentations on masturbation (Ellis, 1965b, 1965d). Throughout all this heated opposition to my sex views, I have consistently used RET on myself and refused to make myself enraged, depressed, or anxious. Only appropriately sorrowful and disappointed!

My most outstanding contributions regarding RET include the following: (1) Founding RET, the first of the modern major cognitive-behavioral therapies; (2) strongly pushing and popularizing RET and CBT with professionals and helping make this "new kid on the block" one of the popular therapies extant; (3) nicely using RET on myself and thereby stubbornly refusing to make myself miserable when founders of cognitive-behavior therapies that started a decade or more after RET claimed an originality that was hardly theirs; (4) refusing to upset myself when very popular do-it-yourself books—especially Dyer's *Your Erroneous Zones* (1977)— made fortunes promulgating RET without any acknowledgment that RET ever existed; (5) publishing the first research study of RET and CBT (Ellis, 1957b) after I had practiced it for two years; (6) as probably the busiest practitioner of RET in the world, continuing to learn from my thousands of individual and group sessions every year, and remaining open to revising the major rational-emotive theories and practices over the years; (7) building an Institute for Rational-Emotive Therapy that is very active in clinical training, research, and other areas, and that has a number of active affiliates in the United States, Canada, Mexico, England, Holland, Germany, Italy, India, and Australia.

Reflections on Clinical Psychology: Past, Present, and Future

Clinical psychology's past—and when I began my graduate work in 1941, its past still largely existed—was concerned mainly with diagnosis rather than with psychotherapy. In my first job in a well-known mental hygiene clinic in 1948, I was not allowed to do any therapy—that was the sole prerogative of the clinical psychiatrists. I only did psychological testing and a little vocational counseling. Even in the testing area, I was the first clinical psychologist to use the Rorschach and other projective tests.

I frankly resented this part of clinical psychology and rebelled against it by sneaking in some therapy without reporting it and by arranging a part-time private practice in which I mainly did psychotherapy and sex therapy. When I became chief psychologist of the New Jersey State Diagnostic Center and later of the entire Department of Institutions and Agencies of New Jersey, I supervised the psychologists under me in both diagnosis and therapy and actually arranged for most of our psychiatrists to do diagnosis and consultation. In New York City where I practiced, however, almost all psychotherapy was psychoanalytic, and practically all of the reputable analysts were psychiatrists. This was because, until about 1949, the psychoanalytic societies admitted very few psychologists for training; and most psychologists, like myself, who wanted to be analysts had to find unconventional analysts who would train them and help set them up in practice.

Clinical psychology, in the days when I got into the field, was not only heavily psychoanalytic but also exceptionally Freudian. Although I was largely psychoanalytic myself in the 1940s, I objected then—and still do—to the Freudian theories about the Oedipus complex, specific stages of sexual development, sexual origins of neurosis, rigid transference interpretations, and other dogmas, and I forthrightly said so at the time (Ellis, 1949c, 1950a). I also heavily assaulted psychologists' devout reliance on paper-and-pencil personality tests and (as noted earlier) made myself a great reputation by doing so.

I was—and still am—highly skeptical of many of the formulations dear to the heart of most clinical psychologists of the 1940s and 1950s. I didn't take intelligence tests too seriously, although I thought they had some degree of validity. I rarely used personality tests with my clients, figuring that listening to them carefully and asking them some direct questions would be sufficiently diagnostic. I practiced classical analysis with free association and lengthy dream interpretation for a while, but found these and other analytic techniques too inefficient, so I veered to psychoanalytically oriented psychotherapy, using more direct questioning and faster interpretations. I found most psychotherapists to be highly speculative, dogmatic, and antiscientific. I discovered that sending the mate of a person I was seeing to another therapist frequently created much confusion and conflict. So in 1950 I started doing conjoint marital therapy, as well as seeing whole families jointly. Even when still practicing psychoanalytically oriented therapy, I added some behavioral components like skill training and homework assignments (Ellis 1955a, 1955b).

On the whole, my impression of the clinical psychology, and especially the psychological treatment, of the past is that it was in its formative stage, was not very original or creative, debased itself with psychoanalytic traditionalism, and was often unscientific. Controlled experiments in psychotherapy were rare. In New York therapy was largely psychoanalytic, but in the 1940s and 1950s universities began to train psychologists in nondirective Rogerian therapy and, to my mind, that made psychologists' treatment even more inefficient and ineffective (Ellis, 1948a). After being trained in Rogerian methods in my graduate work at Teachers College, and later in my psychoanalytic training, I found more reason than ever to return to the honest directness that I first started to use in 1943 in sex therapy.

Let me conclude by answering some important questions that the editor of this book, Gene Walker, has aptly asked about my lifelong absorption in clinical psychology and psychotherapy.

What were early interests that led to your interest in psychology? Mainly my physical illness (nephritis) as a child and the severe headaches it seemed to produce; and my anxiety over potential failure and disapproval. I became determined to use the best-known psychological and philosophic methods not to make myself needlessly miserable over *anything*.

What individuals, books, and ideas shaped your development as a psychologist?
First, the philosophic writings of Epicurus, Epictetus, Marcus Aurelius, Spinoza,
Ralph Waldo Emerson, Henry David Thoreau, Bertrand Russell, John Dewey,
Thorsten Veblen, Paul Tillich, A. J. Ayer, and other philosophers. Second, the
psychological writings of William James, Sigmund Freud, Alfred Adler, John B.
Watson, Ivan Pavlov, B. F. Skinner, Erich Fromm, Harry Stack Sullivan, Karen
Horney, and others. Third, the sexological writings of Havelock Ellis, Ivan Bloch,
August Forel, W. F. Robie, Th. Van de Velde, and other liberal sex therapists.

*Throughout your career, what were the guiding ideas and principles for your
work?* Science, efficiency, honesty, revolutionism, and passionate skepticism.

*Could you describe some of the problems that confronted you in the research and
other work that you did?* Mainly I was confronted with the problem of coming up with
hypotheses, especially in my sex and RET research, which were stoutly opposed
by many other psychologists, and being forced to think rationally and behave forthrightly in spite of their great opposition.

*What were your thoughts and feelings surrounding these problems and how did
you resolve them?* I never did feel depressed or self-deprecating, but at times I felt
angry because I told myself that my detractors were (and still are!) foolish and unfair
and that they absolutely *must not* be the way they clearly were. But I used RET on
myself and successfully gave up just about all my anger at *them* while I remained
sorry and displeased at their *behavior*. I accepted these sinners and did not condemn
them for their sins!

Were there colleagues who greatly supported or opposed your work? Yes, both!
Most clinical psychologists—in fact, the great majority—vehemently opposed, first,
my liberal sex views and then, even more so, my RET theory and practice. The
psychoanalysts, the Rogerians, and the behaviorists all ranted and fumed against
RET. But I stubbornly refused to upset myself about this and actively continued to
practice, supervise, and teach. A small group of colleagues strongly supported me,
became RETers, and have continued to support me throughout the years. Later,
especially after 1970, I developed a large number of RET and CBT supporters. But
even many of the CBT theoreticians and practitioners, for various reasons (including,
probably, envy and personal ego-inflation), keep misquoting me and accusing me of
all kinds of skullduggery. Tough! But hardly awful or horrible!

What sort of lifestyle did you have as a clinical psychologist? Most busy and quite
enjoyable! I have seen more individual and group clients than almost any other living
psychologist; briefly supervised thousands of therapists and intensively supervised
hundreds of them; given over 3000 talks and workshops here and abroad; and
published over 600 articles, over 50 books, and scores of audio and video cassettes. I
still enjoy most of this activity and look forward hopefully to much more of it. If other
pursuits—such as opera, ballet, and play-going—came an unclose second, too bad!

Are there things you would do differently if you had it to do over? Of course, since I have made many errors and presumably would learn by them and try to correct them. On the big issue, however, of whether I would criticize other clinical systems and procedures less, I doubt that I would change to make myself more popular. I still believe that a main goal and service of a clinician and scientist is to definitely—but not damningly or angrily—expose other mistaken and ineffective systems. So I would probably still determinedly do so in spite of the flak that I would thereby draw against myself and my views. *Vive* passionate skepticism!—which, I think, is at the very heart of good science.

As far as my personal life is concerned, I would again do many things quite differently, and not do what I actually did—such as marry my first and second wives, both of whom I loved considerably (and am still friendly with), but with whom I was not really compatible. However, I do not regret the experience I had with both of them, because for the most part I enjoyed them; and I learned what *not* to do in my subsequent love relationships.

The one thing in my personal life that I definitely *would* do over again would be to live together with Janet Wolfe, with whom I have cohabited for almost a quarter of a century. Janet and I are both loving *and* compatible—a rare combination! Our mutual warmth, trust, caring, support, humor, and playfulness have been, and still are, a most *rational* addition to my existence. Janet has also added immeasurably to the development and growth of RET and the Institute for Rational-Emotive Therapy. Without her extraordinary directing of the affairs of the institute for the last 15 years, and the removal of innumerable administrative burdens from my shoulders, it and I would have been severely handicapped. Congratulations are in order to Janet for supporting me and RET so beautifully and to me for having the perspicacity to start and maintain my loving relationship with her!

References

Bandura, A. (1969). *Principles of behavior modification.* New York: Holt, Rinehart & Winston.

Bard, J. (1980). *Rational-emotive therapy in practice.* Champaign, IL: Research Press.

Bartley, W. W. (1962). *The retreat to commitment.* New York: Knopf. Rev. ed., 1985.

Beck, A. T. (1967). *Depression.* New York: Hoeber-Harper.

Beck, A. T. (1976). *Cognitive therapy and the emotional disorders.* New York: International Universities Press.

Beck, A. T. (1988). *Love is not enough.* New York: Harper & Row.

Bernard, M. E. (1986). *Staying alive in an irrational world: Albert Ellis and rational-emotive therapy.* South Melbourne, Australia: Carlson/Macmillan.

Bernard, M. E. & Di Giuseppe, R. (Eds.) (1989). *Inside rational-emotive therapy.* Orlando, FL: Academic Press.

Bernard, M. E. & Joyce, M. R. (1984). *Rational-emotive therapy with children and adolescents.* New York: Wiley.

Burns, D. D. (1980). *Feeling good: The new mood therapy.* New York: Morrow.

Burns, D. D. (1989). *Feeling good handbook.* New York: Morrow.

Dryden W. (1984). *Rational-emotive therapy: Fundamentals and innovations.* Beckenham, Kent: Croom-Helm.

Dryden, W. & Ellis, A. (1989). Albert Ellis: An efficient and passionate life. *Journal of Counseling and Development, 67,* 539–546.

Dryden, W. & Trower, P. (Eds.) (1986). *Rational-emotive therapy: Recent developments in theory and practice.* Bristol, England: Institute for RET (UK).

Dyer, W. (1977). *Your erroneous zones.* New York: Funk and Wagnalls.

Ellis, A. (1945). The sexual psychology of hermaphrodites. *Psychosomatic Medicine, 7,* 108–125.

Ellis, A. (1946). The validity of personality questionnaires. *Psychological Bulletin, 43,* 385–440.

Ellis, A. (1947a). A comparison of the use of direct and indirect phrasing in personality questionnaires. *Psychological Monographs, 61,* 1–41.

Ellis, A. (1947b). Personality questionnaires. *Review of Educational Research, 17,* 101–109.

Ellis, A. (1948a). A critique of the theoretical contributions of nondirective therapy. *Journal of Clinical Psychology, 4,* 248–255.

Ellis, A. (1948b). Review of A. C. Kinsey, W. B. Pomeroy, & C. E. Martin, *Sexual behavior in the human male. Journal of General Psychology, 27,* 289–290.

Ellis, A. (1948c). A study of trends in recent psychoanalytic publications. *American Imago, 5* (4), 3–13.

Ellis, A. (1949a). Some significant correlations of love and family behavior. *Journal of Social Psychology, 15,* 61–76.

Ellis, A. (1949b). A study of the love emotions of American college girls. *International Journal of Sexology, 3,* 15–21.

Ellis, A. (1949c). Towards the improvement of psychoanalytic research. *Psychoanalytic Review, 36,* 123–143.

Ellis, A. (1950a). An introduction to the scientific principles of psychoanalysis. *Genetic Psychology Monographs, 41,* 147–212.

Ellis, A. (1950b). Love and family relationships of American college girls. *American Journal of Sociology, 55,* 550–558.

Ellis, A. (1950c). The sex, love and marriage questions of senior nursing students. *Journal of Social Psychology, 31,* 209–216.

Ellis, A. (1951a). *The folklore of sex.* New York: Charles Boni. Rev. ed., New York: Grove Press, 1961.

Ellis, A. (1951b). Introduction. In. D. W. Cory, *The homosexual in America* (pp. ix–x). New York: Greenberg.

Ellis, A. (1953). Is the vaginal orgasm a myth? In A. P. Pillay & A. Ellis (Eds.), *Sex, society and the individual* (pp. 155–162). Bombay: International Journal of Sexology Press.

Ellis, A. (1954a). *The American sexual tragedy.* New York: Twayne. Rev. ed., New York: Lyle Stuart and Grove Press, 1962.

Ellis, A. (Ed.) (1954b). *Sex life of the American woman and the Kinsey report.* New York: Greenberg.

Ellis, A. (1955a). New approaches to psychotherapy techniques. Brandon, VT. *Journal of Clinical Psychology Monograph Supplement,* Vol. II.

Ellis, A. (1955b). Psychotherapy techniques for use with psychotics. *American Journal of Psychotherapy, 3,* 452–476.

Ellis, A. (1956). An operational reformulation of some of the basic principles of psychoanalysis. In H. Feigl & M. Scriven (Eds.), *The foundations of science and the concepts of psychology and psychoanalysis* (pp. 131–154). Minneapolis: University of Minnesota Press. (Also: *Psychoanalytic Review, 43,* 163–180.)

Ellis, A. (1957a). *How to live with a "neurotic": At home and at work.* New York: Crown. Rev. ed., Hollywood, CA: Wilshire Books, 1975.

Ellis, A. (1957b). Outcome of employing three techniques of psychotherapy. *Journal of Clinical Psychology, 13,* 344–350.

Ellis, A. (1958). *Sex without guilt.* New York: Lyle Stuart. Rev. ed., New York: Lyle Stuart, 1965.

Ellis, A. (Ed.) (1959a). *The place of value in the practice of psychotherapy.* New York: American Academy of Psychotherapists.

Ellis, A. (Ed.) (1959b). *What is psychotherapy?* New York: American Academy of Psychotherapists.

Ellis, A. (1960). *The art and science of love.* Secaucus, NJ: Lyle Stuart.

Ellis, A. (1961). Frigidity. In A. Ellis & A. Abarbanel (Eds.), *The encyclopedia of sexual behavior* (pp. 450–456). New York: Hawthorn Books.

Ellis, A. (1962a). *The American sexual tragedy.* Rev. ed., New York: Lyle Stuart and Grove Press.

Ellis, A. (1962b). *Reason and emotion in psychotherapy.* Secaucus, NJ: Citadel.

Ellis, A. (1963a). *The intelligent woman's guide to manhunting.* New York: Lyle Stuart and Dell. Rev. ed., *The intelligent woman's guide to dating and mating.* Secaucus, NJ: Lyle Stuart, 1979.

Ellis, A. (1963b). *Sex and the single man.* Secaucus, NJ: Lyle Stuart.

Ellis, A. (1965a). *The case for sexual liberty.* Tucson, AZ: Seymour Press.

Ellis, A. (1965b). *Sex without guilt.* Secaucus, NJ: Lyle Stuart; and North Hollywood, CA: Wilshire Books. Orig. ed., 1958.

Ellis, A. (1965c). The treatment of psychotic patients with rational-emotive psychotherapy. In *Symposium on therapeutic methods with schizophrenics* (pp. 5–32). Battle Creek, MI: Veterans Administration Hospital. Reprinted, New York: Institute for Rational-Emotive Therapy. Rev. ed., 1989.

Ellis, A. (1965d). *Suppressed: Seven key essays publishers dared not print.* Chicago: New Classics House.

Ellis, A. (1968). *Is objectivism a religion?* New York: Lyle Stuart.

Ellis, A. (1969). A weekend of rational encounter. *Rational Living, 4* (2), 1–8.

Ellis, A. (1971). *Growth through reason.* North Hollywood, CA: Wilshire Books.

Ellis, A. (1972a). *How to master your fear of flying.* New York: Institute for Rational-Emotive Therapy.

Ellis, A. (1972b). What does transpersonal psychology have to offer the art and science of psychotherapy? *Voices, 8* (1), 20–28.

Ellis, A. (1972c). *Psychotherapy and the value of a human being.* New York: Institute for Rational-Emotive Therapy.

Ellis, A. (Speaker) (1973a). *How to stubbornly refuse to be ashamed of anything.* Cassette recording. New York: Institute for Rational-Emotive Therapy.

Ellis, A. (1973b). *Humanistic psychotherapy: The rational-emotive approach.* New York: McGraw-Hill.

Ellis, A. (1973c). Is transpersonal psychology humanistic? *Association for Humanistic Psychology Newsletter,* May, June, pp. 10–13.

Ellis, A. (Speaker) (1973d). *Twenty-one ways to stop worrying.* Cassette recording. New York: Institute for Rational-Emotive Therapy.

Ellis, A. (Speaker) (1974). *Rational living in an irrational world.* Cassette recording. New York: Institute for Rational-Emotive Therapy.

Ellis, A. (1975a). Comments on Franks's "The limits of humanism." *Humanist, 35* (5), 43–45.

Ellis, A. (Speaker) (1975b). *RET and assertiveness training.* Cassette recording. New York: Institute for Rational-Emotive Therapy.

Ellis, A. (Speaker) (1976a). *Conquering low frustration tolerance.* Cassette recording. New York: Institute for Rational-Emotive Therapy.

Ellis, A. (1976b). RET abolishes most of the human ego. *Psychotherapy, 13,* 343–348. Reprinted, New York: Institute for Rational-Emotive Therapy.

Ellis, A. (1976c). *Sex and the liberated man.* Secaucus, NJ: Lyle Stuart.

Ellis, A. (1977a). Fun as psychotherapy. *Rational Living, 12* (1), 2–6.

Ellis, A. (Speaker) (1977b). *A garland of rational humorous songs.* Cassette recording and song book. New York: Institute for Rational-Emotive Therapy.

Ellis, A. (1977c). Why "scientific" professionals believe mystical nonsense. *Psychiatric Opinion, 14* (2), 27–30.

Ellis, A. (1977d). *Anger—how to live with and without it.* Secaucus, NJ: Citadel Press.

Ellis, A. (1979). *The intelligent woman's guide to dating and mating.* Secaucus, NJ: Lyle Stuart.

Ellis, A. (1980). Psychotherapy and atheistic values: A response To A. E. Bergin's "Psychotherapy and religious values." *Journal of Consulting and Clinical Psychology, 48,* 635–639.

Ellis, A. (Speaker) (1982a). *Rational-emotive therapy: A documentary film featuring Dr. Albert Ellis.* Film. Champaign, IL: Research Press.

Ellis, A. (Speaker) (1982b). *Solving emotional problems.* Cassette recording. New York: Institute for Rational-Emotive Therapy.

Ellis, A. (1983a). *The case against religiosity.* New York: Institute for Rational-Emotive Therapy.

Ellis, A. (1983b). The philosophic implications and dangers of some popular behavior therapy techniques. In M. Rosenbaum, C. M. Franks, & Y. Jaffe (Eds.), *Perspectives in behavior therapy in the eighties* (pp. 138–151. New York. Springer.

Ellis, A. (Speaker) (1984). *How to be happy though human.* Cassette recording. New York: Institute for Rational-Emotive Therapy.

Ellis, A. (Speaker) (1985a). *A guide to personal happiness.* Cassette recording. Washington, DC: Psychology Today Tapes.

Ellis, A. (1985b). *Overcoming resistance: Rational-emotive therapy with difficult clients.* New York: Springer.

Ellis, A. (Speaker) (1986a). *Effective self-assertion.* Cassette recording. Washington, DC: Psychology Today Tapes.

Ellis, A. (Speaker) (1986b). *Rekindling romance.* Cassette recording. Washington, DC: Psychology Today Tapes.

Ellis, A. (1986c). Fanaticism that may lead to a nuclear holocaust. *Journal of Counseling and Development, 65,* 146–151.

Ellis, A. (Speaker) (1987a). *How to stop worrying and start living.* Cassette recording. Washington, DC: Psychology Today Tapes.

Ellis, A. (1987b). The impossibility of achieving consistently good mental health. *American Psychologist, 42,* 364–375.

Ellis, A. (1987c). Integrative developments in rational-emotive therapy (RET). *Journal of Integrative and Eclectic Psychotherapy, 6,* 470–479.

Ellis, A. (1987d). A sadly neglected cognitive element in depression. *Cognitive Therapy and research, 11,* 121–146.

Ellis, A. (1987e). The use of rational humorous songs in psychotherapy. In W. F. Fry, Jr. & W. A. Salameh (Eds.), *Handbook of humor and psychotherapy* (pp. 265–288). Sarasota, FL: Professional Resource Exchange.

Ellis, A. (1988a). How can psychological treatment aim to be briefer and better? The rational-emotive approach to brief therapy. Paper presented at the Fourth International Congress on Ericksonian Approaches to Hypnosis and Psychotherapy, Dec. 10, San Francisco.

Ellis, A. (1988b). *How to stubbornly refuse to make yourself miserable about anything—yes, anything!* Secaucus, NJ: Lyle Stuart.

Ellis, A. (Speaker) (1988c). *He who hesitates is lost.* Cassette recording. Washington, DC: Psychology Today Tapes.

Ellis, A. (Speaker) (1988d). *Briefer and better ways of helping yourself emotionally.* Cassette recording. New York: Institute for Rational-Emotive Therapy.

Ellis, A. (1989a). Ineffective consumerism in the cognitive-behavioral therapies and in general psychotherapy. In W. Dryden & P. Trower (Eds.), *Cognitive psychotherapy: Stasis and change* (pp. 159–174). London: Cassell.

Ellis, A. (1989b). Is rational-emotive therapy (RET) "rationalist" or "constructivist"? Keynote address to World Congress of Cognitive Therapy, Oxford, England, June 29. Also in A. Ellis & W. Dryden, *The essential Albert Ellis.* New York: Springer.

Ellis, A. (1989c). Comments on my critics. In M. E. Bernard & R. DiGiuseppe (Eds.), *Inside rational-emotive therapy.* San Diego, CA: Academic Press.

Ellis, A. & Abarbanel, A. (Eds.) (1961). *The encyclopedia of sexual behavior.* New York: Hawthorne Books.

Ellis, A. & Abrahms, E. (1978). *Brief psychotherapy in medical and health practice.* New York: Springer.

Ellis, A. & Becker, I. (1982). *A guide to personal happiness.* North Hollywood, CA: Wilshire Books.

Ellis, A. & Bernard, M. E. (Eds.) (1983). *Rational-emotive therapy approaches to the problems of childhood.* New York: Plenum.

Ellis, A. & Bernard, M. E. (Eds.) (1985). *Clinical applications of rational-emotive therapy.* New York: Plenum.

Ellis, A. & Brancale, R. (1956). *The psychology of sex offenders.* Springfield, IL: Thomas.

Ellis, A. & Conrad, H. (1948). The validity of personality inventories in military practice. *Psychological Bulletin, 45,* 385–426.

Ellis, A. & Conway, R. (1967). *The art of erotic seduction.* New York: Lyle Stuart.

Ellis, A. & Dryden, W. (1987). *The practice of rational-emotive therapy.* New York: Springer.

Ellis. A. & Dryden, W. (1989). *The essential Albert Ellis.* New York: Springer.

Ellis, A. & Grieger, R. (Eds.) (1977). *Handbook of rational-emotive therapy,* Vol. 1. New York: Springer.

Ellis, A. & Grieger, R. (Eds.) (1986). *Handbook of rational-emotive therapy,* Vol. 2. New York: Springer.

Ellis, A. & Harper, R. A. (1961a). *A guide to rational living.* Englewood Cliffs, NJ: Prentice-Hall.

Ellis, A. & Harper, R. A. (1961b). *A guide to successful marriage.* North Hollywood, CA: Wilshire Books.

Ellis, A. & Harper, R. A. (1975). *A new guide to rational living.* North Hollywood, CA: Wilshire Books.

Ellis, A. & Knaus, W. (1977). *Overcoming procrastination.* New York: New American Library.

Ellis, A., McInerney, J. P., DiGiuseppe, R., & Yeager, R. J. (1988). *Rational-emotive therapy with alcoholics and substance abusers.* New York: Pergamon.

Ellis, A. & Sagarin, E. (1964). *Nymphomania: A study of the oversexed woman.* New York: Macfadden.

Ellis, A., Sichel, J., Yeager, R., DiMattia, D., & DiGiuseppe, R. (1989). *Rational-emotive couples therapy*. New York: Pergamon.

Ellis, A. & Whiteley, J. M. (1979). *Theoretical and empirical foundations of rational-emotive therapy*. Pacific Grove, CA: Brooks/Cole.

Ellis, A., & Yeager, R. (1989). *Why some therapies don't work: The dangers of transpersonal psychology*. Buffalo, NY: Prometheus.

Ellis, A., Young, J., & Lockwood, G. (1987). Cognitive therapy and rational-emotive therapy: A dialogue. *Journal of Cognitive Therapy, 1* (4), 137–187.

Emery, G. (1982). *Own your own life*. New York: New American Library.

Ferenczi, S. (1952). *Further contributions to the theory and technique of psychoanalysis*. New York: Basic Books.

Glasser, W. (1965). *Reality therapy*. New York: Harper & Row.

Goldfried, M. R. & Davison, G. C. (1976). *Clinical behavior therapy*. New York: Holt, Rinehart & Winston.

Greenberg, L. S. & Safran, J. D. (1984). Integrating affect and cognition: A perspective on the process of therapeutic change. *Cognitive Therapy and Research, 8,* 591–598.

Grieger, R. & Boyd, J. (1980). *Rational-emotive therapy: A skills-based approach*. New York: Van Nostrand Reinhold.

Grieger, R. & Grieger, I. (Eds.) (1982). *Cognition and emotional disturbance*. New York: Human Sciences Press.

Guidano, V. F. & Liotti, G. (1983). *Cognitive processes and emotional disorders*. New York: Guilford.

Hauck, P. A. (1973). *Overcoming depression*. Philadelphia: Westminster.

Hauck, P. A. (1974). *Overcoming frustration and anger*. Philadelphia: Westminster.

Hauck, P. A. (1984). *The three faces of love*. Philadelphia: Westminster.

Hite, S. (1976). *The Hite report*. New York: MacMillan.

Kinsey, A. C., Pomeroy, W. B., & Martin, C. E. (1948). *Sexual behavior in the human male*. Philadelphia: Saunders.

Kinsey, A. C. Pomeroy, W. B., Martin, C. F., & Gebhard, P. H. (1953). *Sexual behavior in the human female*. Philadelphia: Saunders.

Lazarus, A. A. (1971). *Behavior therapy and beyond*. New York: McGraw-Hill.

Mahoney, M. J. (1974). *Cognition and behavior modifications*. Cambridge, MA: Ballinger.

Masters, W. & Johnson, V.A. (1960). *Human sexual response*. Boston: Little, Brown.

Masters, W. & Johnson, V.A. (1970). *Human sexual inadequacy*. Boston: Little, Brown.

Maultsby, M. C., Jr. (1971). *Handbook of rational self-counseling*. Lexington, KY: Rational Self Help Books.

Maultsby, M. C., Jr. (1986). *Coping better . . . anytime, anywhere*. New York: Prentice-Hall.

Meichenbaum, D. & Goodman, J. (1971). Training impulsive children to talk to themselves. *Journal of Abnormal Psychology, 77,* 115–126.

Pillay, A. P. & Ellis, A. (Eds.) (1953). *Sex, society and the individual*. Bombay: International Journal of Sexology Press.

Popper, K. R. (1985). *Popper selections*. D. Miller (Ed.) Princeton, NJ: Princeton University Press.

Raimy, V. (1975). *Misunderstandings of the self*. San Francisco: Jossey-Bass.

Walen, S. R., DiGiuseppe, R., & Wessler, R. L. (1980). *A practitioner's guide to rational-emotive therapy*. New York: Oxford.

Walsh, R. (1989). Psychological chauvinism and nuclear holocaust: A response to Albert

Ellis and defense of non-rational emotive therapies. *Journal of Counseling and Development, 67,* 338–340.

Weinrach, S. G. (1980). Unconventional therapist: Albert Ellis. *Personnel and Guidance Journal, 59,* 152–160.

Wessler, R. L. (1984). Alternative conceptions of rational-emotive therapy: Toward a philosophically neutral psychotherapy. In M. A. Reda & M. J. Mahoney (Eds.), *Cognitive psychotherapies: Recent developments in theory, research and practice* (pp. 65–79). Cambridge, MA: Ballinger.

Wessler, R. A. & Wessler, R. L. (1980). *The principles and practice of rational-emotive therapy.* San Francisco: Jossey-Bass.

Wiener, D. (1989). *Albert Ellis: Passionate skeptic.* New York: Praeger.

Wilber, K. (1989). Let's nuke the transpersonalists. *Journal of Counseling and Development, 67.*

Hans J. Eysenck, Ph.D., D.Sc.

Professor Emeritus of Psychology
University of London, England

◆

Maverick Psychologist

It is odd in many ways that I should end my career with a chapter in *The History of Clinical Psychology in Autobiography.* My interests as a youngster were exclusively in theoretical physics and mathematics. Within psychology my interest was in the experimental and psychometric domains, and as I shall relate I got into clinical psychology entirely by accident. Last but not least, I am probably as unlike the typical clinical psychologist as it is possible to be, never having treated any patients, and having done most of my life's work in other areas like behavioral genetics (Eysenck & Martin, 1988), the experimental analysis of the reminiscence phenomenon (Eysenck & Frith, 1977), conditioning and learning theory (Eysenck, 1976), and the study of individual differences, with particular reference to personality and intelligence (Eysenck & Eysenck, 1985). Yet, as I hope to make clear, there is some mad logic underlying my life's work, and leading to the studies which caused my inclusion in this volume, and to my being given the Distinguished Scientist Award by the APA for my work in behaviour therapy.

Historians take autobiographies with a grain of salt, and obviously what I shall say here, while true as far as I can make it, is inevitably tinged with subjectivity, and must equally inevitably look at things my way. More objective and balanced accounts will be found in the histories of behaviour therapy by Kazdin (1978) and Schorr (1984). A wider view of those areas of my work and life not covered here can be obtained from my chapter in Volume 7 of *A History of Psychology in Autobiography* (Eysenck, 1980), and from my autobiography, *Rebel with a Cause* (Eysenck, 1990). A more objective account of my life and work, warts and all, will be found in H. B. Gibson's *Hans Eysenck: The Man and His work* (1981).

In reading autobiographies, I tend to skip over any extended accounts of early life, family background, and school years because they do not normally seem very informative or interesting. Consequently I will keep my own account brief. I was born in Berlin, Germany, on March 4, 1916, in the middle of the First World War. My mother was an aspiring actress, and my father was in the army, of course, having previously served some time in the navy. He too was getting into the acting profession. My father came from a Catholic family in South Germany, while my mother came from a Protestant family in Silesia, a part of Prussia. Thus my genes incorporated the two great religions that had divided Germany since the time of the Thirty Years War, as well as the two parts of the country, North and South, which have always been held to embody the militaristic and the cultural faces of Germany, respectively. Fortunately neither of my parents took religion very seriously, and neither did I; it has never played any part in my life. I had no voice in being christened, of course, but I had to be bribed with the gift of a bicycle to allow myself to be confirmed. That was the end of my interest in matters religious.

After I was born my parents pursued their careers all over the country, and I was brought up (if that is the right word) by my grandmother, who when young had a brilliant career predicted for her as a singer and actress, but who became crippled in an accident (the end effect being entirely due to the criminal incompetence of the doctors who operated on her). I saw very little of my parents, who divorced when I was 4, and who had little feeling for me, an emotion I reciprocated. My grandmother was, to use a term not applicable to many people, a "good" woman, unselfish, caring, altruistic, and altogether too good for this world. Halfway through the Second World War she was murdered by the Nazis in a concentration camp, after having been hidden for about a year by two Catholic sisters who shared her religious convictions. Even now I cannot bear to think about the suffering she must have gone through in that time.

When I said my grandmother brought me up, that is merely to use a conventional phrase. I was a headstrong lad from the beginning, and she was quite incapable of enforcing any discipline, so I grew up rather like "Topsy." I was quite good at school, without ever doing any work. I was bored by most of the teaching I received, and soon found out that I was a good deal brighter than any of my teachers. This did not make me particularly popular with them, as neither then nor now have I ever had the ability to disguise my true feelings. Furthermore, practically all the teachers were right-wing or even followers of the growing Nazi party, while in my maverick fashion I was full of socialist ideas. I received wildly differing marks for my essays, for instance, depending on whether the teacher liked or didn't like my ideas. I remember one teacher almost having apoplexy when we were asked to write an essay on a famous German hero. I picked Frederick the Great, mercilessly dissecting his "achievements" and concluding that he was "an autocratic, warmongering poofter." This did not go down well!

My teachers also didn't like my flippant attitude, often expressed in satire. When we were asked to write an account of the Nibelungen story, the sacred Germanic myth, I made a farce of it by interpreting it in psychoanalytic terms—not that I knew anything about psychoanalysis, but the symbolism made popular by Freud was then all the rage, and I had heard about it. Such incidents as Hagen plunging his spear into the place in Siegfried's body where a leaf had settled when he was bathing in the dragon's blood, which made him invulnerable, but leaving that particular part open, was an obvious invitation to such interpretations.

I was interested in astronomy and subatomic physics, and particularly the theory of relativity and quantum mechanics. Our teaching in physics was execrable, and I paid no attention to it. However, at the suggestion of the head master I jumped a class, and he made it a condition that I would have special coaching in mathematics because it is not easy to make up the year if you jump in that way. My parents hired a Ph.D. who had been studying with Einstein, and instead of the boring mathematics we were doing at school, I persuaded him to teach me the principles of modern physics, which I found much more interesting.

I developed an almost pathological hatred of Hitler and all that he stood for—racism, warmongering, the *Führerprinzip*—and spoke out very openly against all this. Apart from the Jewish boys in the class, practically all the others were Nazis at heart, and I would have had a hard time if I hadn't been big and strong and quite experienced in street fighting. I was also pretty good at sports, at least those that involved a ball, I played tennis (I won tournaments), football, field hockey, ice hockey, handball, Schlagball (a peculiarly German game halfway between baseball and cricket), and during a spell at an English school I even learnt to play cricket!

The final year of my school career coincided with Hitler's first year as chancellor, and when I made my application to the university I was told that I would be accepted only if I joined the S.S. This was not a condition usually made for entrants, but I expect they had heard of my outspoken criticisms, and thought that membership in the Death's Head Brigade would change my outlook. Of course I refused—the very thought was anathema to me, and in any case I knew that I couldn't keep my mouth shut, and would end up in a concentration camp in no time at all. So I decided to leave Germany and become an exile. There really was no choice for someone with my political and social attitudes and ideals, but I knew it would be a hard wrench, and so it turned out.

My mother had become a well-known film star and had married her director and producer. Max Glass was a mid-European Jew who had been a professor of aesthetics at the Sorbonne in Paris, but had decided to use his talents in order to become rich instead. He was very well known for his work in films, and produced some of the most artistic and imaginative films for Terra, second only to UFA among the ranks of German film producers. Being Jewish he had to flee Germany, and of course my mother went with him to Paris. I spent some time in France, at my mother's suggestion, studying French literature and history at the University of Dijon. However, I preferred England, where I had already been several times, and finally went to London.

Before taking up an account of my career in England, let me just finish my account of my parents. When the Germans overran France, my mother was in the southern part, having fled from Paris a few days before. The Petain government collaborated with the Nazis and imprisoned all German refugees, but she escaped from her concentration camp by bribing some of the guards and made her way across the Pyrenees to Madrid, where Max Glass was waiting. They went to São Paulo in Brazil for a few years, then to New York, and after the war finally settled again in Paris, where they lived until he died. For the final three or four years of her life, my mother came over to London to be with her only child; she died of old age at 94. My father stayed in Germany and became a member of the Nazi party (as he had to do in order to pursue his profession as *conferencier* and actor, but took no part in the war; he died at the age of 80.

When I arrived in London I found that the University of London required me to pass a special entrance examination, and I took courses at a commercial college, Pitman's College, to prepare for these exams. I also learned shorthand, typing, and other secretarial skills, in case I had to earn a living that way. I passed the entrance examination, but when I went to enroll in the physics faculty I was told I had taken the wrong subjects and was therefore ineligible. This is a favourite ploy of the University of London, which is perhaps the most bureaucratic of all universities; in Germany, once you are qualified to enter the university you have a completely free choice of courses, lectures, and examinations. I hadn't known about these conditions, and asked whether there were any science subjects I could take. "Oh yes," they said, "There is always psychology!" I answered rather weakly, "What on earth is psychology?" "Oh," they said, "You'll like it!" This is how I got into psychology, which was the one subject in the faculties of both arts and sciences. I have often wondered what would have happened to me had I gone into physics, but of course there is no answer to such a question.

I entered the Department of Psychology at University College in 1935, under Professor Cyril Burt, later to be knighted for his services to education. In some ways this was a lucky choice, as he was probably the foremost psychometrician of his age, with only Leo Thurstone and Godfrey Thomson to rival him. The teaching faculty was quite small, containing, besides Burt, J. C. Flugel, a professional psychoanalyst who taught social psychology, and S. J. Philpott, who taught the experimental classes. Burt had succeeded Charles Spearman, whom I also got to know.

In those years I still had an almost photographic memory, being able to read and visually reproduce a page almost at will. My mode of studying was perhaps a trifle unusual. I would get a number of textbooks, read them through, and know it all. I could easily answer any exam question by simply calling up the image of the page that contained the answers. This is a useful capacity for doing well at exams, but of course no use at all for serious research work. However, I soon found that I knew more psychology than my teachers, except in their own specialized areas. Burt of course knew far more psychometrics than I did, Flugel knew far more psychoanalysis, and Philpott knew far more about Jung—oddly enough for someone who taught experimental psychology, he was a confirmed follower of Jung. Altogether the department was very psychoanalytic—Burt himself had been a founding member of the British

Psychoanalytic Association, and had only one criticism to make of Freud, to wit, that the notion of unconscious ideas was contradictory, because ideas are defined as being conscious! I could even then think of more trenchant criticisms.

As we all know, there is in psychology a dualism that has always threatened to destroy psychology as a unified science. On the one hand we have the experimentalists, often very narrow in outlook, who pay no attention to individual differences, personality, intelligence, and such concepts; on the other hand we have the psychometricians, who are interested in individual differences but pay no heed to the experimentalists' concerns. In England this opposition was manifested in the hostility existing between the London school, which, under Spearman and Burt, specialized on the psychometric side, and the Cambridge school which, under Sir Frederick Bartlett, specialized in the narrowest kind of experimental psychology, paying no attention to individual differences. The narrowness of teaching characterizing both sides is shown by the fact that Burt allocated one hour (!) to the teaching of conditioning and learning theory; he gave that lecture himself, although he quite plainly knew very little about either. On the other hand, I have had graduate students from Bartlett's laboratory who couldn't even calculate a correlation, and had had just one hour's teaching in statistical methodology!

It seemed obvious to me that both sides were wrong in neglecting the expertise of the other, and that what was required was the unification of psychology to bring the two sides together. This immediately made me unpopular with both Burt and Bartlett, and indeed Burt developed a quite unreasoning hatred of me that lasted to the end of his life. This hatred, which is well documented in Hearnshaw's biography of Burt (1979), showed itself in many odd ways. Burt was the editor of the *British Journal of Statistical Psychology,* and in one issue published a review of my first book, *Dimensions of Personality.* This was signed by a well-known British statistician, and was about as devastating a review as I have ever seen. A few years after it appeared, I happened to meet this statistician, and he told me that in fact he had written a very good review, but that Burt had completely rewritten it an published it under his name! This is hardly normal behaviour, and in my autobiography I give many other such examples (Eysenck, 1990).

Nevertheless, in 1938 I got my first degree, with first-class honours; Burt told me later that it was the best set of exam papers he had ever seen. (A little while after that he also told me that he hadn't been able to read my writing, and only gave me a first because I had done so well in class! This was a typical Burtian method of having it both ways, regardless of what the truth might be.)

On the day I received my degree, I married Margaret Davies, a pretty young girl from Winnipeg, Canada, who had graduated in mathematics and was working in London as a secretary. I got her interested in psychology, and she did an external degree and finally a master's degree. She was very bright and hardworking; to be able to do all this while also holding a full-time job and running a home certainly required a great deal of efficiency. We had one son, Michael William Eysenck. He took up psychology and has done very well, becoming a professor at one of the schools of the University of London. We have written several books together, including one popular (*Mindwatching,* 1985) and one serious (*Personality and Individual*

Differences: A Natural Science Approach, 1985). He is probably a better experimentalist than I am, but with rather narrower interests.

When war broke out the University of London went to Aberystwyth, but I couldn't leave Margaret and had to stay in London. I did my Ph.D. on the topic of experimental aesthetics, motivated both by my interest in art and also by the fact that in the absence of the department and its technical facilities I had to work on something that did not require apparatus. Picture reproductions and similar stimulus materials were available, however, and I got my Ph.D. in 1940, two years after the B.A. My D.Sc. had to wait until 1964; this is a degree given by the University of London for outstanding quality and quantity of publications in one's chosen subject.

I had not then been in England long enough to be naturalized, so I was declared an "enemy alien." I escaped internment by the skin of my teeth, arguing with the police officers who came to take me away and getting away with it. I had tried to join the armed services but was rejected, first by the air force, then by the navy, and finally by the army—they just didn't want to know. I was finally accepted by ARP (Air Raid Precautions)—groups of people set up all over the country to deal with air raid casualties and all the problems and difficulties caused by the bombing of London and other towns. This time itself would make an interesting story, but it is not really relevant to the main theme of this chapter. What is relevant is that one day I received a letter from Philip Vernon, who at that time was psychological adviser to the army. He also was interested in experimental aesthetics, and we had met a number of times to discuss these mutual interests. We had become friends, and when a vacancy occurred at the Mill Hill Hospital, where Aubrey Lewis (later Sir Aubrey) was director of research, Philip recommended me. The Mill Hill Emergency Hospital was a wartime psychiatric institution for the armed forces. The traditional Maudsley Hospital had been split up at the beginning of the war into two parts, one going to Mill Hill, the other to Sutton, in order to provide psychiatric services for the army, the navy, and the air force, and it was here that my career in abnormal and clinical psychology began. I knew nothing, or very little, about abnormal psychology, and it was pure chance that led me to this particular venue.

A few words may be apposite regarding the Maudsley Hospital and the Institute of Psychiatry. The Institute of Psychiatry is the postgraduate medical school associated with the Bethlem Royal and Maudsley hospitals, and is a member of the British Postgraduate Medical Federation of the University of London. The Maudsley Hospital was established in 1914 by the London County Council at the insistence of Henry Maudsley, who contributed to the cost of building; in 1924 the Maudsley Hospital Medical School was granted full recognition by the University of London. Early in 1948 it was renamed the Institute of Psychiatry and admitted to the British Postgraduate Medical Federation. Later in the same year the Maudsley Hospital was amalgamated with the Bethlem Royal Hospital (the former "Bedlam," probably the oldest mental hospital in the world) to form a joint teaching hospital. The institute now comprises professorial departments of psychiatry, psychology, neurology, neuropathology, physiology, biochemistry, and biometrics, as well as child and adolescent psychiatry.

A few words about Sir Aubrey Lewis, whose plans for the institute led to the developments just outlined. He was born in Australia, studied medicine there, and later turned to psychiatry. He spent several years in Germany and the United States, acquiring a reputation for profundity and a wide knowledge of psychiatric theories and practices. He was an extremely intelligent man, and one who didn't suffer fools gladly; he could be very cruel indeed to registrars and others who didn't measure up to his ideal of the scientist-clinician. His main aim was to elevate the status of psychiatry, which at that time was right at the bottom of the medical totem pole. He attempted to do that by associating it with a number of recognised sciences that he considered fundamental to the proper study of psychiatry. He was one of the few psychiatrists in Great Britian who recognised the importance of psychology in this respect, and without his great help and furtherance I would certainly not have been able to achieve anything like as much as I did in fact manage to accomplish.

When I said I didn't know anything about psychiatry, clinical psychology, or abnormal behaviour, that was not quite true. At the beginning of the war I had made the acquaintance of Alexander Herzberg, whose ideas and therapeutic practices had a profound influence on me.

Herzberg was a German psychiatrist of Jewish origin who left Berlin, where he had his practice, to come to London in the early 1930s. He settled in the Swiss Cottage district, near Hampstead, where many refugees congregated. He was not quite 40 when he emigrated, and he died at the early age of 50. He is known mainly for his book, *Active Psychotherapy,* which was published in 1945. He was extremely intelligent, had a genuinely scientific outlook on psychiatry, and soon became the centre of a group of psychiatrists, mostly refugees, who used to meet at his house to discuss the theory and practice of psychiatry. Gradually Herzberg made these informal gatherings into a forum for the discussion of his new methods of active psychotherapy and the use of graduated tasks.

I had just received my Ph.D., and was very glad to be invited to attend these meetings. My interest was more in experimental psychology than in the abnormal field, but with the university gone to Aberystwyth there was little intellectual stimulation to be found, and any serious discussion of psychological problems was welcome. As he makes clear in his book, Herzberg considered himself a psycho-analyst and a follower of Freud. Most of the people who came to these meetings had similar leanings, although some held rather more esoteric views. I had not exactly been impressed by what I had learned at University about Freud, but was willing to listen; these discussions of detailed case histories were exactly what I needed to gain some insight into just what was happening in therapy and how the patients improved (or not, as the case might be).

As his book makes clear, Herzberg put forward many views which marked a departure from orthodoxy, and which may be considered to be precursors of theories associated with behaviour therapy; I doubt if he quite realized how incompatible these views were with psychoanalysis as taught at that time. Consider his statement of the aims of psychotherapy: "to make the patient free of symptoms; . . . to make him safe from relapse" (Herzberg, 1941, p. 19). This is not a Freudian statement; psychoanalysts tend to disregard the symptom and talk almost exclusively of hypothetical background factors and unconscious complexes, the elimination of which they regard as their prime concern. Herzberg's statement is a clear adumbration of the view that neuroses are essentially nothing but the set of "symptoms" shown by the patient, so that the elimination of the symptoms eliminates the neurosis. In discussion I frequently pointed out to him that he was a more radical innovator than he was prepared to admit, but he always smilingly refused to agree, and insisted that he was merely trying to speed up the unduly slow process of orthodox treatment; he never considered himself anything but a true follower of Freud.

In his theory of neurosis, too, Herzberg clearly anticipated the application of Miller's doctrine of approach and avoidance gradients, and his method of treatment was based on a detailed consideration of these gradients. Nor was he ignorant of the facts of spontaneous remission; "neuroses sometimes fade out without any treatment" (p. 20). This fact too was not easily admitted by orthodox analysts, and is difficult to reconcile with Freudian theory. Herzberg simply stated it as a fact of his clinical experience, without realizing the important implications it might have for the theory he nominally subscribed to. Such intellectual schizophrenia is not infrequent in innovators, even in highly intelligent ones; they cling to orthodoxy in their formal statements, while rejecting it in their actual work and theories. Herzberg is an interesting case in point, and his book would repay an extended critical treatment by someone more expert in Freudian mythology than myself.

The main contribution Herzberg made to behaviour therapy, however, was of course his *method of graduated tasks*. Experience had shown him clearly that orthodox Freudian treatment took far too long to be practicable (or advisable) with the great majority of patients; he also found that it was not always (or even usually) successful. (It is interesting to note that J. Wolpe later progressed along exactly the same path, although he of course succeeded in taking the important step of cutting the umbilical cord!) Hence Herzberg's call for more "active" therapy; the very term of course is opposed in essence to all that psychoanalysis stands for. The patient must be made to work, and work successfully, to overcome his symptoms: "there is one psychotherapeutic agent by which we can attack a neurosis . . . ; this is the achievements which we demand from the patient. Achievement is fulfilment of a task by an activity directed to that purpose" (p. 21).

Herzberg insisted that the tasks that he set for his patients must be "graduated"; this term he defines as "arranged according to their difficulty." There is an obvious similarity here to Wolpe's "symptom hierarchies," although Wolpe in the main uses imagery in treatment, whereas Herzberg was concerned with in vivo desensitization. It is for this reason that our early work at the Maudsley used desensitization in actual life situations; it was not until we had the benefit of Wolpe's advice and guidance that we changed over to the use of imagery. (Even now there is little evidence to show that one method is superior to the other as far as effectiveness is concerned, although Wolpe's method is of course very much more practicable.) There is no explicit statement regarding relaxation in Herzberg's paper, but in fact the clinical sessions preceding and following the activities prescribed were used to discuss the events and feelings during the contrived situations, and reassurance and calming talk took the place of relaxation. The de facto similarities are probably closer than they might appear from reading Herzberg's theoretical views, which are somewhat confused; here if ever seems to be a case of "Do as I do, not as I say!"

Does "active psychotherapy" work? It is difficult to form an accurate impression from the data given by Herzberg, particularly as there is no proper control group; furthermore, there seems to have been an unusually large number of patients who broke off treatment (possibly because Herzberg was much less selective in his choice of patients than is usual in psychoanalytic circles). However, when we look at the cases successfully treated it would be difficult to deny that Herzberg is right when he says that "a treatment by practical tasks will probably be short in comparison with purely analytical treatment or, in other words, that tasks will considerably shorten even analytical treatment" (p. 27). It is interesting to note that the number of sessions Herzberg used for his successful cases is very similar to that used by Wolpe; Wolpe, however, had far fewer terminations by his patients. Nevertheless, the shortening of treatment produced by the introduction of graduated tasks is a notable achievement, which one might have anticipated would have had a considerable impact on psychiatry. It is interesting to speculate why in fact there was no such impact.

The first reason that comes to mind is the simple one that Herzberg had no official position, was not connected with any university, and thus had no pupils who might have carried on his tradition, taught others, and extended his research. This is a terrible handicap, made worse by the fact that he was a refugee who had to reconstruct his professional life from the shambles produced by Hitler's thugs. He might of course have succeeded had it not been for his untimely death, which cut short any influence he might have had and left his doctrine in an unfinished state, open to theoretical criticism and virtually unsupported by factual or experimental material. Rebels to be successful must live long; even Bertrand Russell finally got the Order of Merit from the Establishment he so openly despised. But not all rebels live to be almost a hundred, and Herzberg's early death terminated his direct influence.

A third reason, perhaps, was the fact that he worked in England. The rapid adoption of new ideas has never been a characteristic of English establishments, and the almost American insistence on efficiency and success shown in Herzberg's writings received almost as chilling a reception as my own views were to receive a few years later. (Americans, of course, almost never read non-American journals and books, and consequently never encountered his paper or his book; I have looked in vain for any mention of either in American writings.) And last, he wrote in the middle of a war, when few psychologists or psychiatrists had the time or patience to bother with new ideas or methods; they hardly had time to read at all, even if they had the inclination. And when the war was over, Herzberg was dead. *Exoriare aliquis nostris ex ossibus ultor!*

Yet in another sense it may be said that Herzberg's views have not only survived, they have triumphed. My own ideas of behaviour therapy were certainly very much influenced by what I heard and learned from him, and the similarities between his views and mine are apparent. We did, indeed, disagree on one vital point; he regarded "graduated tasks" as merely an adjunct to psychoanalysis, which was supposed to carry the main therapeutic burden, while I suggested to him that theoretically at least this notion could not be derived from the facts. "Let P stand for psychoanalysis," I said, "and let T stand for graduated tasks, and S for spontaneous remission. You assume that $P > S$, but you admit that there is really no evidence for this. You state that $T + P > S$, and although there is no formal evidence for this, I agree that it is a tenable position. But from these equations one could also deduce the possibility that $T > P$, that is, that the treatment by tasks, without psychoanalysis, might be superior to psychoanalysis, so that we could dispense with the psychoanalytic part of the equation altogether and write $T > S$." He agreed theoretically that such a possibility existed, but would not agree that it justified an experimental study of the effects of T in isolation; nor would he consider a clinical trial comparing T with P, with $P + T$, and with S. (He did not of course have the resources to carry out such studies in any case, but it is interesting that he was so encapsulated in the Freudian web that he could not see the need for empirical proof of those parts of his theory which relied on received authority.)

Physically Herzberg was a small man, married to a rather larger woman who produced Continental tea and *Guggelhupf* cake at our meetings. He had a dynamic personality, sparkled with intelligence, and possessed a wide knowledge of literature, science, and mathematics. He was always kind and considerate; although much older and wiser than I was, as well as very experienced in his field, he always talked to me as an equal, and never resented my continued questioning of his basic beliefs. I took all this for granted at the time; is this not the way scientists are supposed to behave? I was to find out later on how exceptional this attitude towards criticism was in a psychiatrist, or indeed in any kind of scientist. Herzberg was imperturbable; he never lost his temper, never showed any emotion, never resented criticism. He also completely lacked any sense of humour; he could never see the point of a joke, or understand the humour in a film comedy.

I once used him as the subject in an experiment on humour, in which the captions had been cut off cartoons and the subject had to write a humorous caption. He looked at the picture (a lady sitting at a makeup table, her face completely missing, speaking into a telephone; the original caption had been "Hello, is that the Acme Vanishing Cream Company?"), frowned, and could think of nothing to say. I prompted him: "Is there nothing odd and unusual in the picture?" He finally said, "Yes, the telephone is not properly connected up." (The artist had drawn just a few hasty squiggles to indicate the connection between phone and handpiece.) This failure to see the obvious (in this case the missing face), but rather to notice the irrelevant discrepancy, carried over into his general social perceptions; he did not feel at ease outside the cognitive, intellectual field, or within the organised, circumscribed social situation. Also, he had to confess that he usually failed to understand what was happening in films. His social perceptions were thus seriously circumscribed. He was a nice person, as well as a creative one; I shall always regret that he did not live to see the flourishing of present-day behaviour therapy. I think he would have approved.

I had been reading about J. B. Watson and "Little Albert," whom Watson used to illustrate the theory that neurotic symptoms arise through a process of Pavlovian conditioning, and I was also familiar with the methods used with considerable success by Mary Cover Jones, his student, to extinguish such conditioned emotional responses. All this research had been done in the 1920s, but there had been very little interest shown by psychiatrists or clinical psychologists, all of whom jumped on the Freudian bandwagon, disregarding the evidence that what I was to call "behaviour therapy" was clearly very much more effective than the type of dynamic psychotherapy they preferred. I was of course aware that there were difficulties in accepting the Watsonian model as it stood. It postulated traumatic events which produced the association between the conditioned autonomic stimulus (CAS) and the conditioned response (CR), but in peacetime neuroses such traumatic events seemed largely lacking. Also, learning theory would suggest that extinction should take place and make impossible the development of long-continued neurotic disorders. This association link between learning theory and neurosis thus linked the field of abnormal psychology with one of my interests in experimental psychology, and I thought that if I ever got the opportunity I would investigate it further.

In thus mentioning my early development of theories of what I called to myself "behaviour therapy," I do not wish to claim any kind of priority over others who developed similar ideas. Priority disputes in science are generally absurd, and have to be settled inevitably on the basis of published material. I am mentioning the facts of the case simply because they illustrate the development of my ideas; it will soon become apparent why they did not result in any kind of published material until 1959, when my first article on behaviour therapy appeared.

The reason for this long period of incubation was the attitude of Aubrey Lewis to psychologists who undertook any form of treatment. He was absolutely opposed to this practice, believing that all treatment should be reserved for psychiatrists with medical qualifications. This did not worry me at the time; I had plenty of other topics to keep me busy, but it was later to lead to a great quarrel which ended our friendship and led to the establishment of behaviour therapy in Great Britain as the prerogative of clinical psychologists.

I had expected Aubrey Lewis to tell me, as essentially his research assistant, which areas to work in, but that was not the way he worked. He left it entirely up to me, and as a complete novice I didn't quite know what to do. I decided to do the same thing I had done when I started in psychology; I simply got hold of the 12 largest textbooks of psychiatry I could obtain and read them through fairly thoroughly. I found after a few weeks that I knew far more psychiatry than most of the psychiatrists working at Mill Hill—not necessarily a very impressive feat, as they had practically ceased reading anything after obtaining their medical degrees! It did impress Aubrey Lewis, however, that I could quote verbatim statements by French, German, British, and American psychiatrists whenever we had a discussion about particular research problems.

In my psychiatric reading I found there was a lot of talk about personality characteristics, which were usually judged in terms of ratings made very subjectively by the psychiatrist, and without any evidence of reliability or validity. Diagnoses were made in the same manner, without any check on their reliability or validity. I decided that one of my first studies would be into the reliability of psychiatric judgements, a task that was made easier by the fact that patients were seen and diagnosed rather independently by more than one psychiatrist. Aubrey Lewis had instituted a system of extensive forms to be filled in by the psychiatrist for each patient, which listed symptoms, diagnoses, personality traits, and many other important variables. This made the study easier, but when I asked the superintendent for permission to carry out such an investigation he obstinately refused on the basis that surely I wasn't suggesting that medically trained psychiatrists could make errors in their judgements!

I did of course carry out the study nevertheless; I think it was the first really large-scale study to look at reliability of psychiatric diagnoses, using several thousand cases. The outcome was a "lemon"—the reliability of diagnoses was very, very poor, amounting to something less than 5% agreement. The superintendent, needless to say, refused me permission to publish these findings. This attitude is illustrative of the defensive mechanisms so common in people who feel themselves vulnerable, and psychiatrists certainly feel vulnerable as compared with surgeons and other more highly valued members of the medical fraternity.

The collection and analysis of all this material did not occupy much of my time. I was interested in more fundamental problems of dimensions of personality and mental abnormality, as opposed to the qualitative distinctions implied by the medical system of diagnosis. There seemed to me two problems involved: that of dimensions versus qualitatively different disease entities; and the number of dimensions involved. Freud of course had adopted a dimensional model, using the concept of regression to define that dimension. Milder regressions produced neuroses, stronger regressions produced psychoses; the model was therefore a unidimensional one, but of course there had been no proof one way or the other. I tried to work out a statistical method that would settle the question once and for all, and arrived at the method of "criterion analysis" (Eysenck, 1950, 1952b).

The essential feature of this method is to take a number (n) of measures which distinguish, say, psychotics and normals with a high level of significance. These measures are then intercorrelated in the "normal" group and separately inter-correlated in the "psychotic" group. If the psychotic group is qualitatively differentiated from the normal group, then there should be no correlations between the measures within either the normal or the psychotic group. If, on the other hand, there is a general diathesis going from the normal to the psychotic group, then a similar pattern of intercorrelation should appear within the normal and the psychotic groups, and, when factor analyzed, these two groups should give rise to identical factors. In addition, factor loadings should not only correlate with each other, but also with the discriminant capacity of the different tests used to distinguish between the normals and the psychotics. Using the method on different populations, and using different tests, I found evidence which seems to me to establish quite firmly that a dimensional model is the only appropriate one, and that at least two dimensions (psychoticism and neuroticism) are needed for the purpose. I also used other methods, such as discriminant function analysis, to establish the same point (Eysenck, 1970).

In choosing the tests in question, I was much aided by a whole series of studies I was doing as a preliminary into the measurement of the major dimensions of personality. It seemed to me very likely that such important disorders as neurosis or psychosis would be based on diatheses or predispositions that could be found in the normal population, and that one could thus form a link between personality dimensions on the one hand and psychiatric disorders on the other. This was the theme of my first book, *Dimensions of Personality* (Eysenck, 1947) and also of my second book, *The Scientific Study of Personality* (Eysenck, 1952a). A large body of work, using questionnaires, ratings, experimental tests, and physiological tests established the existence of three major dimensions of personality, which I called "extraversion-introversion," "neuroticism-stability," and "psychoticism-superego functioning." Their development is described in great detail in the book I wrote with my son, Michael, entitled *Personality and Individual Differences: A Natural Science Approach* (Eysenck & Eysenck, 1985). There is now an enormous body of evidence to suggest that these three factors are very firmly grounded in reality, appear in many different cultural and national groups all over the world, and can be extracted from practically any large-scale collection of ratings or self-ratings, including the 16 PF, the MMPI, the CPI, and others, and may thus lay claim to constituting a paradigm for personality research.

It also seemed to me that personality, and with it the diathesis leading to neuroses and psychoses, had a firm biological basis, so that one would expect a high degree of heritability. At the time this was hotly denied, largely on the basis of the work of Newman, Freeman, and Holzinger (1937), whose study of identical and fraternal twins, and identical twins raised in separation, had resulted in denial of the importance of genetic factors in personality. Their work is subject to very damaging criticism (Eysenck, 1967), and their conclusions do not follow from their data. Thus I found that for identical twins the intraclass correlation for the Woodworth-Matthews Inventory was .56, for fraternal twins it was .37, and for identical twins brought up in separation it was .58. The authors comment that "the Woodworth-Matthews Test appears to show no very definite trend in correlations, possibly because of the nature of the trait and also because of the unreliability of the measure." This comment seems almost unbelievable. If we regard this questionnaire as an inventory of neurotic tendency, as the original authors certainly did, then we would here seem to have definite evidence for the importance of heredity, seeing that identical twins are distinctly superior in point of intraclass correlation to fraternals. Moreover, and this is a particularly interesting feature of these data, identical twins brought up in separation are if anything *more* alike than are identical twins brought up together! These data suggest a heritability of very roughly 50%, which is not different to that which is now widely accepted for practically all aspects of personality (Eaves, Eysenck, & Martin, 1989).

One of my doctoral students, Don Prell, and I carried out a study of neuroticism in identical and fraternal twins, using a variety of different tests (Eysenck & Prell, 1951), and I also carried out an investigation of extraversion-introversion, using the same methodology (Eysenck, 1956). Both studies found a very substantial degree of heritability, and although by modern standards the number of twins used was very modest, and the methods of analysis were certainly not up to present-day requirements, the results have been replicated many times. A very detailed account of modern work, particularly our own, has been recently published in *Genes, Culture and Personality: An Empirical Approach* (Eaves, Eysenck, & Martin, 1989). This book deals not only with personality but also with clinical features like anxiety and depression and their relation with neuroticism, involving both genetic and environmental factors, and much else which is relevant to abnormal psychology, but which would be too technical to go into here.

In the climate of the 1950 and 1960s, this stress on genetic factors was not well received. I still recall with some amusement a quotation from *The Theory and Practice of Psychiatry,* a widely used textbook by Redlich and Freedman (1966). They made only one comment on the importance of genetic factors in mental disorders: "The importance of inherited characteristics in neuroses and sociopathies is no longer asserted except by Hans J. Eysenck and D. T. Prell" (p. 176). The statement itself was of course completely untrue; I have quoted ample evidence even from these early days for genetic effects in the causation of neurotic disorders (Eysenck, 1967). The quotation merely illustrates the deliberate refusal of many leading psychiatrists and psychologists to look at the evidence and to acknowledge the importance of genetic factors.

But all this is taking us a little ahead of my time at Mill Hill. That period came to an end when the war finished and I was transferred, on the same Rockefeller grant that had supported me at Mill Hill, to the Maudsley Hospital, when the wandering psychiatrists returned to their home. Lewis was very set on establishing the profession of clinical psychology in Great Britain, and he had decided that I was the person to carry out this task. There were a few psychologists working in mental hospitals—Philip Vernon himself had worked in the Children's Department at the Maudsley for a while—but there was no organization, no training facilities, and no recognized profession. Lewis was organizing the creation of the Institute of Psychiatry, and he suggested that there should be a sub-Department of Psychology within the Department of Psychiatry, under my leadership; I was to be given the rank of Reader (associate professor) at the University of London. I agreed, and we arranged that I would go to the United States to study clinical psychology, its organization and contents.

I had been invited by Morris Viteles to come to the University of Pennsylvania at Philadelphia, as a visiting professor, and I accepted the invitation. For the first time I was to have a proper job, be paid a proper salary, and become a recognised teacher at the university. This was certainly a leg up from the very insecure and poverty-stricken existence of the research assistant existing on "soft" money and completely dependent on the people to whom the grant was paid.

That same year (1950) marked another important event; I separated from Margaret and married a student of mine who had come from the fields of chemistry and mathematics to the more congenial study of psychology. Sybil was the daughter of the famous violinist Max Rostal, and we started our life together in Philadelphia—not perhaps the most romantic of cities, but a happy contrast to life in England, which was then still characterized by severe rationing, the almost complete absence of capital or any goods to buy, and the general aftermath of a very bloody war indeed.

We spent a happy time in the United States, travelling all over the country and visiting different departments to see what was going on in clinical psychology. I also gave lectures on the personality research I had been doing in England. My book had become widely known in the United States, and it was quite comical to experience at every university I visited a seduction scene in which the chairman would whisk me away to some quiet corner and offer me a job, either in the department or as the head of the clinical section. I found this amusing because I really had no experience whatever in clinical work, and while my salary would have been very much better, and living conditions even more so, I felt it was my duty to stick to my promise and return to England. It would be interesting but pointless to consider what might have happened had I stayed in the United States!

My investigations showed me that there were three major facets of clinical psychology in the United States. The first was that psychology was subordinate to psychiatry, the psychiatrist determining the content and the method of the psychologist's work and calling on the psychologist not as a colleague but as a hired hand. To put it crudely, the psychiatrist was the master, the psychologist did as told. This was not my idea of the function of the clinical psychologist in Great Britain, and I refused to consider the possibility of starting a profession built on that model.

The second facet I found was that psychologists did psychotherapy, usually of a "dynamic" or Freudian kind, imitating psychiatrists, whose model was very much the same. There seemed to be no basis in fact for these methods of treatment, and I made it my business to look into it. The outcome was my paper on the effects of psychotherapy (Eysenck, 1952c) in which, on the basis of published evidence, I showed that there was no basis for the belief that psychotherapy of any kind, or psychoanalysis in particular, did better than spontaneous remission as far as serious neurotic disorders were concerned.

Mine was not the only voice querying the effects of psychotherapy—others like Denker, Landis, Salter, Wilder, and Zubin had also raised the question, but they had done so *sotto voce,* whereas I stated my conclusions clearly and unequivocally. There were over a dozen replies, mostly very critical, in many different journals; all criticized a point I had not made, namely that psychotherapy had been proved to be ineffective. I had very carefully argued that the evidence did not support the view that psychotherapy was effective, and I had also drawn attention to the poor quality of much of the material that was available. Had I said that the material *proved* the inefficacy of psychotherapy, criticism would have been justified. But all I had really stated was that the evidence was insufficient to prove the efficacy of psychotherapy, and the more people denigrated the available evidence, the less it could be used to affirm the efficacy of psychotherapy!

The history of this debate is long and rather boring. A number of summaries suggest that more recent studies have proved me wrong; but in reality these summaries arrive at such a conclusion by *suppressio veri* and *suggestio falsi.* Rachman and Wilson (1980) have summarized the evidence, and also present a critical review of work of those who, like Bergin and Luborsky, apparently arrived at a different conclusion, by means already characterized. Rachman and Wilson conclude that my early article, and subsequent reviews of later evidence leading to the same conclusion, are still essentially correct, and that evidence for the efficacy of psychotherapy is still lacking.

This may seem to violently contradict the conclusion drawn by Smith, Glass, and Miller (1980) in their meta-analysis of studies on the effect of psychotherapy. Thus they conclude that "psychotherapy is beneficial, consistently so, and in many different ways. Its benefits are on a par with other expensive and ambitious interventions, such as schooling and medicine. The benefits of psychotherapy are not permanent, but then little is" (p. 183). When we look at the evidence, however, we find that they have indulged in a gigantic confidence trick. Fundamental to their conclusion is their Table 5-1, in which they compare 18 different types of therapy on the basis of the average effect size. This measures the difference from groups receiving no treatment, and as all the results are positive, their conclusion would seem to follow. However, a careful reader might note that their "treatment" number 18 is called "placebo treatment"; in other words, rather than using the placebo treatment as a control, which is the only acceptable way it can be treated, it is used here as if it were a genuine kind of psychotherapy! The actual effect size of the placebo treatment is .56, as compared with psychodynamic therapy, which has an average effect size of .69—an insignificant difference! What Smith, Glass, and Miller actually find, therefore, is that psychodynamic therapy gives very much the same results as placebo treatment—hardly a very positive conclusion!

When we note additionally that their statistics show that length of treatment is completely uncorrelated with effectiveness of treatment (which contradicts an underlying hypothesis of psychodynamic therapy), and that the duration of training of the therapist is completely uncorrelated with the success of the therapy (which again contradicts the tenets of Freudian psychotherapy), we begin to see that their conclusion may be more an expression of hope than of fact.

What they claim to have shown is that "different types of psychotherapy (verbal or behavioural; psychodynamic, client-centred, or systematic desensitization) do not produce different types or degrees of benefit" (p. 184). They carefully fail to add to this list of different types of treatment the term "placebo," although the placebo effect is not very different from the average effect of all the types of treatment they have investigated. If it is true, as Luborsky once put it, that "Everyone has won and all must have prizes" (Luborsky, Singer, & Luborsky, 1975), then this will simply illustrate the "Alice in Wonderland" atmosphere of all these analyses. But of course what they say is not true; Smith, Glass, and Miller give evidence that behavioural treatments are significantly better than others, although they try to argue themselves out of this statistical conclusion by a completely unacceptable argument.

Much of this, of course, lay in the future, but I decided that in the absence of evidence for the efficacy of psychotherapy I could not justify its inclusion in the list of things to be taught to clinical psychologists in Great Britain, and neither could I justify clinical psychologists using these methods. Up to this point, therefore, I agreed with Aubrey Lewis that the use of psychotherapy by psychologists was not justified; I went beyond him in also arguing that its use was not justified by psychiatrists either!

It might be thought that while there was no real evidence for the efficacy of psychotherapy, at least it could do no harm. But this is not true; there is much evidence that psychotherapy very frequently actually does do harm (Mays & Franks, 1985). Strupp, Hadley, and Gomez-Schwartz (1977) were the first to draw attention to this crucial factor in the evaluation of psychotherapy, and it is certainly a point that should never be forgotten. I still find it totally unacceptable that a method of treatment that can do great damage to the patient, that demands high payment and much time from the patient, and that has never been shown to benefit the patient, is taught to budding psychiatrists and clinical psychologists as a panacea and is recommended to patients ignorant of the facts and unable to judge what they have been told.

The third facet of American clinical work was the universal acceptance of so-called projective techniques, like the Rorschach technique and the Thematic Apperception Test (TAT), as methods of clinical diagnosis. Having surveyed the evidence, I wrote a summary article pointing out that there was little if any evidence for the reliability or validity of these methods, and that in the absence of proper validation they should certainly not be used in clinical practice. To convince my colleagues at the institute, I had a simple experiment carried out in which the Rorschach was administered to 50 severe neurotics and 50 perfectly normal people, and the records given to experts to simply sort out which was which. None of them succeeded beyond chance! If experts cannot even mark the difference between the Rorschach record of the severe neurotic and the perfectly normal person, can they be trusted to make the much finer distinctions required in clinical practice? In their book *An Experimental Approach to Projective Techniques,* Zubin, Eron, and Schumer (1965) came to pretty much the same conclusion, on the basis of a much wider survey of the evidence than I had undertaken. Of course, neither their efforts nor mine have had much influence on clinical psychologists.

However that may be, when I returned to England I was determined that clinical psychology as I was planning to set it up would be exactly the opposite to what I had seen in the United States. I was determined that psychologists would be the equals of psychiatrists, not their servants. I was equally determined that psychotherapy was not to be their *modus operandi,* and that they should not be using projective methods. In all this I had the support of Aubrey Lewis. However, my approach did leave open the crucial question of what in fact they would be doing.

To this question my answer was as follows. It seemed to me that the contribution to psychiatry which was made by genetics was based on the academic discipline of genetics. Similarly, the contribution made by biochemists was in terms of their knowledge of biochemistry. Much the same was true of all the other basic sciences that were being taught at the institute. Psychology, it seemed to me, should not be an exception. Our contribution must be based on the psychological knowledge that had been accumulated by theoreticians and experimentalists over the past century, particularly in the fields of learning and conditioning, memory and forgetting, personality and intelligence, and various other, perhaps somewhat less directly relevant, areas of research. In particular, diagnostic testing should use more experimental techniques relevant to the individual case, and most of all psychologists should contribute to the treatment of patients by making use of the methods of behaviour therapy.

Behaviour therapy is based on the principles of learning theory and conditioning, and these are an essential part of psychology as a scientific discipline. Everyone seemed to be agreed that neuroses were acquired, although there was a genetic background for them; it seemed to follow that we should make our contribution by looking at the process of learning or conditioning and at the means of reversing it. My acquaintance with the work of Herzberg (directly), and of Watson and Mary Cover Jones (indirectly), suggested to me that the means were at hand for improving our methods of treatment. This, it seemed to me, would be the central piece of our conception of clinical psychology, and should be the mainstay of our teaching.

There were, of course, two difficulties in all this. The first was that behaviour therapy as such did not yet exist, and you cannot teach a nonexistent discipline! The second difficulty was that Aubrey Lewis would almost certainly oppose any efforts to work along these lines, or to permit clinical psychologists to carry out behaviour therapy.

In all this, Lewis was certainly in rapport with the general attitudes of psychiatrists at the institute. As an example, I may perhaps mention my adventures in trying to suggest the "bell and blanket" ("bell and pad" in the U.S.A.!) method of treatment for enuresis to the head of the Child Guidance Department at the Maudsley. Dr. Cameron was a dyed-in-the-wool psychoanalyst, who treated children suffering from enuresis with long-continued psychoanalysis; a look at his success rate suggested that it was considerably less effective as a method of treatment than doing nothing whatsoever! However, when I suggested to him that as a clinical experiment we might try the bell and blanket method, he exploded. "I'm not going to let anyone torture my children and give them electric shocks!" he exclaimed, although of course no shocks are involved in the treatment, which requires nothing but an alarm bell linked with the blanket to wake the child up in the initial stage of bedwetting. He seemed completely impervious to fact or logic, and incapable of understanding what was involved. Fortunately, after his death a few years later, his successor allowed us to introduce the method, which of course is now universally used in all psychiatric hospitals in Great Britain. This then was the authentic voice of the fundamentalists who held most of the leading consultant positions in the Maudsley Hospital and at the Institute of Psychiatry; the task seemed a difficult one, but I decided to undertake it nevertheless.

I had collected a group of students and staff members who were keen to try out these new methods on individual patients, who helped in developing behaviour therapy as a discipline, and who worked out new methods where necessary. Prominent in this group were Gwynne Jones, Irene Martin, Bob Payne, Jimmy Inglis, Jack Tizard, Gordon Claridge, Cyril Franks, and many others who later became well known in behaviour therapy. There were a few psychiatrists friendly to our cause, like Linford Rees, who helped us by sending suitable cases for treatment. In addition, psychologists had always been more closely involved with the treatment of children than with adults, and so we had a chance to try out our methods on some of the children in the Children's Department. We had fortnightly or monthly meetings at my house where we discussed theory, talked about progress in the treatment of individual cases, and generally began to form a coherent and mutually supportive group.

In this group my part was that of coordinator, theoretician, and motivator. I did not take part in the actual treatment of cases, considering that to do so would take me away from my research activities, which to me seemed to be more in line with my capacities than would actual treatment.

Gradually we arrived at certain general principles, which governed ways of treating individual patients, and finally felt that we had something to offer. In 1958 I gave a lecture to the Royal Medico-Psychological Association, the senior psychiatric society in England at that time, on the topic of behaviour therapy, assisted by Gwynne Jones, who spoke about some of the cases he himself had treated. My talk, which was published in the *Journal of Mental Science,* (Eysenck, 1959b) gives what I believe to be the first detailed account of the principles of behaviour therapy. I mentioned ten points (listed in Table 1) on which behaviour therapy differs from psychotherapy. To my mind, these are still useful in marking off two paradigms which are irreconcilable, and between which empirical decisions about effectiveness, experimental support, and theoretical consistency can be made.

Table 1

Differences between psychotherapy and behaviour therapy (Eysenck, 1959)

Freudian psychotherapy	Behaviour therapy
1. Based on inconsistent theory, never properly formulated in postulate form	Based on consistent, properly formulated theory leading to testable deductions.
2. Derived from clinical observations made without necessary control observations or experiments	Derived from experimental studies specifically designed to test basic theory and deductions made therefrom.
3. Considers symptoms the visible upshot of unconscious causes ("complexes")	Considers symptoms as unadaptive conditioned responses.
4. Regards symptoms as evidence of repression	Regards symptoms as evidence of faulty learning.
5. Believes that symptomatology is determined by defense mechanisms	Believes that symptomatology is determined by individual differences in conditionability and autonomic lability, as well as by accidental environmental circumstances.
6. All treatment of neurotic disorders must be *historically* based	All treatment of neurotic disorders is concerned with habits existing at *present*; their historical development is largely irrelevant.
7. Cures are achieved by handling the underlying (unconscious) dynamics, not by treating the symptom itself	Cures are achieved by treating the symptom itself; that is, by extinguishing unadaptive conditioned responses and establishing desirable conditioned responses.
8. Interpretation of symptoms, dreams, acts, etc., is an important element of treatment	Interpretation, even if not completely subjective and erroneous, is irrelevant.
9. Symptomatic treatment leads to the elaboration of treatment	Symptomatic treatment leads to permanent recovery, provided autonomic as well as skeletal surplus conditioned responses are extinguished.
10. Transference relations are essential for cures of neurotic disorders	Personal relations are not essential for cures of neurotic disorder, although they may be useful in certain circumstances.

Later I will deal with the problems raised by the emergence of cognitive behaviour therapy; here let me only note the reception my intentionally mild and factual presentation received. Many of the psychiatrists present jumped up and down in fury, yelled at me, and almost threatened to lynch me. They had to be restrained by the chairman, a Scottish psychoanalyst, who had to remind them that I was their guest and should be treated accordingly. It was a curious exhibition of mass hysteria, indicating that the belief that a training analysis (which practically all of these psychiatrists had had) leads to a greater degree of sanity and emotional control was a delusion! At question time, Gwynne Jones and I were treated with undisguised hostility. There seemed to be a general feeling that we had violated some unwritten commandment and had behaved altogether irresponsibly in curing our patients by means not sanctioned by the founder of psychoanalysis.

The publication of the paper called forth a number of rejoinders, most of them suggesting that this was merely a method of treating symptoms, which would lead to a return of the symptom, or to symptom substitution. There was of course no basis for these suggestions, and our work has shown that in fact symptom substitution or recurrence is very unusual in behaviour therapy, probably less so than in psychoanalytic treatment! All in all, I commented that it was rather odd for those who could not *even* cure symptoms to accuse us of *only* curing symptoms! This remark, too, was not well received.

We had now, as it were, come out of the closet, and war was declared by Aubrey Lewis himself when he heard what we had done. His reaction was oddly emotional for a man of his intelligence and indeed wisdom. As an example of his reaction, let me take the case of one of his registrars, who had an adult patient who wet his bed. Ignorant of the methods of bell and blanket treatment, he consulted one of our psychologists, who had had a great deal of experience of this type of work. When Aubrey Lewis heard of it, he wrote to all his registrars saying that under no conditions were they ever to ask a psychologist for advice on methods of treatment! So although all the experience in behavioural treatment was on our side, psychiatrists were not to benefit by it in case this should encourage psychologists to go on treating neurotics! Aubrey Lewis was not opposed to behaviour therapy as such; indeed, he valued it highly and wanted psychiatrists to use it. He was merely opposed to psychologists administering the treatment, in spite of the fact that they alone had the necessary theoretical background in learning theory and conditioning, and that psychiatrists simply could not be expected to add another couple of years to their lengthy training in order to become masters of the technique, which required extensive knowledge of psychological principles. I think that Aubrey Lewis was aware of the irrational nature of his prejudice but could not bring himself to abandon it. This was a great pity, because the resulting conflict destroyed our friendship.

Theoretically I should have had no chance of winning the contest. Aubrey Lewis was head of the Institute of Psychiatry, effectively if not in name; he had the management committee in his pocket, because he was a member of it and I was not; he had the dean and the secretary on his side, having appointed both; and he voiced the view of most of the consultants, who wanted to restrict treatment to medically qualified personnel. Although I was at the time a full professor, in charge of a separate department, we were both part of the British Postgraduate Medical Federation, who would of course pay far more attention to a medical professor than to a nonmedical professor. And most important of all, he was a master of academic infighting, having always succeeded in pushing through his plans without ever having registered a single failure. I had no experience of this kind of administrative dogfight; I had concentrated entirely on research, writing, and teaching, leaving all the committee work to Lewis. Suddenly I had to fight this very unequal battle in which he was trying to reduce the size of the psychology department or even eliminate it, and in any case make it impossible for us to carry out any treatment of patients in the future.

For once in my life I had to get out of the ivory tower and remember some of the street-fighting skills I had acquired while battling the Nazis. There were two weaknesses in Aubrey Lewis's case. The first was that my unit was entirely independent of his. I had learnt enough in the United States about the dependence of psychologists on psychiatrists to insist on this, and it was procedurally difficult for Lewis to breach this independence. Second, Lewis was very sensitive to anything that might rebound to the discredit of psychiatry; his aim was to build it up as part of the scientific discipline. This meant that he could not really afford the kind of vicious battle I was quite willing to undertake. I threatened to complain to the Postgraduate Medical Federation; I threatened to write to the senate of the university; I even proposed to go to the vice-chancellor and to the chancellor, an honorary position held by a member of the royal family. I was willing to write to the *Times* and to every other newspaper in the country to expose the machinations which were being initiated to make it impossible for us to research and implement new and potentially very valuable methods of treatment.

There was a lot of infighting on various committees, but my fellow professors in the scientific subjects began to feel that their independence might be endangered if they let Lewis get away with it, and I actually managed to build up a position firm enough to defeat his objectives. It was the first time he had ever lost a battle he had set his heart on winning, and it seemed to destroy him. We carried on our regular weekly discussions as before, pretending that nothing had happened, but of course it was rather like a marriage disrupted by a violent quarrel in which unforgivable things have been said—it could never be glad, confident morning again!

I regretted both the quarrel and the winning. I owed a great deal to Aubrey Lewis, as did British psychology as a whole, and his support had meant a great deal to me. I would have done anything to avoid hurting his feelings, but I still cannot see that I could have done anything different. I believed then, as I believe now, that the business of medicine is to heal; that good methods should supersede bad ones; and that those best qualified by training and experience to use these methods should indeed implement them. I was not interested in receiving credit for starting behaviour therapy in England, but I had to think of the thousands of patients who might now be cured quickly and safely, rather than be made worse by psychoanalysis and allied methods of treatment. It was a battle that simply had to be won, and I believe that the effects of winning it have been beneficial to patients, to psychiatry, and to psychology. But there's always a price to pay, and I wish that Aubrey Lewis had lived long enough to see the beneficial effects of the compromise solution we eventually came to with the National Health Service.

As clinical psychology became universally established, the role of the psychologist as the purveyor of behaviour therapy was more and more widely accepted, and the profession became integrated into the National Health Service. The final act of acceptance was the 1976 Trethowan Report, *The Role of Psychologists in the Health Services.* This report stated that "clinical psychology is a relative newcomer among health service professions, but one which has developed practically in recent years. The concern of clinical psychologists is that of the application of the principles of general psychology to the problems arising in the National Health Service, and in particular to the treatment and care of patients" (p. 1). Note the mention of "treatment" of patients; this acknowledges the place of clinical psychologists as therapists. In its conclusion, the report also acknowledges that "the major fields, or potential fields, for clinical psychology are mental illness, mental handicap, physical handicap, child and adolescent health problems, neurology, general medicine, geriatrics, community medicine and general medical practice," and that "clinical psychologists in the Naitonal Health Service should be recognized as having full professional status" (p. 25). This report marks the end of the battle, and the acknowledgement on the part of the medical profession, and psychiatry in particular, that we were right in the position we took, in opposition to Sir Aubrey Lewis and those who agreed with him.

Of course, all this did not mean that opposition to behaviour therapy ceased completely. As an example of the absurdity of much of this opposition, consider the Zangwill Report (1980), which originated as follows. In the early 1970s, there were increasing complaints about the care of patients in one ward at Napsbury Hospital. After one elderly patient died from injuries received about 5 to 15 days prior to her death—injuries which were not noticed by staff—a committee of enquiry was set up. This committee duly reported in 1973. In brief, they found that the consultant had adopted R. D. Laing's "social" views on schizophrenia and had decreed that patients should take responsibility for themselves. These management practices resulted, effectively, in food and other basic requirements being withheld from some patients at some times. Instead of dealing with the problems as revealed by their enquiry—by disciplining the staff involved in some appropriate way—in the most audacious nonsequitur the Napsbury Committee diverted attention from the dangerous practices based on Laing's theory.

The following quotation reveals all:

> There is no doubt in our minds that physical conditions on Cedar Ward were at times allowed to fall below an acceptable minimum standard, which the public have the right to expect in an NHS hospital. We are aware that similar problems have arisen in regard to other methods of patient-care for chronic schizo-phrenics, such as the technique of operant conditioning and similar forms of behaviour modification. All these methods, like Dr. Scott's, raise problems such as the freedom of the patient, the risk of amateurish application, and the possible lack of protection for patients. In this connection it is noteworthy that the State of Minnesota, in consultation with appropriate professional staff, has prepared official guidelines to deal with these potential difficulties. (para. 23)

The Napsbury Report goes on in similar fashion to recommend,

We think that similar difficulties may arise in relation to other programmes of behaviour modification which, we believe, are being introduced increasingly in NHS hospitals. We, therefore, recommend that the Department of Health and Social Security should consider the desirability of asking the Royal College of Psychiatrists, the Royal College of Nursing, and the British Psychological Society to set up a joint working party to formulate ethical guidelines for the conduct of such programmes. (para. 55)

Out of such amazing logic was the "Zangwill Committee" born. With such unpromising parentage, it is little wonder that the subsequent report is not only unsatisfactory but has the singular honour of being largely repudiated by the parent bodies.

It could be argued that the original Napsbury team genuinely saw implications for patient care beyond the immediate programmes they saw operating. They identified certain key dilemmas which face staff, whatever method of treatment is being implemented. If that was the case, then they should have clearly recommended that a subsequent working party enquire into the ethical problems involved in treating chronic patients in hospitals. By focussing on "behaviour modifications," without even taking advice from psychologists, the investigating team diverted attention from Drs. Laing and Scott, and thereby did a great disservice to chronic patients.

In other words, what happened was that methods associated with one of the most severe critics of behaviour therapy, Dr. R. D. Laing, led to the treatment of patients by Dr. Scott which was so scandalous that a committee had to be set up to look into it; and that by a remarkable sleight of hand, this committee managed to devote its attention to behaviour therapy, which had absolutely nothing whatsoever to do with the original misdemeanour! This case is typical of many similar ones on the part of the dinosaurs who oppose evolution.

My first task had been to establish clinical psychology as a profession, integrated into the National Health Service, with recognised principles of training and a proper career structure. My second task was to publicize its achievements, to make everyone in psychology and psychiatry aware of what was happening. I had argued for the application of scientific methodology to abnormal psychology in my *Handbook of Abnormal Psychology,* the first edition of which was published in 1960, the second in 1972. In the same year I edited *Behaviour Therapy and the Neuroses* (1960a), followed in 1964 by *Experiments in Behaviour Therapy.* In these books I collected most if not all of the papers supplying the evidence for the effectiveness of behaviour therapy. In 1965, Dr. (later Professor) S. Rachman and I published the first textbook of behaviour therapy, *Causes and Cures of Neurosis.* In 1974, I edited *Case Histories in Behaviour Therapy,* which shows in detail how cases were in fact treated by behaviour therapists. And in 1977 I published a popular book, *You and Neurosis,* in which I tried to tell the general public about the principles and successes of behaviour therapy.

In 1963 I persuaded Pergamon Press to publish a new journal, *Behaviour Research and Therapy*; my intention was to define the nature of the new profession of psychology, and in particular behaviour therapy as an applied science. The journal obviously filled a very real need, because within seven years of the publication of its first issue, it had risen to ninth place out of 77 psychological journals, as measured by the impact of its articles. With a Citation/Article Index of 1.184 (an index of the importance of the given journal's articles on psychology, as defined by the *American Psychologist,* 1976, p. 674), *Behaviour Research and Therapy* was rated higher than the APA journals that had overlapping content—the *Journal of Abnormal Psychology* and the *Journal of Consulting and Clinical Psychology.* In his *History of Behaviour Modification,* Kazdin (1978) observed that the journal "provided an identity for individuals working with distinct behavioural techniques, problems, and settings" (p. 187).

Jack Rachman, who collaborated with me in editing the journal, and later became its editor-in-chief, wrote on the occasion of its 25th birthday that

> It succeeded in providing a valuable bridge between European and North American psychologists and psychiatrists . . . the hot debates that enliven the early issues of the journal are matters of historical record, and now that the theory and practice of behaviour therapy and its derivatives, are well established across the world, newcomers sometimes find it difficult to comprehend what the fuss was all about. Behaviour therapy was the first coherent, practical, and scientifically ambitious alternative to the prevailing conception of the psychological basis of abnormal behaviour. It constituted a major challenge to the established psychotherapies and the psychodynamic theory, and was propounded with a confidence that seemed precocious but which turned out to be justified. In recent years, signs of complacency developed and there are too few traces of the earlier willingness to tackle large questions. Many of these questions, and some new ones, remain unanswered and are invitations to ambitious research scientists and clinicians. (Rachman, 1987, p. 1)

The principles of behaviour therapy were helped to spread by the founding of the British Association for Behavioural Psychotherapy in Great Britain, the Association for the Advancement of Behaviour Therapy in the United States, and similar associations in Germany and elsewhere. Former students of mine, like Vic Muyer in Great Britain, Cyril Franks in the United States, and Hans Brengelmann in Germany, were prominent in all of these organizations, which published journals such as the British *Behavioural Psychotherapy* and the American *Behavior Therapist.*

Histories of the development of behaviour therapy sometimes overestimate my contributions to the popularization of the topic, at the expense of the creative effort involved in getting our theoretical concepts together and working out the methods of therapy we were using. This is perhaps the inevitable consequence of the secrecy which had to surround our first tentative steps in this direction, and the fact that we worked as a group. In any case, it is the success of the venture that matters, not the question of individual contributions. And of that success, there can hardly by any doubt.

I did not myself take any part in the later developments, the negotiations with the

National Health Service, or the formation of the association. I have always been a "loner," concerned with research rather than administration, and have always resisted efforts to draw me into devoting time and energy to problems of organization, policy, committee work, and so forth. When asked by the Council of the British Psychological Society to stand for president, and to be in charge of the International Congress of Experimental Psychology to be held in London, I refused, although aware of the honour; my talents lie in research, not in administration. I did later agree to become the first president of the International Society for the Study of Individual Differences, because it seemed important to get this venture off the ground and to associate it with the journal *Personality and Individual Differences,* which I had just launched and was editing; also of course it involved very little in the way of time and energy! Other than that I have always eschewed membership of committees, councils, and other aggregates as far as possible. My experience shows that you can go a long way along these lines if you are determined enough.

Having thus finished my jobs of getting the profession of clinical psychology started and of setting behaviour therapy on its way, I turned with relief to the task that seemed to me even more important, and which was much more congenial to me, that of trying to furnish the new profession with a satisfactory theory on which to build its practices. There was, and always has been, a determined group of practitioners resolute in the belief that theory is unimportant, that eclecticism should reign supreme, and that therapy is an art rather than a science. A. Lazarus and I. Marks are good examples of this breed. Early critics of behaviour therapy, like Breger and McGaugh (1965), Locke (1971), and London, (1972) made two points in this connection, which have been reproduced many times since then. The first is that the methods of behaviour therapy are not in fact derived from learning theory, as Wolpe and I maintained, but are essentially the outcome of serendipity, which I once heard defined as "looking for a needle in a haystack and finding the farmer's daughter." It is curious that this argument is always made by critics who have no practical knowledge of the field, who have never made any of the discoveries in question, and who do not seem to care to base their conclusions on any kind of factual evidence.

Wolpe, Skinner, and the members of the Maudsley group had no hesitation in asserting that the practices we pioneered and advocated are firmly based on scientific principles, learning theory, and the discoveries of laboratory research; the same of course holds for J. P. Watson and Mary Cover Jones. An excellent example of the way in which laboratory discoveries and academic theories can be used in this connection is the 1980 work of Rachman and Hodgson, *Obsessions and Compulsions.* In our 1965 textbook, Rachman and I had already singled out the work of Solomon on obsessional behaviour in dogs as constituting a good paradigm for the possible treatment of compulsive behaviour, and as that book demonstrates, the method worked extremely well. Using "flooding with response prevention," as Solomon, Kamin, and Wynne (1953) had done, it became possible to turn a success rate of practically 0% for psychoanalysis, psychotherapy, leucotomy, electroshock, and other treatments attempted into a success rate of about 90%, an achievement replicated at least twice (Meyer, Levy, & Schnurer, 1974; Foa & Goldstein, 1978). This is only one example; many others could be adduced for the value of animal research in suggesting methods of treatment, and for the value of psychological theory in general.

The critics I have mentioned suggest, in addition, that there is no general theory in the field of learning and conditioning that is widely accepted, maintaining that the laws of learning on which behaviour therapy was said to be based themselves remain to be established. As they have pointed out, fundamental issues, such as the role of mediational events in behaviour change, the nature of responses learned, and the limitations of a stimulus-response analysis, have not yet been resolved. They also make the point that behaviour therapy mistakenly assumed a monolithic learning theory as one of its bases as an applied science. But if learning theory itself had not succeeded and resolved its major issues, then how could it rely on this theory as an established guide (Erwin, 1978)?

It is of course true that there is no final, monolithic, universally agreed theory of learning; but what reasonable critic would expect this? Three hundred years after Newton, we still do not have a monolithic, universally agreed-on theory of gravitation, with at least two quite different theories still in the field—Einstein's relativistic theory of distortions of the space-time continuum, and the quantum mechanics theory of particle interaction. In spite of this failure to achieve a monolithic theory, physics seems to have done quite well in practice, and certainly has not abjured the use of theory in making practical applications! The critics are seeking a degree of perfection here that is unobtainable, and certainly not characteristic of the "hard" sciences, even at their most successful. This point is argued in more detail elsewhere (Eysenck, 1987), but perhaps enough has been said here to illustrate the unreasonableness of the criticisms.

Much the same can be said about another line of criticism, one that is often put forward by cognitive psychologists like Beck, Mahoney, and Meichenbaum. They have attempted to establish what they consider a new and rather different discipline of "cognitive behaviour therapy," but in doing so they have based their arguments on shifting sands. They criticize an outmoded kind of learning theory, such as that put forward by Watson, and pay no attention to recent advances in learning theories that would demonstrate the irrelevance of these criticisms.

It would be quite untrue to say that behaviour therapists from the beginning have failed to pay attention to cognitive principles. Ever since the days of Pavlov and Tolman, learning theory has indeed embraced cognition as a vital part of learning, as evidenced by Pavlov's "second signalling system." We may perhaps also cite Platanov's 1959 work, *The Word as a Physiological and Therapeutic Factor*. Modern theory in the field is equally insistent on the importance of cognitive factors. The following quotation is from Mackintosh's 1984 textbook:

> The view of conditioning as the establishment of new reflexes or the strengthening of S=R [stimulus=response] connections, a view which dominated Western learning theory for half a century, has gradually given way to a view of conditioning as the acquisition of knowledge about the relationship between events in an animal's environment, knowledge which may not be immediately apparent in any change in behavior at all. When a CS [conditioned stimulus] is regularly

followed by a reinforcer, animals can be said to learn that the CS signals the reinforcer. This is achieved by the establishment of an association between some central representations of the two. From studies that have altered the value of a reinforcer after conditioning, it is apparent that the representation of the reinforcer associated with the CS must, in at least some cases, itself be available for modification when their value is manipulated. (p. 56)

Clearly the criticisms of "cognitive behaviour therapists" are based on ignorance of modern learning theory, and assume that when the principles of learning theory are invoked by behaviour therapists, they are those of Watson and the early workers of 60 years ago. This of course is not true; what is meant by "learning theory" is the most modern developments, including S-S (stimulus-stimulus) principles of conditioning, the invocation of cognitive aspect, motivational factors, and so on. For a well-based discussion of modern behaviourism, the reader is referred to Zuriff's 1985 book *Behaviorism: A Conceptual Reconstruction*; and for the relevance of these principles to behaviour therapy, the reader might usefully consider Eysenck and Martin's 1988 *Theoretical Foundations of Behaviour Therapy*.

It may also be worth pointing out that there is in fact no generally agreed-on body of principles that might be associated with cognitive theories. Allport (1975) has characterized the whole field of cognitive psychology in a rather unflattering summary. It is, he maintains,

typified by an uncritical, or a selective, or frankly cavalier attitude to experimental data; the pervasive atmosphere of special pleading; a curious parochialism in acknowledging even the existence of other workers, and other approaches, to the phenomena under discussion; interpretations of data relying on multiple, arbitrary choice-points; and underlying all else a near vacuum of theoretical structure within which to interrelate different sets of experimental results, or to direct the search for significant new phenomena.

In a similar way, M. W. Eysenck, in his 1984 *Handbook of Cognitive Processes,* points out "the extremely diverse and sprawling nature of the current scene" in cognitive psychology. He goes on to say that

at least part of the reason for the growing army marching behind the banner of cognitive psychology is the increased vagueness with which the term is used. Virtually all those interested in perception, learning, memory, language, concept formation, problem solving, or thinking call themselves "cognitive psychologists," despite the great diversity of experimental and theoretical approaches to be found in these various areas. (p. 1)

Taking all these arguments into account, I see no reason to give up the definition of behaviour therapy I adopted in the beginning, namely "the application of the principles of learning theory to the development of abnormal mental states, and the extinction of such abnormal conditioned responses along Pavlovian lines." We have certainly learned a lot since the days of Pavlov and Watson, and obviously all these developments must be taken into account in theorizing about abnormal mental states and advocating methods of treatment. This was implicit in my original formulation, and remains equally valid today. I have not come across any criticism which validly impugns the arguments presented here.

But, it will be said, is it not true that the conditioning theory of neurosis originally advocated by Watson had run into insuperable difficulties? I have already mentioned some of these. In the first place, there is no evidence for the traumatic events that play such an important part in Watson's (and Freud's!) theory of neurosis. Instead of a traumatic unconditioned stimulus (UCS) leading to single-trial conditioning, what we normally find in peacetime neurosis is a relatively mild causative event followed by the insidious growth of fear and anxiety reactions associated with it. In the second place, what we often find in a fully developed neurosis is that what is interpreted as the CR is in fact a great deal stronger then the unconditioned response (UCR), an event for which there is no provision in traditional learning theory. Third, even if neurotic responses were to be interpreted in terms of conditioning, we would expect extinction to follow as a consequence of exposure to unreinforced CSs, and while this may account for a good deal of the spontaneous remission that is observed, nevertheless it leaves us without explanation for the large number of long-continuing neurotic disorders that, in these terms, should be impossible.

Another problem is the failure of the notion of "equipotentiality," adopted originally by Pavlov and Watson; that is, the view that any stimulus can act as the conditioned stimulus with equal ease. Phobias are usually related to a nonarbitrary set of situations that differ markedly from those one would expect from learning theory. Phobias are seldom related to events giving rise to painful experiences in modern life, such as from electrical equipment or dental treatment, but are much more frequently related to relatively rare and often harmless events and organisms. Thus, fear of snakes is about twice as prevalent as fear of dental treatment in a normal population, although presumably many more persons have had actual painful experiences in the latter context (Agras, Sylvester, & Olivean, 1969).

The problem here lies in the notion of "equipotentiality" favoured by Pavlov—the notion that any neutral stimulus can be conditioned to become a CS with equal ease. Seligman (1971) put forward the view that some types of stimuli are "prepared" more than others to become conditioned stimuli for anxiety and fear responses, due to evolutionary developments, and this notion of "preparedness" has achieved a great deal of empirical support. The work on human preparedness has been summarized by Öhman, Dimberg, and Öst (1985), and by the equally impressive work on animals (mainly rhesus monkeys) by Mineka (1987).

It does seem reasonable that fear of snakes for instance, both in humans and in monkeys, should be easier to evoke through a process of conditioning than would fear of flowers, say, because of the greater biological usefulness of this mechanism. Preparedness, in this view, is one step removed from the direct genetic determination of phobic fears, for which there also exists good evidence (Torgersen, 1979). Although some people may have an innate fear of snakes, some, in whom this innate fear is weaker, are merely "prepared" to condition fear readily to snake stimuli, while still others have a low genetic predisposition and would be quite difficult to condition to such fears.

This belief in the biological and genetic antecedents of neurotic reactions may seem incompatible with a behaviouristic view, but even Watson and Rayner (1920) speculated that the long continuance of Little Albert's conditioned fear reaction to rats might have been due in part to some kind of "constitutional inferiority"; it might not have been observed in other children, presumably those not suffering from such an inferiority. The term itself is not defined, but clearly Watson did consider the possibility that individual differences played a large part in the development of conditioned fear reaction, leading to neurotic disorders and phobias, and that these might be of genetic origin. It is unfortunate that this early open-mindedness on the part of the founder of behaviourism has not generally been adopted by his followers! However that may be, the evidence by now is compelling, and must be taken into account by anyone concerned with the origins and cure of neurosis (Eaves, Eysenck, & Martin, 1989).

The other great problem with Watson's analysis is more complicated. Essentially, it relates to the postulation of traumatic events as causing neurosis, and the extinction of these conditioned responses.

The first part of the problem is clinical. War neuroses often do begin with a traumatic event, such as being buried alive by an explosion or witnessing the death or mutilation of a friend. However, in civilian neuroses such events are rare, and in the majority of cases the initiating event is not excessively traumatic, and does not produce an immediate, strong CR. Rather, there appears to be an insidious increase in the anxiety produced by the CS that may take years, or even decades, before a full-blown phobia becomes apparent, or a clinical state of anxiety is reached. This is the major clinical objection to Watson's theory.

From an experimental point of view, a second objection is the simple one that on this account extinction should set in almost immediately, making the development of any long-lasting neurosis impossible. Whatever the CS may be, the subject is likely to encounter it quite frequently and without attending reinforcement. This should produce relatively quick extinction of the CR. Let us consider a person suffering from a cat phobia; he or she is likely to encounter cats in nonthreatening situations quite frequently, and each such encounter should foster extinction. The phobia should thus quite soon disappear. The fact that this does not seem to happen is a powerful argument against Watson's theory (Kimmel, 1975).

A third important point is that in ordinary Pavlovian conditioning there is no way in which the CR could be stronger than the UCR. Yet if we look at clinical cases, as mentioned earlier, the initiating conditioning experience often leads to UCRs and CRs that are rather mild; it is only after the insidious development of the neurosis has taken place that the CRs become so strong as to constitute an actual mental illness. Hence in these quite typical cases of neurosis and phobia, the CR becomes much stronger than the original UCR; on ordinary Pavlovian principles this would seem to be impossible.

What these three objections have in common, of course, is a reference to the development of the CR over time, when the subject is exposed a number of times to the CS only, that is, to the CS without simultaneous reinforcement. Classical conditioning theory would expect extinction under these conditions, but what happens in the case of the development of a neurotic illness seems to be the opposite; that is, an incrementation of the CR. To explain this anomaly, I followed up Grant's (1964) suggestion that there is an important distinction between Pavlovian A and Pavlovian B conditioning, and proposed that the consequences of this distinction are important in regard to extinction (Eysenck, 1985).

Pavlovian A conditioning is exemplified by the textbook example of classical conditioning, that is, salivation on the part of the dog to the sound of a bell that had been repeatedly presented shortly before food was given to the hungry dog. Of the many UCRs presented (approach to the food, ingestion, and so on), Pavlov chose to measure only one, buccal salivation. As Zener (1937) pointed out, it is noteworthy that the CR did not include approach to and attempts to feed upon the bell or other source of the CS. Any approach and reorientation movements were directed to the food source, showing that the CS does not substitute for the UCS, as S-R theorists have often stated. Pavlov maintained that the CS serves as a signal that the food is about to be presented, and this position is also taken by S-S theorists. This approach is now almost exclusively recognized as being more in line with the facts than the old-fashioned S-R approach (Mackintosh, 1984).

Pavlovian B conditioning is directly linked by Grant (1964) to the Watson and Rayner (1920) experiment, but as he points out, Pavlov has priority. A reference experiment for Pavlovian B conditioning could be that in which an animal is given repeated injections of morphine. The UCR in this case involves severe nausea, profuse secretion of saliva, vomiting, and then profound sleep. After repeated daily injections, Pavlov's dogs were found to show severe nausea and profuse secretion of saliva at the first touch of the experimenter.

The major differences between Pavlovian A and B conditioning relate to drive and to degree of similarity between CR and UCR. In Pavlovian A conditioning, no learning takes place unless the subject is in a suitable state of drive, such as hunger in the case of the salivary conditioning in dogs. In the case of Pavlovian B conditioning, the UCS provides the drive or motivation. In Watson's theory, the UCS clearly provides the drive, making his a case of Pavlovian B conditioning.

In Pavlovian B conditioning, the UCS elicits the complete UCR, whereas in Pavlovian A conditioning the organism emits the UCR of approaching and ingesting the food. Thus in Pavlovian B conditioning the CS appears to act as a (partial) substitute for the UCS, which is not true of Pavlovian A conditioning. Expressed in different terms, we may say that in Pavlovian A conditioning typically the CR and the UCR are different (salivation as opposed to approach to and ingestion of food), whereas in Pavlovian B conditioning they are similar or identical (nausea, profuse secretion of saliva, vomiting). As Grant points out, many components of the UCR in Pavlovian conditioning "are readily seen as components of the CS which will be evoked by the preparations of the injection after repeated daily morphine injections" (p. 5). A great deal of interoceptive conditioning (Bykov, 1957) and autonomic conditioning (Kimble, 1961) appears to follow the Pavlovian B paradigm.

These differences between Pavlovian B conditioning can be used to argue that the consequences of CS-only presentation may be quite different in the two paradigms (Eysenck, 1976). In Pavlovian A conditioning, it is meaningful for both the subject and the experimenter to talk about CS-only presentation as the presentation of the CS that is not followed by the UCS. However, in Pavlovian B conditioning this is difficult to accomplish because the CR, which follows the CS, is for all purposes identical with the UCR. Consequently, the phrase "CS-only presentation" is meaningful for the experimenter, who controls the presentation of the UCS, but not for the subject, who experiences the CR as identical with the UCR. In Pavlovian B conditioning, if it be true that the CS-only condition is not necessarily fulfilled (as far as the subject is concerned), then it seems to follow that the ordinary laws of extinction might not always apply. Although the experimenter has arranged the contingencies in such a way that CS is not followed by UCS, under certain conditions (to be specified later) the CR itself might act as a reinforcement equivalent to the UCR, thus producing not extinction but an increment in the strength of the CR. This incrementation has been called *incubation,* and has led to a revised conditioning theory of neurosis (Eysenck, 1985).

There has been much discussion of the incubation phenomenon and the large body of research that supports it (Eysenck, 1976, 1985); there is no space to review the evidence again here. Incubation is a process that is theoretically intelligible in terms of Pavlovian B conditioning, and experimentally verified by many animal and a few human experiments. We also have both theoretical and practical evidence concerning some of the variables that make for incubation rather than extinction, such as strength of the UCR and CR, duration of exposure of the CS-only, personality, and so on (Eysenck, 1985).

The general form of the theory of incubation and extinction in neurotic fear reduction is shown in diagrammatic form in Figure 1. It shows on the ordinate the strength of the CR, and on the abscissa the duration of CS-only exposure. Curve A illustrates the decline in fear/anxiety with duration of CS exposure; there is ample evidence from the animal and particularly from the human field (Rachman & Hodgson, 1980, Figure 14.1) to support the general decline over time of the fear/anxiety reaction. The theory states that on this curve there is a critical point. If CS-only exposure stops before this point is reached, that is, while the strength of the CR is above this level, incubation will result. If at termination of CS-only exposure the strength of the CR is below this critical point, extinction will result. Thus duration of exposure is a critical element in deciding whether incubation or extinction is to result from treatment or experiment, and there is much evidence from the clinical field to support this view (Eysenck, 1985).

If CS-only exposure is continued long enough to provide an increment of extinction, curve A will be lowered on the next occasion, as indicated by curve B, and subsequent increments of extinction will reduce the whole curve below the critical point, as in curve C. Curve A indicates a typical sequence of events when flooding with response prevention is used as a therapeutic technique; curve C indicates the level at which desensitization and modelling proceed.

Strength of the CR and duration of CS-only exposure are not the only critical variables; personality (and the concentration of peptides and hormones that control both personality and fear/anxiety reactions) also play an important part. Note that the theory is also relevant to the acquisition of fear/anxiety responses; if the original

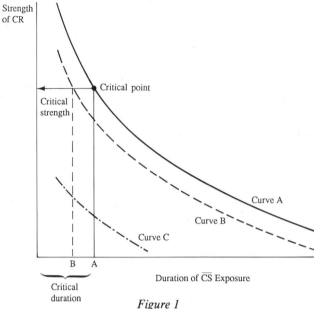

Figure 1

Strength of CR as a function of CS-only exposure (Eysenck, 1979)

CR exceeds the critical point, then incubation will occur and the final CR will be stronger than the original UCR, an event not contemplated in Pavlov's original theory, but clearly apparent in experimental animal studies, as well as characteristic of the development of human neuroses (Eysenck, 1979). The biological underpinnings of this theory in terms of peptides and other biochemical variables are discussed by Kelley (1987).

The theory I have just outlined is too new and too untried to say anything definitive about it. It certainly constitutes an improvement on Watson's original theory, or Mowrer's attempts to reformulate it, and it does account more than any other theory for the facts which are known about neurosis and its treatment. Unfortunately, most behaviour therapists are not interested in theory; but a good deal of research is now going on in an attempt to test deductions from it, and in due course no doubt we will know more than we do now.

In recent years I have become increasingly interested in the application of behaviour therapy to the prophylaxis and treatment of physical diseases such as cancer and coronary heart disease. My interest began in the late 1950s, when I did some work on the personality correlates and determinants of cigarette smoking. This led me to ask whether there were any similar correlations between personality and smoking-related diseases. My first study with David Kissen, a Scottish oncologist, (Kissen & Eysenck, 1962), suggested quite a *high negative relationship between lung cancer and neuroticism (i.e., the absence of neuroticism and other traits characteristic of strongly expressed emotions)*, but it was not until I teamed up with Dr. Grossarth-Maticek, a psychologist born in Yugoslavia who later emigrated to

Heidelberg, that really important results began to emerge. All this work of course has a very long history.

Some four thousand years ago, the Indian Mahabharata declared, "There are two classes of disease—bodily and mental. Each arises from the other. Neither can exist without the other. Mental disorders arise from physical ones, and likewise physical disorders arise from mental ones." Can this be true? It certainly contradicts our Cartesian notion that body and mind are entirely different substances, which cannot influence each other. Nevertheless, as we shall see, Mahabharata was right, and Descartes was wrong.

This is an important debate, which is also relevant to another debate which has been going on in medicine for many, many years. Many modern doctors aim to treat a given disease, but others, going back to Hippocrates, declare that what they should be treating is a patient who happens to have a disease. In other words, it is suggested that factors like stress, social support, personality, anxiety, and depression, and many other similar variables play an important part in whether a person will or will not come down with a given disease, and how that person will react to it. This in turn suggests that treatment and prophylaxis should be concerned with these factors, as well as with the microbes, viruses, and other agents which are involved in the disease.

There certainly is a long tradition linking cancer, for instance, with personality. The theory dates back some two thousand years, and many observant physicians have contributed to its evolution. Cancer-prone people, and patients suffering from cancer, are believed to be over-cooperative, appeasing, unassertive, and over-patient. These people avoid conflict and instead try to harmonize behaviour, do not express negative emotions, particularly anxiety and anger, but rather suppress them, and are compliant with external authorities. Much evidence from recent work suggests that there is some such correlation between cancer and personality, and also that people of this type, once they have contracted cancer, die more quickly than others who are less compliant and more complaining, assertive, and prone to express their anger.

In recent years there has also been a growing belief that there is some relationship between personality and coronary heart disease, as expressed in the well-known concept of "Type A" behaviour originally described by two American physicians, R. H. Rosenman and M. Friedman. People of this type engage in hard-driven and time-urgent work-directed behaviour. They tend to be aggressive, their hostility is easily aroused, and they exhibit competitive achievement-striving, impatience, and explosive speech patterns. Contrasted with this, "Type B" is a more peaceful, normal, and healthy type. The cancer-prone type, differing in many ways from Type A, was subsequently labelled "Type C," so that we are apparently dealing with three different types, the healthy Type B, the cancer-prone Type C, and the coronary heart disease-prone Type A.

The large body of literature on the relationship between these types and disease has been kinder to Type C than to Type A. Prognostic studies, using interviews or questionnaires of Type A behaviour, have not been able to predict coronary heart disease too well, some studies giving positive and others negative results. It is now accepted that the net was cast too wide, and that only *some* of the traits of Type A are relevant to coronary heart disease, particularly hostility, aggression, and anger.

I have recently been closely involved with some prospective studies along these lines. These three prospective studies, carried out over the last 20 years by Dr. Grossarth-Maticek, show that there is a fairly strong relationship between such personality types and disease. A person's type was ascertained by means of a personality questionnaire enquiring particularly into interpersonal stress, such as the loss of a loved one, and the person's reaction to that stress. The questionnaire was administered by an interviewer, who would explain parts of the questionnaire not clearly understood by the respondent, and who would ask for specific examples of the respondent's conduct which would be relevant to the questions in the inventory.

According to their answers, subjects were allocated to Type 1, the cancer-prone type; Type 2, the coronary heart disease-prone type; Type 4, the healthy type; or Type 3, a kind of person characterized by psychopathic reactions not particularly related to cancer or to coronary heart disease, and hence from that point of view reasonably healthy. Type 1 would correspond with Type C, Type 2 with Type A, the Type 4 with Type B, although the characterization of Type 2 omits those aspects of Type A which have not been found to be relevant to coronary heart disease (Eysenck, 1988). Ten years after diagnosis, the people who took part in these studies were again contacted and it was ascertained who was still alive, who had died, and what the cause of death had been.

In the first of these three studies, a small town in Yugoslavia was selected for study, and the oldest person in every other household was contacted. In addition, a number of highly stressed individuals were selected who were not the oldest in the household. In the second study, carried out in Heidelberg, a random sample of people was contacted within preselected age and sex norms. Each of the participants was asked to nominate a family member or a friend who was severely stressed; these people were then contacted and constituted the third group, the Heidelberg stressed sample.

Figures 2, 3, and 4 show the results. In each case the number of people in each of the types is shown. A higher proportion of people died in the Yugoslav study than in the Heidelberg normal group, because obviously cancer and coronary heart disease tend to occur more frequently in older people, and the Yugoslav group was older. Of more interest is the fact that the Heidelberg stressed group, although not older than the Heidelberg normal group, had a much higher incidence of death from cancer and coronary heart disease, suggesting that severe stress of this interpersonal kind was indeed a killer. Differences in smoking and other similar variables were not responsible for this difference.

It is clear that in all three studies Type 1 was more likely to die of cancer than of coronary heart disease and Type 2 of coronary heart disease rather than cancer, while Types 3 and 4 tended to have a rather low level of mortality. Obviously, members of these two groups will also die in due course, many of them possibly of cancer or coronary heart disease; a healthy personality may postpone but cannot avoid death! Nevertheless, the results show fairly definitely that the theories linking personality and disease are correct, as are those implicating stress as a causal factor in death from cancer and coronary heart disease (Eysenck, 1987).

These findings raise two very important questions. If stress, and the way a person reacts to stress, can influence whether or not he or she will later contract cancer or coronary heart disease, is it possible through some form of psychological treatment to alter that person's behaviour in such a way that he or she can avoid illness? The other question is whether, given that a person is suffering from cancer or coronary heart disease, psychological treatment can prolong life. There is now evidence that the answer to both questions is affirmative.

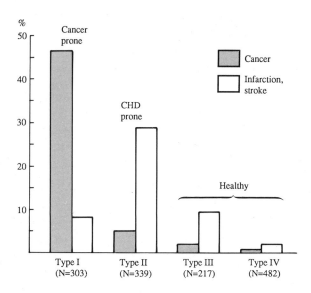

Figure 2
Death from cancer or coronary heart disease as a function of personality type:
Yugoslav study (Eysenck, 1988)

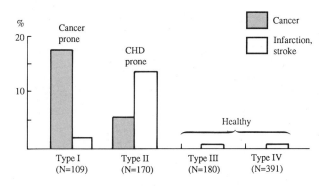

Figure 3
Death from cancer or coronary heart disease as a function of personality type:
Heidelberg normal study group (Eysenck, 1988)

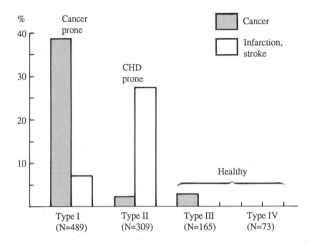

Figure 4
Death from cancer or coronary heart disease as a function of personality type:
Heidelberg stressed study group (Eysenck, 1988)

Both the cancer-prone and the CHD-prone person apparently have difficulty in coping successfully with stress. Thus instead of terminating the stress and going on with successful living in an autonomous manner, these people develop feelings of hopelessness and helplessness, believe that they cannot cope any more, retreat within themselves, show depression and other forms of abnormal emotional reaction, or indulge in angry and hostile behaviour of a socially unacceptable kind. Clearly it is possible to teach these people proper coping mechanisms, which would enable them to escape from the corner into which they have painted themselves; to show them how to get over their depression, how to express their anger and hostility in a socially acceptable manner, and generally how to abandon the neurotic and unsuccessful adaptations they have shown and behave in a more reasonable and rewarding manner. Dr. Grossarth-Maticek worked out a method of behaviour therapy that emphasized the rewarding qualities of the new type of behaviour, and made the person under treatment realize the lack of rewards characteristic of his or her usual response to stress. The actual techniques used employ a variety of devices, including suggestion and hypnosis, the teaching of coping techniques, and many others; this is not the place to describe the methods used, but rather to turn to a discussion of the results achieved (Grossarth-Maticek, Eysenck, & Vetter, 1988).

In the first of a series of studies, 100 cancer-prone and 92 coronary heart disease-prone people were divided into a control group and a therapy group—50 in each group for the cancer-prone people, 46 in each group for the coronary heart disease-prone people. After 13 years, these 192 people were located and it was determined who was still alive, who had died of cancer or coronary heart disease, and who had died of other causes. The results are shown in Table 2. It will be seen that the therapy, which consisted of between 25 and 30 hours of individual treatment, was very successful in preventing cancer in the cancer-prone group, and in preventing coronary heart disease in the CHD-prone group. Obviously psychological treatment, guided by a reasonable theory of the behaviour leading to cancer or coronary heart disease, can change behaviour in the direction of healthier living, and at least temporarily prevent cancer and coronary heart disease.

Table 2

Effects of behaviour therapy on cancer-prone and coronary heart disease-prone subjects (Eysenck, 1987)

| | Cancer-Prone Group | | | |
	Still Alive	*Died of Cancer*	*Died of Other Causes*	*Total*
Control	19	16	15	50
Therapy	45	0	5	50
Total	64	16	20	100
	Coronary Heart Disease-Prone Group			
	Still Alive	*Died of CHR*	*Died of Other Causes*	*Total*
Control	17	16	13	46
Therapy	37	3	6	46
Total	54	19	19	92

The cause of death as shown on death certificates is notoriously unreliable; it may be useful simply to look at the undoubted facts of life and death. This was done for the total group of 192 in Table 3, which shows how many of the 96 people in the therapy group were still alive and how many had died of cancer or CHD, as well as corresponding figures for the control group. For people at risk of cancer and coronary heart disease according to their personality diagnosis, it would clearly pay to undergo a course of behaviour therapy.

Table 3

Effects of therapy on death from cancer or coronary heart disease, in prophylactic studies (Eysenck, 1988)

	Live	*Dead*	*Total*
Therapy groups	82	14	96
Control groups	36	60	96
Total	118	74	192

Another set of subjects was treated by means of group therapy; groups of about 20 people were given behaviour therapy for an average of six hours on two or more separate days. The 245 subjects in the therapy group and 245 matched subjects in the control group were followed over a period of eight years. In the therapy group, 48 people died; in the control group, 180. This difference shows that group therapy, too, can be successful as a prophylactic agent in preventing death from cancer and coronary heart disease.

Finally, an experiment was done on 1200 people, of whom 600 constituted the therapy group, 500 the control group receiving no treatment, and 100 a placebo group receiving a treatment not anticipated to have any results, but serving to show the possible effect on the patient of receiving *some* form of treatment. In this case, treatment consisted of one hour of individual therapy, accompanied by a one-page instruction leaflet explaining the meaning of autonomy training, coping behaviour, and so on. The follow-up results after 13 years demonstrate that the placebo group,

Table 4
Survival of cancer patients treated and not treated by behaviour therapy,
in years (Eysenck, 1988)

Type of Cancer	Number of Pairs of Patients	Survival Time in Years		Comparison of Survival Times
		Therapy Group	*Control Group*	
Scrotal	1	5.8	3.2	+
Stomach	1	4.8	1.8	+
	2	2.4	2.3	+
Bronchiolar	1	1.7	2.4	−
	2	5.6	1.5	+
	3	4.2	1.6	+
	4	3.2	1.1	+
	5	1.7	1.7	=
	6	4.5	1.2	+
	7	5.2	1.0	+
Corpus uteri	1	6.8	4.2	+
	2	4.5	4.8	−
	3	7.2	3.5	+
	4	8.2	3.1	+
Cervical	1	5.5	4.2	+
	2	6.1	4.0	+
	3	3.2	3.3	−
	4	4.5	4.1	+
	5	2.8	3.6	−
Colon and rectum	1	9.5	4.2	+
	2	7.5	2.1	+
	3	6.3	4.9	+
	4	4.8	4.3	+
	5	5.7	4.1	+
Total	24	0 5.07 (average)	0 3.09 (average)	

receiving "dynamic" type therapy and instruction, showed much the same record of death as did the control group, while the therapy group showed far fewer deaths from cancer and coronary heart disease (Grossarth-Maticek, in press; Eysenck & Grossarth-Maticek, in press).

Let us now turn to the question of treatment of existing cancers. Table 4 shows 24 pairs of patients, matched for type of cancer. In each pair one patient was chosen for therapy by the toss of a coin, the other being given no behaviour therapy. Survival time in years is shown for each patient, and it will be seen that those in the therapy group survived on average over five years, while those in the control group survived just over three years. The plus sign (+) in the last column means that the patients in the therapy group survived longer, the minus sign (−) that the patients in the control group survived longer, and an equal sign (=) means that they survived equally long. It will be seen that there are far more plus than minus or equal signs.

Finally, Table 5 shows the results of a study of 100 women who were terminally ill with breast cancer. Half elected to be treated by chemotherapy, while half refused. Half received psychotherapy, half did not, giving 25 women who either had neither type of therapy, or both, or one, or the other. Mean survival time in months is given in the table, showing that those who received no type of therapy survived for only 11 months, those who received both survived for 22 months, and those who received only chemotherapy or behaviour therapy survived between 14 and 15 months. Clearly, behaviour therapy is as effective as chemotherapy in prolonging life, and equally clearly both types of therapy together have a synergistic effect—that is, they prolong life more than adding the simple effects of the two together.

Table 5
Survival of cancer patients in months,
by type of treatment received (Eysenck, 1988)

Behaviour Therapy	Chemotherapy		
	No	*Yes*	*Total*
No	Mean = 11.28 N = 25	Mean = 14.08 N = 25	Mean = 12.68
Yes	Mean = 14.92 N = 25	Mean = 22.40 N = 25	Mean = 18.66
Total	Mean = 13.10	Mean = 18.24	Grand mean = 15.67 N = 100

The results of these studies suggest quite strongly that psychological treatment can have a pronounced prophylactic effect, and that it can prolong life once the person is suffering from a terminal illness. Is there a possibility that behaviour therapy might be used to actually *cure* cancer? A study has recently been carried out in Holland in which eight persons were located who were suffering from cancer that was considered to be terminal, but who nevertheless recovered without treatment. Such cases are rare, but they do exist, and it is interesting that all eight showed very strongly the healthy personality type (Type 4) described by Grossarth-Maticek. It would certainly seem worthwhile to try to determine whether the possibility exists of reversing the progress of cancer in certain types of persons by behaviour therapy. Success is unlikely, but the experiment ought to be made.

How is it possible that stress, or the reaction to stress, can influence a physical disease like cancer in one way or another? The answer probably is that our behaviour does not so much influence the cancer itself but rather the immune system. We develop miniature cancerous growths every day, but they are killed off by the immune system. It is probably the weakening of the immune system in old age that accounts for the greater number of cancers in people over 60. The immune system is very much influenced by peptides and hormones, such as cortisol for instance, and it is well known that this immuno-destructive agent is in turn linked with depression; depression increases cortisol, and increased cortisol destroys and weakens the immune system. In one study of old people in a home, who were suffering a good deal of stress, it was shown that not only did behaviour therapy involving the teaching of coping behaviour prolong life and increase the activity and contentment of the patients so treated, a significant and continued decrease, as compared with the control group, was also found in the amount of cortisol present.

Indeed, it is possible to demonstrate immediate effects on the immune system of quite slight environmental stimuli. Thus in one study pre- and postmeasures of immunoglobulin A were taken. (Immunoglobulin A is a substance that reflects transitory changes in the immune system.) The subjects were shown either humorous videotapes or a control tape. There were significant increases in immune response to the humorous film compared with the control. Perhaps the Marx Brothers have had a more beneficent effect on cancer control than all the medical interventions that have been done!

In another study, an intimate relationship was shown between immunoglobulin A and the mood of students, immune system responses being lower on days of high negative mood and higher on days of high positive mood. There is little doubt about the close relationship between behaviour, mood, and immune system responsiveness, making more credible the possibility of defeating cancer through some form of behaviour therapy.

The work here reviewed opens up possibilities, but it does not suggest final answers. Very little in the way of financial funding has gone into these areas, for a simple reason. Medical people these days are wedded to the idea of treating the disease and not the patient, and there is quite a hostile attitude to the involvement of personality, stress, and other psychosocial variables in the disease and treatment process. These concepts are not familiar to most doctors, they are not taught in medical school, and they do not form part of medical orthodoxy. Hence there is a considerable degree of suspicion and prejudice against these new-fangled ideas which is difficult to break down, and a definite reluctance to support research into these factors. This is unfortunate, because the evidence is strong that these novel ways of looking at the problem may be of considerable help in prophylaxis and treatment. A lengthy process of reeducation seems needed, but in the meantime thousands of people are dying unnecessarily of cancer and coronary heart disease— people whose lives could have been saved had there been a greater readiness to support research in these novel areas. We simply have to give up the notion of body as opposed to mind, and to accept the notion of a body-soul entity, just as physicists have had to give up the notion of time and space as separate entities, and now deal with a space-time continuum.

If these new ideas are at all along the right lines, and the evidence certainly suggests that they are, then the National Health Service in England, and the many health insurance systems in other countries, will need to consider very carefully a problem originally raised by the ancient Chinese, who were supposed to pay their doctors while they were healthy, and to cease paying them when they were ill. This emphasis on prophylaxis and health, rather than on treatment after illness, has a powerful appeal, even though the story may be apocryphal. If we can indeed avoid cancer and coronary heart disease by suitable psychological treatment, or at least postpone their onset by 15 years or more, then we can not only add immeasurably to the sum of human happiness, we can also lessen the financial burden on the National Health Service and on health insurance plans in other countries. The cost of prophylactic treatment is quite insignificant in comparison with the cost of treating patients who are suffering from cancer or coronary heart disease in hospital, carrying out operations, paying for medicines, maintaining the hospitals, paying the doctors and nurses, and incurring all the other costs involved in such treatment.

Considering the ever-increasing financial burden on the National Health Service, it would seem reasonable on the part of the government to look into the possibility of lessening this burden by adopting some form of prophylactic diagnosis of cancer-prone and coronary heart disease-prone personality types, and by providing psychological treatment to prevent the development of cancer and coronary heart disease. The opposition of the medical profession to any novel ideas, and the general inertia of the bureaucracy involved, will almost certainly make the realization of such a plan impossible, but it does seem a pity that novel ideas should not be treated in a more hospitable way.

However that may be, our work is of course still continuing, and we hope to mount a replication of the three studies described earlier, including what has been sadly missing, a repeated assay of the immune system and the number of natural killer cells, as well as other biochemical data. I am of course unlikely to see the end of such a lengthy prospective study, but at least I would like to be connected with its beginnings!

This more or less concludes my association with clinical psychology and behaviour therapy. Clinical psychology is alive and well in Great Britain, with well over a thousand practitioners, a proper career structure, healthily integrated with the National Health Service, and accepted fairly universally by psychiatrists. The practice of behaviour therapy by psychologists is taken for granted by everybody, and in due course we may hope that its use as a prophylactic agent in physical diseases will also be accepted.

How is it that we are so successful in Great Britain, while in other parts of the world, from Israel to France, from South America to Scandinavia, behaviour therapists complain of lack of acceptance, failure to be recognised, and rejection by psychiatrists in general? There was an interesting debate on this topic at the Third International Congress of Behaviour Therapists in Edinburgh in 1988, the majority blaming the nonacceptance of American values, which they thought were a characteristic of behaviour therapy, in their various countries. In the discussion I said that I could not agree with this notion—American values are no more accepted in Great Britain than in the other countries named, particularly at a time, before Mrs. Thatcher, when behaviour therapy had already been accepted, and was growing exponentially. In any case I could not see that behaviour therapy was particularly characteristic of American values—Joseph Wolpe and my colleagues and myself had developed the concept and techniques of behaviour therapy in South Africa and England respectively, and they were only later taken up in the United States.

It seems to me that two things contributed to the success of behaviour therapy in the United Kingdom. First, something I missed in the various countries where it was not doing so well was a spirit of determination and aggressiveness. It seemed to me that in those countries behaviour therapists were trying to lie down with the analysts, like the lamb with the lion in the Bible; this may work in a parable, but it does not work so well in real life. It rather reminds me of the famous young lady of Riga, who foolishly rode on a tiger; as we all know, she ended up as the smile on the face of the tiger!

There is an obvious philosophical, scientific, and practical opposition between psychoanalysis and behaviour therapy, and any attempt to gloss it over is bound to fail, particularly when psychoanalysis has acquired a powerful position in psychiatry and medicine generally. What is needed, it seems to me, is wholehearted opposition, making quite clear the differences between the two, rather than half-hearted attempts to gloss over the chasm that divides them. I have found in general that it is wise to avoid conflict, fights, and dissention wherever possible, but sometimes there comes a moment when this is no longer possible, and then you have to do the best you can to win a fight that has been forced on you.

An example that comes to mind is an event which occurred when I was in primary school, so I must have been about eight years old. We had a new music teacher wished upon us, a Herr Meier, a fat and florid man who took himself very seriously. As an introduction, he wanted each of us to sing for him, and all the other pupils obliged happily. When it came my turn, I stood up and said politely that unfortunately I had no singing voice at all, and there would be no point in my trying to sing. He shouted that everyone could sing, and that I would be no exception, so would I please do as he said. I shrugged my shoulders and started to do the best I could, which of course was pretty awful. He stopped me very soon, shouting that I was obviously trying to take the Micky, and that he would tolerate no such insolence. He ordered me to go up to the dais where he was sitting, grabbed my right hand with his left, and threatened to hit me with the ruler he had in his right hand. When he brought it down I drew back my hand and he hit the table, which seemed to infuriate him even more. He again grabbed my hand, holding it very tight, and lifted the ruler to hit my hand really hard.

Without thinking I leaned forward and sank my teeth into the fleshy part of his hand, beneath the thumb. Even then I was tall and strong, and I bit him really hard. He dropped the ruler, blanched (I have never seen anybody's face go so white so quickly) and tried to withdraw his hand. I hung on like a bull terrier, and the class of course erupted in shouts, screams, and jumpings up and down. At that moment the headmaster walked past and, intrigued by the noise, opened the door and imperiously asked what was going on. He must have been surprised by what he saw—one of his teachers standing up on the dais, with a small boy dangling from his left hand and the class in an uproar! He immediately came and tried to dislodge me, but without success. Finally, with the help of several colleagues, poor Mr. Meier was released and taken home in a taxi. He was away for a fortnight, and never returned to that particular class.

The headmaster clearly did not know what to do with me. Insubordination in the young was not to be tolerated in the Prussian state, but on the other hand Mr. Meier had violated the law of the Weimar constitution, which forbade teachers to hit pupils. In the end, he wisely decided to do nothing; but while I was at primary school the other children always referred to me as the boy who bit his teacher. I remember the whole episode quite well, and I also remember that there was little emotion involved on my part. I was being treated unjustly, and there was simply no way in which I could tolerate such treatment. I did not take into account any of the objective factors of the situation, such as respective size, strength, or power; all this faded into insignificance compared with the absolute need to fight injustice. In many ways what I did then was prognostic of what I was to do later on, though in rather less physical fashion. The reaction was wholly instinctive, but I still feel that I did the right thing. You cannot let people get away with wrongdoing just because they are strong and powerful; whatever the cost, you have to stand up for yourself.

It seems to me that it is the lack of this kind of fighting spirit that accounts for the lack of success of those who have tried to establish behaviour therapy in various countries. Rationally we would expect that a method that is so clearly superior in effectiveness, and which is also so much cheaper and shorter than psychoanalysis, would be universally recognized and practised. Failure to act in accordance with such rational consideration is obviously unreasonable, and should be mercilessly and publicly criticized and condemned. Perhaps in due course someone will rise in these countries to firmly plant the flag of insurrection in the hostile ground of psychoanalysis; until this is done, little is likely to change.

The second reason that behaviour therapy has not flourished in many countries is a certain lack on the part of practitioners of simple common sense or political instinct. It was obvious to me, for instance, that I should not go public before I had established my position so firmly that the resulting storm would not be able to shake it. Had I published my paper a year or two earlier, the results would have been fatal. Obviously in battles of this kind one must be careful to choose the right time, the right place, and the right opportunity.

As an example of how not to do it, let me quote the German experience. Hans Brengelmann, one of my former students, had taken the germ of behaviour therapy with him to Germany, and it was growing quite well, leading to the establishment of a national society and a paper devoted to the topic. He was just concluding arrangements with various insurance companies to pay for the treatment of neurotic patients by means of behaviour therapy, when a group of militant left-wing behaviour therapists pushed through a declaration that individual treatment of patients was not the way to get rid of neurosis; the only way to do so was to change society through revolution! As might be imagined, the insurance companies were not particularly enamoured of financing a revolution, and withdrew their offer. Ever since then behaviour therapy has had great difficulty in establishing itself in Germany; having missed the right opportunity, it will have much trouble in becoming accepted. This is but one example of the absurd way in which some people throw away their advantages! It should be sufficient to indicate that good sense is needed as well as aggresiveness in establishing a new method of treatment.

I would like to end this essay by asking what, in the long run, my influence on behaviour therapy has been. Christopher Barbrack and Cyril Franks (1986) have written a very thoughtful chapter, entitled "Contemporary Behavior Therapy and the Unique Contribution of H. J. Eysenck: Anachronistic or Visionary?" in *Hans Eysenck: Consensus and Controversy.* My own views on the matter are perhaps too subjective to recount here, but they do not essentially differ from those of Barbrack and Franks. This is what they say:

> Whether one considers Eysenck a gadfly or guardian angel, it is unwise to dismiss him too casually. Still, when all is told, the conclusion that Eysenck's influence on behaviour therapy is a fraction of what it could be is unavoidable. The reason may be, in part, related to the following: (1) he writes so clearly and specifically that others understand his position and dismiss it for the sake of something they like better even if it is not understood nearly so well; (2) his manner of expression is dogmatic; (3) the material he presents is too technical and demands much effort to read; (4) his approach demands that treatment plans be formulated on the basis of psychological knowledge, that predictions be made about treatment effectiveness and that treatment be assessed against this standard—and it is much easier to "fly by the seat of your pants" and "shoot the breeze" in therapy sessions; (5) behaviour therapists may find data gathering and treatment evaluation tedious and even aversive; and (6) some behaviour therapists may not understand or appreciate the practical value of theory.
>
> We believe that these and other barriers to Eysenck's influence will fall as the knowledge base of behaviour therapy expands. For influence already exerted in behaviour therapy, Eysenck has earned our gratitude. As behaviour therapy contines to evolve, one day Eysenck will receive the full measure of appreciation his unique contribution deserves.

Only history will tell whether this is a correct view of the matter; we all have the right to differ in our predictions, and no one can prove us wrong as yet. My own belief is that Barbrack and Franks have been overly optimistic!

References

Agras, W. S., Sylvester, D., & Olivean, D. (1969). The epidemiology of common fears and phobias. *Comprehensive Psychiatry, 10,* 151–156.

Allport, D. A. (1975). The state of cognitive psychology. *Quarterly Journal of Experimental Psychology, 23,* 141–152.

Barbrack, C. R. & Franks, C. M. (1986). Contemporary behaviour therapy and the unique contribution of H. J. Eysenck: Anachronistic or visionary? In S. Modgil and C. Modgil (Eds.), *Hans Eysenck: Consensus and controversy* (pp. 233–245). London: Falmer Press.

Breger, L. & McGaugh, J. L. (1965). Critique and reformulation of "learning theory" approach to psychotherapy and neurosis. *Psychological Bulletin, 63,* 338–358.

Bykov, K. M. (1957). *The cerebral cortex and the internal organs.* New York: Chemical Publications.

Eaves, L., Eysenck, H. J., & Martin, N. (1989). *Genes, culture and personality: An empirical approach.* New York: Academic Press.

Erwin, E. (1978). *Behavior therapy: Scientific, philosophical and moral foundations.* New York: Cambridge Press.

Eysenck, H. J. (1947). *Dimensions of personality.* London: Routledge & Kegan Paul.

Eysenck, H. J. (1950). Criterion analysis: An application of the hypothetico-deductive method to factor analysis. *Psychological Review, 57,* 38–53.

Eysenck, H. J. (1952a). *The scientific study of personality.* London: Routledge & Kegan Paul.

Eysenck, H. J. (1952b). Schizothymia-cyclothymia as a dimension of personality. 11. Experimental. *Journal of Personality, 20,* 345–384.

Eysenck, H. J. (1952c). The effects of psychotherapy: An evaluation. *Journal of Consulting Psychology, 16,* 319–324.

Eysenck, H. J. (1956). The inheritance of extraversion-introversion. *Acta Psychologica, 12,* 95–110.

Eysenck, H. J. (1959a). The Rorschach Test. In H. Buros (Ed.), *The Fifth Mental Measurement Yearbook* (pp. 276–278). Nebraska: Gryphon.

Eysenck, H. J. (1959b). Learning theory and behaviour therapy. *Journal of Mental Science, 105,* 61–75.

Eysenck, H. J. (Ed.) (1960a). *Behaviour therapy and the neuroses.* Oxford: Pergamon Press.

Eysenck, H. J. (Ed.) (1960b; 2nd ed. 1972). *Handbook of abnormal psychology.* London: Pitman.

Eysenck, H. J. (Ed.) (1964). *Experiments in behaviour therapy.* Oxford: Pergamon Press.

Eysenck, H. J. (1967). *Biological basis of personality.* Springfield, IL: Charles C Thomas.

Eysenck, H. J. (1970). A dimensional system of psychodiagnosis. In A. R. Mahrer (Ed.), *New approaches to personality classification (pp. 169–208).* New York: Columbia University Press.

Eysenck, H. J. (Ed.) (1974). *Case Histories in behaviour therapy.* London: Routledge & Kegan Paul.

Eysenck, H. J. (1976). The learning theory model of neurosis: A new approach. *Behaviour Research and Therapy, 14,* 251–267.

Eysenck, H. J. (1977). *You and neurosis.* London: Maurice Temple Smith.

Eysenck, H. J. (1979). The conditioning model of neurosis. *The Behavioral and Brain Sciences, 2,* 155–199.

Eysenck, H. J. (1980). Hans Jürgen Eysenck. In G. Lindzey (Ed.), *A History of Psychology in Autobiography,* Vol. 7 (pp. 153–187). San Francisco: W. H. Freeman.

Eysenck, H. J. (1985). Incubation theory of fear/anxiety. In S. Reiss & R. R. Bootzin (Eds.), *Theoretical issues in behavior therapy* (pp. 83–109). New York: Academic Press.

Eysenck, H. J. (1987). Personality as a predictor of cancer and cardiovascular disease and the application of behaviour therapy in prophylaxis. *European Journal of Psychiatry, 1,* 29–41.

Eysenck, H. J. (1988). The respective importance of personality, cigarette smoking and interaction effects for the genesis of cancer and coronary heart disease. *Personality and Individual Differences. 9,* 453–464.

Eysenck, H. J. (1990). *Rebel with a cause.* London: Harrap.

Eysenck, H. J. & Eysenck, M. W. (1981). *Mindwatching.* London: Michael Joseph.

Eysenck, H. J. & Eysenck, M. W. (1985). *Personality and individual differences: A natural science approach.* New York: Plenum.

Eysenck, H. J. & Frith, C. D. (1977). *Reminiscence, motivation and personality.* New York: Plenum.

Eysenck, H. J. & Grossarth-Maticek, R. (in press). Creative novation behaviour therapy as a prophylactic treatment for cancer and coronary heart disease: 2. Effects of treatment. *Behaviour Research and Therapy.*

Eysenck, H. J. & Martin, I. (Eds.) (1988). *Theoretical foundations of behaviour therapy.* New York: Plenum.

Eysenck, H. J. & Prell, D. (1951). The inheritance of neuroticism: An experimental study. *Journal of Mental Science, 97,* 441–465.

Eysenck, H. J. & Rachman, S. (1965). *Causes and cures of neurosis.* London: Routledge & Kegan Paul.

Eysenck, M. W. (1984). *A handbook of cognitive processes.* Hillsdale, NJ: Erlbaum.

Foa, E. B. & Goldstein, A. (1978). Continuous exposure and strict response prevention in the obsessive-compulsive neurosis. *Behavior Therapy, 17,* 169–174.

Gibson, H. B. (1981). Hans Eysenck: The man and his work. London: Peter Owen.

Grant, D. A. (1964). Classical and operant condtioning. In A. W. Milton (Ed.), *Categories of human learning.* New York: Academic Press.

Grossarth-Maticek, R. & Eysenck, H. J. (in press). Creative novation behaviour therapy as a prophylactic treatment for cancer and coronary heart disease: 1. Description of treatment. *Behaviour Research and Therapy.*

Grossarth-Maticek, R., Eysenck, H. J., & Vetter, H. (1988). Personality type, smoking habit and their interaction as predictors of cancer and coronary heart disease. *Personality and Individual Differences, 9,* 479–495.

Hearnshaw, L. S. (1979). *Cyril Burt: Psychologist.* London: Hodder & Stoughton.

Herzberg, A. (1941). Short treatment of neuroses by graduated tasks. *British Journal of Medical Psychology, 19,* 19–36.

Herzberg, A. (1945). *Active psychotherapy.* New York: Grune & Strattan.

Kazdin, A. E. (1978). *History of behavior modification.* Baltimore: University Park Press.

Kelley, M. J. (1987). Hormones and clinical anxiety. In H. J. Eysenck & I. Martin (Eds.), *The theoretical foundations of behavior therapy* (pp. 403–432). New York: Plenum.

Kimble, G. A. (1961). *Hilgard and Marquis' conditioning and learning.* New York: Appleton-Century-Graff.

Kimmel, H. D. (1975). Conditioning of fear and anxiety. In C. D. Spielberger & I. A. Sarasan (Eds.), *Stress and Anxiety,* Vol. 1 (pp. 214–237). New York: Wiley.

Kissen, D. M. & Eysenck, H. J. (1962). Personality in male lung cancer patients. *Journal of Psychosomatic Research, 6,* 123–137.

Locke, E. A. (1971). Is "behaviour therapy" behaviouristic? *Psychological Bulletin, 76,* 318–327.

London, P. (1972). The end of ideology in behavior modification. *American Psychologist, 27,* 913–920.

Luborsky, L., Singer, B., & Luborsky, L. (1975). Comparative studies of psychotherapies: Is it true that everyone has won and all must have prizes? *Archives of General Psychiatry, 32,* 995–1008.

Mackintosh, N. J. (1984). *Conditioning and associative learning.* Oxford: Clarendon Press.

Mays, D. T. & Franks, C. M. (1985). *Negative outcome in psychotherapy.* New York: Springer.

Meyer, V., Levy, R., & Schnurer, A. (1974). The behavioral treatment of obsessive-compulsive disorders. In H. R. Beech (Ed.), *Obsessional states.* London: Methuen.

Mineka, S. (1987). A primate model of phobic fears. In H. J. Eysenck & I. Martin (Eds.), *The theoretical foundations of behavior therapy* (pp. 81–112). New York: Plenum.

Newman, H. H., Freeman, F. N., & Holzinger, K. J. (1937). *Twins.* Chicago: University of Chicago Press.

Öhman, S., Dimberg, V., & Öst, L. R. (1985). Animal and social phobias: Biological constraints and learned fear responses. In S. Reiss & R. R. Bortzin (Eds.), *Theoretical issues in behavior therapy* (pp. 123–175). New York: Academic Press.

Plantanov, P. (1959). *The word as a physiological and therapeutic factor.* Moscow: Foreign Languages Publishing House.

Rachman, S. (1987). Editorial. *Behaviour Research and Therapy, 25,* 1.

Rachman, S. & Hodgson, R. (1980). *Obsessions and compulsions.* Englewood Cliffs, NJ: Prentice-Hall.

Rachman, S. J. & Wilson, G. T. (1980). *The effects of psychological therapy.* London: Pergamon Press.

Redlich, F. C. & Freedman, D. (1966). *The theory and practice of psychiatry.* New York: Basic Books.

Schorr, A. (1984). *Die Verhaltenstherapie.* Weinheim: Beltz.

Seligman, M. E. P. (1971). Phobias and preparedness. *Behavior Therapy, 2,* 307–321.

Smith, M. L., Glass, G. V., & Miller, T. I. (1980). *The benefits of psychotherapy.* Baltimore: The Johns Hopkins University Press.

Solomon, R., Kamin, L., & Wynne, L. (1953). Traumatic avoidance learning: The outcome of several extinction procedures with dogs. *Journal of Abnormal and Social Psychology, 48,* 291–302.

Strupp, H. H., Hadley, S. W., & Gomez-Schwartz, B. (1977). Psychotherapy for better or worse: The problem of negative effects. New York: Grouson.

Torgersen, S. (1979). The nature and origin of coronary phobias. *British Journal of Psychiatry, 134,* 343–351.

Trethowan, W. W. (1976). *The role of psychologists in the health services.* London: H.M.S.O.

Watson, J. B. & Rayner, R. (1920). Conditioned emotional reactions. *Journal of Experimental Psychology, 3,* 1–14.

Zangwill, O. (1980). *Behaviour modification.* London: H.M.S.O.

Zener, K. (1937). The significance of behavior accompanying conditional salivary secretion for theories of the conditioned response. *American Journal of Psychology, 50,* 384–403.

Zubin, J., Eron, L. D., & Schumer, F. (1965). *An experimental approach to projective techniques.* New York: Wiley.

Zuriff, G. E. (1985). *Behaviorism: A conceptual reconstruction.* New York: Columbia University Press.

Sol L. Garfield, Ph.D.

Professor Emeritus of Psychology
Washington University, St. Louis, Missouri

◆

A Career in Clinical Psychology

I was born in Chicago on January 8 during the great blizzard of 1918. Luckily, the doctor came to our home and remained there until I was born. My parents were both immigrants from Russian Poland. They had met and married in Brooklyn, New York, and had moved to Chicago a short time before my birth. They had migrated to the United States, along with many other Jews from eastern Europe, to escape the pogroms, discrimination, and general lack of opportunity in their native communities. To them, America was a land of opportunity for them and for their children.

My parents had relatively little formal education. From the accounts I can recall, and from the fact that both of them emigrated alone before the age of 20, their formal education must have been the equivalent of our eighth grade. Then as now, educational opportunities for Jewish students in Russia were limited. However, my parents placed a great value on education, and this attitude was one that I developed also.

My father had learned to be a plumber, and he worked at this trade when he first came to the United States. However, he became a grocer early on, and my earliest memories are of our grocery store and of our apartment, which was in the same building. My father was a grocer in one store or another until I was 22 years old and within two years of my Ph.D. Our family was closely knit; my mother, my sister, who was two years younger than I, and I all helped out in the family store as needed.

When I entered the first grade my father's store was in a largely Black neighborhood, and occasionally I was picked on by older children on my way home from school. In second grade I was the only White child in my class. During the middle of that year we moved to an apartment in a largely White neighborhood so that my sister could start school in a more secure environment. Educationally, however, I had done well in the original neighborhood. When I had been in the new school for about half the semester I was advanced to the next grade, and moved up again at the end of the semester.

The move to the new neighborhood when I was about 8 meant that we saw less of our father. Since we no longer lived in back of the store, we only saw him in the evening on weekdays and on Sundays after 12:30 P.M. On Saturdays, my father didn't get home until midnight. There was no such thing as a family vacation, for my father worked every day of the year except for Yom Kippur. On that day, our store was closed and my father remained at home. He was not a religious person in the formal sense, and we did not belong to a synagogue or temple. However, this was his way of acknowledging his Jewish beliefs and identification.

I did very well in elementary school and my progress was accelerated. During the middle grades, my main interests were reading and sports. We did not have any books in English in our home that I can remember; but the public library had plenty, and I was a constant visitor. I particularly enjoyed adventure stories, sports stories, and a series about West Point and Annapolis. On the whole, these early years were happy ones. Although my father worked long hours, as long as he earned a living we were all satisfied. However, the Depression, which followed the stock market crash of 1929, had a very marked impact on my life.

As the economic situation worsened, my dad's business slowly declined. The largely Black neighborhood in which our store was located was hit particularly hard. Cash was scarce, and a great many of my father's customers subsisted on vouchers supplied by the Illinois Emergency Relief Agency. From the time I entered high school in 1931 until about the middle of 1936, I was increasingly concerned about my dad's business and how it affected him. He sometimes lacked the money to pay for the goods he needed and had to borrow small sums from relatives. Several times I loaned him the $12 or $15 that I had saved up. My father, a strict moralist, was proud of paying his bills on time. I perceived that the economic situation was having a strong impact on him as well as on my mother, and this affected me greatly. However, it also fostered a very close and sharing relationship between me and my parents.

Even though our concern and anxiety about my father's business during these years overshadowed other activities, life still went on. Besides school and sports, I took violin lessons, played in the high school orchestra, helped my father on Saturdays, distributed circulars occasionally for a neighborhood movie theater, and read a fair amount. I also acquired my first good books. The Chicago *Tribune* sponsored a 20-volume series of great literature, and I saved coupons that allowed me to buy the books for something like 59 cents a volume over a period of several months. Building my small library became something of a passion, and it has always been hard for me to dispose of books and journals that I no longer need.

During my first two years of high school I was a fairly good student and made the honor society in my second year. However, except for an occasional course in which the teacher gave a lot of homework, I rarely had to take work home, and I developed the view that smart people could get good grades without spending a lot of time on homework. Although this view seemed valid at first, it caused problems later, particularly in my year of physics and in an advanced mathematics course. From being a top student in math I went to being a mediocre one. I also received a very low grade in the last semester of fourth-year Latin, with a warning that I might not graduate. This did have a sobering effect. I studied my daily Latin assignments and graduated on time in February of 1935. I did profit from this experience; and although I didn't become a "real" student until graduate school, I learned that academic progress does require some effort.

Although graduation from high school was considered an important event, it had always been assumed that I would somehow go on to college. No one in my entire family had ever been to college, so there was little information or guidance about this important matter. Also, as far as I can remember, I received little or no information or guidance from anyone at the large high school I attended, even though it was just a short walk from the University of Chicago. Besides relative ignorance of what was involved in selecting a college and what college actually consisted of, our economic situation was also an important factor. Although my father was having a difficult time making ends meet, both he and my mother were extremely supportive of my going to college. It was finally decided that I should apply to the University of Wisconsin in Madison, where I could stay with an aunt and uncle who would require only a nominal payment for room and board. I made the necessary inquiries, secured and sent off the required forms, and was accepted for admission at Wisconsin in February 1935.

College and Graduate Education

The College Years

My first, and also last, semester at Madison was a very trying period for me. I had just turned 17, knew very little about what to expect at the university, and had already used up all my savings. The large state university was so overwhelming that I felt somewhat inferior and out of things. I lived off campus, walking the eight or ten blocks from my aunt's apartment to the university four times a day. I went home for lunch and did not participate in any campus activities, except for an occasional free lecture.

My parents and I had decided that I should be a lawyer, since my father in particular had a very high regard for the profession. I myself had no particular interest or goal in mind, so I readily agreed. I knew I didn't want to be a doctor, and law was the only alternative mentioned. Consequently I listed law as my university and occupational goal, and was quite disappointed on registration day to be told that before I could become a lawyer I had to enroll in something called "arts and sciences." I wound up with botany (a five-credit laboratory course), Spanish (four credits), and English history and English, regular three-credit courses. This curriculum didn't make a great deal of sense to me, but I was told that I was "doing the right thing." Still, I saw my university work as mainly a repetition of the kinds of courses that I had taken in high school.

Despite my disappointment about what I was going to study at the university, I became interested in some of my courses and, to my surprise, actually did very well in botany. This success was due to an excellent professor and lab instructors. On the other hand, history, a subject I actually liked, gave me a rough time until I learned how to take lecture notes in a meaningful way. However, the lack of recreational activities, the lack of money, and the continuing bad news from home about my father's business made it a rough period for me. I knew that the times were especially difficult for my father, and this was my major concern.

Shortly before the semester ended, I learned that my father had had to give up his business and that my family had moved in with an aunt and uncle of mine in Chicago who themselves lived in a four-room apartment. That spring and summer of 1935 stand out in my memory as the most anxious period of my life; without question, the circumstances had a great impact on me. My father was devastated by his situation, and it affected my mother as well. In addition, jobs were scarce, and I was unable to get any steady work to help the family. Finally, in August of that year, my father bought a small grocery store. Before making the final decision, he asked me to spend a day at the store and give him my decision about it. This request meant a great deal to me, because it showed my father's respect for my opinion even though I was only 17.

This little store was important to our family history, and I must say a bit more about it. It was a small store on a corner in the West Side of Chicago where two streetcar lines crossed. In addition to patronage from medical students and nurses from the West Side Medical Center, people waiting for the streetcar would come in for small purchases such as cigarettes, soft drinks, and the like. There were also meager living quarters in back, a bedroom and a kitchen with a large coal stove. My parents and I moved there while my sister remained on the South Side with relatives and continued at the same high school.

Our new store was opened seven days a week from 6:00 A.M. to 11:00 P.M. Obviously the hours were long, but at least they offered the opportunity to earn a living. My father opened the store each morning and took a nap in the afternoon. My mother and I took turns relieving him and helping out at other times as required. Despite the long hours there was a noticeable change in the mood of my family, and I was happy to see my father gradually become his old jovial self again.

The new situation also meant that I could not continue my studies at Wisconsin. It was obvious that I was needed to help out in the store, even though my parents said that the decision was up to me. After some appraisal of educational possibilities in Chicago, I decided to enroll at the Central YMCA College in downtown Chicago. This college was accredited by the North Central Association, the tuition was very moderate, I could reach it in about 15 minutes by streetcar, and classes were available during the evening. By taking courses at Central Y, I would not be losing any time educationally, and when our family's situation changed I could transfer to another college or university. My parents again left the decision up to me, since I was "American born" and knew more about it than they did.

During the three semesters that I attended Central Y on a variable time schedule, a number of important events and decisions took place. The campus, one tall building with an elevator, differed markedly from the large, hilly, graceful campus on Lake Mendota in Madison. However, I adjusted quickly to the change, made a number of new friends, and actually was much happier as a result of our improved economic and family situation. I was also given a battery of tests at the college for education and vocational guidance, including the Strong Vocational Interest Inventory. Later I was called for an interview with a counselor who told me that although I did have interests in common with lawyers, I had stronger interests in teaching and in occupations dealing with people. This interview had a profound effect on me, for I had never considered teaching as a possible professional goal. In fact, I had not thought about any occupation except that of lawyer, which seemed to please my parents. Of course, I was not yet 18 and not overly worldly wise. However, I knew that I did not want to be a businessman or to work the long hours my father did.

As a result of this interview, I decided to read up on both the legal profession and the teaching profession. In the college library I came across a book on the legal profession in Chicago that painted such a bleak future for anyone who had little in the way of economic resources that I couldn't see much sense in preparing to be a lawyer. On the other hand, teaching seemed to offer the possibility of steady employment at a moderate wage. I became preoccupied with the choice of profession. I discussed the matter a number of times with my parents, although I gathered that they still looked up to lawyers more than they did to public school teachers. As usual, they deferred to my preference and said the decision was mine.

The change in occupational goal didn't have a geat deal of impact on the courses I was taking except that I enrolled in the introductory education course the following semester. Although it wasn't the most stimulating course I ever took, it wasn't too bad, and I did receive a grade of "A." I took the usual required courses in history, political science, sociology, the physical and biological sciences, philosophy, and psychology. Except for the instructor's demonstration of hypnosis and brief references to Gestalt psychology and psychoanalysis, the content of the introductory psychology course was difficult to differentiate from my course in human biology. It clearly wasn't anything to make me develop a strong interest in psychology.

At the end of three semesters, my family's financial and psychological situation had changed greatly for the better. Toward the end of this period, we rented a small studio apartment a block from our store, and my sister and I lived there while my parents continued to live in back of the store. My sister also transferred to the local high school and graduated from there. All of these events made things easier for me. In addition, since my sister could now help out in the store, I could think of the possibility of transferring to a better-known college or university. Because the University of Chicago was on the quarter system and I was completing my fourth semester in February 1937, I opted to apply to Northwestern University, in suburban Evanston. I had decided to be a teacher of history and was admitted to the School of

Education at Northwestern as a junior immediately upon completing my last semester at Central YMCA College.

I didn't know it at the time, but my association with Northwestern was to last for five and a half years. Attending classes at Northwestern meant I spent less time in the family store, but I had to spend three hours a day commuting to and from the university. I was able to get to Evanston by taking an elevated train to Chicago's Loop and then taking one or two elevated trains to my stop in Evanston. Although taking these trains during peak traffic times and fighting the crowds was no picnic, I seemed to endure it quite well. I would get up early, get dressed, stop at our store on the way to the train station, eat a quick breakfast, grab my lunch, and I was off. Occasionally I would remain on campus to hear a noted speaker, but these times were few. If I had no pressing assignments, I would join my father in the store. After completing my first semester at Northwestern, I took nine credits in the summer session that followed. In this way, I was able to take additional courses each semester and graduate in June 1938. By doing this I also saved a small amount of money.

Only a few things need to be mentioned about this period at Northwestern. My interest in history continued to be strong, and one of my history instructors suggested that I consider going to the University of Chicago for graduate work. However, I was undecided about my future as a historian, and the courses I had taken in educational psychology and guidance interested me a great deal. Although the professor who taught the educational psychology course was not a particularly good teacher, the textbook was one of the most interesting I had ever read. Written by Sidney Pressey of Ohio State University, it emphasized research in developmental psychology. The course in guidance introduced me to student personnel work, the antecedent to today's counseling psychology. I also enjoyed the practice teaching I did during my last semester, teaching a social studies class for slow learners. The praise of my supervisor, and the grade I received, gave me confidence in my teaching ability.

However, despite my success as a student teacher and my good academic record, I was unable to get a job teaching upon graduation. Although one of my professors had told me that Jewish students experienced more difficulty in this regard than other students, I was still surprised when I did not get one inquiry from the university placement bureau. This, my first serious encounter with discrimination, was an extreme disappointment for me. My parents, who had had worse experiences in this regard, took it in stride and were very supportive. In the summer of 1938, events of great importance were taking place in Europe, and the rise of Hitler and the Nazis was of direct concern to many immigrants in the United States.

My mother had two sisters and a brother still living in Poland with their families. My parents decided that they should visit them before it was too late and also do what they could to try to bring them over to this country. Consequently, shortly after my graduation, my parents left for New York, from where they made a trans-Atlantic crossing to Europe. During the eight weeks or so that they were gone, I ran the store with the help of my sister and of a close friend, a medical student at the University of Illinois. My friend and I slept in back of the store, while my sister lived in the apartment. The faith my parents had in my ability at age 20 to run the store, as well as the successful experience I had of going to the market, purchasing produce and other products, keeping track of financial matters and the like added to my personal confidence. If nothing else, I knew that I could manage a grocery store, and as I have indicated elsewhere (Garfield, 1986), some of this experience was helpful when I was editing the *Journal of Consulting and Clinical Psychology*!

My parents returned from Poland quite depressed, and my father was unsuccessful in his efforts to provide adequate economic guarantees to bring some of my mother's family to the United States. Eventually all of my mother's siblings and their children in Poland were put to death by the Nazis.

In spite of the sadness of that period, life here had to go on and I had to make some decisions about my immediate future. Some of my fellow students had taken jobs as case aides with the Illinois Emergency Relief Agency when they were unable to secure teaching positions. Making a decision was difficult. Although I wanted to be independent, I saw little future in these positions. Instead, I thought that if I could add to my skills, I might have a better chance of securing a teaching position. I might add that I had learned rather late in the game that if one were not a graduate of the three-year Chicago Teachers College program, one had to have two years of teaching experience to be eligible for a teaching position in Chicago. A four-year degree from Northwestern or from the University of Chicago just wasn't adequate.

After some deliberation with my parents, I decided to enroll for a master's degree in guidance and counseling at Northwestern. The tuition was not exorbitant for graduate school, and I could still work in the store and commute from home. This was an important decision, and the events that followed in the next couple of years greatly influenced my later career decisions.

Graduate School

I asked S. A. Hamrin, a guidance professor whom I liked and admired, to be my advisor. Outside of the requirement for 30 hours of graduate work and an M.A. thesis, there were very few specific requirements. I took a course on guidance techniques that emphasized interviewing and vocational tests; a course on tests and measurements; an advanced educational psychology course; and a course called "Psychoeducational Clinic." Several of these courses interested me considerably, and I believe I matured quite a bit as a student. I also became more interested in psychology. The advanced educational psychology course was identical to the course called "Schools of Psychology" given in the psychology department. Our texts were Edna Heidbreder's *Seven Psychotherapies* and R. S. Woodworth's *Contemporary Schools of Psychology.* I became very interested in Gestalt psychology and did my M.A. thesis on the implications of Gestalt psychology for education.

The counseling courses, particularly the practicum aspects, were also of interest, and although I was the youngest person in my classes, I apparently made a good impression on Dr. Hamrin. He had agreed to provide counseling services for about 40 orphans in a state school and home in central Illinois, all of whom were graduating from high school. To assist him he had an older doctoral student, an experienced post-masters-degree guidance counselor, and me. This was a great experience for me in several ways. The night before we left, I was a guest at Dr. Hamrin's home in Evanston. After breakfast at his home, we picked up the other two members of the team and drove about a hundred miles to our destination. During the three days we were there, I gave the youngsters intelligence tests as well as other tests where indicated, helped score tests and assemble case folders, participated in some brief staff conferences, and on the last day was allowed to conduct interviews with several of the students. The latter was a real challenge, since the students' social worker sat in on the interviews. In addition to the counseling experience I received, I felt good about being accepted by the other participants—and also about the small check that I received for my services.

Of even greater significance in terms of the impact it had on my subsequent education and career was the course called "Psychoeducational Clinic." Professor Paul Witty, one of the most distinguished professors at the university, gave this course and also directed a small clinic. The course could be taken for more than one semester; the initial semester focused on learning the 1937 Revised Stanford-Binet test. An identical course was also given in the psychology department. Beyond learning the new Stanford-Binet, which in the late 1930s was practically synonymous with clinical psychology, I also made a positive impression on Dr. Witty. I took another course in educational diagnosis with him, which dealt with the problems manifested by children in school. These two courses, although nominally in the area of educational psychology, actually exemplified much of clinical psychology as it existed in the 1930s.

I did well in my course work, completed my masters thesis, passed my oral exam, and received my M.A. degree in June 1939. I was now equipped to be a social science teacher and a school guidance counselor or psychologist. In addition to the Northwestern University Teacher Placement Bureau, I signed up with a few private placement agencies and waited to see what the future would bring. To my disappointment, it didn't bring much, and it was hard not to be depressed about my occupational situation. I had a good educational record, two degrees, and good letters of recommendation from the faculty. However, the only job notification I received was from one of the private agencies, for a position as social studies and English teacher, guidance counselor, and athletic coach at a town in Georgia. The position was for nine months at a salary of $90 a month. Although I wasn't sure if I was fully qualified for all aspects of the job, I sent in my application the same day I received the notice. I waited expectantly and with increasing apprehension as the days passed. I never even received an acknowledgment of my application.

My lack of success in securing any kind of a job even faintly related to my education and training was very disconcerting. Although I knew I had better-than-average qualifications for a regular position in secondary education, I had to come to grips with the fact that I was going to have a very difficult time securing suitable employment.

Although I had no job lined up for the fall, I was able to secure several part-time jobs at Northwestern during the summer after I received my M.A. I worked as an assistant in the guidance laboratory, which provided practicum experience for summer graduate students taking courses in personal and vocational counseling. I also had a job helping a professor set up and administer a conference on counseling and guidance to be held in Evanston. I was given a considerable amount of responsibility on this project, and the conference was very successful. I participated in parts of it, and tried to learn what I could from participants. I remember supervising the registration desk when Rudolph Dreikurs, the noted Adlerian psychiatrist, made his appearance. He was an invited speaker, and when he came to the desk he announced clearly that he was Rudolph Dreikurs and that he was an Adlerian. He was an interesting person, and the first practicing psychiatrist with whom I had come in contact, but I learned later that not all psychiatrists automatically announce their theoretical allegiance when you first meet them.

During that summer of 1939, I explored via the library and other contacts what job or career possibilities were open to me. It was clear that I would have to consider additional preparation as well as new career paths. On my M.A. program I had learned a certain amount about psychological tests and their applications in psychology and education. I also explored possible positions in the federal civil service system pertaining to test construction and personnel selection. This was one alternative to consider. Another was to go ahead for a Ph.D. in psychology or educational psychology in the hope that there would be less discrimination in higher education than in the secondary school system. I discussed this with the dean of the College of Education, a man I liked and respected. He told me that he thought the faculty probably would not accept me as a doctoral candidate because job opportunities would still be difficult for Jewish graduates, and the faculty would not want me to invest the time and money necessary for such a program under these circumstances. At the same time, he told me that the faculty had a very high opinion of my ability. I appreciated his frankness and gave up on the possibility of acquiring a doctorate.

Toward the end of the summer session, Professor Witty asked me if I would be interested in working on his research project as a paid assistant. At this time I was seriously considering taking courses in research and psychology that might prepare me for a position in the federal civil service system. I discussed with Professor Witty the possibility of my taking such courses as a nondegree student. He agreed to act as my faculty advisor in this regard, and asked if I would like to be his assistant in the psychoeducational clinic as well as helping him on his research project. The former position provided half tuition plus a small stipend. I agreed to assist Dr. Witty in both projects and to take specific courses in terms of my new objective. There is no question that Dr. Witty's offer of help was a significant factor in allowing me to increase my future prospects and, as matters turned out, in eventually allowing me to become a clinical psychologist.

In the fall of 1939, I enrolled as a nondegree candidate and registered for four courses. I took two courses with Witty, one on research methods and the other on the clinical uses of the Stanford-Binet and related tests. I also took two courses in the psychology department dealing with individual differences and statistics. In addition, I demonstrated the administration of the Stanford-Binet and some other individual tests to graduate students, worked with some cases referred to the clinic, helped evaluate the case reports of graduate students, and worked on Witty's research project. This project was a large-scale study of the interests of Black and White high school students in Chicago. A former doctoral student had collected over a thousand questionnaires and had just begun to tabulate the data when he had some argument with Witty and left the university. Under Witty's direction, I began to tabulate various sections of the data. Another faculty member was also involved in the project, but he played a very minor role.

I still commuted daily from our apartment in Chicago and tried to help out in the store, usually on weekends and evenings. My sister had married and moved back to our old neighborhood in the Hyde Park section of Chicago. In spite of being so busy, I enjoyed my courses and the work for Witty. In fact, it was a very good time for me academically. I excelled in all my courses and felt that my professors clearly respected me. Needless to say, this was ego-enhancing and increased my self-confidence, although there were always troubling incidents that did not allow these feelings to get out of hand.

Near the end of the semester, I presented Dr. Witty with tables and computations for a section of the research on which I had been working. He looked at it, said I had done a nice job, and then surprised me by asking if I would like to write the first draft of the article. I was quite excited, and prepared what I thought was a fine description of the research results. I gave the draft to Professor Witty and waited for his words of praise. A week later, he told me he had read my report and then surprised me again by saying, "Sol, you don't know how to write." I can still remember blushing and feeling very crushed, even though the pain was assuaged slightly when he went on to say that I wrote like Professor X. Despite this painful incident, I continued to work on the project, eventually became co-author of three articles, and learned a great deal about writing from Professor Witty, who had several hundred publications to his credit and was an associate editor of the *Journal of Educational Psychology.*

Sometime during that year, the director of research for two of the northshore surburban school systems had accepted an academic position at a university in the southwest. This man also taught measurement and guidance courses at Northwestern. I had met him during the previous summer when I worked at the guidance laboratory and had assisted him as part of my work. He told me that he had recommended me as his replacement to the school boards but that they had raised questions about my being Jewish. He said he hated to tell me this but wanted me to know that he thought highly of my abilities and that other factors were involved in the decision. The schools involved also asked the Northwestern faculty to recommend someone, and they also recommended me, but with no success. Despite my lack of success in securing the appointment, I was encouraged by the positive response of the faculty. This acceptance, as well as my academic success, kept me from being discouraged.

Consequently, I signed up for four courses for the second semester that year, and here again Fate was kind to me. In addition to another semester in the psycho-educational clinic and a course on Dewey's theory of logic, I took a course on psychometric methods and a seminar on personality theory in the psychology department. Having been in two advanced psychology courses with psychology majors, and having excelled in both courses, I was now both more confident and more interested in such courses. The personality seminar, which included about ten other students, mostly Ph.D. candidates in psychology, was taught by A. R. Gilliland, the chairman of the psychology department. I got into a bit of an argument with Professor Gilliland over one question on the midterm exam. When he challenged me to support my position, I came into his office with several books and he was gentleman enough to admit that he had been wrong. Although I was concerned that I might have caused him to perceive me negatively, particularly since I was from outside the department, my fear was groundless. He asked me and another student to assist him in performing a small experiment in relationship to the seminar. By the end of the semester, we were on very good terms and he asked me to consider pursuing my graduate work in the psychology department. However, other events had occurred earlier that need to be mentioned.

Shortly after this semester began, Witty had suggested that I apply for a university fellowship to pursue a Ph.D. program with him. I was pleasantly surprised by this suggestion, but I told him what the dean had told me earlier. He said that on the basis of my record I should apply anyway. Encouraged, I discussed the matter with another faculty member, who told me that I would lose nothing by applying, and that if I did not receive a fellowship I definitely should not continue as a student. I then submitted my application for the fellowship, and some weeks later was informed that I had been selected as a university fellow. Obviously, this was an important event in my life. Beyond the tuition and stipend provided by the fellowship, the award also signified faculty support.

As the semester drew to an end in June 1940, it seemed that all kinds of things were happening to me, most of them positive. I had participated in research projects; one article was in press and two others were in the process of being prepared for journal submission; I had been well accepted by the graduate students in psychology, who were nearer to me in age than those in education; and Professor Gilliland had asked me to consider transferring to the psychology department and assisting him on a research project. Also, by this time I was the main worker in the psychoeducational clinic. After some thought, I decided to keep on with the fellowship in educational psychology and to take mainly psychology courses, since there were only a few required seminars in the former area—and this is pretty much what I did for the next two years.

Although there were a number of positive features in my life situation at this time, I also began to come to grips with the requirements for the Ph.D. degree. The language requirements were of particular concern to me. At that time, all Ph.D. candidates at Northwestern had to pass written examinations in German and French. I had studied neither language in high school or college, and it was common knowledge among the graduate students that the German exam had kept more people from getting a Ph.D. than any other single cause. Therefore I thought I had better try to pass the German exam first and thus evaluate my chances of eventually completing the degree requirements.

I secured a series of German readers, graded in difficulty and using English cognates, and began my self-study of the language. At first, at the simplest levels, I seemed to make good progress. However, when I looked at a German book or journal, I was completely stymied. In addition to studying German that summer, I supervised some graduate students who were administering tests in one of the Evanston schools and was also hired to analyze test data from a four-year experimental program in a high school.

The latter was a worthwhile experience in several ways. I gained additional experience in organizing, analyzing, and preparing a research report. I also noted the deficiencies in the project itself and how they seiously limited the conslusions that could be drawn. Since the study had been overseen by some of the education faculty, I took some pleasure, at the tender age of 22, in pointing out the inadequacies in the design of the study and offering a few suggestions for future reasearch. That summer I also took a psychology course called "The Human Organism," for which I wrote a paper on the maturation hypothesis. The subject greatly engrossed me, and the visiting professor praised the paper. Finally, my parents sold our store that summer and later that year bought a rooming house. My help at home thus was no longer required, and I began to spend more time at the university, eventually taking a room in an off-campus rooming house.

I have gone into what may appear to be considerable detail in describing my first two years of graduate work. However, this was a very significant period of my life and one of the turning points that helped shape my future life and career. I can describe my last two years of graduate school much more briefly.

During my third year, I took the required research seminars in education and also took courses in experimental psychology, personality research with Gilliland, and adolescent psychology. In addition, five psychology graduate students and I met with Gilliland to ask if he could arrange a course for us with some clinical practicum experience. (It should be mentioned here that the kinds of clinical psychology programs that came into existence after the Second World War did not exist in 1940.) Gilliland cooperated fully, and this clinical course was given by Dr. Phyllis Wittman, the chief psychologist at Elgin State Hospital, which was 35 miles from the university. We spent one day a week at the hospital, and once a week Dr. Wittman came to the campus for a two-hour seminar. As far as I can remember, everyone who participated in this special course eventually received a Ph.D. degree.

At first, visiting a mental hospital and seeing "real live" patients was an exciting experience. In fact, Jim Morton, a Black graduate student who had his own car, and I made several extra trips to the hospital on Saturdays. However, our enthusiasm gradually dimished. This hospital had over four thousand severely disturbed patients and only two psychologists, whose main functions were testing and research. In fact, there was almost no emphasis on treatment. Although Dr. Wittman was a very able and enthusiastic psychologist, working with psychotic inpatients did not appeal to me. I thought that working with children and adolescents would be more interesting.

During that year, I passed the German exam on my second try. When informed that I had passed, I was extremely euphoric, a feeling that has been equaled on only a few other occasions during my life—when my wife agreed to marry me, when I was discharged from the army, and when my first book was accepted for publication. Having passed the German hurdle, I was confident that I would be able to complete the remaining requirements and receive my Ph.D.

I was also pleased when Dr. Gilliland asked if I would work on his research project on the selection of airplane pilots. Gilliland had some previous contacts with a pilot training center and had recently received a grant from the National Research Council to develop and evaluate procedures for selecting suitable candidates for pilot training. A fellow graduate student who was interested in industrial psychology, Harold Wisely, had already agreed to participate, and he and I would be the research assistants. I readily assented, and we worked out a design that included a variety of physiological and motor performance tests, particularly in terms of evaluating responsiveness to stress. I will say a bit more about this research later.

This third year of graduate school, and my first year as a Ph.D. candidate, was a busy one. I developed a number of friendships with graduate students in psychology, including Ralph Heine, Alan Rosenwald, Julian Pathman, Greg Kimble, and George Lovell. I also made a few friends in the Ph.D. seminars in education, but with one exception these did not last very long after I left Northwestern. During the year, my attitude toward my educational program and the work I was doing underwent a rather significant change. Previously I had been primarily motivated by the eventual goal of obtaining a reasonably secure job. Now I was genuinely interested in and enjoying what I was doing and what I was learning. I also felt more confident in my abilities, and the respect I received from my teachers and my fellow students meant a great deal to me. I truly wanted to get my Ph.D. and felt that this would be sufficiently satisfying even if I *never* secured a position in my field. Being awarded a university fellowship for the next year also had a positive effect on me.

This change in my view of future goals and my increased self-confidence probably increased my motivation, for I passed my French exam during the following summer and began to prepare for my preliminary examinations. In addition to written and oral examinations, each candidate had to present a dissertation proposal. Gilliland had suggested the possibility of using part of his project for my dissertation, but I wasn't that positive about the project at that time. Also, after considering many possible topics and being strongly encouraged by a visiting professor of educational research, I decided on a study that would evaluate the ability of teachers to apply psychological principles. Wickman's (1928) famous study comparing the judgments of teachers and mental health workers may have been an influence in this regard. I developed a number of vignettes describing children's behaviors, which were followed by judgments about the behaviors and possible explanations for the judgments given.

In the fall of 1941 I took my preliminary examination and passed, although the nine members of my oral examining committee, which included Witty and Gilliland, thought my proposal was going to be difficult to carry out. However, they said they would give me the opportunity to try it. Their comments as well as the world situation at that time did cause me to think seriously again about my dissertation decision. I had received an educational deferment from the draft until April 1942. With the uncertainty of the draft plus the possiblility of real difficulty in securing the participation of teachers and psychologists in my project, I decided to explore the possibliity of selecting some features of Gilliland's research project as a possible dissertation. I finally developed a proposal that was accepted and became my dissertation, although I had to have another meeting of my dissertation committee to approve the change. Also, since the data upon which the dissertation would be based were considered confidential, we had to get permission from the National Research Council before the dissertation could be approved.

All went well with the dissertation, which was titled "Certain Physiological and Motor Reactions to Disorganizing Stimuli with Special Reference to Their Use as Aids in the Prediction of Flying Ability." Although the title was long, the completed dissertation was just 58 pages. There is no need here to describe the study in any detail. Although I learned about GSR and blood pressure recordings, about stress reactions, and about using logarithmic measures when analyzing physiological data, I never returned to this area again. However, I greatly appreciated the cooperation I received from the education faculty, the psychology department, the graduate school, and the National Research Council. Although nominally a university fellow in educational psychology, I was conducting a study in experimental and physiological psychology, and two of the three members of my dissertation committee were psychology department professors. The international situation in late 1941, along with our potential entry into the war, undoubtedly had some influence on campus activities, but I was impressed with how helpful everyone was to me during that period.

Besides working on my dissertation, I also took Claude Buxton's graduate course on learning, Sam Beck's newly offered course on a projective technique called the Rorschach Test, and courses on research and child development. Beck was not a faculty member at Northwestern, but arrangements were made for him to give the course in the evening. His own book was not yet in print, so we had no text, and all answers about scoring and interpretation came from Beck personally. Almost all of the graduate students interested in clinical psychology took that course when it was first offered that year.

I completed my dissertation in the spring of 1942 and approval was granted by the National Research Council for a final oral examination on the dissertation. However, the examining committee had to be limited to five faculty members, who agreed to keep the proceedings secret. In addition to my dissertation commmittee, a professor of counseling and a professor of aeronautical engineering constituted the committee. The orals went well, and I received my Ph.D. degree in June 1942. However, the abstract of my dissertation had to be kept secret and was not delivered to Northwestern until after the war was over in 1946, when it was published in the university Ph.D. abstracts.

In the meantime, I had received another deferment until October 1942 to complete my educational requirements. With the requirements completed, I was awaiting induction into the armed services. I taught tests and measurements during the summer session at Northwestern, prepared a special report of the Northwestern University project on pilot selection for the National Research Council, and along with Harold Wisely, my partner on the research project, went to see Morris Viteles in Philadelphia about possible military-related assignments concerning pilot selection. Viteles was then director of the National Research Council Committee on the Selection and Training of Aircraft Pilots. However, nothing came of this, and after the summer session I returned to stay with my parents in their rooming house. During this period of waiting for induction, I read a large number of books I had purchased but had never had the time to read, including *War and Peace* and *The Brothers Karamazov.* I should also mention that about two years previously I had taken a civil service examination for positions dealing with test construction in the civil service system. A few days after I received my notice to report for induction of military service, I also received a job offer from the civil service. It was my first real job offer, but I had to decline it in favor of accepting the job offer from the army. On December 8, 1942, I passed my physical examination and was inducted into the army, where I served for 40 months.

Career: The Early Years

The Military Experience

Although my term of duty in the army seemed interminable at the time, I need not devote much space to describing that experience. Even though I had my Ph.D. degree and both the American Psychological Association, which I had joined a year earlier, and the federal government had procedures for designating "scientific and professional personnel" for special consideration, I was first assigned to basic training in the infantry at Fort McClellan, Alabama. At the conclusion of basic training, I was sent to the army classification school at Washington and Jefferson College in Pennsylvania. I tried both there and during basic training to apply for the Adjutant General's Officer Candidate School (OCS) but wasn't allowed to do so for reasons that weren't clear to me. Essentially, I was told that I had to be part of a regular unit. However, when I completed the eight-week classification course I was told that I had been selected to go the Adjutant General's Personnel Consultant Assistant School in Maryland. Personnel consultants were officer clinical psychologists, which is what I wanted to be. I told the officers at the classification school that I didn't want to be trained as a psychological assistant, since I wanted to apply to OCS and therefore preferred to be assigned to an army unit. However, my request was denied.

Nine of us were sent to this school for a five-week course to learn about the tests used in the army as well as some recognized psychological tests. One of my friends, a Ph.D. candidate in educational philosophy, was one of the faculty, and he and others tried to arrange for me to appear before an OCS board. However, although the OCS that I wanted to attend was in the same camp, a colonel there decided that if I were accepted for officer's training, the valuable training I had received at army school would be wasted.

After a couple of misassignments, and after six months during which I felt I had contributed absolutely nothing to the war effort, I was finally assigned to the Philadelphia Induction Station as an enlisted personnel consultant. I was assigned to the psychological section, where we tested and screened inductees. Basically, we focused on non-English-speaking, illiterate, and mentally retarded draftees, using nonverbal and some individual tests of mental ability.

I remained in Philadelphia for a little over a year and was promoted to staff sergeant and chief noncommissioned officer of the psychology unit. I didn't particularly like working under officers who had less training in psychology than I did, but I was treated well by the two psychology officers and by the other officers in charge of the induction station. There were also several compensations in the assignment. I shared a hotel room with another soldier, the induction station was not too far from the University of Pennsylvania, I attended a number of concerts, and I made several trips to New York and saw some theater productions on Broadway.

The induction station acted as the point of entry for all the military services, and each of the services was to get approximately equal percentages of men with different levels of skill. This was to ensure an equal distribution for each of the main services, including the Coast Guard. A top noncommissioned officer from each of the four services sat at a table and made ratings of occupational skill or level as the potential inductees passed through the examining line. Although they used the same rating scale, these officers had no specific guidelines. After I had been there a few months and had been made a corporal, I was called into the commanding officer's office and told that a higher headquarters had analyzed the records from our station and found them wanting. In essence, the problem was a lack of reliability among the raters who judged the level of occupation among the inductees. I was then asked, or rather ordered, to leave my current assignment and be the sole rater of occupational level or skill. Although I really didn't know a great deal about this area, of course I had to comply.

For several months I interviewed every person who came through the Philadelphia Induction Station and rated him in terms of occupational skill or level. In a relatively short time I learned about the major occupational groups in the Philadelphia area, could distinguish a spot welder from an arc welder in terms of skill, and could do the job quite quickly. In a short time I interviewed thousands of men and prepared a brief rating guide. When I went out to lunch, the whole line at the induction station at my point in the process stopped, and didn't resume until I returned. It was probably the most important, or at least imposing, position I ever had, but I had no thought of making a permanent assignment out of it. I trained one of the other soldiers in the psychology unit in the use of the guide I had prepared, observed him until I felt he was able to do the job, and then returned to my former activities.

I was impressed with the fact that each month we saw individuals from every district of greater Philadelphia and that the differences between the groups was immense. On days when the inductees came from the more affluent suburbs, there was very little for our unit to do. Practically every inductee was a high school graduate, spoke English, and was not mentally deficient. On the other hand, on certain days we hardly had a free moment. I was surprised that there was so much illiteracy among people living in a large northern urban area. I did some informal investigating and discovered that most of the illiterates were actually recent migrants to the North who had received limited schooling in the South. I got permission to do a systematic study of this observation, developed an interview schedule, trained the staff, and began to collect data. However, before I could get a complete month's data, I was ordered to stop the investigation because it was taking too much time and slowing up the induction process. I did try analyzing our data, but soon gave up because we did not have an adequate sample.

I had come to Philadelphia in the summer of 1943, and by the time I was ready to apply for the Adjutant General's OCS, I learned that they were no longer taking applications. I also heard from Paul Witty, who was now an army major in Washington, that there were rumors about authorizing direct commissions for psychologists. However, as of the summer of 1944, there was still no clear indication of this development. I was also one of the few enlisted men in the induction station at this time who was not classified as "limited service." I had been kept on because I was considered to be in a scarce and essential classification. Nevertheless, I wanted to be an officer and learned that they were still accepting applications for the Quartermaster Corps. I applied, was accepted, and spent 17 weeks at the OCS at Camp Lee, Virginia. During the 10th week of OCS I heard officially that psychologists could now be commissioned as second lieutenants in the Adjutant General's Department. I received word from the chief psychologist of the Third Service Command, which included Pennsylvania, who told me to continue in OCS and that I would be requested specifically by the service command and assigned to psychological duties. In November 1944, I was commissioned a second lieutenant in the Quartermaster Corps.

After leaving Camp Lee, I reported to the headquarters of the Third Service Command in Baltimore, where I met the chief psychiatrist, Colonel Henry Brosin, a wonderful man despite the fact that he was a psychoanalyst. He made me feel wanted, and offered me the choice of working in two different hospitals, pointing out their strengths and weaknesses in an honest fashion. I chose to go to the station hospital at the Aberdeen Proving Ground in Maryland. As the first psychologist at the hospital, I was something of a rarity until people got to know me. The neuropsychiatry service consisted of three wards, one of which was a closed ward. In addition, we had an outpatient clinic three days a week for soldiers referred by the dispensary physicians.

During my 14 months at Aberdeen, I became deeply involved in all of the activities of the neuropsychiatry service. I read everything available in the hospital library on psychiatry, psychotherapy, and psychoanalysis, as well as buying books of my own. I was appointed director of group psychotherapy and also conducted most of the individual psychotherapy. After a few months, the chief of the neuropsychiatry service was replaced by Major Irwin Schatz, an experienced psychiatrist who was also a diplomate in neurology. We became good friends, and I learned a great deal about psychopathology and neurology from him. He also shared a number of clinical responsibilities with me, so that I was not limited to a narrow psychological or psychometric role. Although we had a young psychiatrist on the service, Major Schatz and I had adjoining offices on the locked ward and he consulted with me more than with the other psychiatrist.

During my stay at Aberdeen I conducted intake interviews, made rounds, lectured to the medical staff of the hospital, participated on discharge boards, and on a few occasions even performed as weekend neuropsychiatry officer of the day. I was also designated as chief psychologist when another psychologist and a psychological assistant were added to our service. Furthermore, during the last couple of months that I was there, when the military activities were winding down and cases were few, I saw every case with Dr. Schatz. Afterward we would discuss the case together, and I learned a great deal from this experience.

Two other events that occurred during 1945 also need to be mentioned. In the spring, I was sent to Fort Sam Houston in San Antonio, Texas to attend the Officers Clinical Psychology School. I had to change trains in St. Louis, and as I waited in the milling crowd I observed another army officer observing me. I wondered if he might be going to San Antonio as well, but he was wearing the insignia of the Armored Corps, a far cry from the Adjutant General's School. Of course, I was wearing the Quartermaster Corps insignia, which also bore no relationship to my assignment. After a short while, he came over and, to my surprise, asked if I were going to the Officers Clinical Psychology School. He then introduced himself, and that was how Julian Rotter and I met. He claimed that his superior clinical skills enabled him to pick me out as a clinical psychologist, whereas I claimed it was due to my impressive bearing and intelligent visage. In any event, we became close friends during the five-week period of the school. I was asked to be on the faculty of the school when our class was finished, but the Third Service Command would not release me, and I returned to the hospital at the Aberdeen Proving Ground.

During the summer of that year, while on a short leave in Chicago, I met Amy Nusbaum. She was a graduate of Antioch College and had just completed her first year of teaching in a private suburban school. I found her to be attractive, intelligent, and properly appreciative of my talents. Consequently, I talked her into marrying me, and we were married on December 25, 1945. We have been very happily married since that date, and my choosing Amy as my wife has simply confirmed my confidence in my own clinical skills.

The Early Post-War Period

I was discharged from the army in April 1946 and returned to Chicago. I had already submitted an application for a position with the new clinical psychology program in the Veterans Administration (VA) and once in Chicago I answered a couple of other job inquiries. Although I would have preferred a position working with children, and had an interview at the Louisville Child Guidance Clinic, when I received a definite offer from the VA in May for a position in a neuropsychiatric hospital in Mendota, Wisconsin, just outside of Madison, I accepted. A close friend of mine had accepted a position on the psychiatric staff there earlier, so at least I knew someone there.

At that time, the VA program was an exciting one. In addition to modeling itself after the army psychology program and describing the main functions of the psychologist as diagnosis, research, and therapy, the VA had developed a cooperative training program in clinical psychology with selected universities. Again, I was the first psychologist the hospital had ever had, and I did my best to acquaint the medical and nursing staffs with the activities and contributions of psychology. In addition to the usual diagnostic testing and research duties, I conducted both individual and group psychotherapy, mainly with psychotic patients. I attended all the diagnostic case conferences and presented my psychological evaluations at these meetings. I felt that my work was well received and respected.

I remained at Mendota for 14 months. During that time, I added another staff psychologist and accepted my first two trainees from the University of Wisconsin. Ann Garner, then Ann Magret, was the faculty member directing the clinical program, and she sent me two excellent trainees, Leonard Eron and William Fey. Len Eron has remained a lifelong friend. As the local Rorschach expert, I taught the trainees about projective techniques and the like. I was proud of the fact that both of these trainees published their first research articles with me. Not only did I see research as one of the three main functions of the clinical psychologist, I thought it was important enough to devote several evenings a week to it as well as Saturday mornings. Since the field of clinical psychology has changed so noticeably in the last 20 years or so, at least in the United States, I want to say a bit more here about clinical research.

Although research was listed in the VA job description for clinical psychologists, most of the psychologists I knew did not engage in research. The reason usually given was that they were too busy with their clinical duties to have time for research. I personally never found this to be true and felt that this tendency was a discouraging feature of our field. Perhaps my own training, and particularly my interactions with Paul Witty, had influenced me to see research as intimately related to clinical work. As a beginning graduate student I was overly impressed with the value of psychological tests. There seemed to be a psychological test for every conceivable human trait or skill. However, only after several discussions with Witty did I become fully sensitive to the need to demonstrate the validity and usefulness of the tests to be used in clinical work.

Thus, when I was chief psychologist at Mendota, I kept records on every patient we examined and later analysed the validity of our appraisals. The trainees also participated in these activities, and we published studies that threw considerable doubt on Wechsler diagnostic patterns, on measures of mental impairment, and on certain features of the Thematic Apperception Test. As I saw it, we had a responsibility to test and validate our clinical procedures, and it was our research skills that made our profession unique. Furthermore, the clinical directors under whom I worked seemed impressed by my research efforts, rather than viewing them as distractions from my clinical work.

In the fall of 1947 I was offered a position as assistant professor of psychology at the University of Connecticut. In addition to my teaching duties, I was to set up a Ph.D. program in clinical psychology. Shortly after accepting this position, I received a call from James G. Miller, chief of psychology in the VA asking me to reconsider and accept a position as chief psychologist at the Winter VA Hospital in Topeka, Kansas. In addiition to being a promotion, the position in Topeka was considered an important one because of its affiliation with the Menninger Clinic. David Rapaport was there, and a large number of psychiatrists were being trained there. Although I had a call from the Topeka hospital telling me of their interest, I decided to stick to my decision and honor my commitment. So my pregnant wife and I drove to the rural area of Storrs, Connecticut, where the university was located.

Although this new setting was quite different from the psychiatric hospital in Mendota, there were a few commonalities. In both I had to plan and set up a new clinical psychology program, and in both I *was* the program until I could hire additional staff. In one I oriented hospital staff to clinical psychology, organized referral procedures and the format of psychological reports, and collaborated with university personnel. In the other, I oriented university personnel to the requirements of a doctoral program in clinical psychology, organized the program and wrote course descriptions, and developed relationships with potential practicum agencies.

The psychology department was small at that time, but it had some excellent people. I developed close and lasting friendships with Charlie Osgood, later a distinguished president of the APA, and with Olga deCillis, later Olga Engelhardt. I also recommended the appointment of Henry Ricciuti, whom I had met at the Officers Clinical Pyschology School, and he joined me as a clinical faculty member the next year. We were a young and enthusiastic group. During my first year at Connecticut I was offered an assistant professorship at a higher salary, at the University of Michigan. However, I decided to stay on at Connecticut, where I was promoted to associate professor my second year.

I organized a psychological clinic at Storrs, and along with Ricciuti tried to offer all the essential courses for a clinical program. I taught graduate courses on the Wechsler, projective techniques, psychopathology, and psychotherapy, in addition to teaching undergraduate courses in abnormal psychology and the psychology of adjustment. Each semester I had to prepare new courses, see clients, and supervise students. There was little time for research, and I realized that academia wasn't all it was cracked up to be. Clearly, clinical research was more readily and meaningfully conducted in clinical centers.

Our first daughter, Ann, was born in Willimantic, the town nearest to the university campus. She added a new and most welcome dimension to our life. At the same time, several of my colleagues and I did not feel we were getting the administrative support necessary for developing a doctoral program in clinical psychology. After several meetings with the dean and others, Osgood, Ricciuti, and I decided to leave. For over a year, one of the senior psychiatrists with whom I had worked at the VA hospital in Mendota had been writing to urge me to accept the position of chief psychologist at the VA Mental Hygiene Clinic in Milwaukee, Wisconsin. He was now the director of the clinic and was not fully satisfied with his staff of psychologists. I had hoped to join Osgood in moving to the University of Illinois, but a position there did not materialize. Consequently I accepted the job in Milwaukee, and we moved there in the summer of 1949.

Although the Milwaukee VA clinic was not the most stimulating place I ever worked, in retrospect it was a worthwhile experience. Some years later Lowell Kelly told me that I had made a serious mistake in not accepting the position at Michigan. Certainly the University of Michigan Department of Psychology was very large and prestigious. However, by not going there and later going to the clinic in Milwaukee, I was able to secure additional clinical experience that generally was not available in a university psychology department. In particular, psychotherapy became a primary activity of mine, and as I worked with outpatients my interest in the psychotherapeutic process deepened. It was during this period also that I observed at first hand the phenomenon of premature termination, an event that was rarely mentioned in the psychotherapy books.

I was also impressed by the great disparity between the theoretical discussions of my psychiatric colleagues and the daily realities of the clinic. The party line was that we were engaged in intensive psychodynamic therapy. However, during a lull in the clinic's intake, I conducted a study of all the closed cases (Garfield & Kurz, 1952) and discovered that the median length of this intensive therapy was actually just six sessions! My experience here also indicated that most clinicians had little interest in evaluating their work, and that the traditional psychotherapy offered was not particularly appropriate for most of the patients we saw. I should also mention that I supervised trainees from the University of Wisconsin, several of whom became well-known psychologists.

After two years in Milwaukee, during which time our second daughter, Joan, was born, I was appointed as one of the three directors of psychology training units in the VA, with an office in Chicago. The other two were located on the East and West coasts. These newly created positions were designed to give psychology training in the VA more autonomy and visibility. I was responsible for planning and administering psychology training in Illinois and Wisconsin. This involved working with the universities of Chicago, Illinois, and Wisconsin, as well as with Northwestern University and most of the VA installations in the two states.

Since the position was a newly created one, I had to work out my own procedures, schedule visits and interviews, and the like. Essentially, I was working with 64 trainees, about 20 university faculty consultants, a number of VA psychologists, and hospital and clinic administrators. In the beginning, it was something of a challenge to keep all parties participating in a manner that I considered positive and at the same time to make sure that the bureaucratic aspects of the program were functioning well. For example, all entering trainees had to fill out standard civil-service forms, and although they were assigned to different clinical units throughout my region, they received their reimbursement checks from my office. I also enjoyed visiting the four universities and the various installations. Since the Chicago area had over half of the trainees and a concentration of facilities, I spent most of my time there. However, I visited the other two universities and the other hospitals at least twice a year.

Once I had the program functioning well, the job became less demanding. During this time, I was able to renew old friendships and make some new ones. William A. Hunt, the chairman at Northwestern, had me appointed to the psychology faculty as a lecturer. I regularly taught the graduate course on the use of individual intelligence tests, and also taught the introductory Rorschach course and a course on interviewing. Since I was a full-time VA employee, I taught these courses in the evening.

In addition to my teaching activities, I made arrangements to carry a few cases in psychotherapy at the Chicago VA outpatient clinic and to supervise a couple of students. Jack Watkins was the chief psychologist there, and my old friend Ralph Heine was the assistant chief. During my stay in Chicago I also carried out two studies with Heine, one on staff evaluations of psychological test reports (Garfield, Heine, & Leventhal, 1954) and another on nurses' interests in psychology. We were quite critical of psychological reports that were full of clichés and untestable statements of personality dynamics, and our study indicated that a number of psychiatrists, social workers, and even psychologists shared our view.

Although this chapter is getting considerably longer than I anticipated, there are several aspects of my six years as training unit chief that I believe deserve some mention. Although I wanted to leave the VA toward the end of this period, it was clear that on the whole the best clinical training in psychology was taking place there. Aside from the financial support provided to students, the VA also provided the equivalent of two full years of supervised clinical training on a half-time basis. Furthermore, the VA installations, particularly in the Chicago area, had large psychology staffs, all of whom had Ph.D.s, and many of whom had received their training in the VA.

As compared with other clinical facilities, the psychology positions in the VA were good ones, and psychologists were given more opportunities and responsibilities in working with patients than was true elsewhere. The psychologists I knew were all engaged in psychotherapy, and in the early 1950s this was still a new activity for psychologists. A number of very bright and capable graduate students were trainees in my unit. I can't list them all here, but of those in the Chacago area I can mention Robert Carson, Sarnoff and Martha Mednick, Allen Rechtshaffen, David Ricks, Craig Affleck, and Lawrence Kohlberg. Credit is due James Miller initially, and later Harold Hildreth, who provided the leadership for the program during this early period.

The cooperative relationship between the universities and the VA was also a positive feature of the program and tended to emphasize the two aspects of graduate training. University faculty served as consultants to the VA installations and could be used in different ways, depending on the situation and their particular skills. In the Chicago area I was able to arrange a training program that most of the participants grudgingly did admit provided the broadest training. Prior to this time the University of Chicago and Northwestern students tended to work at the VA installation nearest their university. I was able to work out a systematic program for both groups of trainees. They first began training in the large psychiatric hospital at Downey, Illinois. This hospital, with over 20 psychologists, seemed the best place to introduce trainees to working with psychiatric patients. It was also the only VA hospital in my region that had a ward for female patients. At the end of their first year, the trainees were transferred to the large general VA hospital at Hines, Illinois, or to the West Side Hospital in Chicago. During their third or fourth year the trainees were assigned to the large outpatient clinic in Chicago. The fourth year was an elective one, and modifications were possible if dissertation research was begun in a given setting. In this way, the trainees were exposed to a variety of settings and patients.

I worked in the Chicago area from 1951 to 1957. During this period both of my sons, Stan and David, were born; the Garfield family now numbered six. Because of fiscal uncertainties, the psychology training units, now numbering 13, were transferred from the regional offices where they had been housed to psychiatric hospitals. Thus, around 1954 my office was moved to the VA hospital in Downey, Illinois, about 35 miles from Chicago. In many ways Downey was a unique hospital at the time, and it had a very fine, progressive director. During that period, psychologists were assigned as ward administrators on several wards, and some research programs were also undertaken. There was also a large psychiatric residency program directed by Jules

Masserman, a well-known professor at Northwestern University. As part of this program, Masserman arranged an outstanding lecture and interview series. I heard and observed Karen Horney, Karl Menninger, and Frieda Fromm-Reichman, as well as a number of other distinguished psychiatrists.

Before leaving Milwaukee, I had started working on an introductory clinical psychology textbook. There were only a few existing clinical books, and I thought that I could write one that was up to date and would give students a good introduction and overview of the field. I worked on this project mainly in my spare time, and the book was finally accepted and published by Macmillian in 1957. It was well received, and was a popular text for a few years. Also in 1957, many changes were taking place in the VA. The training units were being abolished, in part as an economy measure, and Hal Hildreth, who had instituted many innovations in VA psychology, was leaving to work at the National Institute of Mental Health. I also had been wanting to leave the VA and after serving for a short while as coordinator of psychological services at the Downey VA Hospital, in November 1957 I accepted a position as associate professor and chief of the Division of Medical Psychology at the Nebraska Psychiatric Institute in Omaha, Nebraska. Once again, my family had to move to a new home in a new location.

The Nebraska Psychiatric Institute

I worked at the Nebraska Psychiatric Institute (NPI) from 1957 until the summer of 1963. That period of almost six years was an interesting and important part of my professional career. NPI was both a unit of the Nebraska State Hospital system and a part of the University of Nebraska College of Medicine. Cecil Wittson was professor and chairman of the department of psychiatry, director of NPI, and head of the State Department of Mental Health. He was "Mr. Psychiatry" in Nebraska and had a number of unusual achievements to his credit. He was a member of the National Advisory Council of the National Institute of Mental Health, a supporter of research on mental health, and was devoted to building a high-quality research and training center for Nebraska.

When I was there, NPI was in a modern new building with inpatient wards for adults and children, outpatient offices with one-way vision screens, and a new research wing, including beds for specific research projects. In particular, Wittson was a pioneer in the use of TV and related electronic devices. On the grand round presentations on Monday morning a patient would be interviewed on the ward, and the interview would be shown on a large-screen television in the NPI auditorium. The interviewer would later appear in the auditorium to discuss the session and to answer questions. There was also a two-way electronic hookup between NPI and the three regular state hospitals in Nebraska. The Friday visiting lecture series was broadcast to the hospitals, and the personnel there were able to question the speaker. During my six-year stay, a number of prominent psychiatrists, psychologists, and related scientists visited NPI for a two- to three-day period. They met informally with staff, residents, and other trainees, and gave formal lectures on Friday afternoons. Harry

Harlow, Leon Festinger, Joseph Wolpe, John Anderson, and Maurice Lorr were among those invited by the psychology division.

Initially my main task was to strengthen and reorganize the psychology division. I brought in Craig Affleck, a former trainee, to head the adult psychology unit, and eventually added two more new appointees. Similar changes were made in the children's unit, and later I also added a statistician to our division. All of the psychologists except the statistician and a physiological psychologist carried out both clinical and research activities. Once these appointments and arrangements were made I designed an internship training program, and we soon obtained APA accreditation and internship stipends from the National Institute of Mental Health.

The years in Omaha were busy ones, during which I was involved with many teaching and research activities. Our division of medical psychology was active in a number of projects. Along with Malcolm Helper and Robert Wilcott, I carried out one of the first systematic evaluations of the effects of Chlorpromazine on emotionally disturbed children. With Craig Affleck, I conducted a number of studies dealing with premature termination and potential prognostic factors in psychotherapy. Milton Wolpin and I studied client expectations for psychotherapy, as well as correlates of success in medical school.

NPI was also awarded a center grant for research and training in mental retardation, and several of us became active in this area. We had access to the large state institution for the mentally retarded at Beatrice, Nebraska, and we conducted studies there. Affleck and I appraised the entire population of the institution and discovered 24 residents who upon reexamination were found not to be retarded (Garfield & Affleck, 1960). These individuals had been institutionalized for an average of 12 years. A biochemist colleague and I also studied all of the cases of phenylketonuria there (Garfield & Carver, 1960). Thus, in addition to my participation in other projects, I was involved to some extent in the ongoing emphasis at NPI on mental retardation. In fact, I published several papers in the *American Journal of Mental Deficiency,* and as a result was appointed an associate editor. I also was promoted to full professor in 1959.

In addition to our internship in clinical psychology, we gave short courses on testing to junior and senior medical students during their clerkships in psychiatry, provided instruction to nursing students, and gave 12-hour courses to the psychiatric residents during each of their three years in training. At the request of Dr. Wittson, I also developed a 10-hour course on behavioral science, which I taught in collaboration with Affleck and Wilcott.

During my tenure at NPI I continued to see patients in outpatient psychotherapy, conducted a few groups as co-therapist with adolescent inpatients, supervised the research projects of some interns, and participated in the diagnostic evaluation of selected cases. Although heavily involved in research and teaching, I never neglected my clinical participation. I also represented the state of Nebraska at the annual meeting of state chief psychologists and conducted a survey of research in state mental health programs (Garfield, 1960).

Outside activities provided additional stimulation and opportunities for learning. I was elected secretary-treasurer of APA's Division of Clinical Psychology (1960 to 1963), and also served a second term on the APA Council of Representatives. During this period I was also appointed a member of the Committee on Clinical Drug Evaluation of the National Institute of Mental Health. This was a particularly interesting experience for me, since for most of that time I was the only psychologist on the committee, and my knowledge of psychopharmacology was limited. I learned a lot and met a number of outstanding individuals. My participation on this committee also played a part in my leaving NPI in 1963. George Ulett, director of mental health for the state of Missouri, was also a member of the committee, and he discussed his plans for the soon-to-be-developed Missouri Institute of Psychiatry (MIP) in St. Louis. Max Fink, a newer member of the committee, was to be appointed director of MIP. Their enthusiam, plus the opportunity to devote most of my time to my own research in the area of psychotherapy, made the new institute appear very attractive.

Although my stay in Omaha had been productive and I had been well treated, I felt that I could broaden my research experience by accepting a position as "principal scientist" at the new institute. I was also offered an appointment as research professor of psychology at Washington University. In addition, my response on several visits to St. Louis had been positive. So, in the summer of 1963, the Garfields once again packed their belongings and moved to their new home in Clayton, a suburb of St. Louis.

Career: The Later Years

Despite my high expectations, my stay at MIP was disappointing and lasted just one year. After encountering certain roadblocks, I concluded that I would not be able to do the research on psychotherapy that I wanted to do. Instead, I conducted and participated in three other studies, one dealing with prognostic factors in schizophrenia and two in collaboration with psychiatric colleagues in the area of psychopharmacology. I also taught a graduate course in psychopathology at Washington University (WU), which I enjoyed. I was somewhat depressed, however, that I had moved my family to St. Louis and that I was dissatisfied with my work situation. I asked about a position at WU, but was told that there was no opening at my level.

Fate must have been looking out for me, for in March 1964 I was unexpectedly invited to visit Teachers College (TC), at Columbia University in New York City, as a candidate for the position of professor and director of the clinical psychology program. A few weeks later I was invited back, with my wife, for a final interview. At the same time I was also offered a professorship by WU, but our decision in favor of TC was clear. I was elated at receiving the TC appointment, but I was also aware that moving our four children to new schools twice in one year would be very hard on them, and on my wife. This was the most difficult move we ever made; happily, however, there were no serious repercussions.

Teachers College, Columbia University (1964 to 1970)

My position at TC was unlike any of the others I had held, and the experience was both challenging and rewarding. Instead of having to set up a new program or revitalize a problematic one, I was to direct a well-functioning and prestigious program. Applied psychology at TC since the time of E. L. Thorndike had developed remarkably. The department of psychology, consisting of over 40 full-time faculty, had a number of distinguished members, including Lawrence Shaffer, Robert Thorndike, Arthur Jersild, Morton Deutch, Donald Super, Albert Thompson, and Joseph Shoben. The clinical program, under the earlier leadership of Shaffer and then of Shoben briefly, was a well-established program with seven full-time faculty, a number of part-time faculty, and a training clinic with a part-time psychiatrist and a full-time social worker. The model for training was the scientist-practitioner model, with which I was in hearty agreement. The situation here clearly differed from most of my previous work situations, and the tasks that confronted me were also different. In fact, the style and tempo of life in New York City also differed tremendously from any other place that we had lived.

The clinical program at TC had many positive features. Besides what I have already described, I was impressed with the high quality of the students, the cooperative attitude of faculty and administration, and the high regard accorded the program, not only within TC but also within Columbia University. The graduate students admitted to the clinical program were among the top students admitted to the entire graduate school at Columbia, and this was apparent in their work. However, like most graduate students, they were generally more interested in clinical practice than in clinical research.

There was a definite increase in the pace and variety of my activities during this time. In the year before moving to New York I had become president-elect of the Division of Clinical Psychology of the APA, and during my first year there I became president of the division. The APA was in the process of planning a national conference on the professional preparation of clinical psychologists, and I was very much involved with the planning of that conference, which was held in Chicago in the fall of 1965, just before the APA convention. The planning of the conference stimulated considerable interest and controversy among different groups of psychologists, and this took a fair amount of my available energy. Furthermore, as director of the clinical program at TC I was a central participant in the activities pertaining to the students' practicum and internship training. Besides being an active consultant to several VA hospitals, I was the coordinator of the practicum in counseling and psychotherapy for students in clinical, counseling, and school psychology. I was also able to secure a few paid part-time practicum assignments for students interested in working with children.

I clearly saw my major responsibility as the training of clinical psychology graduate students, with research and scholarly work as secondary. Furthermore, since my experience with most other clinical programs had revealed inadequate practical training, I was particularly sensitive to this feature of the program. By comparison with other programs, TC's program was excellent, with real practica in assessment and psychotherapy. However, I was not satisfied with the internships the students had selected in the past. After discussing my views with the clinical faculty, it was agreed that I would meet with each student preparing to do an internship and approve the centers to which he or she would apply. This took extra time and made me unpopular for a while (at least), but several students in later years thanked me for helping them to get the best training possible. Before I came to TC, most students took any available internship in the New York area, even if it was lacking in quality. During my tenure, the "west of the Hudson policy" was put into effect, and students sought the best internships regardless of location. Besides helping the travel industry, I believe I helped to broaden the experience of a number of students. I recall two of our students being accepted for internships at the University of Colorado Medical School in Denver. When I lectured there during the middle of their internship year, they told me that they had learned it was possible to live in a city without a subway system!

Despite the fact that the TC clinical program was an established and recognized program, I saw the need for some modifications. Psychotherapy was focused exclusively on adults with heavy psychoanalytic emphasis. In addition, there appeared to be little awareness of the community mental health movement and the importance of prevention with regard to psychological disturbance. After my first year I was able to bring about some changes and to hire new faculty to provide instruction and supervision in the areas of child psychotherapy and community mental health. Also, Allen Bergin, the junior member of the clinical faculty when I arrived, expressed interest in teaching a course in behavior therapy. I supported his interest, and he taught the first course in behavior therapy the following year.

In addition to the activities already described, I taught two graduate courses, supervised four students in psychotherapy, presided at the weekly supervisors' lunch conference and the discussion seminar that followed, supervised a few students in research, prepared the annual NIMH training grant and APA report, wrote student recommendations for internships and jobs, attended faculty meetings, lectured at other institutions, participated in professional meetings, wrote an occasional paper or chapter for edited books, saw some clients in therapy, and served as a part-time field selection officer for the Peace Corps. I was also on the editorial boards of several journals. Without question, these years at Columbia were the busiest and most demanding of my life. I recall that when I reached my home in suburban New Jersey after a day in New York, I was mixing a martini before I took off my coat!

A few other events during these years were significant. One was my developing friendship and collaboration with Allen Bergin. Although I had not met him before coming to TC, we related well to each other, we shared an interest in empirical clinical research, and we had great mutual respect despite our differences in age, background, and status. Around 1967, Allen came into my office with his usual yellow pad and said that he would like to collaborate with me on a few projects. The result of this proposal was our research project with Richard Prager on evaluating outcome in psychotherapy and plans for a handbook of psychotherapy. The research project demonstrated that different methods of evaluation lead to different types of results (Garfield, Prager, & Bergin, 1971). For example, therapists' evaluations made at the end of therapy were much more favorable than were the differences between pre- and posttherapy scores. The *Handbook of Psychotherapy and Behavior Change* came out in 1971 (Bergin & Garfield) and was very well received. Two subsequent editions have been published (Garfield & Bergin, 1978, 1986), and there has been some discussion about a fourth edition. Bergin and I maintain our friendly and collaborative relationship, and we take some pride in the *Handbook*.

Despite all the very positive features and experiences associated with TC and Columbia University, some developments occurred in 1968 that had a strong impact on me. I refer here to the student uprising at Columbia University, led by Mark Rudd. The barricading of university buildings, the obstruction of university activities, and the associated violence were appalling and depressing. It was a sad experience to witness this attack on one of America's great universities. Although the buildings involved were on the other side of 120th Street and thus did not involve TC directly, the uprising did have an effect on the entire university. Classes were canceled for a couple of days, and all sorts of faculty and student-faculty meetings were held. Each major program had student-faculty meetings and committees, and the psychology department had a two-day meeting to discuss various issues of governance and student participation.

In the years that followed, the student-faculty committees and meetings took a considerable amount of time and, as far as I was concerned, interfered with my responsibilities in directing the clinical program. These activities also appeared to split the clinical faculty into two groups and to change the atmosphere of the program. I felt that training and research were taking a back seat to student-faculty discussions about how the program should function.

Consequently, although previously I had found my position to be very stimulating and satisfying, I now felt otherwise. I had received several inquiries concerning other job possibilities and actually explored two of them, but did not feel that they would be completely satisfactory. During my stay at Columbia I had received several calls from the chairman of the psychology department at Washington University in St. Louis, but did not view that department very favorably, particularly after making a visit there to advise them on their clinical program. However, in the spring of 1969, a new chairman, Tom Sandel, was appointed at Washington University, and he came to New York to talk to me about a position as clinical director there. After his visit, I visited Washington University again. This time I was impressed with the evident desire on the part of the faculty to have me come and the free hand promised me to develop the program. I was also promised the opportunity to hire or bring with me a senior faculty person.

I planned to take a sabbatical semester from TC in the spring of 1970 and then to move to St. Louis in the summer of 1971. However, one of the administrators at TC thought my plan wasn't fair. Rather than get involved in controversy, I resigned effective July 1, 1970 and moved on to Washington University in St. Louis. We moved back to the same suburb where we had lived before and the younger children were reunited in school with former friends.

The Clinical Psychology Program at Washington University

I have sometimes wondered if making as many moves as I have has actually had a negative effect on my professional activities. Beyond the effort involved in packing, unpacking, moving, buying and selling homes, getting new driver's licenses, and the like, there is also the time spent in meeting new colleagues and adapting to new situations. However, in spite of the amount of time that is consumed by a move and therefore not available for professional activities, I also believe that the range of experiences I have had has broadened my perspective and understanding. Be that as it may, the situation at Washington University (WU) was extremely different from the one at TC.

Although WU had had an APA-approved clinical program for many years, the program had been administered by the departmental chairman, an experimental psychologist, and a clinical committee of five or six members. For several years there had been considerable student dissatisfaction and, more recently, critical evaluations from the APA concerning accreditation and from NIMH concerning the university's training grant. The department had been told that a full-time director of the clinical program was essential. This explained the university's search for someone to head the program.

I spent the entire summer of 1970 writing up the new clinical psychology program, consulting with faculty, interviewing students, and making contacts with practicum agencies. Unlike TC, there was no departmental clinic and there were no adequate practicum courses. Thus I had to rely on practicum placements in the community, many of which did not meet my standards. I also set up some transition courses so that advanced students could get concentrated practical clinical training before departing for their internships. I had the files of all the clinical students sent to my office, where we maintained them and kept them up to date. I adapted several procedures that had been used successfully at TC, and developed others. I also wrote out the new clinical brochure in a manner that was both informative *and* accurate, and prepared applications and reports to APA and NIMH.

My hard work the first year paid off. We received full accreditation from APA and our training grant was renewed. Some of the original clinical faculty left for a number of reasons, and I was able to add several new faculty members and strengthen the program. By the end of the second year the clinical program was running smoothly, but I became aware of some dissatisfaction on the part of a few of the nonclinical faculty members. This feeling was partly related to the significant change that had occurred in the department relative to the clinical program. The clinical faculty held its own meetings, selected its own students, kept its own student records, and had the best graduate students in the department. In the eight years that I directed the program, only one clinical student failed the doctoral qualifying program, and he passed it the second time. This was in marked contrast to the rest of the department. However, what I believe irritated some colleagues was that I limited admission to the courses on diagnosis and therapy to our clinical students. This was done because all such courses contained some practicum training, and the faculty could supervise only a limited number of students. This practice also stopped students not admitted to our program from securing clinical training through a back-door procedure and made recruitment more difficult for some of the other faculty members.

Two other activities during my tenure as clinical director should also be noted. I brought order to the clinical records and reduced the median time for completing the program from seven to five years. I was surprised to note, for example, that some students had gone on internships in previous years and had never returned to complete the program, although their files were still in an active status. I also devoted considerable energy to helping three of the clinical faculty secure tenure. I was the only tenured member of the program until this occurred, and I considered this reliance on junior faculty and the resulting lack of stability to be a serious problem. I was glad to be able to help improve this situation.

After the first few years I was free to devote more time to scholarly activities and to other professional matters. In 1974 I was asked by the Division of Clinical Psychology to give a three-day postdoctoral institute on "Current Issues in Psychotherapy," to be held just before the annual APA convention in New Orleans. I found working with experienced clinicians and clinical faculty members in this way to be a stimulating and satisfying experience, and I was pleased to be asked to conduct a similar institute the next year when the APA met in Chicago.

For six years I was on the executive board of the Council of University Directors of Clinical Programs, and I was also elected by the members of the clinical division to another three-year term on the APA Council of Representatives. I also rewrote and updated my 1957 clinical text and published a new text in 1974. Along with Rick Kurtz, I conducted a study of clinical psychologists (Garfield & Kurtz, 1976) and compared it with an earlier study conducted by Lowell Kelly (1961). One finding of note was the increase in the number of clinical psychologists who identified themselves as eclectics. Another was the clear difference in value systems between research-oriented clinical psychologists and those whose main concern was practice. This difference has remained and even intensified since then, and has constituted a serious problem for the APA.

In the summer of 1976, I took my first sabbatical leave. I had made up my mind that I was going to remain in one place long enough to enjoy the academic privilege of a sabbatical. My wife and I rented an apartment in London for one semester. Living there was a great experience. I was able to devote every morning to working on a book on psychotherapy that I had thought about for several years. By the end of the five months' leave I had completed the first draft of *Psychotherapy: An Eclectic Approach,* which was published early in 1980. Being free of administrative duties was a new and satisfying experience. I also gave some lectures, visited my old friends Max Hamilton and Michael Gelder, renewed contacts with Phil Feldman, and met John Davis and David Shapiro. I had started working with Allen Bergin on the second edition of our *Handbook,* and did some work on it in London. The final hectic work on revisions, tardy manuscripts, preparing indexes, and the like occupied most of my time in 1977, but we made the deadlines and the second edition was published in the summer of 1978. Again, the reviews were positive.

That year I also accepted appointment as editor of the *Journal of Consulting and Clinical Psychology* for the period 1979 to 1984. I valued this honor, but I also realized that it carried significant responsibility. For this reason, as well as others, I decided to give up directing the clinical program. Thus, for the first time in my career, I was not in an administrative position. To a great extent, my time was my own. Editing the *Journal* took up a considerable part of my time, but I enjoyed the challenge. This had always been my favorite journal, and I did my best to maintain its high quality. During my six years as editor, my interactions with authors, associate editors, and the other editors and editorial staff of APA journals were generally very pleasant. I tried to emphasize high quality and clinically relevant research articles and also introduced special sections of four or five invited articles on a specific topic. During that period, I received, examined, and processed 5834 manuscripts (Garfield, 1986).

There are just a few other events that merit some mention here. In the fall of 1978 I attended a meeting in Bethseda, Maryland to discuss the planning of a collaborative study of the treatment of depression to be sponsored by NIMH. Subsequently, I was appointed to the advisory committee for that project and have participated in that role since that date. It has been a fascinating experience to participate vicariously in this very important research project, which compares two forms of psychotherapy and the anti-depressant imipramine. The use of therapy manuals, the specific training and monitoring of the therapists during the study, the collaboration of three large psychiatric centers, the comprehensive evaluation procedures, and the centralized coordination and data processing all made this a unique and innovative study. The deliberations of the advisory committee with project investigators and NIMH staff, along with appraisals of the problems and results evident during the study, clearly illustrated the complexity of research on psychotherapy and the lack of unanimity about many aspects of psychotherapy.

In 1982 I also accepted appointment to the NIMH Psychosocial and Behavioral Treatment Review Committee, of which I was chairman from 1984 to 1986. Like most review committees, this committee met three times a year to process research grant applications in the area of psychotherapy. Although reading many lengthy grant applications could become tedious, it also gave me an overview of current research endeavors in psychotherapy. The divergent points of view of the 12 committee members also made the meetings interesting, and the total impact was definitely educational.

In the spring of 1982 I met with Allen Bergin to consider a third edition of our *Handbook of Psychotherapy and Behavior Change.* We were gratified at the reception of the first two editions, and we were assured by the publishers and others that a third edition was merited. The book had become a standard reference as well as popular graduate text on research in psychotherapy. After our meeting and several conferences by phone, we finally agreed on the contents and possible authors for the new edition. We decided to reduce the size of the book by roughly 100 pages and to have 19 chapters instead of 23, hoping this would also reduce the price of the book and make it more readily available to graduate students. We omitted the chapters dealing with research on psychoanalytic therapy and on research with children. Both of these areas had produced relatively little research since the previous edition, and the work on brief psychodynamic therapy would be covered in the chapter dealing with research on brief psychotherapy. We condensed the chapters on behavioral and cognitive therapies, substituted a chapter on developmental perspectives on psychotherapy for the previous chapter on psychobiological foundations, restored the chapter on educational and vocational counseling, and added a new chapter, "Behavioral Medicine and Health Psychology."

Editing and producing a new edition of the *Handbook* is always a very demanding task, particularly in meeting the standards we set for our authors and ourselves and in meeting our publication deadline. All manuscripts are reviewed by Bergin and me as well as by one of our consulting editors or other outside consultants, and the authors are given detailed feedback and recommendations for revision. The revisions are again reviewed by the co-editors, and by other reviewers as necessary. Since most of the authors are highly respected researchers, one cannot treat them as graduate students when providing them with reviews of their chapters. Most of the authors have been very cooperative in working with the editors, but occasionally a problem or difference of opinion has arisen. However, these few incidents were resolved successfully and excellent chapters secured. I should also add that Allen Bergin and I have worked together extremely well for over 20 years, reaching agreement amicably on most problems. He took major responsibility for the first edition, while I have had major responsibility for the other two editions.

During this time I also revised my clinical psychology text, and the new edition was published in 1983. Thereafter, I concentrated mainly on the third edition of the *Handbook,* which was published in July 1986. Before its completion, I had decided to retire from my position as professor of psychology. I was 68 and could have waited until age 70 before retiring, but I wanted to be free of any restrictions on what I might do with my time. I certainly did not see this decision as signifying a complete break with psychology. I was still on the editorial board of five journals, and along with Arnold Goldstein and Leonard Krasner I was co-editor of a new series of clinical books for Pergamon Press, *Psychology Practitioner Guidebooks.* I also had some tentative ideas for a book on brief psychotherapy. My wife and I love to travel, and I wanted to be free to travel when the spirit moved me. The department of psychology at WU was nice enough to honor me with a surprise symposium featuring four distinguished friends of mine, Jerome D. Frank, Leonard Eron, Ralph Heine, and Allen Bergin. It was a wonderful occasion that my wife and I were able to share with our four children and my sister and brother-in-law, as well as with colleagues and friends.

Since officially retiring in 1986, I have taught the basic graduate course in psychotherapy once and have given a series of lectures on psychotherapy at WU, completed a few articles and some chapters for edited books, reviewed several books for two journals, delivered a few lectures here and abroad, published a book on brief psychotherapy for the Pergamon *Psychology Practitioner Guidebook* series (Garfield, 1989), and have visited a number of places, including China, Thailand, Singapore, and Malaysia. I should also have mentioned that a year before retiring, I went on a lecture tour to New Zealand and Australia for ten weeks, a most enjoyable trip. I know of no better way than a lecture tour to combine business with pleasure.

Reflections on Clinical Psychology: Past, Present, and Future

In the preceding pages I have tried to provide a sketch of my life, with emphasis on my professional training and career. It was a fortunate coincidence that the large-scale expansion and development of clinical psychology after 1945 coincided with my own career as a clinical psychologist. Changes that were totally unpredictable have taken place, and the field itself has been transformed. From my perspective some of the changes have been for the good and some clearly have not. When I joined the APA in 1941 and attended my first convention that year, which incidentally was held at Northwestern University, the APA was a scholarly and scientifically oriented organization of around three thousand members. Clinical psychology played a relatively small role in the APA and there were no organized clinical programs of the type that exist today.

In the intervening years the APA has grown to over sixty thousand members, clinical psychology training programs have mushroomed within and outside of universities, clinical psychology has shown the largest growth of any area in psychology, and professional concerns have dominated American psychology. The conflicts and tensions between scientifically oriented members and those interested primarily in private practice have increased and threatened to split the organization. This conflict has led some distinguished scientists to resign from the APA and has caused a number of us to feel both saddened and alienated.

One of the aspects of post–World War II development that I found particularly important was the combination of science and practice that distinguished the developing field of clinical psychology. As mentioned in the Boulder Conference report (Raimy, 1950), clinical psychology was developing as a unique profession combining both science and practice, and it was this feature that most of us valued and tried to foster. The scientist-practitioner was the declared goal of all of the university training programs and was the feature that clearly differentiated clinical psychology from the other mental health professions such as psychiatry and social work, "lesser professions" devoted only to professional practice. This model was the source of considerable enthusiam and pride among many clinical psychologists at that time. We viewed our profession as scientifically oriented, requiring the use of research-validated procedures and providing services to all segments of the public without a dominant interest in our own economic aggrandizement. At the same time, we defined our areas of professional competence and did not want to be viewed as mere adjuncts to other professions.

Thus, although many of us were active in state psychological associations, supported certification and licensing of psychologists, and did not want to be dominated by any other profession, we were not primarily interested in private practice and were not antipsychiatry. In fact, I still believe that a collaborative clinical setting potentially provides the most comprehensive type of service to people seeking psychological or psychiatric help.

Over the years, however, the situation has changed noticeably, and this change became quite apparent in the early 1960s. Some individuals strongly voiced their dissatisfaction with the training they had received in graduate school and wanted more practical training included in university programs. Through various local and other organizations they were vocally critical of the planning for the Chicago Conference of Professional Training and wanted a greater say in activities of this type, claiming that the universities had always dominated them. Despite this oppositional activity, which did postpone the meeting for several months, the conferees at the Chicago Conference in 1965 voted overwhelmingly for the Boulder model of the scientist-practitioner. Three other models were presented, the "Professional Psychologist," the "Research Clinician," and the "Psychologist-Psychotherapist," but the "Scientist-Professional" model received the most support (Hoch, Ross, & Winder, 1966).

Although the deliberations of the Chicago Conference appeared to indicate that there were no strong challenges to the dominant scientist-practitioner model, the years since then have indicated otherwise. Although the professional training program instituted at the University of Illinois in 1968 for the doctor of psychology degree (Psy.D.) was eventually discontinued, a large number of free-standing professional schools of psychology, as well as a smaller number attached to universities, have since come into being. These programs, offering either Psy.D. or Ph.D. degrees, admit large numbers of students and, unlike university programs, graduate large classes every four years. It seems apparent that the emphases and value system of these two types of programs are quite different, and I wonder how long they can co-exist. A recent conference on training recommended that all new professional training programs be affiliated with universities after 1995 (Resolutions, 1987). However, the outcome of this recommendation is uncertain.

Along with these developments, the conflict in values between researchers and practitioners has become more acute within the APA. What was once a scientific and socially oriented organization has become politicized and concerned with lobbying, legal suits, and competition with psychiatric and medical groups. The composition of the APA has changed, with the professionals now outnumbering the scientifically oriented and research-oriented members. Members are elected to office on the basis of organized political action rather than on the basis of their visible contribution to psychology. Instead of psychologists bringing their research expertise to the field of mental health and contributing to the advancement of knowledge in areas pertaining to abnormal behavior and personality, clinical psychologists currently are clamoring to be allowed to prescribe drugs and admit patients to hospitals. Instead of pride in the uniqueness of their profession, such clinical psychologists appear to be trying to emulate psychiatrists. Instead of evaluating the utility of psychoanalysis and fostering more efficient treatments, clinical psychologists, with financial backing from the APA, have won a legal battle to be admitted to psychoanalytic institutes, just like medical analysts. And they are very proud of the achievement! They believe that now they will be able to charge higher fees and receive greater respect. Thus, the domain of concern and inquiry for clinical psychologists has shifted greatly in recent times from what it was when I entered the field.

It is very difficult to predict future events, especially when one does not have a crystal ball. This is particularly true in the case of clinical psychology, which has exhibited so many unpredictable changes over a relatively short time. However, if the current conflict within psychology continues, and if an increasingly large number of professionally trained clinicians are little influenced by research-oriented clinical psychologists and the reasearch tradition in psychology, then I believe that the field will lose its unique identity and its current role and status related to research in the mental health area.

I would like to elaborate on this point. In the 1940s, the three main functions of the clinical psychologist were usually listed as diagnostic testing, psychotherapy, and research. Of these, diagnostic testing was clearly the primary activity and psycho- therapy a new and highly coveted activity that had been administered mainly by psychiatrists. Although projective techniques were also of recent origin, they were incorporated in test batteries and generally received the same kind of empirical evaluation as other psychological tests. When I taught projective techniques, for example, students became acquainted with problems in reliability, validity, and normative data as well as with methods of administration and interpretation. Furthermore, as clinical psychologists became more actively involved in psycho- therapy, they provided a greater emphasis on research and evaluation. Increasingly over the years our research competence and participation has been recognized by governmental agencies, medical schools, and other groups. This research competence in psychotherapy has actually strengthened our right to be major participants in this area, and many innovations have come from research-oriented psychologists as well as research-oriented psychiatrists.

Psychotherapy has become the primary activity of a majority of clinical psychologists, and it has also become better known and accepted by the public at large. In many ways psychotherapy has become a growth industry, and the number of different forms of psychotherapy has increased to over four hundred (Kazdin, 1986). Most of these forms of psychotherapy have never been evaluated in any systematic manner. At the same time, with few exceptions, the psychotherapies that *have* been evaluated have been found to have roughly comparable levels of efficacy. Findings such as these have real implications for practice and research in psychotherapy. With the present concerns about the rising costs of health care and the emphasis on account- ability, the need for a critical evaluation of psychotherapeutic approaches and for the devising of efficient and effective procedures is very evident. To attain such a goal, both systematic research and new creative formulations are required.

The recent emphasis on professional training without an equal emphasis on research training will not be adequate to meet the aforementioned goal. Most students today appear primarily interested in learning clinical skills, particularly psychotherapy. They do not show the same interest in attempts to evaluate therapy or in learning about possible limitations on the effectiveness of psychotherapy. In many programs, one particular approach to psychotherapy is emphasized and any questioning of the adequacy of the approach is fraught with danger; yet a questioning of current beliefs and an attempt to evaluate them is essential if a field is to progress. As mentioned before, despite the fact that there is still no empirical evidence to demonstrate the effectiveness of psychoanalysis (Garfield, 1981; Rachman & Wilson, 1980), some psychologists have devoted considerable effort to securing admittance to psychoanalytic institutes in order to become psychoanalysts.

I find some recent developments in clinical psychology both interesting and perplexing. Among these developments are the proliferation of psychotherapeutic schools and the adherence by clinicians to one approach. Relatively early in my career, I was intrigued by the possibility that common factors were operating most of the psychotherapies. The dissertation research of my friend Ralph Heine (1953), comparing Adlerian, psychoanalytic, and Rogerian therapies, lent some support to this view. I even devoted ten pages to a discussion of "Common Aspects of the Psychotherapeutic Process" in my first clinical psychology text, *Introductory Clinical Psychology* (Garfield, 1957). The emphasis on common factors was a central feature of *Psychotherapy: An Eclectic Approach,* published in 1980. However, in the years in between, although there was some recognition of "nonspecific factors" in psychotherapy as something to account for in research, little attention was paid to the possibility of common factors in psychotherapy. During this period, the number of psychotherapeutic approaches increased tremendously and the bulk of the research studies evaluating the efficacy of psychotherapy indicated few differences among the approaches evaluated. The recent NIMH collaborative study of depression appears to have secured comparable results (Elkin, 1986). However, clinicians have been reluctant to come to grips with these findings.

I have a strong conviction that in the long run the proliferation of psychotherapies will diminish, and a relatively small number of empirically validated procedures will characterize the practice of psychotherapy. An attempt has been made recently to promote integration in psychotherapy, with an organization and a journal devoted to this effort. I refer to the Society for the Exploration of Integration in Psychotherapy and the *Journal of Integrative and Eclectic Psychotherapy.* Whether this development will have a significant impact remains to be seen. However, if the history of medicine has any implications for clinical psychology and psychotherapy, research findings will gradually reduce the number of competing schools and approaches, and most will fall by the wayside. In a comparable manner, independent professional schools will gradually have to give way to research-oriented institutions such as the universities. If clinical psychology can hold on and not be discarded by the great research universities, then it may continue to be a unique research-oriented profession in the mental health field and be recognized for its contributions to the advancement of knowledge and clinical practice. If, on the other hand, clinical psychology neglects its research tradition and devotes its main energy to guild issues, it may be superseded by some existing or new profession. Only time will reveal its future course.

References

Bergin, A. E. & Garfield, S. L. (Eds.) (1971). *Handbook of psychotherapy and behavior change.* New York: Wiley.

Elkin, I. (1986). *NIMH Treatment of Depression Collaborative Research Program.* Paper presented at the annual meeting of the Society for Psychotherapy Research, June 19, Wellesley, MA.

Garfield, S. L. (1957). *Introductory clinical psychology.* New York: Macmillan.

Garfield, S. L. (1960). Research survey: State mental health programs. *American Psychologist, 15,* 319–320.

Garfield, S. L. (1974). *Clinical psychology: The study of personality and behavior.* Chicago: Aldine.

Garfield, S. L. (1980). *Psychotherapy: An eclectic approach.* New York: Wiley.

Garfield, S. L. (1981). Psychotherapy: A 40-year appraisal. *American Psychologist, 36,* 174–183.

Garfield, S. L. (1986). Editing JCCP 1979–1984: Some observations and reflections. *The Clinical Psychologist, 39,* 17–20.

Garfield, S. L. (1989). *The practice of brief psychotherapy.* New York: Pergamon Press.

Garfield, S. L. & Affleck, D. C. (1960). A study of individuals committed to a state home for the retarded who were later released as not mentally retarded. *American Journal of Mental Deficiency, 64,* 907–915.

Garfield, S. L. & Bergin, A. E. (Eds.) (1978). *Handbook of psychotherapy and behavior change,* 2nd Ed. New York: Wiley.

Garfield, S. L. & Bergin, A. E. (Eds.) (1986). *Handbook of psychotherapy and behavior change,* 3rd Ed. New York: Wiley.

Garfield, S. L. & Carver, M. J. (1960). Phenylketonuria: A further study. *Journal of Nervous and Mental Disease, 130,* 120–124.

Garfield, S. L., Heine, R. W., & Leventhal, M. (1954). An evaluation of psychological reports in a clinical setting. *Journal of Consulting Psychology, 18,* 281–286.

Garfield, S. L. & Kurtz, R. (1976). Clinical psychologists in the 1970s. *American Psychologist, 31,* 1–9.

Garfield, S. L. & Kurz, M. (1952). Evaluation of treatment and related procedures in 1216 cases referred to a mental hygiene clinic. *Psychiatric Quarterly, 26,* 414–424.

Garfield, S. L., Prager, R. A., & Bergin, A. E. (1971). Evaluation of outcome in psychotherapy. *Journal of Consulting and Clinical Psychology, 37,* 307–313.

Heine, R. W. (1953). A comparison of patients' reports on psychotherapeutic experience with psychoanalytic, nondirective and Adlerian therapists. *American Journal of Psychotherapy, 7,* 16–23.

Hoch, E. H., Ross, A. O., & Winder, C. L. (1966). *Professional preparation of clinical psychologists.* Washington, DC: American Psychological Association.

Kazdin, A. E. (1986). Comparative outcome studies of psychotherapy: Methodological issues and strategies. *Journal of Consulting and Clinical Psychology, 54,* 95–105.

Kelly, E. L. (1961). *Clinical psychology—1960: Report of survey findings.* Newsletter, Division of Clinical Psychology, 1–11.

Rachman, S. J. & Wilson, G. T. (1980). *The effects of psychological therapy,* 2nd Ed. New York: Pergamon Press.

Raimy, V. (Ed.) (1950). *Training in clinical psychology.* New York: Prentice-Hall.

Resolutions approved by the National Conference on Graduate Education in Psychology (1987). *American Psychologist, 42,* 1070–1084.

Wickman, E. K. (1928). *Children's behavior and teachers' attitudes.* New York: Commonwealth Fund.

Molly Harrower, Ph.D., D.H.L.

Professor Emeritus
University of Florida, Gainesville, Florida

◆

Inkblots and Poems

British Beginnings

If I begin at the very beginning, I would have to say that I was born in Johannesburg, South Africa. Although true, this would be misleading; for I was the child of Scottish parents who at that time happened to be traveling internationally in connection with my father's business. As soon as I was deemed old enough to travel—6 weeks or so, it is said—we embarked on the long sea journey back to England. Thus all that my unusual birthplace has done for me is to make explanations necessary when I fill out various forms, and to complicate my entry into the United States some 20 years later—this because the United States regards the place of birth as the determinant of nationality, whereas in Great Britain nationality is always that of the parents.

While there is something arbitrary about my place of birth, the village of Cheam, 12 miles south of London, in which my family settled and in which I grew up, provides the genuine backdrop for my British childhood. The house we lived in had title deeds going back to the year 1672, and each subsequent owner had recorded what he had done to add to its "beautifying." Beautiful, yes; but abysmally cold and drafty in winter.

Cheam village itself figured rather prominently in old historical records. In the time of Henry VIII, Cheam was a place for the hunting of wild boar, and the royal court would depart from London to hold masques and theatrical performances in a large estate known as Nonesuch Palace. In a house a few doors from our own, built in the 1500s, a hidden room was recently discovered, on the walls of which King Charles I, apparently hidden there by his supporters before his execution, had written the Cavalier watchword, "Remember."

My father and mother were about as different as two human beings could be. My father, the youngest of a large family, came from a small village in Perthshire, Scotland. His mother died when he was very young, and he was brought up by an older sister. He showed the oversensitivity and sometimes withdrawal of having been a lonely, isolated child. He was shy and reserved, and this reserve affected me deeply. His silences meant disapproval to me, and not for years did I discover how this hangover had affected my life. I never heard my father tell a single story about his life as a young person. I also see now that he was afraid to express the great tenderness he obviously felt. Our relationship developed along the safe, unemotional grounds of sports—golf and cricket particularly—and our cultural heritage, Gilbert and Sullivan. I became a good cricketer (later playing for London University), and even appeared in a film entitled *Eve at the Wicket*! I became letter- and note-perfect in all Gilbert and Sullivan operas, and much later produced two amateur performances in the United States. My happy memories are of our outings to see some of the great cricket matches between England and Australia, and the intense enjoyment of attending all performances of the opera when the D'Oyly Carte Company came to London.

One such excursion was so packed with excitement that I feel I must record it. The company had been absent from England for some 15 years, and its first-night performance was a national event. The only way to obtain a seat was to stand for a day and a night in a queue for unreserved tickets. To my amazement, my father announced that he and I (aged 13) would undertake this vigil. Since it had seemed to me that everything I had yearned for until that moment had been pronounced too adventurous to be considered, this spectacular change of policy for such an occasion still leaves a glow of pleasure, even after 70 years. And it was well worth it! Sitting on our camp stools wrapped in our tartan rugs, we waited. The whole group, like my father and me, knew every word and every tune, and we sang spontaneously all through the night.

My mother's family and her childhood experiences were entirely different from my father's. She had innumerable stories to tell about the escapades that she and a brother undertook. Many of her memories revolve around the dynamic character of her father. He was at once businessman, Greek scholar, art critic and collector, traveler, and writer. I never knew him, but it is as if his overflowing personality reached me through the stories my mother told. He apparently was a legendary, fun-endorsing person. As a young woman my mother traveled all over Europe with him, obviously reflected much of his philosophy, used his art teaching in lectures of her own, and transmitted to our generation his richness and appreciation of life. He discovered many important, previously unknown artists, and brought the first painting by Corot to Scotland. One of the happiest moments in my mother's life was when *she* discovered an unrecognized Rembrandt in a small gallery in Italy—a rare find.

One of the stories from my mother's childhood I could never hear often enough. It was about one of my grandfather's cousins, James Y. Simpson, a major medical figure who invented chloroform. As the story is told, there was a dinner party at my grandparents' house, and Simpson was among the guests. The ladies at such parties always retired to the drawing room after the meal, while the gentlemen stayed on with their wine and cigars. On this particular occasion it seemed that the gentlemen were dallying much longer than usual before the host's "Shall we join the ladies?" rallied them for more polite conversation.

The parlormaid was summoned by my grandmother and dispatched to remind the gentlemen of their expected appearance. She returned with the excited remark, "They're a' under the table wi' th' chlorie!"—being interpreted, "They're all under the table, under the influence of chloroform." James Y. Simpson had been experimenting, and they had all succumbed to "th' chlorie."

I suppose you could stretch a point to say that the reason this was my favorite story was because of my early interest in consciousness and unconsciousness, and experimentation in general!

To return to my parents: my mother used to tell me that it was she who had finally proposed to my father, after finding him standing outside her door in an agony of apprehension. She thereby put at his disposal for the 40 years of their married life her undivided and unswerving loyalty and love. Her only moments of conflict came when, as a result of my inevitable adolescent storms demanding independence, she was torn between her devotion to him and her understanding of me. She was courageous and buoyant; she exuded faith in my father, despite his depressions and misgivings. By far the stronger and, to my mind, richer personality, she nonetheless dissolved herself into an atmosphere, so to speak, in which he might feel safe.

Humorously aware of "dear Dad's difficulties"—he was always fearful for us, something we children resented—she never missed an opportunity to point out to us his innate artistic ability. After some spontaneous statement of her own, to which he could only make a studied critical remark, she would point out her own impulsiveness and extol his attitude with some comment like, "Dear Dad is always so sensible."

Looking back, I see that it was my mother who created the home in which my younger brother John and I grew up. But at the time by far the most important person in our childhood universe was our nurse.

The upbringing of a child in Britain in the early 1900s differed from that of a comparably situated American child in two important ways—the early nursery years, on the one hand, and the banishment at 7 for boys, and 10 or 11 for girls, to boarding schools. The nursery was indeed a world apart, geographically separated in the house and psychologically separated in the child's mind. The "children's hour" is no literary phrase: we made an excursion from 5 to 6 each evening to see our parents in the drawing room, but we lived upstairs in the nursery.

British nursery life is an enigma to many people in the United States, and I have spent much time discussing it. I can easily take either side in an argument as to which is the "better" way to bring up a child. How is it possible, I have been asked innumerable times, that you can have so little "home life" in the sense that Americans know it? What must it be like if the child's mother seems to have so little input in the early development?

This way of life can be made to look quite unnatural from the outside, but for us children it was the norm. It goes without saying that much depends on the character of the nurse in charge, for it falls to her not only to set the stage for acceptable behavior, but to give rise to all important concepts such as kindness, justice, and fair play, by her example. Our nurse was young, energetic, resourceful, and humorous. But deep down, the thing that so endeared her to us was the knowledge that she was tough and could not be fooled. Children love to get away with murder, but secretly they despise those whom they can fool.

Our nurse had an uncanny knowledge of the infant makeup. On one occasion I was watching John, my brother, aged 1 to my 4, being bathed. My mother brought up some friends to see the baby. As the slippery little figure was picked out of the tub to the admiration of the guests, I remarked, "I wish he were mine." The guests and my mother cooed their appreciation of my sisterly love. But the clear-eyed nurse remarked cold-bloodedly afterwards, "I know what you wanted him for. You want to beat him up." This vindictive thought had, of course, been uppermost in my mind; and while I protested vehemently, the fact that she *knew* was a tremendously important factor in my feelings toward her.

My younger brother John is not easy to bring into my life story, for we have seen so little of each other. We probably overlapped in consecutive shared experiences for little more than five years. Three years my junior, his baby schedule isolated him from many of my early activities with other children; and when he was 7, he was sent off to school in the accustomed manner.

During our few years of joint ownership of the nursery, we seem to have been involved in elaborate fantasy lives, which we communicated to each other, but retained as personal preserves.

John had a family of "Wumps." The Wumps were, to start with, real entities: they were small shawls, wound into the shape of a roll of paper toweling. (These shawls were, incidentally, worn by us children for protection against the cold as we moved from one freezing, unheated part of the house to another. There was, of course, no central heating of any kind in the 17th-century dwelling, and only utterly inadequate fireplaces in each room; and far worse were the spaces to be traveled of corridors and stairways from the nursery to the drawing room, with nothing to alleviate the icy cold.)

The Wumps, liberated into fantasy, were part of Mr. John's army. They had names like Scancie-Scoman and Rattabooda. They had endless adventures, and to this day we refer to small dwellings as "Wumpy houses."

My fantasy "family" consisted of purple horses. The chief horse, Zel, had yellow spotted wings, and I later captured him in a verse that showed him able to do all the things I would have liked to do, and none of the things I considered myself forced to do.

I think of Zel
My purple horse
With yellow spotted wings.
He can do fifty million sums,
And all his other things
When I think thoughts.

He never starts his tea with bread and butter
He can have fifty million bits of cake.
He's always asked to walk right in the gutter.
His mother likes it when he stays awake.
He never has to wash before his dinner
Because he knows that twice a day's enough.
His nurse is happy when he's getting thinner
He does not have to eat that treacle stuff.

And when he's tired of them and his own garden
He does not have to stay in it all day,
He spreads his wings and tells me he is coming
And then flies fifty miles away.

(Harrower, 1929)

Returning for vacations from our respective schools, at slightly older ages, we were sports-oriented. We had a cricket pitch on the lawn, and a complicated putting layout to improve our golf. We made a theatre out of the large hayloft above the stables, where we gave amateur performances. The area we used for a stage had a trapdoor, which opened into a large pile of straw. Most satisfactory dramatic effects could be produced by a character's sudden disappearance into the underworld; the audience, of course, displaying the appropriate exclamations of surprise! There were chutes down which hay could be dropped into the mangers, which one could slide down; and rooms for storing the harvest of pears and apples—a hideout with many possibilities.

Leaving for school, the Unknown, was an occasion for the stiff upper lips of all concerned. My first year away from home at age 11 was, I regret to say, a total failure. It is somehow skipped over in the family annals, for at the end of the year I was removed from the school. I possess my diary, written in 1918. The word "misable" appears on almost every page. It was at the end of World War I, and the food supply in England was very low; what we got to eat was worthy of my detailed recording. But basically the record is one of the impact of "ragging" (hazing) on the defenseless.

The most dramatic of my experiences remains etched on my mind. For a minor, prearranged "offense" I was lifted up by some tall girl and told to hold to the lintel of a big doorway and to hang there. As I dropped down, I tore my hand open on a nail. This of course was not supposed to be part of the punishment, but it posed a great problem. I was charged on pain of reprisals not to show my hand to "Matron"; anyway, regardless of reprisals, to "blab" was out of the question. When the hand became infected, some appropriate story had to be invented.

It was never *incidents,* however, that made me unhappy; rather, it was the unpredictable decisions of older girls to "send her to Coventry." Not to be spoken to, for what seems like an eternity, can undermine one more than physical demonstrations of dislike. Of course, the code demanded that none of this ever reach the ears of parents or teachers.

Luckily for me, my body came to my rescue. I developed hives, weals so enormous that I was advised to leave school on the basis of having some strange skin disease. The concept of psychosomatic medicine was far from being formulated in those days, and the idea that acute unhappiness could be related to gross physical symptoms was unknown. I profited greatly from this disturbance, for both my mother and I could hold our heads up when I was removed. Clearly, nothing would have been more shameful than to be unable to "take" one's prescribed fate at that stage in life.

How children react to such hazing is influential in their development. For me, I think, it provided an empathy with the underdog, and a sense of the damage that an arbitrary or prejudicial outlook can do. Having been excluded has provided understanding of what exclusion can mean. I cannot generalize, of course, but one of the most sensitive of my psychiatric colleagues told me years later that such experiences, which he also had had at a vulnerable age, had influenced his choice of a therapeutic role in later life.

For the next six years I was sent to another school, also away from home. Godolphin School Salisbury was run on the so-called house system; the idea was that fewer excesses of "ragging" could be perpetrated if there were fewer children in one unit. This was largely true as far as physical affronts were concerned, but there were still plenty of opportunities for the subtle and systematic disapproval of weaklings. If one has to develop the kind of self-sufficiency and independence necessary to cope with such isolation at an early age, then such apparently unusual actions as coming to America alone and without funds at age 22 are more understandable.

Although I was not acutely unhappy, my six years at Godolphin School Salisbury were certainly not joyful ones. Returning to school after a vacation, we all made out large calendars, with the number of days to be lived through until the next release.

I wanted so desperately to succeed, and never really understood what seemed repeatedly to lead to my downfall. I would laugh at the wrong time, I would speak in the wrong corridor; I once shouted at the top of my lungs for sheer joy, on a walk on Salisbury Downs, miles from anywhere, and was promptly reported. I was caught in a "scandal" involving the discussion of "beastly things." This discussion included the question of why a cock has a comb. It took me years to discover the answer to my question, which is that the comb is a secondary sex characteristic, and when it turns red it indicates sexual maturity!

I was caught writing a letter in prep-time (arch crime), on school property (a notebook). This was so serious an offense that I was sent to the headmistress. "You have got such an honest face," she said sadly. "It's a pity that you don't live up to it."

It was not until my last few months in school that my turbulent career took a turn for the better. The last in a succession of house mistresses seemed to approve of the ugly duckling, giving me a break that faith in one's abilities invariably does. As a result, I left school, a young and immature 18, almost in a haze of glory. I had won the poetry prize, judged by an outsider; had captained my house cricket team to first place for the first time in its history; and, to the open amazement of all the teachers, had passed the entrance examinations into Oxford and Cambridge—in the subjects that had been considered worthwhile my attempting. To have asked me to take an examination in mathematics was considered unfair, it having been pronounced for some reason that my mind was not attuned to these mysteries.

However, no one had at any time even considered the possibility of my going to college, so my next move was in line with the accepted tradition: I was sent to a finishing school in Paris. I deeply resented the idea of being "finished." In my rather one-sided view, I was being sent, against my will, into a den of not iniquity, but frivolity. I was being asked to ally myself with girls whose avowed and explicit purpose was to spend money, to buy clothes, and to "catch a man"—while *I* yearned to "Do Something" with my life.

As a protest against these trivialities, I renounced all pleasures such as trips to the best Paris shops, dinners in well-known restaurants, afternoon teas with exquisite little cakes, operas, theatres, and arranged dances, and dedicated myself to proving the triumph of mind over matter. I decided to become thin and ethereal. I followed this program so successfully that I was delighted, but my parents were concerned. It was decided that for the stormy petrel, as my mother always called me, Paris was a mistake. Something else would have to be arranged.

So I was sent to a "wholesome family in Switzerland." I was to attend school there, and to participate in the activities of the serious-minded family. Here I acquired a reasonable amount of French, and since the family outdid me in their desire for the good and wholesome life, I could relax.

Several events stand out as milestones in this period. One was the first time I heard the word "psychology." It was in church, from the lips of a rather progressive young Swiss clergyman. The gist of his sermon was that *science* had demonstrated that one could actually make of oneself what one wanted, that there was factual evidence for the belief that one could control one's destiny in the sense of becoming the kind of person one wanted to be. To a condemned "black sheep" like me, such words were revolutionary. The word *psychology* became a legitimate open sesame, Science and the Good Life brought together. The world spun on a new axis. I *could* be what I wanted: I *would* be what I wanted!

The emotional impact of the word *psychology* bore fruit in action. I returned from Switzerland determined to go to college and was accepted for a course in journalism at Bedford College, one of the several colleges that made up the University of London. The journalism course covered five subjects, one of which was psychology. This was taught by Dr. Beatrice Edgell, who had worked with Külpe in Germany, taking her Ph.D. with him in 1906, a remarkable accomplishment for a woman at that time.

The glow from my newfound interest in psychology must have been evident, for Dr. Edgell invited me to become a full-time psychology student, shifting from journalism to a new degree program, the academic diploma in psychology.

College life was even more fulfilling than I had anticipated. My extracurricular activities included being captain of the college cricket team. I was chosen to play the role of Hamlet in the first-year students' production of that play. I acquired a tutor with whom I spent many hours of much more insightful study than was possible in the more orthodox curriculum of the diploma program. Under the guidance of my tutor, I tackled such essay subjects as "The Unscientific Nature of Behaviourism," "An Attempt to Understand Consciousness," "In Search of a Clear Understanding of Time," and "A Study of the Act of Thinking."

In contrast, consider these examples of questions from the college course in practical psychology: "Measure the subject's accuracy in making the pitch of a sound equal to that of a standard of 750 vibrations," and "Find the subject's difference threshold for the distance between two points on the skin when the standard is 3 cms. Use the Limiting Method."

The next two summers also provided a wonderful experience: I was a student at the Margaret Morris School for dancers and artists in the south of France. As part of the summer program we were taught painting by J. D. Ferguson, one of the foremost members of the flourishing Scottish School. We novices took part as extras in performances put on by the experienced Margaret Morris dancers.

Many well-known artists and writers dropped in to visit and to pay their respects to J. D. Ferguson and Margaret Morris. I was quickly absorbed into a community of artists, writers, social reformers, and delightful eccentrics who formed the outer circle of Margaret Morris's friends and dance school.

Among the outstanding figures in my mind were Max Eastman, who was well known in the field of literature, and C. K. Ogden, the Cambridge scholar who developed Basic English and was editor of the series "Philosophy, Psychology and Scientific Methods," in which both Köhler and Koffka had published. *The Mentality of Apes* (Köhler, 1927) and *The Growth of the Mind* (Koffka, 1928) were important contributions to Gestalt psychology.

Ogden needed a Girl Friday; I was looking for a job; we made the connection.

My work with Ogden has been described elsewhere (Harrower, 1978, 1984). A long article in *Life* magazine was devoted to his work and eccentricities (Dennis, 1957). He is relevant to my development in that he formed one of the major connecting links in my life story. After I had worked with him as associate editor of *Psyche,* on hearing that I was eager to go to America, he wrote to Kurt Koffka, who had just arrived in America himself, suggesting that I might be included in the group of psychologists Koffka was planning to bring to his research laboratory at Smith College.

Koffka replied that he would accept me and suggested that I double as secretary for the group. I therefore learned speed-writing promptly!

Why did I want to go to America? Mainly because my tutor at Bedford College was an American and I needed to endorse America in a battle royal that had developed between my parents and this friend. Smoldering with indignation and full of enterprise, I wrote a book of children's poems (Harrower, 1929), and asked for money for a passage to America in lieu of advance royalties. I also arranged for a job at the Aloha Camp in Vermont, as counselor for horseback riding and putting on a Gilbert and Sullivan opera, a combination made in heaven! So off to the States at age 22.

American Adventures

I arrived in America in the summer of 1928. My camp experiences were all that I could have hoped for, but by the fall I was ready to embark on serious psychology, and proceeded to Smith College to work with Koffka.

The research laboratory that was to be my intellectual home and place of work for the next few years was clearly an unusual place. It was in a sense autonomous and not part of the general academic establishment. It had been founded with money raised by Smith alumni to celebrate President Nielsen's 15 years in office. The idea behind it was that it should be the working place of a succession of outstanding scholars in different fields, each for a five-year period. Psychology was the first discipline chosen, Kurt Koffka the first recipient. All publications were to appear in a special series, *Smith College Studies in Psychology,* and also in the prestigious German periodical *Psychologische Forschung,* of which Koffka was an editor.

The "lab" was 100 percent international. There was Huang, a brilliant Chinese student, who was working on the effects of magic on the child mind: when does a child get the idea that something has happened contrary to the laws of nature, and through this, how does the child arrive at the idea of what is a law? There was Alexander Mintz from Russia, interested in color contrast and brightness thresholds; Marthe Sturm from France, studying after-images; Tamara Dembo, a student of Kurt Lewin's, with a Ph.D. from Berlin, working on frustration and incomplete tasks; Eugenia Hanfmann, trained in Jena; Fritz Heider from Vienna; and Grace Moore, to become Grace Heider, engaged in a study of transparency, form, and color. Some of these names will be recognized as contributors to present-day psychology.

When the projects were lined up for the first year, as I had no research in progress of my own, I was assigned as Koffka's assistant to work on the perceptual problems of his special interests. Thus, I dedicated two years to making thousands of meticulous observations and measurements in a study eventually published as "Colour and Organization, Parts I and II," *Psychologische Forschung*[1] (Koffka & Harrower, 1931, 1932).

Koffka expected everyone to keep strict hours of attendance, and certainly we all worked hard. But there were hours when our investigations were set aside. At teatime the whole group would meet for far-ranging informal discussions. I began to see new vistas in psychology and philosophy, and was able to absorb the meaning of Gestalt theory from its very source. I was also exposed to a level of psychological investigation that I had never encountered before. I saw dedicated students concentrating on highly technical problems of perception; whether this was something I wanted to devote my life to, I still was not sure.

My initial appointment at Smith College with Koffka had been for one year, no conditions attached. But reappointment meant a certain commitment to science and psychology. Did I want to become a serious student? If so, somehow I must be routed

---

[1]This working partnership lasted in various ways until Koffka's death in 1941; details can be found in *Kurt Koffka: An Unwitting Self-Portrait* (Harrower, 1983).

toward a doctorate—not an easy matter, as my educational background was clearly unorthodox. Moreover, Smith was not primarily known as a higher-degree granting institution.

Before the academic complications were faced, the first prerequisite was for Koffka to be satisfied that I could independently come up with ideas for an acceptable dissertation. This, as it happened, was the least of my worries, as I was now keen to develop and follow ideas of my own, sparked by the stimulation of the group at the lab. I wanted to know the answer to a question.

The question that concerned me at that time was whether some of the general principles of Gestalt theory, which were proving so important in the study of perception, could be utilized in what was spoken of in those days as the "higher mental processes," namely thinking and reasoning.

The concept of organization had proved vital in studies of perception. Could it be equally stimulating and meaningful when applied to thought processes? Koffka was delighted with the idea, and I went to work that year to test my hypotheses experimentally.

After two years at Smith I received an unexpected offer to teach at Wells College for a year. This was far too valuable an opportunity to be disregarded, even though it meant an interruption in my work at the lab. Of course, teaching proved a valuable experience, but I came back to Smith at the end of the academic year eager to complete my project, now entitled "Organization in Higher Mental Processes" (Harrower, 1932).

However, fate decreed that my work on my doctorate was to be postponed once again, by an even more unexpected offer from the University of London. I was invited for a year to hold the position of senior lecturer in psychology at Bedford College. This offer resulted from the sudden, tragic death of psychology professor Victoria Hazlett, who was burned in a laboratory accident. I was nominated for this appointment because my original mentor, Professor Beatrice Edgell, who was shattered by the tragedy and who was due to retire in one year, needed someone whom she knew well as her colleague in the department in her final year. Thus I profited from two unusual teaching opportunities before I gained my Ph.D.

On returning from London for what turned out to be my final year at Smith, I still faced the formidable Ph.D. examination. My dissertation had been accepted, but the orals and the written examination still had to be undertaken. Five examiners were appointed and five days of written papers were decreed. The examiners were Edwin Boring of Harvard; Arnold Gesell of Yale; George Humphrey of Queens University, Canada; Koffka, representing the research lab; and Harold Israel, a member of the Smith psychology department. It was also decreed that I must remain in seclusion in the dean's house while taking the examination, the rationale being that I might otherwise make a trip to the library to look up some fact I had forgotten! Considering the level at which the papers were to be written, and the caliber of the examiners, this seemed to me a senseless precaution, but it nonetheless added to the tension and strain.

At the height of the discussion about the making of an acceptable Ph.D. from Smith, Koffka had to leave for a research project with Alexander Luria, the noted

Russian psychologist. They were to spend the summer in Uzbekistan, in Asia, making a study of the Uzbek natives. It was gratifying and interesting to me to be able to help with the plans for the expedition and to prepare test material for it, but Koffka's absence at the time of my big ordeal was a blow.

What sort of questions were asked in a Ph.D. examination in 1930? Here are a few from the first of five days of questions:

1. Discuss the statement, "Visual acuity is an affair not of the sense of light (Lichtsinn) but of the sense of space."
2. How can the Liebmann effect be used to prove that optical illusions are facts of organization?
3. State Berkeley's argument that depth cannot be *seen* and show why it is wrong.
4. Contrast Hering's geometrical theory of the nuclear plane with a dynamic theory of the perception of surfaces.
5. What is anisotrophy of visual space? What fact seems at first sight to be incompatible with it?
6. "Similarity is identity of parts." Discuss this proposition in the two provinces of perception and thought.
7. What difference does it make whether we explain thinking by determining tendencies or by organization?

With my Ph.D. finally behind me, I was ready to work as a Gestalt psychologist. I had the personal blessings of Koffka, Köhler, and Wertheimer to go forth and teach the gospel of experimental psychology from the Gestalt point of view.

But something happened that radically altered my perspective and changed what I was looking for as the life work of a psychologist. A close friend emerged from drastic surgery a changed person. How changed? This friend, dean of a college, was, prior to the operation and exhaustive illness, a vibrant, dynamic, and enterprising person. I had been influenced by her and admired particularly her courage, her way of handling difficulties, and her indomitable spirit. As a result of this physically stressful period, she lost much of this orientation and became someone who I would have to describe as manipulated by, rather than challenging, fate. I felt a need to protect such a person, a feeling that psychology should be able to contribute to the restoration of the former self.

At this moment the watertight world of perception, color contrast, and visual acuity collapsed, and there was born the need to seek a place—a hospital perhaps—where a person, a patient, rather than a retina, could be studied and perhaps helped.

It took some time to find a sponsor for this "crazy" notion and to work out the details necessary for such a project, but in 1936 the Rockefeller Foundation backed me with a fellowship to work as an *experimental* psychologist at the Montreal Neurological Institute, working under the renowned brain surgeon Dr. Wilder Penfield.

The extent to which this idea was considered alien can be seen in the fact that my original proposal was altered in the following way. I had stated that my project would involve studying the *"psychological effects of surgical operations,"* the impact of surgical shock. "Psychological" was penciled out and "physiological" was written in, with the statement, "Surely this is a mistake. There can be no psychological effects from a surgical operation or procedure."

Although somewhat disappointed that teaching experimental psychology was not to become my aim and ambition, Koffka nonetheless responded wholeheartedly in favor of this change in direction of goals and interests. Having been successfully interviewed in Montreal, and about to make a final choice, I wrote to Koffka, asking,

> Well, what do you think? Shall I accept the challenge and go to the cold north where there are no nice holidays and where I shall have to start from scratch and be busy and hectic and nervous, but perhaps contribute something which—all things considered—in the abstract and depersonalized, I believe to be one of the big things that can be contributed?

Koffka's reply shows that he was all for the new venture.

> Your exciting note came this morning. Thinking only of you, your ability, your interest, your adaptability and the potential good you can do, I say unhesitatingly YES. I am sure that though the beginning may be difficult, and you may at first often feel discouraged, it will turn out to be your greatest success. You have two qualities that fit you for such a position: human sympathy and original imagination and inventiveness. These, together with your indomitable activity, will carry you through triumphantly. I understand that the choice for you is not easy.[2]

I took the risk, and Alan Gregg of the Rockefeller Foundation charted my course: six months to be spent with Kurt Goldstein, neurologist, brought to the United States from Nazi Germany by the Rockefeller Foundation and established at the Montefiore Hospital in New York; the rest of the three-year fellowship to be spent at the Montreal Neurological Institute at the invitation of Dr. Wilder Penfield, who was interested in the idea of a psychologist working in the medical field. It was further suggested that I spend the intervening months following an intensive program in the field of German literature, in preparation for work with Kurt Goldstein.

Immersion in the Medical Environment

Goldstein and the Montefiore Hospital

In September 1937, after a final "long vacation" abroad, which was heavily interlaced with the study of the pertinent German articles, I arrived with some trepidation at the Montefiore Hospital in the Bronx. All the authorities whom I had

---

[2] The original letters between Kurt Koffka and me are to be donated at my death to the Archives of the History of American Psychology, along with all other material of potential historical interest.

consulted over the previous months about my upcoming project had been adamant about one thing: the need for some initiation period, some preliminary exposure to hospital routine, some dealing with patients. In addition, all agreed that Kurt Goldstein, just arrived from Germany as a scholar in exile, was the person *par excellence* to be my teacher.

So much stress had been put on this that I had the feeling that there must be something very special involved in relating professionally to patients. Having no notion what this might be, I felt vulnerable and ignorant in the face of the mighty world of medicine.

Vitally important as the three months with Goldstein turned out to be, interestingly enough, "dealing with patients" was never a question of his teaching or my explicit learning. I knew almost immediately that I could, by being my natural self, relate to any ill person whom I met or worked with. Goldstein recognized this, and we established a rapport that gave me much-needed confidence.

This is not to say that I did not learn daily how to adjust and cope with the new and strange environment, and even more important, with the feelings that at times swamped me. Almost immediately I ran into a (to me) quite unexpected problem, a confrontation about the fact that I was a woman. How come I did not know that the world had two levels of citizenship? And that hospitals were bastions of male supremacy? One has to remember that my experience up to that point had been in essentially female-dominated universes. I had been embedded in situations that were virtually devoid of sex distinctions. Bedford College, although part of the larger unit of London University, was Bedford College for Women. Smith College, here in the United States, was known nationally as a stronghold of outstanding women scholars. As for our "lab," there were actually more women than men, and discrimination along those lines by Koffka would have been unthinkable.

On my first day at Montefiore Hospital, I received the information that I could not eat in the doctors' dining room. Because I was a psychologist? No, the other psychologists in Goldstein's lab were permitted to go there. The implication was clear: doctors were men! However, after an interview with the superintendent, in which the question was not raised, within an hour Goldstein was notified that I could eat in the dining room after all. My policy remained, lie low and don't use up energy by fussing, things will work out.

Goldstein's offices and examining rooms were tucked away in the basement of the huge rambling structure, a veritable maze of corridors to be traversed. On arrival, one found a general feeling of relaxation and friendliness; a higgledy-piggledy setup, was my way of describing it. Aside from the four or five people working with Goldstein, there was a constant flow of visitors, for he was internationally known. Heated discussions could be heard in several languages, and the feeling was that systematic research of the kind that an academic lab promotes would be difficult to achieve.

Goldstein's teaching turned out to be highly personal. Being his student meant being his shadow, going with him everywhere, being with him as he spoke to patients, discussing the notes he wrote about them. The experience must have been similar, I think, to that of the apprentices of old, where the master conveyed his techniques indirectly, by example. For Goldstein, a patient's mental distress was to be taken seriously and diminished as far as possible. He lived the frustrations of his handicapped patients. In 1918, he had written about his work with the brain-injured as being governed by the need to help the patient regain a place in the world of normal affairs. His specific interest was to discover what a patient could do and to find work for him in that field. This availability, and his capacity to listen to what the patient was trying to say, was in sharp contrast to the inevitable hard-boiled atmosphere of a busy metropolitan hospital for chronic disease. As I followed Goldstein on his rounds, I saw how patients appreciated him, but picked up the unmistakable antagonism evidenced by interns and residents at his personal and leisurely interest in patients as people.

The first impact of the medical world is disturbing—it evokes strong emotions, and these feelings must be lived through if one is to survive and contribute. This is nothing new; every medical student, sooner or later, to some degree is in danger of being overwhelmed and has to put up protective barriers. My letters epitomize my first feelings: "I cannot become callous to the suffering I am seeing, and I am frightened by the frightfulness of the cancer ward and the autopsies. I feel like King Edward—I want to abdicate and crawl away somewhere and hide." (Edward VIII had abdicated in 1936.)

While working with an individual patient, Goldstein taught several important ideas. From his actual demonstrations on the wards, it was possible to pick up some of the basic theoretical concepts to be found in his writings—for instance, the danger of trying to superimpose a theoretical point of view on a patient's performance, thereby blunting or distorting accurate observations.

Sometimes Goldstein would point out the importance of wrong answers, of failures in test situations, and how these wrong answers give clues to the individual's understanding of the total situation. A wrong answer was more important in understanding a defect than the correct one. My Gestalt training made me temperamentally akin to all of this, and my own interest in wrong answers was endorsed at that point. Throughout my professional life, particularly in the Wechsler Comprehension and Similarities test, I have used wrong answers as if they were projective material, that is, as revelations of special pressing needs, strong enough to override logic.

My own experimental work dealt with the study of the difference between normal and brain-injured patients in perceptual achievement with ambiguous figures (Harrower, 1936, 1939). I had modified the Rubin Profile-Vase figure to have a series of figures in which both the profile and the vase were made more and more explicit. Soon I found significant differences in the two populations. Patients were often unable to make anything out of the completely ambiguous figure. They would also show marked perseveration of the first response, despite the increased articulation of the alternate part of the field—that is, seeing the profiles rather than the vase to begin with, the patient would continue to see them despite additions to make the vase more visible, and vice versa.

Patients tended to introduce concrete familiar objects belonging to their own immediate experience. For example, a farmer called the vase area a "mound of hay." This was an excellent example of the loss of the abstract attitude, the most general characteristic that Goldstein found among the brain-injured, and thus confirmed and reinforced this theoretical point of view.

Around this time, I wrote to Koffka,

Goldstein now wants everything dropped so that I should go ahead with my figure-ground experiments. He thinks of course, that the more articulated figure will be seen regardless of all other factors. I like him tremendously; he has a kindness and humanity which is like manna from heaven in this impersonal place. I understand him intuitively; partly through my training and partly from temperament. He told me himself that I must be like him because I can get things done so quickly.

A little later, I wrote,

Goldstein called me out this afternoon to discuss my figure-ground article. He was much excited by its possibilities, but finds too little attention is paid to the patient's attitude (quite true, but this is a complete problem in itself). Anyway, I am to work on it now, getting any material I want. We had several good ideas about it together; possibly making three-dimensional figures with depth between the profile and the vase in an attempt to see if the nearer or more palpable one is chosen by the patient. Goldstein feels the brain damaged patients have both less "fluctuation," as he calls it, the capacity to alternate their perceptions, and also the opposite—more fluctuations, so that the whole experience becomes unstable.

A vital component of adjustment to the medical framework was understanding the technical language of the "foreign" environment. Listening to Goldstein talk gave me a familiarity with new concepts and ideas.

Part of the bargain of working with Goldstein was to correct his English in his lectures at the New School, and to revise the translation of his book, *The Organism* (Goldstein, 1939). By and large, Goldstein did very well with the English language, but he frequently used one word that constantly baffled his audience. It sounded like this: ree-al-mee. Finally, I got him to pronounce it properly with the following jingle: With good Kurt Goldstein at the helm, there will be peace throughout our realm.

It was during the months with Goldstein that I became acquainted with the Rorschach test, a procedure that was to occupy me actively from then to the present day. Bruno Klopfer, who along with Samuel Beck became the undisputed authority of these years, paid weekly visits to Goldstein's lab. I was immediately struck by the research and clinical possibilities of the method, but I certainly did not know to what extent I would be using it, speaking about it, teaching it, researching it, and enjoying it in the years to come!

The transition to Montreal at the end of three months did not go as smoothly as had been planned on the Rockefeller schedule. Goldstein wanted me to stay longer. His team—of which I was, of course a member—had been spending one day a week on Welfare Island, where rich material of neurological interest was to be found. In December, new cases of alexia and of aphasia of various forms had arrived. In addition, Goldstein offered me a paid job revising the translation of his book, a task I had already been doing in odd moments.

Penfield and Goldstein met to discuss my future program. Penfield felt that only I could be the judge, and should stay on if I was getting what I wanted. However, he was due to leave on an extended speaking engagement in the spring and wanted personally to initiate me into the work that he was most interested in, what he described as "changes in consciousness." This would involve collaboration in his studies of stimulation of the cortex during a new operative procedure for focal epilepsy. I had strong conflicting loyalties, for I was indeed getting much from Goldstein, but I accepted the need to uproot again in light of my total program.

If I were to generalize now, from the perspective of many years, what an initiation period involves, it would be epitomized somewhat like this: It is important to develop protection from overinvolvement emotionally, yet to retain a basic sensitivity to the patient's needs as a person. One must become accustomed to a new language and new concepts, so that as far as possible the household words of the "foreign environment" become one's own. One must acquire enough perspective to be able to use and adapt one's own professional expertise in the new field. For a psychologist, this means the confidence to devise and use appropriate experimental situations. Trivia must be coped with, so that they do not consume unnecessary energy. One must recognize one's own personal style, give it its due, and accept it. Feeling comfortable with oneself evokes comfort in the patient.

Wilder Penfield and the Montreal Neurological Institute

My first months in Montreal provided a second period of initiation, at least as valuable but sharply contrasting in many ways with the previous months with Goldstein.

Nothing could have been more startling than the difference in atmosphere between the Montefiore Hospital and the Montreal Neurological Institute, for the whole staff at the institute was unified, dedicated, and untiring. One was immediately caught up in an *esprit de corps* the like of which I have never again encountered. Goldstein had shared his daily routine and his ideas at every stage with me, but Penfield was far too busy to pay attention to any individual; as one of his initial letters to me had stated, "It's no use your coming here unless you can be original. This is no place where you can ever be told what to do." In this atmosphere I thrived.

Penfield's attitude toward the doctor-patient relationship was also clearly stated in the first interview I had with him: "The patient does the suffering." That is, a psychologist or research worker should not be weakened by taking into account the subjective experiences of the patient being studied. One might say of this contrast to Goldstein's teaching that Goldstein was a physician with a scientist's interests, Penfield a scientist, concerned for but not empathetic with the patient.

My tasks at the Montreal Neurological Institute were varied and flexible, since there were as yet no established duties for a psychologist. My first and most vivid memories are of being closeted under a tentlike structure of sterile green drapes to work with a conscious patient while the surgeon stimulated the exposed cortex, which appeared through an aperture in the drapes. These patients, who suffered from epileptic attacks, were undergoing an operation for the removal of suspected pathological tissue, hypothesized at that time to be responsible for the attacks.

Different parts of the cortex were stimulated to see if the exact area could be found that would trigger an attack. If such an attack was precipitated, this area would be surgically removed.

What Penfield needed at this stage was a psychologist to observe what actually went on in the patient's experience while this artificial excitation of the brain took place. I had to improvise and ask questions that would elicit answers most helpful to the surgeon.

If a patient was describing an experience (evoked as if from nowhere by the external electrical stimulant), I had to ask questions that would enable the patient to contrast this highly unusual immediate experience with comparable experiences from everyday life. If, for example, the patient said that she was hearing the voices of children, I would ask, "Are they your children? Are they saying anything they've said before? Is an old experience happening again, or is it something new?" Theoretical questions of the storage of memory traces were involved here.

Although this was a unique opportunity, it was not an easy task, and in the early days was almost as much of a strain on the psychologist as on the patient! Valuable research material, however, was also derived from pre- and postoperative personality assessments of these epileptic patients.

At that time, there was controversy over the legitimacy of the concept of the "epileptic personality." Some Rorschach workers claimed to have demonstrated a recognizable test entity to support the clinical position. My studies showed exactly the opposite, namely that people with focal seizures, resulting from scar tissue, reflected a wide variety of personality patterns, with a scatter identical to unselected "normals" (Harrower, 1941a, 1941b). Moreover, the ego strengths evidenced in some of the Rorschach records could be shown to be related to the way in which the patient coped with problems arising from the seizures. Psychological tests also proved useful for counseling as well as diagnostic purposes. When the test findings were shared with the patients they were able to utilize their psychological assets and understand some of their own difficulties. Psychology was demonstrating its uses in ways that were relevant to the day-to-day problems of a patient at the institute.

Other activities included long-term follow-ups of aphasic patients, charting their recovery week by week in terms of increased understanding and better use of language. I also participated in experiments designed to detect malingerers and hysterically blind individuals by using an apparatus that reversed the visual field. One minor triumph was my detection of one previously unrecognized color-blind eye, in this particular case ruling out the suspected malingering.

As personality tests proved increasingly meaningful, I was assigned to examine all incoming patients suspected of tumor, with retesting 14 days postoperatively. I thereby acquired over the years, some hundred documented cases of what became known as the "organic personality."

There was very little understanding at the institute in those days of the genuine suffering of a psychologically disturbed patient. Anxiety was seen as a failure in the school of the stiff upper lip. Emotions were for controlling. It was as if the institute collectively breathed a sigh of relief when an organic condition was found in what had first been diagnosed as a psychogenic problem. Thus, a technique like the Rorschach, which could show a demonstrable pattern reflecting the psychological counterpart of cerebral pathology, was very favorably looked on. When the Rorschach began to show this picture consistently in cases that were silent clinically and neurologically, this fact became worthy of note. I will never forget the occasion when the tests showed this cerebral pathology pattern in a patient diagnosed as psychotic. An exploratory operation revealed a large frontal lobe tumor. Penfield announced this achievement at ward rounds. I must have blushed scarlet, for one of the interns whispered, "Can you turn any other color?"

As I said before, one saw very little of "the Chief," but he conscientiously read and discussed by letter any psychological article that was to appear as from the institute. For instance, he was interested in literary style: "The first paragraph is the best opportunity in a chapter to reach the reader. It should be a decoy, a stimulus, a surprise, and a literary masterpiece! Like a sonnet and written at a time of inspiration, of which you have had your share."

Penfield would attend presentations of cases where the psychological results were presented, and often left before the discussion, stating in one letter, "I tried to call you last night. I hope the dicussion went off well. Your presentation was excellent. I deserted by intention hoping for some initiative from the others in that way."

The most remarkable characteristic of these discussions by letter was his ability to admit when his original point of view had been wrong. He had placed great faith in standard IQ tests to show changes after his removal of tumors. When the IQ showed no change, he was at first loath to admit that other tests, for example the Rorschach, could show a difference in the patient's mental and emotional status; but once convinced he would urge the publication of findings even if they refuted his original stand.

Penfield's final and genuine enthusiasm for psychodiagnostic evaluation at the institute led to his strongly endorsing my application for a research grant from the Canadian National Research Council to develop what has become known as the Group Rorschach. This version of the Rorschach technique was first used as a screening process in the Canadian recruiting system in 1939, before it became known in the United States. Standardizing this procedure and supervising its use in many research projects was particularly satisfying to me because of my need to unify the experimental and the clinical approach (Harrower, 1944).

How fared the only woman and the only nonmedical research Fellow? Very well indeed at the institute; but the question of a woman psychologist eating in the doctors' dining room, which had greeted me at the Montefiore Hospital, had its counterpart at McGill University. The authorities at McGill refused to allow any woman faculty member to set foot inside the Faculty Club. Shortly after my arrival, I found that this rule had been modified and that three of us women had "passed" some standard set by a censorship committee.

However, when we did set foot inside the hallowed portals, this notice awaited us: "Ladies are asked to pass as quickly as possible to the quarters allotted to them, and under no circumstances to linger on the stairs or in the hallways."

Somehow the words "to linger" aroused me, and I succumbed to an impulse to mount the famous stairway and, lingering, drop a handkerchief into the hallway below.

It will have become clear from these illustrations of the status of women in the late 1930s that I had been caught in the prevalent pattern of women as second-class citizens. Yet I do not feel that I as a person was in any way handicapped in anything that concerned my major objective—namely, to bring psychological understanding to areas where it did not exist. My various mentors responded to clearly expressed requirements if it was within their power. Perhaps at some point in my hard-to-describe-or-formulate career, it may even have been helpful to be a woman rather than part of the larger masculine gestalt.

Transitions, Decisions, and the Analytic Experience

The years in Montreal were productive and personally satisfying. Some time after my arrival I married Theodore ("Erick") Erickson, a neurosurgeon at the institute. Our married life was greatly enriched by our close camaraderie with the other married Fellows on the hospital staff. Weekend skiing was the order of the day, and we spent many weekends enjoying Canada's national sport. There was a built-in friendship between Fellows at the institute; our common dedication was a strong bond. To be a Fellow was indeed to belong to a very special group.

Professionally, there were constant challenges. My department had enlarged to include other psychologists. An internist, Dr. Donald Ross, was appointed to the department with the special responsibility of bridging the gap between psychology and medicine, something I had always longed for.

Canada's entry into World War II in 1939 had provided an opportunity for me to envisage, develop, and standardize the Group Rorschach, which was then used as a screening procedure in recruiting centers (Harrower, 1943a, 1943b, 1944). This opportunity bore fruit later, and has been important at various stages in my career.

It was with great reluctance, therefore, that I had to leave the institute after four years when my husband was appointed as neurosurgeon at the University of Wisconsin in Madison—where, alas, the nepotism ruling prohibited husband and wife from both being associated with the university. "Sorry, no academic position for wives."

There followed many months of frustration and isolation. Luckily, when the United States entered World War II, I was financed by the Josiah Macy, Jr. Foundation to respond to invitations to work with the Rorschach in the armed forces, an assignment that led to official appointments later as consultant to both the U.S. Army and the U.S. Air Force.

These years were a difficult period in my life, a time of basic issues to be faced. My confrontation with these issues led me to leave Madison, move to New York City, and undertake a personal analysis. Erick and I were divorced the following year.

Few experiences really provide new vistas, but analysis did just that. In my personal life and in my psychodiagnostic and therapeutic work I gained a new depth, a genuine new dimension. I have captured some of this experience in a poem that is included later in this section; but first I must be prosaic and concrete.

I have to distinguish between three phases of my analytic experience. To begin with, I had a few vitally important emergency sessions while I was caught in the turmoil of indecision surrounding my divorce.

The conditions under which a person enters any form of therapy are of great importance. There must be a feeling of need. By that I mean the individual must be vulnerable and admit that vulnerability. When I entered therapy, I was unhappy. Even more appropriate, I, who had not known there was such a thing as fear, was experiencing acute anxiety. I could not predict when a massive apprehensiveness would overwhelm me. I was not able to make basic choices. I was indeed ripe for treatment.

These initial "emergency" sessions also contained a very positive experience. I was able to respond quickly, able to face insights and to leap forward. I dealt with my inability to move from the pseudosecurity of my home—to leave Madison—and gathered a more honest understanding of my role in the situation. Once the hidden aspects of the problem had been forced into the open, I developed the single-mindedness necessary to make the move. I was free of anxiety.

After the finality of the divorce, a new phase of my life began. I was accepted by an anaylst, Dr. Alvan Barach,[3] for a regular program of three sessions a week for over a year. Toward the end of this phase I passed over into what was considered a period of training for my own therapeutic work, for it had come to me by that time that I intended to work as a therapist as well as a diagnostician in my practice.

The residue of my analytic experiences enabled me to proceed with confidence and excitement into my new life in New York City as a clinical psychologist in private practice, at that time a new professional entity.

I am sometimes asked if I changed much during analysis. That is a hard question to answer, and probably better observed from the outside. I had the feeling, rather, of being *restored* to a more appropriate self, not of changing. My recollections are more in terms of sudden insights, rather than of behaving or acting differently. I saw, for instance, how I had for years interpreted my father's silences as disapproval of me, rather than as the result of his own shyness. I saw how this belief had become ingrained and was an inhibitory influence on my spontaneity, particularly in professional meetings, where I would hold back from speaking. I suspected condemnation, unless overtly reassured. Gradually I came to see situations for what they actually were.

My training sessions were an opportunity to discover how I could with ease and enjoyment relate to the people who came to me for help. I saw that I could never learn rules that were to be played out correctly on a therapeutic chessboard. My strength lay in trusting my natural reactions. When I had reached a point of solidarity and

---

[3]Alvan Barach (1895–1977) was in respiratory therapy and was the developer of the first practical oxygen tent. Described by colleagues as "the father of oxygen therapy," Dr. Barach wrote four books on his specialty, more than three hundred articles for professional journals, and a novel, *The Spectacle of a Man.* Psychoanalytically trained, he took a few individuals for personal analysis and therapeutic training.

belief in my own ways of working, and could defend them, my analyst gradually disclosed his own ideas, which were remarkably similar.

Dreams had been very important in my own analysis. I have often used them as the core of my work with patients. I find that dreams can be an advance guard, sounding out the undiscovered territory before any idea of tackling a problem has consciously come to light. I am still amazed at how dreams lead the way, step by step, until the major areas that must be faced have been handled.

My experience in group therapy, and eventually in leading therapy groups, occurred much later. It belonged to those years in New York City when I was in private practice, had become established in the therapeutic field, and was much freer to further my own professional interests.

I had been invited to co-lead a group session with a well-known group therapist. However, in keeping with my belief in experiencing the totality of any new professional undertaking, I decided first to become a regular member of a patient group composed of men and women of different ages and occupations confronting many different problems. I have rarely enjoyed a professional challenge more.

There are some things that individual therapy simply cannot achieve, particularly getting insight into how one looks to others. How one comes across or is envisaged in the different psychological worlds of the group members can be a shock. The unexpectedness and novelty of the experience delighted me as a professional person and evoked again all the naive reactions necessary for being ejected into a new orbit of feelings.

A group is always warned by the therapist of the arrival of a new member, but no details are given; speculation is rife and preferences about the kind of new member hoped for are discussed. As I entered a room full of sharp-eyed strangers, I was greeted by the youngest member with the cry, "Oh, no, not another *mother*!"

But a very special relationship is set up among members of a therapy group who work together for some time. The therapeutic skills of patients (with no professional connections with the mental health field) develop a fine edge. I remember more penetratingly accurate remarks coming from the group members themselves than from the therapist; for by design, where possible, the thrust must come from within the group itself.

Achieving a comfortable position as one shuttles between accepting help, as the needy person, and giving support to another is one of the intangible bonuses that one carries out of the group experience into everyday life. Learning to give and to receive with equal grace is not always easy.

I include here the poem mentioned earlier. It was written for, and then recited at, my final analytic session. One of my hampering experiences had been a hesitation to speak in public. Thus the task I had set for myself was to recite this poem—without notes, of course—as a tribute to my analyst. This need to overcome unnecessary hesitation had so occupied me that I gave no thought to the fact that I had written good poetry, and I was startled to be told it was a very moving poem. This poem is also of interest, I think, in that it bridges the gap between personal and professional needs. I was not only in analysis to gain insights into my own life and behaviour; I was also a psychologist in training to become an analytically oriented therapist.

Last Hour

I awoke this morning
Having recaptured in sleep
The fragment of a prayer:
Said, conscientiously, as a child
Day by day
But long since forgotten, shelved, in disuse.
For the God of childhood
No longer demands of me
That I punch a prayerful time-clock
In order to register attendance
As a worshiper of love and beauty.

And the fragment runs:

That we may show forth praise
Not only with our lips

But in our lives;
By giving up ourselves to service

And by walking in holiness and righteousness
All our days.

"That *we* may show forth praise,"—Who are *we*?
All those who have been privileged to struggle
Toward a fuller understanding,
All those who have been willing to recognize
The devious petty pilferings of parts of the self;
Those parts which competence, control and pride
So neatly cover.

All those who have demanded exposure
Of the falsehoods within,
Those falsehoods justified by reason and logic
And condoned by communal complacence.
We would show forth praise.

Praise? Yes, praise is important
For praise is jubilant and exultant.
Praise is energy cleanly channeled
With nothing lost from leakage or clogging.
Praise is carried in the clearest notes of the horn,
In the inspired and economic movements of the dance.
In the most exalted moments of love.
We would show forth *praise*.

Not only with our lips

But in our lives

How, with my lips,
Can I recapture—recapitulate—
All that has grown within me?
Hard, now, even to believe
That glimpse of an abyss—which brought me here.
Those moments when the ground was no longer solid,
Where hesitancy and doubt, like double images,
Confused the simplest choice or action.

Where fear had no focus,
And by this very feature
Turned to terror.
And from there?
To Hours when the couch appeared
As an exposed and isolated island;
No, as a little left-over fragment
In interstellar space
On which telescopes were trained
For scrutiny and censure.
And where silence seemed
A vast, impenetrable, secret, timeless condemnation.

And from there?
To Hours of establishing a new perspective.
Back on the sunny earth,
Warm and tangible.
Hours of disentangling the present from the past,
The genuine from the counterfeit,
The life-giving from the life-destroying,
The facilitating from the hampering.

Hours when the distance between couch and chair
Was no longer measured in terms of light-years, miles, yards, feet,
For suddenly there was no longer emptiness and distance
There was communication in the very act of thinking.

And from there?

To Hours which passed as the sweep of the second hand
Across the face of the clock.
So crowded, so crammed, so chaotic the press of ideas
Which jostled each other for the chance of exposure
To objective scrutiny.
Hours when the pieces of an emotional puzzle
Lay all assembled, but in disarray
Awaiting deft handling

To give them meaning and coherence.

And from there?

To Hours of acute longing
To be held only in a reassuring presence;
As by strong arms in night sickness.
To Hours of willingly accepted blindness
That one might know what it means to be led.
To Hours of dependency
That one might know what it means to trust implicitly,
To Hours of relinquishing even one's own identity
That one might know what it means to believe.

Not only with our lips
But in our lives

These Hours are part of life, ingrained in me—
Only their shadows do my lips recapture.

By giving up ourselves to service

By giving up?
Yes, but not with resignation or with stifled bitterness;
Not in renunciation or from subservience or duty.
Rather with abandon and relaxation,
With concentration on the central values
And disregard of the peripheral.

By walking in holiness and righteousness all our days.

This may belong to an old idiom,
And the words may now be different
But not so the meaning:
To embody a new way of life at all levels,
At all times, and with all persons,
To make use of the linear coordinates
Of relentless honesty and love
In all complex human equations,
That have been learned
In the scrutiny of simpler actions.
To walk forward in faith with those who share
This core of experience—and to extend it to others.
For with this as a new birthright
I become heir to a goodly heritage.

(Harrower, 1969)

Private Practice

The climate of opinion in the post–World War II era was favorable to the fight against mental illness, and in consequence favorable to the emergence of the clinical psychologist. In the first place, psychiatrists' offices were deluged with applications from returning veterans. Internists also, alerted to psychosomatic problems, were seeing physical symptoms in the light of the repercussions of war-triggered emotional stress.

In addition, multidiscipline research was the order of the day; and this rapport between disciplines provided opportunities for psychologists who had been active in the armed services in World War II. Some of these psychologists had formed realistic working relationships with psychiatrists despite the legal battle over therapeutic "turf" that was soon to develop.

The first World Federation of Mental Health conference was planned for 1948; and already, in 1946, the so-called commissions—interdisciplinary groups dealing with specific mental health problems—were in full swing. The commission I worked on at this time dealt with the problems of prisoners of war, including the Nazis (Harrower, 1976a, 1976b).

Radio programs had experts speaking on various mental health topics. There was a movement to dispel the skeleton-in-the-closet orientation to the everyday problems of living. An attempt was made on such programs to make emotional problems seem as "natural" as having a toothache or a headache.

It was within this framework that I was able to open the first full-time practice of psychodiagnostics and consulting, later to include psychotherapy "officially," after the problems of certification had been worked out.

I was in private practice for 22 years, from 1945 to 1966. By private practice I mean that I was my own boss, able to arrange my own time, and varying somewhat each year, giving different proportions of the day to diagnosis, therapy, research, or consultation. I had learned in my own analysis that my optimum pattern of working required as flexible and free a schedule as possible.

There were so many challenges in a diagnostic practice in the early days, it is hard to keep track of them now: selection of a battery of tests that would be reasonable and practical; determining how long an interval to allow myself between testing and getting the report to the therapist; the development of visual aids so that I could share with the therapist as much as possible the major impacts of the test findings; and developing different types of reports, depending on whether the referring physician or psychiatrist was sophisticated analytically or without analytic training.

There were one or two never-to-be-forgotten cases, one quite dramatic and revealing. A former GI, suspected of having a brain tumor, was brought to my office from the New York Neurological Institute. He had an enormously engorged red eye, and his final answer on the Rorschach to card X was "two red is-lands." (Red eye?) Something in his pronunciation alerted me to get free associations. A ghastly story was explosively precipitated. The patient remembered that during the war he had smashed the testicles of a prisoner he had taken, and had for months been haunted by

the nightmare of "two red eyes" glaring up at him. When the psychological significance of his own red eye dawned on him, and with proper treatment, his symptom
disappeared.

At the other extreme, there was an amusing case of a Latin American dictator's
daughter, who while being tested and subsequently treated was accompanied by a
contingent of policemen from her country—flamboyantly dressed gentlemen, like
those in the chorus of a comic opera. These attendants stood by each day, poker-
faced, on the landing outside my office, naturally causing excitement for the small
children from the other apartments on the floor.

Taking stock some time later, I found that between 1945 and 1958 I had done
extensive diagnostic work-ups on over 1600 patients, referred to me from as many as
200 different therapists—but more of this later.

From the therapeutic point of view, private practice allowed me to develop my
belief that projective material in and of itself is a highly significant factor in self-
understanding; and with the development of projective counseling, I was able to
explore and formulate the kind of cases where the sharing of insights from the tests
was appropriate and where not (Harrower, 1956a; Harrower, Vorhaus, Roman, &
Bauman, 1960; Harrower, 1968).

I also developed my own variation of poetry therapy. I used some of my published
poems to show how a poet might cope with a disturbing experience similar to that of
the patient—in this instance, the omnipresence of obsessive thoughts. This poem was
often reassuring to people who feared that they were unique in their struggle.

> There is a vacuum created when the mind
> Will of a sudden cease its arduous tasks.
> Then as an angry mob that no one asks
> To enter, breaks all barriers; or as wind
> Will howl and rush down through a canyon'd street
> As monstrous tidal wave, or thunder's roar
> Will fill the gap that nature does abhor,
> So do my thoughts with wild insistence beat,
> To splinters shattering will's fragile door,
> Breaking the locks of resolution's setting,
> Crumbling the walls built to enforce forgetting,
> Leveling the props that pride has raised before.
> Should my mind rest one minute of the hour
> Tornado-like these thoughts will show their power.
>
> *(Harrower, 1946)*

I worked a lot with couples held in the vise of divorce uncertainty. I used examples
from their test findings to show each of them how some of their major disagreements
were part and parcel of their coherent but divergent personalities. This was not to say
that such divergences meant that the best solution was a separation; rather that their
discords could be better handled if better understood.

It should be added here that the satisfactions of private practice were intimately bound up with a happy, or I should say memorable, second marriage. In the early 1950s, close friends introduced me to Mortimer Lahm, a widower.

Mortimer had developed his own successful business and understood my need to develop my own practice. We each had a busy schedule, but managed to incorporate and dovetail our common interests. We took our yearly vacation in the winter during Mortimer's less busy season, returning each year to the same small Florida town, where we acquired many friends. During the summer, we took long weekends at my cottage on Long Island—good swimming, and we both played golf.

Mortimer's green thumb brought a rose garden miraculously into existence (I had been no gardener); and I, a noncardplayer, even learned bridge to a point where I was able to play duplicate with him. We visited places in Europe we had each previously explored, and my mother welcomed us to her home in Scotland.

While I could extol Mortimer's praises *ad infinitum* myself, I feel that the following discussion of him, from a book by Jo Coudert, gives an objective description.

> There is a man I enormously like and admire and for no reason based on things held in common, since he is a most successful businessman and is decades older than I, but I find it a joy to be with him because he is so exactly himself. He knows so well who he is that he needs no reflection of himself from you and can go to the heart of interesting matters instead of putting out feelers to explore whether you are friend or foe and whether you are accepting his image of himself or are about to threaten it. I doubt that he even makes the assumption that you will like him because, if he thought about it at all, he would consider this your decision, not his. He is himself, for you to accept or reject as you wish. And because he needs nothing from you in the vein of tacit indications that he is a fine and likable fellow, he totally allows you to be yourself. Not doubting that he is a person, he does not doubt that you are, which means that, although he is a complicated man, his relationships are not; they are easy, varied, and deep.
>
> (Coudert, 1965)

To return to private practice: one of its greatest advantages lay in my being available for part-time jobs and special consulting positions. I have chosen several examples, differing in professional problems and in the length of time required to complete them.

Army

Consultation for the United States Army was mostly a teaching assignment, and a very excellent and interesting one. During the summers of 1947 through 1949, the surgeon general's office sent a team of specialists to teach the heads of various army hospitals a psychosomatic, psychiatric, and psychological approach to medical problems. Three headquarters where chosen—Letterman Hospital in San Francisco, Fitzsimmons in Denver, Colorado, and Walter Reed near Washington, D.C. My team was headed by psychiatrist and analyst Dr. Lawrence Kubie, and was composed of four other psychoanalytically oriented psychiatrists, an internist, a psychiatric social worker, and myself. Each of us lectured everyday, so the program was a tight and concentrated one. The most valuable aspect for me was the fact that so much of the work was practical. By this I mean that I gave a battery of tests to the patient under consideration that day, who had also been assessed by a psychiatrist and an internist.

Thus I learned to administer and evaluate tests fast, to be willing to forgo traditional scoring, to orient my answers to the immediate questions that our group of students asked, to disregard unnecessary items in a test battery in any given case, and to correlate my findings with those of my medical colleagues on the team.

Through listening with the "third ear" to the kind of questions that physicians asked when they were genuinely perplexed at some aspects of the projective tests, I was able to write *Appraising Personality* (Harrower, 1952), which is a dialogue between a psychologist and a physician. I based the questions asked by the hypothetical physician in this book on actual class discussions. After 40 years, I am still in touch with some of those physicians, who have never relinquished their active interest in the psychological approach.

Air Force

By contrast to the relative uniformity of the consulting jobs in the army, consulting with the U.S. Air Force was a series of usually unexpected, differing assignments. One of the most challenging was the request to come up with a projective technique, or some psychological device, that would indicate when a hospitalized pilot or navigator, temporarily sidelined because of intense fatigue and severe anxiety, was ready to return to duty.

To be more specific, I was assigned to Colonel Roy Grinker at Don Cesar Hospital in Florida, and under considerable stress myself, produced the Stress Tolerance Test (Harrower & Grinker, 1946).

My aim was to see to what extent potentially disturbing pictures,[4] depicting devastating war incidents, would still precipitate anxiety in pilots who were receiving psychotherapy in the hospital—or, to put it another way, to what extent the individual had been able to *depersonalize* his experiences, so that he could comment on the pictures per se, rather than relating to the nightmare of his personal involvement.

Here are some examples of the kind of answers given by patients still overpowered by their experiences:

Failure or refusal to reply
Personalization: "My copilot dead . . . civilians we killed"
Evasion through cynicism: "Touching scene, ha ha"

---

[4] The pictures were by the great artist Thomas Hart Benton. We had permission to make slides from them.

Response in terms of tiny details only: a hand (body disregarded); a spot (on the slide)

Univerbal responses: "Pity, death, nightmare, war"

Expression of feeling: "Grief and anguish; it's happening too much"

Synesthesia; sight gives rise to experience of sound or heat: "Roar of the engines; heat"

The diagnostic value of this test was indisputable. We were able to predict and screen out for further treatment those pilots and navigators who were not ready to return to duty. Therapists were able to endorse our findings in short order.

But in one way even more interesting was the general question of the relationship of acute anxiety to perceptual distortion. The test showed that the capacity for objective assessment broke down; powerful inner needs took over; distortions occurred. This was particularly clear in the personalization of answers. The slides became representations of actual experiences, or the slides became the vehicle onto which overwhelming feelings of guilt were projected: "The civilians I killed"; "My brothers dying"; "Havoc from the bombs I dropped."

In the same way, answers such as "heat," "saltwater taste," "sickish feeling," "noise of explosion," "roar of engines" showed the breakdown of even basic sensory modalities. What was seen evoked sound, taste, heat in the place of a visual response.

The closeness of diagnostic procedures and their therapeutic value was shown in this instance by the fact that patients discovered spontaneously that they could lessen their own anxieties by exposing themselves repeatedly to the Benton pictures. Pilots who had already taken the test would ask permission to sit in again and simply be exposed to the slides as new groups were tested (Harrower & Grinker, 1946).

Another assignment for the air force related to the mental condition of Gary Powers, the U-2 pilot shot down in 1961 and held prisoner by the Soviets. The question at headquarters was whether Powers was being kept drugged while in captivity. This was important, since the State Department's method of handling the case would differ depending on the answer. The only materials available to the air force were handwritten, censored letters from Powers to his wife. I was asked whether graphology could give any answers.

I am not a trained graphologist, but have always had the greatest respect for the technique in the hands of experts. So I set up a hypothetical experimental situation, supposed to be part of a study I was making at that time on medical students at the University of Texas. Many of my colleagues knew of this study, and graphologists had already shown interest in making independent assessments of handwriting to be compared with the findings of my full battery of tests. I therefore asked three outstanding graphologists, Dr. Meta Steiner, Dr. Klara G. Roman, and Dr. Frank Victor, to reply to a question concerning "Student X." I asked them to select from a list of possibilities the one that would be apt to account for his failure in his medical studies. This list included, among other things: that his intelligence score fell short of that required; that he had personal problems in regard to authority; that he was taking drugs; that he lacked motivation; or that he was depressed.

All three experts felt that depression was the major reason for the failure. All other alternatives were categorically ruled out. It was later discovered that no drugs had been administered to Gary Powers. Thus this unusual "experiment" provided a satisfactory answer; no charges were made against the Soviets.

Consulting with the State Department

This assignment is of interest because it came about through Mrs. Eleanor Roosevelt's growing interest in a psychological approach to international problems. She became convinced that psychology and psychiatry should play a part in the United Nations and in training those who are concerned with the fate of nations. She discussed her idea with Dr. Frank Fremont-Smith, then head of the Josiah Macy, Jr. Foundation. It was arranged that a small team—two psychiatrists, an anthropologist, and myself—would give a series of lectures in our respective fields. We were to lecture to career diplomats, many of whose names I have since seen as ambassadors to various countries.

In the discussions that followed our lectures, we attempted to orient ourselves to the kind of problems the State Department faced with its personnel. We were told that one of our number would be selected as a consultant, and surprisingly, psychology is not *always* at the bottom of the totem pole, nor are women always discriminated against, for I was the one selected. I continued as a consultant after our lectures had been given.

One of my duties was to sit in as a nonvoting observer at interviews of aspiring young men and women who wanted to go into the consular service. Seven distinguished members of the State Department would run through routine questioning of these applicants. Then, by a sort of sixth sense, often totally disregarding the answers to the questions, they would come up with their choice that Mr. So-and-so would, or would not, be an appropriate individual to be in charge of a consulate abroad.

My task was to make more explicit the reasons for their choices, so that some kind of rationale could be developed and passed on to subsequent examiners. What concerned me most, however, was that the questions were identical for men and women, thus frequently missing much that women had to offer within the consular framework, and on many occasions forcing women candidates into an artificially competitive role with the male applicants. I felt, on the whole, that less appropriate candidates were often chosen.

Another task was to handle personal crises in the State Department staff that in other organizations would have been dealt with by a personnel department— complaints of unfair treatment, lack of promised promotion, and so on. A third responsibility was to be available for personal problems arising among those in the upper echelon, the senior members of the department. My job was different from comparable consultations that I had in big business. First, one had to break down an atmosphere of studied secrecy that, in the abstract, made any idea of discussing personal problems unthinkable. Although I enjoyed my trips to Washington, and although the task was interesting while it lasted, I do not feel that psychology left a permanent mark on the procedures and thinking in the Department of State!

Children's Court

I spent four years (1952 through 1955) as research director, on a part-time basis, in the Children's Court of Manhattan. This experience allowed me to try out some new procedures, some new variations or adaptations of the projective techniques.

The court project, so-called, was a study financed by the Field Foundation, of 200 first offenders. Our team, approximately 12 in number, was made up of psychiatrists, psychologists, and social workers. One adaptation of established procedure that I thought necessary, and that subsequently proved useful in other experimental projects, was to get probation officers and judges to list the questions they actually wished to be answered by a psychological evaluation.

When I arrived, a backlog of incomplete cases from the past six months bore witness to the fact that psychologists, even competent ones, found the writing of reports a time-consuming affair. Yet, when all was said and done, what the judge wanted to know were very concrete things, such as, Is this child psychotic? Yes or no. Is he dangerously aggressive? Is he unduly anxious? Is he intellectually retarded? Does he have any specific intellectual potential? As we trained ourselves to draw up a list of such questions and to answer them briefly in our evaluation, the backlog of cases began to diminish (Harrower, 1955).

One thing that was beginning to impress me in the use of the projective tests was the fact that one cannot get the most out of any person's test dossier without reference to the test findings of the mate, the sibling, the gang, or the close companions. Our diagnostic studies in court began to be centered on gangs and were oriented toward utilizing the healthy potential of the individual members. We wanted to discover which member was the active gang leader, and we attempted to assess his relationship to the others. We found similar structures in many gangs: an intellectual leader, an active leader, and various passive yes-men. We set up therapeutic situations in which the various leaders could lead in a constructive direction.

The idea of interrelating test findings has permeated my work with married couples, with small groups, and with whole families; and it is closely allied to the interaction testing developed by Roman and Bauman and to the consensus Rorschach as reported in 1960 (Harrower, Vorhaus, Roman, & Bauman, 1960).

Consultant to the National Multiple Sclerosis Society

In 1949 I was asked by the National Multiple Sclerosis Society to visit a number of multiple sclerotic patients in south Florida, where, it was thought, a large enough population might be found willing to participate in a psychologically oriented interview. With no special format in mind for a systematic interview, I followed the leads of these patients as they described how their lives had been affected by their illness. These patients allowed me to perceive, to catch a glimpse of, the World According to MS.[5]

---

[5] I have been a member of the Multiple Sclerosis Medical Advisory Board since 1949, and I still respond personally to MS patients who write to me concerning their problems.

The results of these interviews found expression in two manuals—one directed to MS patients themselves, the other to physicians and caregivers. In the booklet directed to patients, *Mental Health and MS* (Harrower, 1953), the emphasis was on general ways to cope: ways to obtain fulfillment of basic needs, and ways to circumvent difficulties inherent in the life situations of MS patients.

In the manual directed to physicians and caregivers, *Psychological Factors in the Care of Patients with Multiple Sclerosis* (Harrower & Herrmann, 1953), I used the experience that I had gained from these interviews in another way. I had found that there were three difficulties in adjustment that seemed to relate specifically to the experienced world of the multiple sclerotic patient as distinct from the handicapped in general.

The first of these has been called the concept of *marginality,* first mentioned by Barker, Wright, and Gonick (1946), which epitomizes the period at the beginning of the MS illness when the patient can neither live in the world of the normal, healthy individual nor find a place as an accepted and recognized invalid.

A second experienced difficulty, again more often seen in MS patients, can be described as feelings of *uncertainty* and intense anxiety that accompany a delayed, tentative, or questionable physical diagnosis.

The third characteristic relates to *loss of control,* whether from bladder incontinence or from inappropriate laughing and crying. These loomed large as experienced difficulties to the patients who were interviewed.

During my years of association with the National Multiple Sclerosis Society, I undertook one large experimental study in which 144 MS patients were compared with controls drawn from patients with polio, tabes, Parkinson's disease, and neurosis. Despite the refinement of current psychological work in this field, the original studies provided some valid comparisons (Harrower & Kraus, 1951).

When I became active in the National Multiple Sclerosis Society, I also began urging the initiation of group therapy sessions, under the direction of an experienced therapist. One of my major problems in the 1950s and 1960s had been to convince the "establishment" of the usefulness of various kinds of psychotherapeutic endeavor. The latest information from the society today, I am glad to say, is that at the present time there are 425 counseling groups led by a professional, and approximately 1000 self-help groups in existence (Nielsen, 1988).

Unitarian Study

The possibility of classifying records of normal subjects on a battery of tests played an important part in a 20-year research and service investigation involving theological students.

In this project, started in 1953, I have collected test records (with seven or eight projectives) on all candidates seeking to enter the Unitarian-Universalist Church as ministers; the total number of subjects is around 1500.

The project has gone through several stages, both in the method of administering the tests and in the writing of the reports. Based on my experiences in the Children's Court of Manhattan, a list of specific questions relating to the most vitally needed information was devised. This list was made in collaboration with Unitarian-Universalist ministers involved in screening the candidates. I was concerned that only questions that could legitimately be answered by a psychodiagnostic battery be included; and, equally important, that pertinent questions from the Unitarian-Universalist point of view be formulated by the church's selection committee.

Over the years, we found that helpful material was elicited by this particular set of questions:

Is this candidate open to others?
Is he preoccupied with self?
Does he relate to both sexes and various ages?
Are there psychological blocks indicated?
To what extent do these blocks hinder growth?
What is this candidate's energy level?
What is his intelligence level?
To what degrees are anger and rebelliousness shown?
Does he relate to long-term values?
Is his self-discipline adequate?
How is sensitivity handled?
Is he aware of his sexual identity?
What is his attitude toward authority?
Does he show aberrant behaviour?
Can he sustain close family relationships?
What are his chief areas of vulnerability?
Does he have any patterns of thinking that may make communication with others
 more difficult?
Other comments in light of the above.

Public Speaking

Although public speaking cannot be considered in quite the same way as the consulting assignments, it was a major part of my applied professional activities, particularly in the 1940s and 1950s.

I am looking at a list of titles of 128 lectures that I gave during that period to academic institutions, learned societies, multidisciplinary groups, Rotarian luncheons, women's clubs, high schools, and PTAs.

These lectures have become part of my attempt to turn over to the Archives of the History of American Psychology relevant material pertaining to the growth of a new profession. A few of these titles, and some sample audiences, are given here:

The application of Clinical Psychological Tests to a Fuller Understanding of
 Somatic Disease (Academy of Medicine)

The Measure of Psychological Factors in Marital Maladjustment (Academy of Sciences)

The Emergence of a New Profession (Custer Institute)

Pre-parole Psychological Examination (Department of Institution and Agencies, Trenton, New Jersey)

The Role of the Clinical Psychologist in Mental Health (Yale University)

Society's Changing Concept of Psychology (Austin, Texas)

Psychiatric and Psychological Concept of Normality

A Psychologist Looks at Literature (Montreal, 1941)

The Inter-relation of Psychology with Psychiatry and Medicine

Psychologists Leave the Ivory Tower (Cornell)

Common Goals in Religion and Psychiatry

Problems of Personality with Reference to the Family (Town and Country Leadership Summer School, University of Wisconsin, 1942)

Problems of Psychology in an Organic Stronghold (Montreal, 1939)

The Psychologist and the Community

Psychology—Its Place in Our Schools

Guiding Children and Youth Towards a Well-Adjusted Life (New York State Parents and Teachers Association)

The Family in Growth and Conflict (Scarsdale High School)

Tensions (Women's Club, Nutley, New Jersey)

A Clinical Psychologist Looks at Brief Therapy (Post Graduate Center, New York City)

The Role of Psychodiagnostics in Psychotherapy

A Clinical Psychologist in Industry (Gulf Oil Company)

Clinical Psychology: Changing Roles and Change in Responsibilities

The Struggle for Certification

In the 1950s I was deeply involved in the problems of certification and licensing. For several years I was chairman of the Joint Council, a group composed of psychologists with varying backgrounds and academic training. When this group dissolved, I spent three years as chairman of the Advisory Council in Psychology to the University of the State of New York Education Department. This council worked closely with the authorities in Albany and collaborated in formulating the official documents with reference to certification. We also appointed the eight examiners whose task it was to decide who was entitled to be certified.

Although one of the most meaningful endorsements hanging on my wall came from the psychologists of New York "In appreciation of her services in securing Legal recognition for the Profession of Psychology," I was never happy in this type of committee work. When the matter was legally settled in 1957, I gave away several file drawers of material pertaining to this undertaking to the widow of one of the board members, who was writing about her husband's activities in the certification field.

The Big Follow-Up

The years of private practice and consultation were fascinating, adventurous, and fulfilling, but the old experimentalist's attitude was beginning to stir and I was becoming increasingly uncomfortable because I felt there was little empirical evidence, based on test findings, to justify some of our pronouncements. To have faith in an instrument, one must use it for many years before it is possible to acquire adequate follow-up material. Now I felt that, having been in practice for 12 years, and having maintained a close connection with the therapists who had referred my patients to me, it was up to me to discover how accurately I had predicted the possibility of a patient improving, or not improving, in various types of therapeutic situations, and what "type" of projective person improved under what conditions.

I was also haunted by the endless emphasis, both psychiatrically and in psychological reports, on the pathological facets of the individual, and I resented the fact that there was no parallel terminology that indicated strengths. I felt that we needed a scale of mental health endowment, just as we have a scale of intellectual endowment. Finally these pressures reached the point where I decided to terminate my practice. I was fortunate enough to get a grant from the Ittelson Foundation to set up a large-scale follow-up study.

I feel that the next few years were perhaps the most rewarding way of working with the projectives. Of 1600 patients to whom I sent questionnaires, it was possible to trace 1463. I was also able to extract from 176 of the 200 therapists (some reluctant, some hesitant, some willing, some eager) reports on a four-point scale as to whether or not the patient had improved (no improvement, slight improvement, moderate improvement, maximum improvement). In addition, I found out what type of therapy the patient had received, and the length of time he or she had been involved in therapy.

While these results were coming in, I attempted to classify, or group together, individuals with "comparable" performance on a total test battery of the projectives. This was a truly challenging task, as so many variables were involved.

It took several years to arrive at and substantiate the concept of "richness" versus "impoverishment," justified by a *uniform* performance on all the projectives on the one hand, and to see the need for a second scale where assets and liabilities were *uneven,* on the other (Harrower, 1970).

Details of this systematic study can be found in *Psychodiagnostic Testing: An Empirical Approach* (Harrower, 1965a). Some of the major findings, however, may be mentioned here. From the returns, it became clear that psychoanalysis, strict classical analysis, was contraindicated for those at the lower end of the scale of *uneven test findings.* Conversely, good mental health potential as reflected in the upper ends of both scales correlated with success in almost all forms of psycho-therapy and analysis, regardless of the length of time the patient was involved in treatment.

"Retirement"

In the fall of 1966, my husband Mortimer's routine physical examination disclosed a potentially serious problem: indications of an aneurysm of the aorta. At that time only Dr. Michael DeBakey in Houston had handled such cases successfully—but his schedule was booked months ahead. It was clear to me that Mortimer's condition and possible operative procedures would require every moment of my time and every ounce of my energy.

When I entered this marriage, I had set up clear priorities. Our life together took precedence over any professional commitment. I had to be completely free from conflicts. I closed my office and resigned from all my part-time positions and obligations.

After five months of illness and several major operations, Mortimer died in March 1967.

I came to Gainesville in 1967 in that mixture of shock and numbness that only those who have lost the mainstay of their life can understand. I was living in a grief-dominated world, performing in what seemed to me an automatic and unnatural way. I was relieved, but somewhat disbelieving, when no one seemed to notice—neither the new friends I was making nor the students in my classes.

I had been invited to come to the University of Florida by Wilse Webb, the head of the Department of Psychology, as a visiting professor, to teach projective material, principally the Rorschach, in any way I chose. For the previous four years, I had been teaching evening classes in the projectives at the New School for Social Research, and my husband had always picked me up after class and taken me to some special restaurant for dinner. The idea of continuing that schedule through the long winter without his protective presence seemed too much to cope with after his death, and I had resigned from the New School.

Gainesville in some way provided a protective presence of its own. After a couple of years the "visiting" aspect of my work was discarded, and for nine years I was able to devote a full half-time to this teaching assignment. I was able to continue and develop my Instruction-Insight Method (see the brief discussion that follows, in the reference to my book, *The Inside Story*), and enjoyed close friendships with many students, friendships that still flourish today.

On reaching the age of 70, I decided to return to full-time writing, research, some private patients, and enjoying the climate of opinion at the university, which was so much to my liking. At that point I became professor emeritus; and, I suppose a chapter on retirement should truly begin.

Since 1976 I have had another 13 years of working full-speed ahead on my own projects, while at the same time keeping close to a host of academic activities. During these years, I have published 3 books, and 14 articles have seen the light of published day.

Kurt Koffka: An Unwitting Self-Portrait (Harrower, 1983) I had wanted to write for many years. It was based on an unusual collection of over two thousand letters that Koffka and I exchanged over a 13-year period. In this book I sought to have Koffka, indirectly and unwittingly, give a picture of himself not necessarily seen in his 700-page *Principles of Gestalt Psychology* (Koffka, 1935), or even in his many lectures. To have successfully used this legacy (both correspondents having kept virtually all letters received) was satisfaction of a rare kind.

The Therapy of Poetry (1972) was another book that called to be written. I had felt when writing my own poems that poetry can provide a strong therapeutic by-product. As I wrote in the introduction to that book,

> Long before there were therapists there were poets, and from time immemorial man has struggled to cope with his inevitable inner turmoil. One way of so coping has been the ballad, the song, the poem. Once crystallized into words, all-engulfing feelings become manageable, and once challenged into explicitness, the burden of the incommunicable becomes less heavy. The very act of creating is a self-sustaining experience, and in the poetic moment the self becomes both the ministering "therapist" and the comforted "patient."
>
> This, in essence, is the burden of my song. This idea has grown with me over the years. It has become more than an idea; it has become a way of living. One can afford to be hurt, one can afford to reach for the stars, if there is a built-in safeguard against crippling depression or disorganizing excitement.
>
> (Harrower, 1972)

In my third book written in retirement, *The Inside Story* (1987), I sought to make available to others the way of teaching projectives that brought with it personal insights as well as the handling of a useful clinical tool. In this I had the interested help of Dawn Bowers, who had experienced the Instruction-Insight Method as a student in one of my classes. As I had written earlier,

> The student should know his own performance in the projectives, so that he will not unconsciously ally himself with patients with similar psychodiagnostic patterns or, conversely, react with undue severity to the producers of test protocols diametrically opposite to his own. The point is rarely emphasized, but this author considers it of prime importance. The psychodiagnostician badly needs to understand his own productions on all the test instruments that he uses. Moreover, he should have the opportunity to go over and discuss a report written on his test production by an experienced and wise psychodiagnostic practitioner. Unless this is done, he will find himself automatically assuming that somehow or other his own productions constitute a base line of normality. He will too readily read pathology into test profiles that are dissimilar to his own and, conversely, will find condoning circumstances where striking similarities pertain.
>
> (Harrower, 1965b)

While I have been happily busy, I do not think of my University of Florida days as a time in which I was pressing myself to perform when I might have been enjoying a more leisurely life. Leisure is well used in Gainesville. Golf on the University of Florida course, daily swimming in my own pool, and several highly challenging faculty seminars in which to listen or to speak are equally opportune. All this time I have gone back to my cottage at the eastern end of Long Island, a cottage loaded with memories of 43 summers, shared with my husband during the years of our marriage and also with my mother, who came over from Scotland with great delight for special visits.

But this chapter was to have been about, and it *is* about "retirement" as I envisage it. For some time I have been battling the concept, which I have found distressingly common in patients, that the loss of the job diminishes the stature of the person. Generally accepted concepts of retirement seem to reinforce this misunderstanding. What has to be emphasized is that the interests in the field that led to job satisfaction are still an integral part of the retiree. Success in a job is the creation of the person, who remains the achiever.

I vowed years ago that I would never be involved in any activity in which some external agent could arbitrarily force me to stop what I was doing, or force me to forgo avid interests and mental aliveness.

Retirement, for my two parents, meant diametrically opposite things. My father retired early—at 60—from business, and became much more himself, turning to painting, music, and the enjoyment of solitude. He was able to disregard the external demands made by the business world. My mother, at 60, started an extraordinary career of free-lance lecturing in art to public school audiences—a career that she did not stop until she was 84. So in different ways my parents used retirement as a time to do what called out insistently to be done, satisfying their own respective inner needs.

Do I have time to sit on the proverbial porch in the rocking chair and take a bird's-eye view of my life? Not much! But perhaps some questions can be answered at leisure if one is in the mood to envisage the passage and patterns of one's life in tranquility.

The following question is perhaps a good one to begin with. By answering it I took part in a study entitled Vigor in Old Age.[6]

How do you, mentally and physically, maintain a high level of vigor, interest, and activity? I am separating my answer to this question into two parts: first, unconscious or spontaneous aspects of my lifestyle evolved without awareness but which, on scrutiny, appear to further optimal functioning, mental and physical; second, what I might call specific strategies that I have developed over the years and that can be recognized as such and adhered to.

A high level of vigor (or energy) must have something to do with inherited physical

---

[6]This study was undertaken by Dr. George Caranasos, the Ruth S. Jewett Professor of Medicine in Geriatrics at the University of Florida.

stamina. It may also relate to basic training and the rigorous physical demands of British public school life (ages 10 to 18).

I have never experienced myself as "energetic." There is a feeling of wellness or illness but energy, per se, does not seem to have a psychological correlate. It is others who tell me that I am energetic, who presumably are making a comparison with their own experiences. I *do* experience, when ill, the lack of normal lifestyle and the *absence* is somehow more of an "entity" than is the familiar, day-by-day living that has no specific name.

I am aware of the need to keep fit. My body *demands* sleep and exercise. I have been conscious of weight but rarely systematically diet. As a teenager I refused the English breakfast, gave up desserts and cakes, and have retained this as part of my diet to this day.

I smoked for a few years in the 1930s, never inhaled, gave it up in the 1940s, and haven't smoked since.

Exercise has been another demand of my body. I have never had to seek it; rather, I have had to be careful that it did not totally monopolize my life. During childhood and adolescence I played cricket all summer, lacrosse all winter, three hours a day demanded by school custom. As an adult, cricket has obviously given way to golf, swimming, and dancing (ballroom and square). I also do creative dancing on rainy days in my house, which can accommodate the space. I don't drag around when I feel sick. My policy, when possible, is to go to bed when I get a fever; and I have grappled with enough colds and flu in my life to have a personal care program to shorten the miseries.

For me, maintaining a high level of interest is easy. I envisage interests as large magnets that pull me toward them and demand to be dealt with or achieved.

These interests may relate to intellectual activities (I refuse to label them as "work") or leisure. The most general concept I can use to describe basic intellectual interest: psyche to soma—psychological experiences paralleling physiological processes. More concretely expressed, my work at the Montreal Neurological Institute on brain damage and loss of functions; years of adapting psychological diagnostic methods to pick up finer changes in behavior and conscious awareness; understanding the patients' psychopathology in therapy in relation to observable clinical symptoms, and so on. My lifestyle could be described as geared to the pursuit of these interests.

Other fundamental satisfactions derive from friends and the achieving of close personal relationships. There is also a great interest in the world of music, my large collection of records and cassettes to which I am constantly adding. I have a compelling and abiding interest in animals and in studying the unique rapport that can be developed with them.

Also in younger days one of my main interests was in acting. Before coming to this country, in addition to many amateur performances, I played a Shakespeare part on a London stage.

Reverting to childhood once again, I remember while very young being struck by the need to do something to bypass some of the disabilities of aging. The words of my French governess *"Si jeunesse savait, si vieillesse pouvait"* (If youth only knew, if age only could) stirred a realization that I must somehow manage always to be able to *"pouvoir."* At this same age, I remember looking at a large picture of Whistler's Mother (the sad-looking lady draped in black), which was used for enormous posters for an insurance company with the ominous words "OLD AGE MUST COME."

Such memories may have given rise to what I am now able to call specific strategies for remaining "myself" as long as possible—that is, a person functioning well and enjoying life.

The pause that refreshes. As soon as things became pressured in my New York practice, combined with lecturing and public speaking in the early 1950s, I wove into my life the pattern of as much empty time as there was stressful time. To use the Coke ad, "the pause that refreshes." I am aware that to be successful in presenting material to students and in public lecturing, which involves answering questions from the audience, I have to be trigger-happy-quick with my reply. My mind refuses to work in a way that satisfies me unless I am rested. It also became clear that the quality of lectures given too close together is adversely affected. I have the same feeling about pleasurable and exciting events: that they must be spaced in order to be reacted to fully and prevented from becoming stressful.

Refusing to let "ought to" or "should not" interfere with more basic rules of living. I seem to have been successful in avoiding situations where the old concepts of "should not" or "ought to" might have overruled the more basic demand of living constructively and with satisfaction. Divorce in the early 1940s was considered horrendous, "not done," but when my health and stability were threatened, I was able to leave my home even without a job to step into.

I have also refused all my life to let money or position influence my choice of work. With my compass set toward freedom and a personal lifestyle, I have had no difficulty in refusing positions that would have restricted my personal life—for example, turning down a deanship and refusing such jobs as the head of a psychology department. I always preferred to stay with minimum fellowship funding, in research positions important to me, rather than to accept positions with status and salary.

Avoiding the draining effect of internal conflict. Perhaps the most basic strategy of living, from my point of view, is to avoid conflict. When I see patients torn apart, unable to decide what they really want, kept in perpetual indecision, I realize how important it has been in my own life to know clearly what I want—perhaps it would be better stated, to *feel* what I want. I seem to be able to be convinced, deep down, of the right road to take. The sharpest conflicts, I think, arise in connection with decisions that involve close personal relationships and professional fulfillment. In this area my close relationships have always been the most important. A major decision of this type comes to mind. Some time ago I was offered the position of head of research in the psychological and psychiatric field at Einstein Medical School in New York. The possibilities of collaboration in areas of my chief interest were enormous. At that time, however, I was about to enter into my second marriage and felt that these two important occurrences, both all-absorbing, could not coexist. I turned down the Einstein offer.

Some Final Thoughts

Our editor, Dr. Walker, has suggested that some additional questions be answered if they supplement material already presented in the chapter. From his list I have selected the following two questions.

What sort of lifestyle did you have as a clinical psychologist? My lifestyle has been no different from what I would have chosen in any other profession. I feel strongly that there should be a minimum of difference between how one behaves professionally and how one behaves personally. I cannot assume a role of any kind. It is one of the most fundamental experiences for me to be myself—whatever that is—at all times. When working with Kurt Goldstein, I discovered that there is no mysterious behavior associated with "working with patients," as I had been warned; and that was a major relief and a personal endorsement.

I needed to have an office physically close to, or in, my home. I achieved that in New York City for over 25 years. I commuted, so to speak, across a landing between two apartments on the same floor. On two other occasions, as soon as I was established professionally, I had an eight-room apartment that combined office and home.

Allowing a personal lifestyle to evolve also demands the capacity to say "no" to attractive offers that might deny essentials of one's own lifestyle. I remember four occasions when I gained much from seeing the whole picture. I was invited to the University of Rochester to be interviewed for a position as dean of women. My name had been suggested by a well-known academic psychologist, and I was assured that the position would include time for research and for teaching perhaps one course. I went to Rochester, and had one of those idyllic weekends, staying at President Valentine's house and finding great rapport with him and his wife. The salary, I remember, was a colossal $6,000 a year—which, compared to my Rockefeller Fellowship of $1,800, was like winning a lottery. I was tempted. But when I returned to the Montreal Neurological Institute and reported my experience to Dr. Penfield, he brought me up short by saying that he considered it astonishing, in view of how hard I had worked to get to the institute, and in view of what I was achieving in my field with him, that I should consider quitting now! This statement startled me, but conveyed the wonderful news that "the Chief" valued my ideas and my execution of them. I realized that my basic idea was what I had hoped it would become—a kind of breakthrough. Of course, I withdrew my name from the Rochester position.

While in private practice in New York City, I was interviewed for the position of president of a small women's college. One of its trustees, whose judgement I valued, had submitted my name. However, this time a "no" response was easy, as my philosophy was at variance with some of the essential points required of a woman president. I realized in the interviews that I could never live in a crystal bowl; the freedom to be completely off-duty was not built into that job. I had begun to realize my need for privacy and aloneness as part of my day.

Without even going for an interview, I turned down the possibility of a job in a rapidly developing department of psychology. The academic life clearly did not allow me the personal timetable that I enjoyed in doing diagnostic therapy and consultations. Teaching part-time I could incorporate, but I would not have been happy with administrative duties and teaching full-time.

My final example was a close shave. In 1946, an important position in the mental health field came into being: that of executive officer, coordinator for the Preparatory Commission of the first conference of the World Federation of Mental Health, which was to be held in 1948. It would have been a job at the international level, extremely well paid, formulating plans, being active in an international preliminary conference with leaders from many countries. But it would have required two years of total dedication. On being offered it, I accepted the job. Luckily, however, I was in analysis at the time, and had an analytic session on the day of my acceptance. As I heard myself describing this acceptance, I realized that I could not dedicate myself unreservedly to this objective. I could not give up my fast-developing four-way program of consulting, diagnosis, therapy, and research. To resign within a few days of accepting the position was a tough experience. But how glad I was to have been able to understand myself well enough to go through with the withdrawal!

It happened that I was later made vice-chairman of the Executive Committee of the International Committee for Mental Health, as well as chairman of the Technical Advisory Committee for the World Federation of Mental Health, which provided me with an opportunity to participate freely in the ten-day conference itself.

By the time the pattern of a flexible work week was becoming clear, I needed space and time to develop new ideas, to develop my own pattern of therapy, and to keep myself available for short-term opportunities as they came along. I realized that to be relaxed and satisfied with my life as a whole was clearly the way for me to contribute professionally.

Are there things you would do differently if you could? I can't think of one thing I would do differently! By far my most difficult times occurred in my first marriage, and during the illness and death of my second husband; but I can't see how I could have behaved differently in becoming involved in either of these close relationships. I certainly knew enough about myself when I married for the second time—knew enough about the relative importance of even a great career in comparison with the deep personal experiences of a good marriage. As I mentioned in my answer to the question on vigor in old age, I was able to give up a major appointment without conflict when embarking on my second marriage; and lack of conflict, I believe, is also a major and necessary factor in living through tragedies in life.

The experience of the decisions accompanying divorce, learning how parting of the ways can be achieved with a minimum of bitterness, was an enormous help to me in my life as a therapist.

> Life, you will lose a lover when I die!
> For whom have you encouraged more; have I
> Not always claimed
> A thousand burning favors from you,
> Proud, untamed and exquisite enchantress?

You say I should not love you, in my face
You have flung hardships, shown me to my place
For my bold daring;
Yet as you spurn me, with the other hand
You cast the colored splendors of the land
For my own keeping; sun and wind and youth
You give me in each kiss. Ah! Life, in truth
You will have lost a lover when I die . . .
But while I live, leave me this ecstasy.

(Harrower, 1946)

References

Barker, R. G., Wright, B. A., & Gonick, M. R. (1946). Adjustment to physical handicap and illness: A survey of the social psychology of physique and disability. *Bulletin No. 55,* New York Social Science Research Council.

Coudert, J. (1965). *Advice from a failure.* New York: Stein & Day.

Dennis, N. (1957). Treasury of eccentrics. *Life,* December 2.

Goldstein, K. (1939). *The organism: A holistic approach to biology derived from pathological data in man.* New York: American Book Company.

Harrower, M. (1929). *Plain Jane: A book of children's poems.* New York: Coward McCann.

Harrower, M. (1932). Organization and higher mental processes. *Psychologische Forschung, 17,* 56–120.

Harrower, M. (1936). Some factors determining figure-ground articulation. *British Journal of Psychology, 26,* 107–124.

Harrower, M. (1939). Changes in figure-ground perception in patients with cortical lesions. *British Journal of Psychology, 30,* 47–51.

Harrower, M. (1941a). Personality studies in cases of focal epilepsy. *Bulletin of Canadian Psychological Association, 19-21.*

Harrower, M. (1941b). Personality changes accompanying organic brain lesions, III. A study of pre-adolescent children. *Journal of Genetic Psychology, 58,* 391–405.

Harrower, M. (1943a). Directions for administration of the Rorschach group test. *Journal of Genetic Psychology, 62,* 105–117.

Harrower, M. (1943b). Large scale investigation with the Rorschach method. *Journal of Consulting Psychology, 7,* 120–126.

Harrower, M. (1944). *Large scale Rorschach techniques.* Springfield, IL: Charles C Thomas.

Harrower, M. (1946). *Time to squander, time to reap.* New Bedford, MA: Reynolds Publishing.

Harrower, M. (1952). *Appraising personality.* New York: W. W. Norton.

Harrower, M. (1953). *Mental health and MS.* New York: National Multiple Sclerosis Society.

Harrower, M. (1955). Who comes to court? *Journal of Orthopsychiatry, 25,* 15–25.

Harrower, M. (1956). Projective counseling: a psychotherapeutic technique. *American Journal of Psychotherapy, 10,* 74–86.

Harrower, M. (1965a). *Psychodiagnostic testing: An empirical approach.* Springfield, IL: Charles C Thomas.

Harrower, M. (1965b). Clinical psychologists at work. In B. Wolman (Ed.), *Handbook of clinical psychology.* New York: McGraw-Hill.

Harrower, M. (1968). Research on the patient. In *New dimensions in mental health.* New York: Grune & Stratton.

Harrower, M. (1969). Poems emerging from the therapeutic experience. *The Journal of Nervous and Mental Disease, 149,* 213–223.

Harrower, M. (1970). The scaling of mental health potential. In A. R. Mahrer (Ed.), *New approaches to personality classification.* New York: Columbia University Press.

Harrower, M. (1972). *The therapy of poetry.* Springfield, IL: Charles C Thomas.

Harrower, M. (1976a). Were Hitler's henchmen mad? *Psychology Today, 10,* 76–80.

Harrower, M. (1976b). Rorschach records of the Nazi criminals: An experimental study after thirty years. *Journal of Personality Assessment, 40,* 341–351.

Harrower, M. (1978). Changing horses in mid-stream: An experimentalist becomes a clinician. In T. S. Krawiec (Ed.), *The psychologists: Autobiographies of distinguished living psychologists,* Vol. 3. Brandon, VT: Clinical Psychology Publishing.

Harrower, M. (1983). *Kurt Koffka: An unwitting self-portrait.* Gainesville: Florida University Presses.

Harrower, M. (1984). Mentors and milestones. In D. Rogers (Ed.), *Foundations of psychology: Some personal views.* New York: Praeger.

Harrower, M. & Bowers, D. (1987). *The inside story: Self-evaluations reflecting basic Rorschach types.* Hillsdale, NJ: Erlbaum.

Harrower, M. & Grinker, R. (1946). The stress tolerance test. *Psychosomatic Medicine, 8,* 3–15.

Harrower, M. & Herrmann, R. (1953). *Psychological factors in the care of patients with multiple sclerosis.* New York: National Multiple Sclerosis Society.

Harrower, M. & Kraus, J. (1951). Psychological studies on patients with multiple sclerosis. *Archives of Neurology and Psychiatry, 66,* 44–57.

Harrower, M., Vorhaus, P., Roman, M., & Bauman, G. (1960). *Creative variations in the projective techniques.* Springfield, IL: Charles C Thomas.

Koffka, K. (1928). *The growth of the mind.* New York: Harcourt, Brace & Company.

Koffka, K. (1935). *The principles of Gestalt psychology.* New York: Harcourt, Brace & Company.

Koffka, K. & Harrower, M. (1931). Colour and organization, Part I. *Psychologische Forschung 15,* 145–92.

Koffka, K. & Harrower, M. (1932). Colour and organization, Part II. *Psychologische Forschung 15,* 193–275.

Köhler, W. (1927). *The mentality of apes.* New York: Harcourt, Brace & Company.

Nielsen, E. (1988). National Multiple Sclerosis Society. Personal communication, 1988.

General References

Abramson, H. A. (1970). The Fremont-Smith effect: An historical note. *The Journal of Asthma Research, 2* (8).

Harrower, M. (1947). *The evolution of a clinical psychologist: Transactions of the first conference on training in clinical psychology.* New York: Josiah Macy, Jr. Foundation.

Harrower, M. (1955). *Medical and psychological teamwork in the care of the chronically ill.* Springfield, IL: Charles C Thomas.

Harrower, M. (1956). The measurement of psychological factors in mental maladjustment. In V. W. Eisenstein (Ed.), *Neurotic interaction in marriage* (pp. 169–191). New York: Basic Books.

Harrower, M. (1961). *The practice of clinical psychology.* Springfield, IL: Charles C Thomas.

Harrower, M. (1986). The stress tolerance test. *Journal of Personality Assessment, 50* (30), 417–427.

Harrower, M. & Steiner, M. E. (1943). Modification of the Rorschach method for use as a group test. *Journal of Genetic Psychology, 62,* 119–133.

Margaret Ives, Ph.D.

◆

Clinical Psychology over the Years

A short account of my recent ancestral background seems appropriate for a beginning. I am fortunate to have my great-grandmother's "reminiscences," which she wrote just a hundred years ago for my father. Her family were Friends, or Quakers. Her father, Dr. Louis Livingston Seaman, studied in England with Dr. Jenner, who had discovered the cure for smallpox, a disease that had been devastating up to that time. Dr. Seaman introduced the cure into the United States in 1808, but I understand that there were demonstrations in New York against him because he vaccinated his children when they were not ill. Dr. Seaman also studied in Phildelphia with Dr. Benjamin Rush, who was one of the signers of the Declaration of Independence.

Eliza Seaman Leggett, my great-grandmother, started the first Women's Club in Detroit and was active in the abolitionist movement. Even though she died in 1901, in the 1950s she was honored by the City of Detroit for her accomplishements. My mother and I attended the ceremony.

My father, Augustus Wright Ives, was a psychiatrist who practiced for many years in Detroit. He was also professor of neurology and psychiatry at the Detroit College of Medicine (now part of Wayne University). He lived to the age of 92. My mother,

Julia Claire Chandler, taught French and German before her marriage. She had traveled alone to Europe in 1896, at the age of 23, to perfect herself in those languages—an unusual thing for a young woman to do in those days. On the boat, she met an older woman who befriended her and showed her around Paris. Two years later, when Mother called on her in Detroit, she met the woman's son, whom she later married. This young man was my father. Had it not been for Mother's traveling alone to Europe, I should not be here to write this autobiography. I was named after my grandmother, the woman on the boat.

Mother's trip took her to Tours and then to Berlin, where she was admitted to the University of Berlin, the first year that women were admitted. (Women received no credit, however.) She met Mark Twain and his daughter at an embassy party, and attended a concert with Lily Lehmann at which Brahms conducted his First Symphony.

My parents were married in 1901 and I was born on April 10, 1903, the older of two children. We lived on Montcalm Street in downtown Detroit, in a house my father had built. As the city became more industrialized, however, we moved farther north, and eventually moved to Birmingham. When one sees what has happened to Detroit these days, it is good to remember what a beautiful, safe city it used to be. I walked alone half a mile to kindergarten and to the early grades. My father hesitantly consented to my coming alone to his office downtown in the David Whitney Building. I found out years later that he had followed half a block behind me to see if I knew how to cross streets properly. I thought it a miracle at the time when some older boys attacked me with snowballs and there was my father right on hand to take my part.

My brother Chandler and I were very close friends and spent much time together. I do not remember that I ever felt any discrimination because I was a girl. I had some advantages, such as being able to stay up a bit later because I was two years older. We used to play games with our parents in the evenings, some of them educational, like the game of Authors. Discipline was firm and loving. My parents did not approve of corporal punishment.

At the age of 5 I began taking piano lessons with my aunt, Madge Ives, whose family lived a short distance farther north. We developed lifelong friendships with my two cousins, Janet and Tom. In the summer we usually went by train through Canada to the home of my mothers's parents in Ogdensburg, New York on the Saint Lawrence River. While there, we also spent time on my great-uncle's farm near Richville, where my mother had lived as a child. My father could usually manage only a short visit with us because of the demands of his practice. My grandmother Chandler was very fond of my father, her son-in-law.

We spent a couple of summers in a rented cottage on the Canadian shore near Amherstburg. I learned to swim and row early. We also spent time on my great-uncle Mort Leggett's farm near Drayton Plains, Michigan.

I attended public schools in Detroit and its suburb, Highland Park, where we moved when downtown Detroit became overindustrialized. I attended a very good high school there, which prepared me for entrance to Vassar College. For example, I had dropped mathematics after three years and an unusually fine math teacher helped me review so that I passed the entrance examination without much trouble. I had specialized in languages, four years of Latin to qualify for Vassar, three years of French, and a little German. I graduated as valedictorian and had to make my first speech in a large crowded auditorium.

I had been at Vassar less than two months when our great family tragedy occurred. In October 1920, when my brother Chandler was 15, he and two other boys, including my cousin, Tom Ives, went camping on the lake on Uncle Mort's farm. Chandler was drowned there. He was a good swimmer and could handle a rowboat, but a storm came up and the boat sank. Chandler took the shorter route to shore, but swam against the wind and did not make it. His friend took the longer route with the wind and reached shore. Tom was not with them.

I have never completely recovered from this loss, now more than 69 years ago. I still dream about Chandler, and in the dream he is always young and we are doing something together. I believe that my life would have been quite different had my brother lived. As it was, I buried myself in my studies, joined the college choir and the track team, and tried to keep busy. But I did not make many friends among my classmates that first year. I withdrew and was not able to socialize. I made most of my close friends in the next year. Now, many years later, I have been asked to be class correspondent and to write a short summary of class events every three months. I am also on the alumnae/i council. As a result, I am now better acquainted with my classmates than when I was in college.

My four years at Vassar greatly helped my development as an independent person and thinker. I majored in psychology and French and added a bit of Italian. This may have been an unusual combination, but I am glad I did it. I cherish the enriching experience I had at Vassar. I studied with the outstanding psychologist, Margaret Washburn, who was president of the American Psychological Association during my student days. I graduated summa cum laude and Phi Beta Kappa.

After graduation, my classmate Augusta Clawson and I were offered positions as teachers at the Girls' Continuation School in Elizabeth, New Jersey. The students were girls of 14 and 15; most worked in garment factories, but a few were household employees. The average wage was, I believe, about $7.50 a week. The girls were required to attend school one day a week until they turned 16. The principal, Mrs. Hazen, was unusual; she wanted us to instill a love of learning in these young people in any way that we thought best. So, in addition to teaching budgeting in arithmetic, we tried reading Shakespeare and appropriate operas, such as Carmen, and took a group of the girls to New York to see *As You Like It.* This was a wonderful learning experience for us as well as for the girls. I taught at the continuation school for four years before returning to graduate school at the University of Michigan to study psychology.

During this period I was invited by a college friend, Margaret Newhall, to accompany her and her mother and sister to Europe in the summer of 1927. Mrs. Newhall had been born in Germany and knew three languages, German, English, and French, equally well. We spent three months traveling in Germany and France, voyaging up the Rhine from Cologne, stopping along the way to visit Heidelberg and other well-known places. We went to Mrs. Newhall's old home in Reutlingen, where we visited her friends and family, and then went on to Friedrichshafen on the Bodensee (Lake Constance). Then we returned to France by way of Strasbourg. We also spent considerable time in Paris and surroundings, with a side trip to the magnificent Chartres Cathedral. Then Margaret and I left to return home to our jobs, while her mother and sister went on to England. I did not visit Europe again for 33 years.

In 1928 I entered graduate school at Michigan and obtained my master's degree in psychology in 1929. There were no internships for psychologists in those days; but, in addition to the usual academic courses, I spent my afternoons working at the University Hospital, where I gave psychological tests to patients in the Division of Psychiatry. It was not long before I added therapeutic interviews to the testing and, to my surprise, was asked to supervise a fellow student in similar activities. Thus I learned a great deal, and when I was completing my work for the degree, Dr. Walter Pillsbury, chairman of the Psychology Department, recommended me for an opening at the Wayne County Clinic for Child Study at the juvenile court in Detroit.

The chief psychologist at the clinic was Dr. Elizabeth Hincks, a Vassar alumna with a Ph.D. from Harvard. She had studied in Switzerland and had been analyzed by Jung himself. She became a good friend of mine. In addition to psychological testing, I learned to work with and understand young people in trouble with the law. We did a so-called personality interview, which included an inquiry into dreams. For the first two years our work was reviewed carefully by Dr. Hincks and then retyped. Although not so named, this was really an excellent internship. In addition to the four psychologists at the clinic, there were four social workers, four secretaries, and two part-time psychiatrists, who saw patients referred by the psychologists. We held a conference on each patient, wrote the report to the court, and sometimes attended court.

After three years at the clinic, I returned to the University of Michigan in 1932 to study for my doctorate. But in 1935, before I had completed my research, I accepted an excellent position at the Henry Ford Hospital in Detroit. This was a general hospital where we had an opportunity to work with patients of all ages and diagnoses. As an integral part of the Department of Neuropsychiatry, we had a varied program. Our chief, Dr. Emmett L. Schott, has reported that we spent 40% of our time interviewing, 30% in psychotherapy, and 25% in testing. I spent much time on the wards and much with outpatients. There were many referrals from other divisions, especially from pediatrics but also from general medicine, dermatology, metabolism, neurosurgery, gynecology, and even obstetrics. I was glad that my father had emphasized the need for the study of neuroanatomy and physiology if I were to work in a hospital.

During World War II we assisted the draft boards in evaluating difficult selectees. To my surprise, after many physicians had left for the service, the chief psychiatrist, Dr. Thos. J. Heldt, asked me to approve for indexing all diagnoses in the department. This was extremely valuable experience, which enhanced my ability to counsel the large number of servicemen and women at the hospital.

I finally received my Ph.D. in 1938. My dissertation, as was customary at that time, was in experimental psychology. It was entitled "The Flight of Colors, Following Intense Brief Stimulation of the Eye." Dr. Carl R. Brown was my supervising professor, and the dissertation was published by University Microfilms.

This period, among the busiest of my life, provided excellent experience; nevertheless, I left after seven years, because for the only time in my life I experienced serious discrimination on the basis of my sex. My salary was low by comparison with Dr. Schott's, and I was given no raise when I received my doctorate. The lay superintendent explained that I could not expect more because I was a woman. So I left for Saint Elizabeths Hospital early in 1943. Dr. Winfred Overholser, an outstanding psychiatrist, was superintendent, and Dr. Isabelle Kendig was chief psychologist. At that time there were only two staff psychologists for about eight thousand patients, many of them psychiatric casualties from the navy.

At first I spent much time testing all over the hospital, and especially in the maximum security division. I also supervised students and taught psychology to the nursing students. During the 1930s, 40s, and 50s, diagnostic testing was increasing in importance, largely, I believe, because of the advent of projective tests. The training function also grew in importance, and in 1947 formal internships and residencies in psychology were initiated. (In 1944 I had spent two months at the City College of New York working with servicemen and women who were casualties of World War II.)

After Dr. Kendig left in December 1950, I became chief psychologist at Saint Elizabeths. Dr. Margaret Mercer, who soon came to be in charge of training, was largely responsible for the excellence of the program. In fact, our program was on the first list approved by the APA, in 1956.

Throughout the 1950s the number of psychology staff and of interns rose slowly and steadily. Our functions broadened; much more psychotherapy, both individual and group, was occurring, with intern participation. Research increased. There were interdisciplinary training programs, in which outside lecturers participated. Carefully supervised diagnostic testing remained important.

During most of this period, I was on the part-time staff of the psychology department at the George Washington University. I was classified as a lecturer in clinical psychology from 1946 to 1955 and as a professorial lecturer from 1955 to 1970.

I note that I have not discussed my social life in detail. I have said that after my brother's death I was withdrawn for a time, but after that I made many friends. While teaching in Elizabeth I became well acquainted with the family of my Vassar classmate Augusta Clawson, and was persuaded to move to Plainfield where they lived. Since I had no car at that time, Augusta drove us every day to Elizabeth and back. I was frequently invited for Sunday evening supper at their home. Augusta now lives fairly nearby in northern Virginia, and I see her frequently.

While I was a graduate student at the University of Michigan, I became acquainted with George Meyer, a young instructor and fellow graduate student in psychology. We spent a great deal of time together, singing in the University Choral Union and going to concerts, plays, and other social events together. This association, which was pleasant and purely platonic, may have kept me from getting acquainted with more men while at the university. George returned to California after obtaining his degree and I did not see him again. I understand that he is now deceased.

During the period at the Ford Hospital (1935 to 1942), I lived with my parents in Birmingham. During the first three years, I spent much time commuting between Birmingham, Detroit, and Ann Arbor, where I spent weekends and was engaged in research for my degree. This was an extremely busy period, and I was most fortunate to be invited to stay with Dr. and Mrs. Norman Maier at their home in Ann Arbor whenever I was there. We became good friends.

I have always wished that I could have arranged for my mother to have another trip to Europe; she had not been again since her early travels as a young girl. But the 1940s were no time to go to Europe, and my parents both died in the 1950s, my father at the age of 92 in 1953 and my mother at 85 in 1959. In 1940 we had taken a delightful trip together through the southern part of the United States, from the Blue Ridge Mountains into Kentucky and Alabama, then back through Indiana into Michigan. I had also seen quite a bit of the United States when I drove to Yellowstone with a college friend and her parents.

Shortly after I moved to Washington, D.C., my parents sold their Birmingham home and came down to stay with me in Washington and later in Alexandria, where we bought a home. But they were no longer alive in July 1960, when I was invited by friends from Catholic University to accompany them on an automobile trip around Europe. We had all attended meetings of the International Congress of Psychology in Bonn, Germany. My friends left the meetings a few days before I did, and I had an interesting experience trying to catch up with them in Paris. I took a helicopter from Bonn to Brussels and then a plane to Paris. But the plane was late, and when I arrived in Paris the travel agency had closed for the night. The Travellers' Aid found me a place to stay and a taxi. The taxi driver was unusually helpful. He explained that President De Gaulle had just devalued the franc, so that one new franc was worth 100 old ones. If I did not know this, he said, I would be cheated. The next morning, when the travel agency opened, I located my friends. After a short time in Paris we started south, visiting cathedrals as we went. Among them were Chartres, and then Avignon, where the pope had stayed during his short absence from Rome. We crossed into Spain, visited Barcelona and then went down the coast of Portugal, from Porto to Lisbon. Then we came back through Madrid, through southern France, along the coast of the Mediterranean to Marseilles and Nice. Finally we reached Italy, where we visited Milan and had a wonderful time in Venice. At that time the canals were not yet polluted.

Rome was our final destination. We toured the museum at the Vatican and then went to see Pope John XXIII at his summer residence. The large audience included many children, and the pope gave a speech on bringing up children in which he emphasized that children do as their parents do, rather than following dictates that do not conform to the example set. I am very glad that I had the opportunity to see and hear that particular pope.

I came home alone from Rome via London to return to Saint Elizabeths. The 1960s brought many changes at the hospital. The National Institute of Mental Health (NIMH) was increasingly involved with us, at first in research only; but in 1967, three years after Dr. Overholser's death, Saint Elizabeths officially joined NIMH. They had great plans for us; the hospital was supposed to become a national model for the conversion of a large mental hospital into a modern community-based mental health facility. The hospital was divided into units, with psychologists assuming diversified functions. Dr. Margaret Mercer was director of research in clinical psychology, Dr. Katherine Beardsley was deputy director of intramural training, and I was in charge of psychological services. But the grand plan never materialized, and in 1987 the hospital was formally transferred to D.C., and is no longer federal. In the opinion of many people, including me, this was a great mistake. The hospital is no longer world famous and is losing its outstanding reputation. I retired in 1973 at the age of 70.

In the meantime, I had continued to travel. In 1964, I went with a group of mental health professionals on a trip around the world, led by Dr. Henry David. From New York we went to London and Vienna; and thence to Ljubljana, Yugoslavia, where international psychological meetings were held. After the meetings, we continued on to Bulgaria, Romania, and the Soviet Union, visiting Kiev, Leningrad, and Moscow, among other places. I found the people friendly and helpful, willing to go out of their way to show us around. From Moscow we flew to Delhi, in India. Among other places, we visited Bangkok, Hong Kong, Tokyo, the Philippines, and Hawaii, returning by way of San Francisco. It was a wonderful trip.

I visited Europe again twice in the 1960s and attended psychological meetings while there. I visited England, France, Germany, Switzerland, and Yugoslavia. In the 1970s I continued to travel. In the summer of 1971, after meetings in Holland, we visited East Africa, traveling to Nairobi in Kenya, where another professional meeting was held. This meeting was of special interest because mental health professionals from various parts of Africa and Asia attended. Their ideas were in many ways similar to ours in promoting self-esteem and love of one's fellows as necessary for good adjustment.

Then we went off into the wild in Kenya and Tanzania. We saw giraffes on the Serengeti Plain, with Mount Kilimanjaro, the highest peak in Africa, looming in the background. We saw zebras, elephants, monkeys, tigers, and lions among the many animals. We had an excellent driver, who took us to the best and safest places to see the animals. We also visited a Masai village and were happy with the cordial reaction we received from the natives. It was the trip of a lifetime.

In 1972, I again went to Asia with my cousin, Janet Ives Duncan, entering by way of Hong Kong, and visiting Singapore, Thailand, Japan, and the Philippines. After that I remained nearer home for awhile, attending meetings in the United States and in Montreal. But in 1976 I went overseas again for meetings in Paris and spent a few days in London. I took a bus trip around England, visiting Stratford-upon-Avon and Oxford, among other places.

While on my trip in 1972, I learned from my cousin Janet that one of her grand-daughters, Janna, was having drug problems and had been arrested for possession. Because of my position as chief psychologist at Saint Elizabeths, I was able to have Janna paroled to me, on condition that she enter our rehabilitation program at the hospital. This turned out to be one of the best experiences of my life. After considerable time in the program, Janna lived with me for two years, obtained a secretarial job, and attended Northern Virginia Community College. She quit the drugs immediately and absolutely upon entering the program and has never touched them again. She is a wonderful person, and I feel that she is almost a daughter to me. She now lives in California, but in spite of the distance has offered to type this autobiography for me. I only wish she lived nearer.

After my retirement in 1973, I began to see a few private patients. I also served as consultant at Saint Elizabeths, seeing patients there as well. I served on the APA Council and on the Executive Committee of Division 13 (Consulting). I am an APA Fellow of the Divisions of Clinical (12) and Public Service (18) Psychology as well as of Consulting. I am listed in *Who's Who in America*.

In 1977, I was invited to serve as executive officer of the American Board of Professional Psychology (ABPP), of which I had been a diplomate since 1948. So I went back to work for four years before my final retirement in 1981. It was my responsibility to evaluate candidates for the examination and to make sure they met the requirements. This function has now been decentralized.

While working as executive officer I was privileged to participate in June and July of 1980 in a beautiful cruise up the coast of Norway to Bergen, where international psychological meetings were being held. This trip was unusual in that we attended two sets of meetings. We flew from Bergen across the Baltic into East Germany, where we attended the first international psychology conference to be held in East Germany since the war. We stayed at the university and found everyone most friendly and happy to have us. Because we had attended a scientific conference, we had no difficulty passing through the iron curtain into West Berlin.

A week after retiring from ABPP in April 1981, I left for China. This trip, for mental health professionals, was sponsored by People to People International. We reached Hong Kong on May 5 and arrived in Beijing (Peking) the next day. We visited the Department of Psychology at Beijing University on the 7th and spent the next day on a trip to the Great Wall, which I climbed halfway up—a great experience. We visited psychiatric hospitals in Tianking (Tientsin), Nanjing, and Shanghai; in all of these places, patients seemed very much like our own. The Children's Palace in Shanghai, where art and music were taught and games were played, was also very interesting.

We visited steel and silk factories and saw an especially lovely garden in Suzhon. Friendship stores abounded, where we were able to make purchases with special money. I remember best the trip on the beautiful Li River, an all-day trip from Guilin to Yanshuo. The scenery was magnificent, and I took many pictures. We returned home in May by way of Hong Kong.

Later, in August 1981, I attended the meetings of the American Association of State Psychology Boards and the APA in Los Angeles. Afterward I enjoyed a visit with my cousin, Janet Duncan, in Escondido, California.

In July 1982 I went again to Europe, this time to attend meetings in Edinburgh. I was glad to have an opportunity to visit Scotland, see the country, and become acquainted with the psychologists there. During this period of my life I was traveling a great deal, and I believe it was a most valuable occupation, not merely because I was seeing new parts of the world; I was also getting to know colleagues in many places, to exchange ideas and enrich my experience.

So I continued to travel and to attend international psychological meetings on my trips. We went to Denmark in 1984 and to England in 1985 for meetings in Brighton, a beautiful city, which I especially enjoyed visiting as a regular tourist.

In 1986, I had the unusual opportunity to visit friends in Adelaide, Australia. On the way I stopped over two nights in Sydney and took a tour bus to explore the city. I was fortunate to meet people on the tour from Birmingham, Michigan, and we went to the famous opera house in the evening to hear the Sydney symphony. It was July 4th, and to our surprise the orchestra played an all-American concert with all kinds of music, from popular to classical, to celebrate the 200th anniversary of our change from the Articles of Confederation to a constitutional system.

The next ten days I spent in Adelaide with my very good friends John and Rollene Wells. John had been my minister for several years at Mount Vernon Unitarian Church in Alexandria. When I visited them, he had a temporary exchange pulpit in Adelaide; somewhat to my surprise, I discovered that there are many Unitarians in that area. We had lunch with a group, went to a church service, and spent considerable time touring the area in the Wells's car.

I will end this account of my travels to professional meetings with my 1984 trip to Egypt in the company of my good friend Mary Wells, the daughter of John and Rollene Wells. Ten years previously, when I was at ABPP, Mary, then an undergraduate student, had come to assist me. She was an excellent assistant, and I believe that her experience at ABPP had something to do with her subsequent decision to become a psychologist. At the time of the international psychological meetings we attended in Cairo, Mary was working toward her doctorate in psychology at the George Washington University. Before the meetings we took a beautiful trip up the Nile to Aswan, an experience I shall always cherish. At the meetings, I was again pleased to find that the African and Asian psychologists present were also discussing ways of improving their clients' self-esteem and interest in their fellows.

Mary and I spent a few days in Paris on our way home, staying by choice in a hotel where the proprietor spoke little English. Even those few days were very good for our fluency in French. Since I had not been in France for some time, my vocabulary had suffered.

This account has made it appear that I spend most of my time traveling, but this is a misconception. The fact that I live alone and have no close relatives nearby makes me a bit lonely sometimes, and I like to be out and doing things. But I am not neglected. I have already spoken of my close friends, the Wells, but I must sadly report that John Wells has recently died after a brief illness. I keep in close touch with Rollene and Mary.

On my trip around the world in 1964, I became acquainted with Henry David, the trip leader, a well-known psychologist who was then associate director of the World Federation for Mental Health and was stationed in Geneva. He now lives in Bethesda, Maryland, and I see him and his wife, Tema, frequently. They are wonderful friends, and I often accompany them to concerts and other events. I especially enjoy the concerts, have season tickets to the National Symphony, and spend much time listening to classical music on the radio. Also, I sing in the choir at the Unitarian Church.

I have a "time-sharing" apartment at Club Land'Or on Paradise Island in the Bahamas, where I spend a week every May. My apartment easily accommodates three people, and I always take one or two relatives or friends. The apartment has an ocean view, and we spend much time exploring the beautiful surroundings on foot or by car, both on the island and in nearby Nassau and vicinity. I have become well acquainted with some of the other people who vacation on the island and feel privileged to go there.

Although I am no longer employed, I do have a small private practice. I volunteer one day a week at Common Cause and one day at the Fairfax County Jail, working with individual prisoners. I cannot see most prisoners over a long period, because they are likely to be transferred, but I do seem to be having some success, judging in part by some letters I have received. One letter said that the young man thought of me whenever he was feeling low or depressed, because I had given him a slightly better opinion of himself. The very low self-esteem of most of these men is appalling, but to be expected, I believe.

I recently attended my 65th reunion at Vassar College. There were 16 of us from the class of 1924, and everyone went out of the way to make us, the oldest ones returning, comfortable. I am glad to have had the opportunity to attend Vassar, and am pleased with what is happening with present-day students. They are much more involved in the community than we were, and apply what they learn from books to practical everyday problems in Poughkeepsie and elsewhere.

I have not said much about my relatives. Had I written this autobiography several years ago it would have been different, but except for my cousin, Janet Duncan, all my surviving relatives are younger than I. None is more closely related than a cousin, and no one lives nearby. As I have already described, my cousin's granddaughter Janna lived with me for a couple of years in the 1970s. Although she now lives in California, we communicate frequently, and she is responsible for typing this autobiography. I spent the Christmas holidays in Tucson with the Duncans in 1987.

On my mother's side of the family, I have many cousins living all over the United States and elsewhere, but only one is a member of my generation. That is Jennette Murton Edelstein, my mother's sister's daughter. She lives on Long Island, near New York City, and we keep in close touch. When I go up that way, I am likely to stop by for a few days' visit, and she does likewise when she comes to Washington. I know her children well; the oldest, Judy, stayed with me while in training for the Peace Corps. She was later stationed in Turkey, and I had a very interesting visit with her there in 1970. That summer I also visited Judy's sister, Cynthia, and her husband, Leslie Cornell, an archeologist who was working on a dig at the Sea of Galilee in Israel. He is now associate professor of archaeology at Depauw University in Greencastle, Indiana.

Another cousin, Barbara Chandler Kimm, lives in Syracuse. (My mother grew up in Ogdensburg, in the same part of northern New York.) I visited my grandparents there frequently throughout my childhood and later, especially during the summers. This area has the advantage of rarely becoming too hot, although the winters can be very cold. Barbara and I keep in fairly close touch and stay with each other occasionally in Syracuse or Alexandria. I also visit friends who bought my grandparents' home in Ogdensburg; I feel very much at home there.

I am sorry that neither the Ives nor the Chandler name in our branch of the family will survive the present generation. There are no surviving Ives men, and the only Chandler man in the generation following mine has no children. There has been a preponderance of women in our immediate family, although there are of course other men more distantly related.

Thus ends my biographical sketch. I supplement it by admitting that I have not published a great deal, nor have I done as much good research as I should have liked. Perhaps I allowed myself to become too busy with clinical duties, teaching, and administering an ever-growing department at Saint Elizabeths Hospital. When I arrived in 1943, only two psychologists, plus two interns, were employed at the hospital, and when I left in 1973 there were more than 40. As I mentioned earlier, the functions were eventually divided into separate units, with the result that I was officially in charge of services only. Nevertheless, we all worked well together, and evidently psychology is still held in high esteem at Saint Elizabeths.

At present, I keep very busy with my volunteer and other activities. Also, I remain in good health.

Alan O. Ross, Ph.D.

Professor of Psychology
SUNY–Stony Brook, Stony Brook, New York

◆

Memories and Reflections

Early Influences

The invitation to contribute a chapter to this collection contained the suggestion that I describe the early influences that led to my interest in psychology, but it did not reveal how I might identify these influences. Thus, rather than speculating about the earliest antecedents of my career choice, I shall recount some of the events I remember from my childhood, leaving it up to the reader to decide what bearing, if any, these experiences may have had on my ending up as a university professor of psychology whose major interest is in clinical child psychology.

Great Expectations

Twenty years after I was born in the German city of Frankfurt am Main, the date of my birth was to become known in the United States as Pearl Harbor Day. By my parents' reckoning I arrived just 3 years and 26 days after the First World War had ended on Armistice Day, now celebrated here as Veterans Day. I identify the date of my birth in terms of the beginnings and ends of wars because my life has been

importantly influenced by the antecedents, correlates, and consequences of the
armed conflicts that have marked and marred the twentieth century.

My parents met at the University of Heidelberg, where both attended medical
school. The Kaiser's war interrupted their studies and sent my father to the Russian
front, where he served as a medical officer for four years while my mother worked in a
military hospital as a medical assistant. They married when the war ended. Father
opened an office for the internal and general practice of medicine, but Mother did not
resume her interrupted medical training.

Higher education had long played an important role in my family. My paternal
great-grandfather held a doctorate in philology (linguistics), which he had earned at
the University of Marburg. One of the heirlooms in my possession is a letter of
reference, written in 1849 for this ancestor of mine by Robert Wilhelm Bunsen, the
inventor of the Bunsen burner, who was then professor of chemistry at Marburg. As a
Jew, my great-grandfather found a university career closed to him and nonuniversity
teaching positions difficult to obtain. To find a job he moved to Homonna, a small
rural community in Hungary, where he taught German and eventually married one of
his students. Some years later the couple returned to Germany, where the attitude
toward Jews had turned more favorable (for the time being), so that my ancestor was
able to secure a position teaching linguistics at the University of Mainz.

My grandfather, who was born during the sojourn in Hungary, studied medicine at
the University of Vienna, where he earned his doctorate in 1881. He settled in
Frankfurt and eventually became one of that city's most respected and best-known
ophthalmologists. By the time I came to know him, he had been awarded the honorific
title *Geheimer Sanitätsrat,* which roughly translates as "Privy Councillor of
Health." The weight of that title was reflected in Grandfather's bearing. I remember
him as a dignified, proud, and unapproachable figure. When my mother prompted me
to show him my first report card, on which I had made the equivalent of "B" in every
subject, Grandfather produced a Latin document from the drawer of his desk. He had
received it when, at age 17, he had graduated from gymnasium, the rough equivalent
of our high school plus a year of college. Grandfather pointed to the word *praecellentes*
next to every subject, translating it for me as "outstanding." His had been a straight-
"A" record and, as he had obviously intended, I was duly awed—and, in view of my
"B's", not a little deflated.

This academic family history would not be complete without my mentioning that
as a young girl, my maternal grandmother had wanted to go to medical school. In her
day, however, the only place in all of Europe where a woman could study medicine
was at an institution for women affiliated with Oxford University. Family lore has it
that when Grandmother asked her father to let her go to Oxford, he nullified her
career choice with a pun, "Wenn Du nach Oxford gehst ist ein Ox fort." (If you go
away to Oxford, an ox will have gone away.) It may be that she was attempting to
gratify her own foiled ambition when she prevailed on her only child, my mother, to
study medicine. Great must have been her disappointment when war, marriage,
children, and not a little negativism deflected my mother from that path.

For as long as I can remember, I have been aware that there have been doctorates
in my family for three generations, that I had a straight-"A" grandfather, that both my

parents had gone to university, and that everyone expected me to follow in these footsteps.

Childhood Memories

A STAB AT AUTONOMY. The years immediately following Germany's defeat in the First World War were marked by runaway inflation, accompanied by shortages of housing, food, and jobs. I must have been barely 2 years old when my mother set a bowl of hot cereal before me and left the room, telling me not to touch the food because it was too hot. Next to the cereal stood a tall, rectangular can with black and gold decoration, depicting a Chinese landscape. Once it had been a container for tea, now it held sugar. Knowing that Mother would pour some of the sugar over my cereal when she returned, I decided to take things into my own little hands. I got the can open, but when I tried to pour the sugar it tipped over and the entire contents spilled onto the cereal. This waste of valuable sugar and ruination of much of the cereal caused quite an uproar. I do not recall what specific consequence my mother brought to bear, but whatever it was it served to make this event most vividly memorable.

My parents were generally quite permissive, and physical punishment was not one of their child-rearing methods. This permissiveness is exemplified by an incident that occurred when I was about 6 years old. My brother, who is four years my junior, and I were amusing ourselves by running the wheeled coal scuttle back and forth on the tiled kitchen floor of our third-floor apartment. It made a lot of noise and undoubtedly damaged the floor, but our mother, who was present in the kitchen, made no attempt to stop us. Eventually the landlord, who lived below us, came running up, banging on our apartment door and yelling anti-Semitic epithets. This scared us into finding a less noisy activity.

FIRE-SETTING AND OTHER MISCHIEF. That my parents did not use physical punishment can be illustrated by an event that took place around the same time as the coal-scuttle story. On Sundays it was the custom of our family to go on an outing. It was a custom, incidentally, that was maintained well into my late adolescence, keeping me from participating in weekend activities with my peers. On one of these excursions we had gone for a walk in a nearby forest. My parents and a friend of father's were walking ahead, my brother and I loitering behind. I had brought from home a purloined box of matches, and when we passed some small piles of dry leaves and twigs I threw lighted matches into them. One of the piles caught fire. Fortunately, it was quickly seen by a passer-by, with whose help my father and his friend extinguished the flames. Although my father's friend advocated sterner measures, my father limited himself to giving me a lecture about the danger of playing with matches and the disaster that might have ensued from my actions. The lecture must have been effective. I have no other act of fire setting in my personal history.

While my father limited his interventions to didactic lectures, my mother made effective use of anxiety induction and guilt arousal to control my behavior. Her principal strategy was the "silent treatment." She simply stopped talking to me when I had aggrieved her and relented only after I had rendered a contrite apology.

Some years after the fire-setting incident, when I was about 13 years old, I sneaked into my father's medical office and filled a small bottle with ether. This bottle I took to school, where I let my classmates sniff it, no doubt to impress them; for I had no idea of the implications of ether sniffing and did not learn of its mood-altering potential until many years later. Not too surprisingly, one of the teachers got wind of this activity, the principal was notified, and a telephone call to my father ensued. When I got home my father gave me a lecture about the effects of ether and told me to keep out of his office. Again, the lecture was effective. I never again experimented with controlled substances.

This list of juvenile offenses would not be complete without my reporting on a brush with shoplifting, about which my parents never knew. I was 11 or 12 years old when a classmate with whom I often walked part of the way home from school had to stop at a small-appliance shop to pick up an item his family had left there for repair. I accompanied my friend into the store, a small, one-man operation. Among the items displayed on the counter was an attractive, pocket-size flashlight. A curtain separated the store from a back room, into which the proprietor went to fetch the repaired appliance. While my friend and I were alone, I pocketed the flashlight. No sooner had I done so than the storekeeper, who had apparently kept an eye on us, came charging out from behind the curtain and in a quiet but threatening voice told me to put it back, adding "Junge, Junge, lass Dich nicht erwischen!" (Boy, oh boy, don't ever let yourself get caught!) I quickly obeyed and meekly left the store.

Just as the man said, I never again permitted myself to get caught. Better yet, I never again attemped a theft. I use the self-revelation of this episode in almost every course I teach because it illustrates so well not only how behavior can be a function of its consequences, but also how a single trial in which theft is associated with high anxiety can keep a guilt-reared youngster from ever stealing again. In fact, as I tell my students, I still experience some anxiety each time I recite (or write about) that man's sudden appearance from behind his curtain.

Neither of my parents ever used physical punishment, but I clearly recall the one and only spanking I received from my second-grade teacher, Herr Otto Kirmse, who was testing our class on the multiplication tables. One by one we were called on to stand up and recite the multiples of a given number. As usual, I awaited my turn with much anxiety; when it came, my assignment was to recite the table of seven. All went well until I came to seven times seven, when my mind went blank. At that Herr Kirmse walked up to me, lifted me up by the suspenders of my baby-blue coveralls, and gave my behind a single whack with his ruler, saying, "Seven times seven is forty-nine." I never forgot this product and can visualize the situation as if it had happened yesterday. Here was a most effective use of pain infliction, but I have at times wondered whether my lifelong difficulties with anything having to do with numbers, be it algebra, statistics, or getting the correct change at a gas station, might not date from that traumatic experience.

The School Years

In my day, eight years of school attendance were compulsory for everyone, beginning at age 6, but kindergarten, though a German invention, was voluntary. All 6-year-olds entered public school (*Volksschule*), which lasted for eight years; but after four years those who were academically qualified could transfer to that uniquely German institution, the gymnasium. There one typically remained for nine years, after which those who graduated were eligible to attend a university.

AN EARLY CAREER CHOICE.   When I was little and as yet unimpressed by my family's academic tradition, I used to surprise and probably shock inquisitive ladies who asked me, "And what do you want to be when you grow up?" by answering, "A nursery school teacher." That was definitely not an acceptable aspiration for little boys in the Germany of the 1920s. Though I had a small number of age-appropriate friends, two to be exact, I had always enjoyed being around children younger than I, and for many years my brother had been my favorite playmate. My unusual career objective thus had a sound basis; but the patronizing reactions of my interlocutors, coupled with the tolerant bemusement of my mother, soon taught me to keep that occupational choice to myself.

I did not begin my formal education until I was 6 years and 9 months old because I had not turned 6 until December and my mother chose not to send me to kindergarten, preferring to keep me at home for as long as possible. In fact, I grew up believing that only "bad" mothers send their children to kindergarten. I recall voicing that idea in an education course in college, much to the amusement of my classmates.

Given my family background, it was not long after I had entered school before it became obvious to me that I was slated to go to the university so that I could enter one of the professions, most likely medicine or law. This prospect literally gave me nightmares all through elementary school because I knew I would have to pass a difficult, state-administered, comprehensive examination. What an anxious little boy I must have been.

As it turned out, my anxieties had been misdirected, for my education was interrupted after eight years by events that were far more immediate, far more realistic, and far more anxiety arousing than my dreams about the *Staatsexamen*.

THE INTERRUPTED EDUCATION.   The gymnasium I entered after completing four years of elementary school happened to be, not too surprisingly, the same one to which my father had gone. As with everything else in German society, there was a prestige hierarchy among the educational institutions, and Lessing Gymnasium was one of the two most prestigious in the city. Not ony did it hold to highly selective admission standards, but it still taught the "humanistic" curriculum, which dated from the Middle Ages and required the study of Latin and Greek by the 10-year-olds who entered its gates. (Those gates, by the way, were inscribed with the motto "Mens sana in corpore sano" [A sound mind in a healthy body].)

Admission to the Lessing Gymnasium was based on an interview with the director of the school. This man not only knew that my father was an alumnus, he also happened to be a member of the Freemasons, a secret society in which both my grandfather and my father were leading figures. Under these circumstances, I now suspect, my admission to the school was probably assured; but my difficulty with numbers, reflected in the equivalent of a "C" on my report card from elementary school, prompted the director to give me a test in arithmetic. I saw catastrophe looming when he announced this, but discovered to my relief that his notion of a test was to ask me the ages of my parents, who were sitting next to me. I had no idea how old they were, but was quick-witted enough to invent a number, giving both of them the same fictitious and highly improbable age—25! I could not understand why everyone laughed, but the answer was accepted. I had been lucky in my choice of number, because the second and last question was how old my parents were together. Twenty-five plus twenty-five; that much arithmetic I could handle. Had I known their true ages, 40 and 41, I might never have had to study Greek.

LEARNING DISABILITY.   I am one of those people who save every piece of paper that comes their way; you never know when it will come in handy. Thus I still have in my possession every report card I ever received. The equivalents of grades on my report cards from gymnasium are expressed in terms of "Very good," "Good," "Sufficient," "Flawed," and "Inadequate." I shall refer to these categories by the letter grades "A" through "F" that are used in most of our colleges. These grades of mine make interesting reading because they document the development of and recovery from what now would be called a learning disability.

My first report card from the gymnasium is dated September 1932. My performance in the preceding three months had earned me an "A" in German and "B's" in Latin, arithmetic, biology, and geography. I shall omit references to drawing and handwriting, at which I was not much better then than I am now. By September 1933 I had dropped to "C's" in German, Latin, and arithmetic, maintaining "B's" only in geography and biology. A year later (September 1934), a "D" appears in written Latin, and by September 1935 I had failing grades in Latin and French, "B's" only in German and (surprisingly) mathematics, and "C's" in the remaining subjects. That report card bears the warning, "Must make a major effort if he is to be promoted." Elsewhere on this document is written, "Difficulties in his mental ability to perform have arisen, which he is trying hard to overcome."

One month later, in the middle of the school year, and for reasons I shall discuss anon, I transferred from the public gymnasium to a small private school that catered primarily to Jewish students. The effect of this transfer on my "mental ability" bordered on the miraculous. By spring of 1936 I was earning "A's" in geometry, algebra, physics, history, and geography and "B's in German, French, and English. Unfortunately, that institution operated only through the eight years required by the compulsory education law. My schooling thus came to a premature and abrupt, though temporary, end when I was 14 years old.

In retrospect, it is easy to explain the rapid deterioration and miraculous recovery of my academic performance. I had entered gymnasium in 1932. Hitler came to power in January 1933, abruptly changing not only the atmosphere in that school but the life of my family. What follows may or may not be relevant to my becoming a clinical psychologist; it *is* relevant to my becoming a clinical psychologist *in the United States*.

I had always been a shy and rather introverted child. My report cards consistently praised my good comportment, and one of them makes favorable mention of my diffidence. Such a child would probably not have been too popular in an all-boy diffidence. Such a child would probably not have been too popular in an all-boy school where the students' ages ranged from 10 to 18. The moment that anti-Semitism was given official sanction by government policy, life for such as I became more and more unbearable. Although the teachers, including those who sported swastika pins on their lapels, remained civil and fair, I had much cause to fear attacks from my classmates during recess and on the way home. As other Jewish students withdrew from the gymnasium to emigrate or to attend the sectarian school operated by the Hebrew congregation, I became progressively more isolated and more frequently the target of such attacks.

Ever considerate, I did not want to worry my parents and never mentioned any of these experiences, even though they asked me from time to time whether I also wanted to transfer to the Jewish gymnasium. A little hero, I had decided to stick it out, much like my parents, who had thus far decided against emigration. Meanwhile my grades deteriorated.

Keeping problems to myself so as not to worry my parents was nothing new for me. When I was about 5 I did not tell my parents for several days about a pain in my abdomen, until a spontaneous cry of pain alerted them and I had to undergo emergency surgery for an appendix that was about to rupture.

My experiences in school were of course not the only events going on around me in those early years of the Nazi regime. A large percentage of the patients in my father's medical practice were employees of the municipal streetcar system. Within a month after Hitler's rise to power, my father lost these patients because they were not permitted to go to Jewish physicians. These streetcar workers were gradually followed by other patients as newspapers, schools, department stores, factories, and eventually all employers came under control of the Nazi Party. The diminishing practice brought diminishing income and with that a move from a reasonably comfortable apartment in the university district to more crowded quarters in a working-class neighborhood.

When my grades first showed signs of deterioration, my parents had gone to talk to my homeroom teacher. He recognized the source of my stress and recommended that they not talk about politics in front of me. Little chance of that being effective, when all I had to do to know what was going on was to look out the window and see on the door of the bar across the street the official decal that announced, in mock-Hebrew letters, "Jews Are Here Not Desired."

It was not only my classmates' behavior that was a source of misery for me; official school policy, dictated bv the municipal authority, also did its part. It was all done gradually, step by step, like the turning of a screw. At first Jewish students were not allowed to attend school assembly; later we were excluded from the weekly sessions of political indoctrination; then came a city-wide sports rally that was "for Aryans only." I stuck it out until the day my classmates returned from an assembly where they had been informed that henceforth Jewish students would have to sit in the back of the classroom. They proceeded to enforce that new rule in the way of 13-year-old boys, and when I got home I told my parents that I wanted out. It was then that they enrolled me in the small private school, where my grades recovered and where I finished my obligatory years of school attendance.

To Work at 14

My parents were not exactly overjoyed to have me stop going to school but, as with other things in those days, they had no choice. With my father's help I got a job as office boy in a still Jewish-owned company engaged in the manufacture and wholesale of brassieres and corsets. It was a stimulating place for a 14-year-old boy. I had all manner of fantasies about the fitting room and the attractive model who tried on the new designs. Although I was employed in the bookkeeping office, carrying messages gave me access to the manufacturing floors of the building, and because I expressed an interest in that aspect the owner assigned a friendly woman to teach me to use the sewing machines. My motivation for learning how to run a seam and make buttonholes was more than an adolescent's curiosity about ladies' underwear; it also had to do with wanting to have a skill that might secure me a job in case we emigrated, a possibility that my parents had finally come to consider.

My work in brassieres and corsets had a very salutary effect on my self-esteem, which the gymnasium experiences had badly undermined. Though only an office boy, I was entrusted with all sorts of responsible tasks, such as taking large cash deposits to the company's bank, entering the boss's inner sanctum with the day's mail, and carrying important verbal messages all over the plant. Last but not least, I was earning the money with which to buy my first typewriter. I had two good years, but it could not last. In July 1938 the Jewish owner's business was confiscated, and by September the government-installed new owners found a reason to terminate my apprenticeship contract, which then had one more year to run. The reason: I had smoked a cigarette in the men's room, an act that was *strengstens verboten,* or so they said.

I worked briefly as a stock clerk for a wholesaler of lace; but then came November 10, 1938, and the infamous *Kristallnacht,* during which all synagogues were set ablaze and the storefronts of the remaining Jewish merchants were smashed. My father and I were arrested (protective detention, they called it). He ended up in the Buchenwald concentration camp, but I was let go after 24 hours in jail because I was not yet 17; not yet, that is, by less than a month! The Nazis went by the rules, and at this time the rule was that all Jewish males between 17 and 60 were to be carted off.

I had been lucky; but so, it turned out, was my father—they released him from Buchenwald after four weeks. Again, they had a rule. If you had served in the front lines during World War I, and if you could document that you were going to emigrate within six months, you could go home. Father qualified, but the emotional scars from that experience stayed with him for the rest of his life.

Emigration

Although my father's army service probably saved his life, it had also been part of the reason why our family had remained in Germany all these years. The first people who emigrated after Hitler assumed power were those whose lives were in danger because of past political activities or who had lost their source of income by not being allowed to work. My father was in neither of these categories. Freemasonry, although immediately outlawed, was deemed apolitical, and he could continue to practice medicine because front-line veterans were allowed to retain their medical licenses. With his source of income reduced but not totally blocked, he believed that we could outlast the regime of that vagrant house painter from Austria who had temporarily, he thought, usurped control of the Fatherland. He was a patriot, my father, proud of his army service on the Russian front and of the medals he had been awarded. His family could trace its German roots to 1787; why should he flee? The answer came to him only gradually, as more and more of his patients were prohibited from using his services. We finally left in March 1939, just in the nick of time; in September the war broke out, and nobody got out of Germany after that.

At the time, most countries of the world had closed their borders to the refugees from the Nazi terror. Turkey, Singapore, and Uruguay were among the few exceptions. The British had closed Palestine, and the quota system that controlled immigration to the United States had generated a long waiting list. As at a supermarket delicatessen counter, we had been issued a number, but there was a long line ahead of us waiting to be served. It was on the basis of that number, however, that Great Britain granted us temporary asylum, and it was there that my family traveled, accompanied by two suitcases and four pieces of hand luggage. All else had to be left behind. *Omnia mea mecum porto* (All I own I carry with me), said Bias of Priene, one of the Seven Sages of ancient Greece, when he fled his homeland with even less than we were allowed to take along. He was referring to what he had in his head. We might well have quoted him, for the one thing no one can take away is what you have learned and your capacity to learn more.

Recovery and Reconstruction

In the beginning of our stay in England, my brother and I lived in Eastleach, a tiny Cotswold village, where the local Anglican clergyman had opened his home to us strangers. Nobody in that village spoke German, and our host's knowledge of the language was limited to the invective *Schweinehund,* which he had learned while in a German prisoner-of-war camp 20 years earlier. Building on the little we had learned in school, my brother and I acquired proficiency in English rather quickly. During those months I came close to fulfilling my childhood wish of becoming a nursery school teacher, for I was charged with taking care of the clergyman's youngest child, a boy with a congenital muscular condition that required him to be pushed around in a stroller. The waiting list for the United States moved slowly, and when we had overstayed the four months to which the clergyman had committed himself we joined our parents in Oxford, where a caring British lady gave both financial and emotional support to our family.

With that women's help I was able to enroll in the Schools of Technology, Art and Commerce, an institution somewhat like our technical high schools. My studies in (not at) Oxford proved important to me for two reasons. First, this experience demonstrated to me the validity of the good grades I had earned after I had moved from the gymnasium to the private school; I had never been sure whether these grades were the result of my performance or of the teachers' sympathy. The school in Oxford used a percentile grading system, and in my one semester there I received 79 in geography and 73 in English and French, together with the comment, "Is a highly intelligent, capable and conscientious student." This comment gave my academic self-image a much-needed and potent boost. The second reason that attending this school proved important was that it allowed me to perfect my typing, which is one of the most useful skills I ever acquired. In fact, as I shall relate shortly, it is a skill that may have kept me from getting killed during World War II.

Our immigration quota number was finally called in February 1940, allowing us to enter the United States—again, not a moment too soon. In May, following the rout of the British army and its evacuation from Dunkirk, the British arrested and deported every male who had come from Germany because they feared that Hitler had infiltrated an unknown number of spies and saboteurs among the legitimate refugees they had so generously accepted.

After a convoyed crossing of the U-boat-infested Atlantic, my family landed in Boston, setting foot on United States soil on Washington's birthday, 1940. *Gone with the Wind* was playing in the first-run movie theatres, and the flags were flying. I like to imagine that it was to celebrate our arrival.

The Land of Opportunity

Though the ship had landed us in Boston, our destination was New York City, where we had relatives and friends who had emigrated earlier. After a night in a Times Square hotel (across the street Bert Lahr and Ethel Merman were starring in *DuBarry Was a Lady*), all four of us moved into a single furnished room with bath in a rooming house on West 85th Street, between Central Park West and Columbus Avenue. The following day we were visited by the distant relative who had facilitated our immigration, thereby saving our lives, by signing a crucial affidavit assuring the U.S. government of her readiness to support us, lest we became a burden on the public purse. This lady arrived from Scarsdale carrying a food basket, and when my mother, to make conversation, asked where she had bought it, she replied, "At Gristede's, but you mustn't shop there, it's too expensive." This still comes to mind whenever I allow myself to do something a bit extravagant.

In those days, the image of the United States was still that of the melting pot. Everyone's goal was assimilation. You learned to speak English as soon as possible, changed your name so that it didn't sound foreign, adopted "American values," and on the soon-to-be-acquired Zenith radio you listened to the "Lucky Strike Hit Parade." We dove into this melting pot with enthusiasm. Brother went off to public school, Mother took a job as a practical nurse in a nearby private nursery school, and Father studied English so that he might be permitted to take the state's medical licensing examination. In 1940 there were only two states in all of the USA that admitted foreign-trained physicians to their examination: Ohio and New York. Although we would have preferred to move to Ohio, Father eventually passed the exam in New York—another reason for settling there.

As for me, the course was clear. I had to work in order to supplement the few dollars the nursery school paid my mother and the pin money my father was getting for delivering to that nursery school the leftover food that a famous restaurant, The 21 Club, was donating for the lunch of the children and staff. Because of my experience in cutting and sewing at the corset and brassiere factory, I started looking for a job in the garment industry. It was a time of high unemployment, and the search was not easy. During one job interview I used the British expression "manufactory" instead of "factory" in describing my experience, whereupon this potential employer said to me through his cigar, and in his heavy Eastern European accent, "Why don't you go to school and learn English before you try looking for a job." Most helpful.

After a couple of weeks of frustrating search I obtained a job as stock clerk in a wholesale house that dealt in the feathers and artificial flowers with which milliners decorated the hats women were still wearing in those prewar days. My first pay envelope (another of the documents I saved) shows that I earned $12 for the 40-hour week. I proudly turned my pay over to my parents, keeping for myself only $1.20 for carfare and other expenses. In those days one could still ride the subways for a nickel.

THE HAND OF CHANCE.   Sometimes I speculate about what might have become of me had it not been for the first of a series of chance encounters that affected the course of my life. One day in 1941, one of the society ladies who served on the board of directors of the nursery school inquired of my mother about her family. When Mother bemoaned the fact that one of her sons was working as a stock clerk, the board member suggested that I attend high school in the evenings and earn my diploma. We had had no idea that there was such a thing as an evening high school. I looked into it, and that fall entered New York Evening High School. Upon an evaluation of the report cards I had so prudently preserved, I was given credit for most of my previous education; but in order to obtain a high school diploma I had to pass the New York Regents examination in English and take courses in American history and civics. To flesh out my program I took French, arithmetic, shorthand, and typing, receiving "A's" in all subjects and winning the silver medal in English at the end of my senior year. I graduated in January 1943 and was drafted into the U.S. Army that very month.

Soon after that, I received my first book about psychology. At the time I was dating one of the daughters of Anne Roe, who practiced the (to me) mysterious profession of psychologist. After the war, Dr. Roe was to become the head of the New York state clinical psychology internship system. At any rate, she is the very first psychologist I ever met, and when I visited her house just before leaving for the army she gave me a little paperback book by E. G. Boring, *Psychology and the Fighting Man* (1942), which contained what little there was in the psychology of that day that had relevance to human behavior. I remember one bit of advice from that book: to see better at night, use your peripheral vision, because there are more rods there than cones, and they are more sensitive to light.

In the U.S. Army

I received infantry training in a camp near Macon, Georgia where, by virtue of a special law that accelerated the citizenship process for aliens in the armed forces, I became a U.S. Citizen after six weeks of service. I learned the use of rifle and bayonet with a group of men who later suffered heavy casualties when they fought their way onto Omaha Beach on the first day of the Normandy invasion. I was not with them because back in training camp I had violated that first G.I. rule, "Never volunteer for anything," by raising my hand when they were looking for someone who knew how to type. This was a stroke of luck, for as a result I was sitting behind a typewriter when all the others were shipped out at the end of their training.

The next lucky event came one (literally) dark and stormy night when I was sitting in what the army called an "orderly room," typing a letter home. The door suddenly opened, and in stepped a young officer who was seeking refuge from the heavy rain. He was from a different unit, and I had never seen him before and would never see him again. While he was trying to dry off, we struck up a conversation. When he asked why I was not trying to become an officer by applying to Officer Candidate School (OCS), I told him that I had only a high school diploma, not a college education. He said, "All you need for OCS is a high school diploma," stepped out the door and disappeared into the darkness. I promptly filled out the application that was to bring about another turning point in my life. In mystical moments, I am inclined to think of that second lieutenant as a divine messenger.

Able-bodied infantry soldiers were not meant to spend the war behind typewriters in the heart of Georgia, and when the first soldiers, injured in the fighting in North Africa, returned to the United States, they freed men like me for combat duty. My replacement arrived on the same day as my orders to report to Officer Candidate School, and these orders superseded others that would have sent me into combat. Had my mother not heard about evening high school; had I been drafted two weeks earlier; had I not known how to type and volunteered that fact at the right moment; had the rain not driven that young lieutenant to seek shelter; had the orders for OCS been delayed—who knows what would have happened to me. These coincidences and other I have yet to relate have convinced me that the direction one's life takes is largely determined by chance. Yet it was I who chose to go to high school; I who chose to admit to knowing how to type; I who chose to submit that OCS application. Without these choices, the chance events could not have made a difference. Hence I continue to make choices, lest chance should find me unprepared.

The OCS that turned me into a second lieutenant was that of the Transportation Corps, the branch of the army that is responsible for seeing to it that men and material get transported to the right place at the right time (most of the time). One of the skills they tried to teach at OCS was how to give instructions; they called it leadership training, and it was to serve me well. My first assignment was to a camp near New Orleans, where soldiers were trained to work as stevedores, loading and unloading ships. There I discovered that I was able to stand in front of a group of people and to lecture to them from notes written on 3 × 5 cards. This was my first experience at teaching, and I found not only that I was able to do it and that I was good at it, but that I enjoyed it as well.

After a year in Louisiana I was ordered to the Pacific theatre of the war, slated to participate in the invasion of the Japanese mainland. Again luck intervened, this time in the form of the supersecret device that the bomber *Enola Gay* dropped on the city of Hiroshima while our troopship was steaming from San Francisco to Hawaii for refueling. We were anchored in Pearl Harbor, of all places, on August 14, 1945, the day Japan surrendered, and we celebrated all night under the glare of the colored flares that every vessel in the harbor was shooting into the sky. I doubt whether there was anyone aboard who worried about the ethics of President Truman's decision to drop the bomb. I know that I did not become troubled about it until many years later.

Contrary to our hopes and expectations, the troopship did not turn around but steamed on, eventually landing me in a demolished and demoralized Japan, where I participated for a year in that unique and remarkable occupation with which the autocrat MacArthur brought democracy to the conquered land. For me that year turned out to be another step along the circuitous route that led to my becoming a clinical child psychologist.

I was assigned to the Transportation Corps unit that operated the Port of Kobe, where troops, food, and supplies arrived and through which obsolete equipment and weary soldiers departed on their way back to the States. My job was that of statistical control officer, which fortunately, considering my difficulty with numbers, entailed no more than seeing to it that the enlisted men under me counted the bags of rice and rusty Jeeps that passed through the port, and sending these sums to Tokyo. The important part of the job, the part that influenced my career choice, was that no ship could depart until I had certified the accuracy of the count. A big ship is the largest movable object that humans have ever constructed. Having the movement of such a ship depend on his word was for this 23-year-old lieutenant a thrilling and gratifying experience. When the time came to think about what I would do after my discharge from the service, I decided that the civilian equivalent of that army job might not be a bad deal. I had read about an occupation called "traffic manager" and, in the absence of expert guidance, made that my career goal.

Higher Education

A Business Career Aborted

How does one become a traffic manager? After a few inquiries I found some correspondence schools and small proprietary agencies that promised to prepare one for that occupation, but on closer inspection I found them not very confidence-inspiring. A better way, I thought, would be to go to college, major in economics, and move from that to making big ships leave port at my say-so. I doubt that this plan was realistic, and I find it remarkable that at a point when I badly needed career counseling I had no idea that there was such a thing, nor where to obtain it had I known. At any rate, nothing ever came of that plan because the line was too long when

I went to register at the business campus of the City College of New York ("CCNY–Downtown"), which is now the Baruch College of CUNY.

Having stood in too many lines during my army years, I was not about to stand in line just to get into college. I got back on the subway and went to the uptown campus of CCNY, where the line was short and they let me register as a nonmatriculated student in the evening session because I did not have my high school diploma with me. Attending college in the evening enabled me to return to my former employer, the flower and feather merchant, who by law was required to rehire a veteran who had been in his employ when drafted. They immediately promoted their former stock boy to salesman, gave me a sample case, and sent me out to Seventh Avenue, the jungle that is New York's garment district. I quickly discovered both that I make a lousy salesman and that I hate that kind of work. Instead of calling on potential customers I spent most of my time "on the road" sitting in a cafeteria reading a book and nursing a cup of coffee until it was time to return to the shop, my samples undisturbed. After four months of this charade I left that job by mutual consent to attend the day session at CCNY full time.

It was thus that I began college in earnest in the spring of 1947, when I was 25 years old. Still planning to become a traffic manager, I took Economics 1, expecting eventually to transfer "downtown" for my business degree. I got a "C" in Eco 1, the only "C" on my entire college record. Together with my success as a salesman, this spelled the end of my business career. What now?

Psychology

An "A" in Introductory Psychology, which Gertrude Schmeidler taught with knowledge, skill, and enthusiasm, offered the answer to my quandary. I toyed briefly with the idea of combining psychology and business in something I thought of as the "psychology of advertising," but then, remembering my early interest in little children, I decided to become a child psychologist. All went smoothly. I did my senior honors thesis under Gardner Murphy, whose interest in extrasensory perception, combined with my interest in children, led to my very first publication (Ross, Murphy, & Schmeidler, 1952). This article described my study of spontaneity and ESP in children, reporting that I had found neither. These negative results were published because Murphy believed that in as controversial a field as ESP even negative results should be put on record and, by virtue of the fact that he was the editor of the *Journal of the American Society for Psychical Research,* they were. In my senior year I was elected to Phi Beta Kappa, and I graduated in June 1949, magna cum laude with honors in psychology.

GOALS, CHOICES, AND DECISIONS.   When it was time to think about graduate school, I asked Professor Murphy's advice on where to go to study child psychology. This was before midlife crises and aging became objects of study; before the field became known as developmental psychology. Among my mementos is a piece of paper on which Murphy had written "Berkeley, Kansas, Clark, Yale, T.C." (the latter refers to

Teachers College of Columbia University). I applied to all of these schools. Here is the opening paragraph of the personal statement I submitted with my applications (another one of my mementos):

My vocational objective is college teaching and research in child development. I hope to obtain a teaching position at an institution which has a child development center connected with it so that I can do research and teach at the same time. As possible alternatives I have positions in child guidance, counseling or as school psychologist in mind. My interest lies primarily in studying ways of healthy development and in guiding parents and children along those lines.

Given the vicissitudes of life, I find it remarkable how close my actual career came to meeting this youthful objective.

Kansas, Clark, Yale, and "T.C." offered me admission. Berkeley later informed me that they had lost my application. As a veteran, I was entitled to government-paid tuition and a generous subsistence allowance. Financial considerations thus played no role in my decision about which of these offers to accept. I chose Yale because I viewed it as the most prestigious and because Kansas was too far, Clark too small, and Teachers College too close to home. Another chance event awaited me when I arrived at Yale in September 1949.

CLINICAL PSYCHOLOGY.   I was standing in the hallway with another incoming student, who had also graduated from CCNY. We were waiting to have mailboxes assigned to us, or some such thing, when a member of the faculty passed by, introduced himself, and asked each of us what aspect of psychology we expected to specialize in at Yale. "Child psychology," I said. "But we don't have a program in child psychology," said he. Seeing my consternation, he asked what subjects I would expect to study if they had a child psychology program. City College had not prepared me for that question, so I improvised. "Tests and measurement, statistics, personality, intelligence testing, social psychology," I ventured. "Oh," he said, "that's what we teach in our clinical program; you want to be a clinical psychologist!" It turned out that my interlocutor was Seymour Sarason, who had recently founded and was director of Yale's clinical program.

And that is how I became a clinical psychologist. I had only the vaguest idea what a clinical psychologist was, because that specialty was fairly new in those days and had not been mentioned in any of my undergraduate courses. If, instead of meeting Sarason on that first day, I had run into Frank Beach, Carl Hovland, or Neal Miller, I might have become a physiological, social, or experimental psychologist instead.

When I got back to New York during the Thanksgiving break, I looked up Gardner Murphy to ask him why he had recommended that I apply to Yale to study child psychology. He answered, "Because Arnold Gesell is there." Arnold Gesell, a well-known pediatrician who had written some widely read books on child rearing, had indeed been at Yale, but he had left two years earlier under less than harmonious circumstances, taking with him not only his entire staff but all of his equipment. Even while still at the university, he had never interacted with anyone in the psychology department, and no one knew of any graduate student who had ever worked with him. Undergraduate advisement was no better then than it is now.

CULTURE SHOCK. When I was a college student, department chairmen held their positions for decades and had far more influence over their departments than they have now when, in most places, a reluctant member of the faculty is elected to be chair for a three-year term and often can't wait to be relieved. At City College during my days there psychology was dominated by the highly respected and widely known Gardner Murphy. Under Murphy's influence, experimental psychology employed the molar concepts of the Gestalt school, physiological psychology was organismic, and personality was biosocial. When I graduated I knew very little about learning theory, other than that Pavlov had discovered classical conditioning while working with dogs and that Thorndike had studied instrumental learning with cats in puzzle boxes.

I was therefore due for quite a culture shock at Yale, where I discovered that they considered Clark Hull, not Gardner Murphy, to be the world's foremost psychologist. I had never heard of Clark Hull and his hypothetico-deductive theory of learning, knew nothing of the controversy between Hull and Tolman about latent learning, and was a stranger to the contributions of Kenneth Spence and O. Hobart Mowrer, whom the psychologists at Yale viewed as their foremost alumni. The Psychology Department at Yale, in the person of Neal Miller, soon introduced me to the Theory of Learning and the explanatory powers of drive, habit strength, fractional anticipatory goal response, and other mysterious constructs. As I look back, I find it remarkable how fragmented and parochial our field was in those days, when each department taught its own brand of psychology as if there were no other.

It was also a function of this parochialism that in my four years at Yale I never heard of Skinner, whose 1938 *Behavior of Organisms* had been around for ten years, five years longer than Hull's own 1943 *Principles of Behavior.* I recall how Neal Miller quickly changed the subject when a student who had taken Fred Keller's course at Columbia said something about Skinner's work.

CLINICAL TRAINING. The Boulder Conference took place in August 1949, a month before I began my graduate studies, and Seymour Sarason had been one of the participants. Having returned from the mountain, Sarason was intent on structuring his program according to the model agreed upon at Boulder. Yale was going to prepare clinical psychologists who were scientist-practitioners. One of the means for this preparation was to have students take their internship during the third year of graduate work so that they could return to their university for the fourth year and conduct dissertation research on one of the clinical questions they had encountered as interns. That fond hope, it turned out, rarely materialized. Dissertations had little to do with clinically relevant issues, and the internship was soon moved to the last year of graduate study, when the topic of the dissertation had long been decided upon.

In those days the training of clinical psychologists still focused mostly on assessment; that is, on administering such tests as the Rorschach and the TAT. Psychologists were just beginning to do therapy, and the fight with psychiatry over this issue was in full swing. In view of this, the high point of Yale's clinical program was the one-semester psychotherapy course. It was taught by John Dollard and based on the book he had written in collaboration with Neal Miller, *Personality and Psychotherapy,* which appeared in 1950. This book was an effort to translate psychoanalytic constructs into the terms of neo-Hullian drive reduction theory.

In the one and only treatment case I carried in my entire time in graduate school, I did what I had been taught by John Dollard, who supervised me: I listened to my client, occasionally said, "uhum" to reward appropriate verbal responses, and once in a while ventured an interpretation, intended to reveal to her that her unconscious sexual conflicts, stimulated by ambiguous social cues, were motivating maladaptive responses that were rewarded by anxiety reduction. Or some such formulation. The main thing was that all points of our guiding paradigm, drive—cue—response—reward, had been touched on in this "interpretation." Each session was taped on reel-to-reel equipment that filled half a room, and verbatim transcripts of my interviews and Dollard's supervisory comments later formed the basis of *Steps in Psychotherapy: Study of a Case of Sex-Fear Conflict,* which Dollard, White, and Auld published in 1953.

Ilse

By far the most important consequence of my decision to go to Yale is that it led to my meeting and marrying Ilse Wallis. Ilse was a graduate student at the Smith College School of Social Work, which had assigned her to a family agency in New Haven for her field placement. Looking for housing, we had independently decided to move into a student-run, 16-person cooperative, called Walden House, which—unusual for those days—accepted both men and women.

It was the perfect setting in which to get to know one another. Everyone took turns cooking, cleaning, washing dishes, and making repairs. We took all our meals together, and held lengthy meetings in which we set house policy. In this close and frequent proximity, Ilse and I were able to discover our similarities in attitudes, interests, backgrounds, and values—similarities which I now know to be the principal ingredients of a successful relationship and which, if one adds mutual support and respect, assure a harmonious and lasting marriage.

We were married in 1950, and our first daughter, Judy, arrived two years later. I have a picture of me in cap and gown, holding 1-year-old Judy in my arms on the day I received my doctorate.

The U.S. Army—Again

When I had been discharged from the army in 1946 I had chosen to retain a reserve commission because I mistakenly feared that I would have to start all over again as a private if another war were to break out. Sure enough, in 1950 another war did break out. It was fought in Korea and euphemistically referred to as a "police action on behalf of the United Nations." I was in my second year of graduate school when other students with reserve commissions were called to active duty. By then I was 30 years old and married, had lost my infatuation with big ships, and could not see another interruption of my education, let alone a separation from my wife.

To avoid being recalled to the Transportation Corps I signed up for the army's Clinical Psychology Internship Program, which had just been established to fill that service's need for clinical psychologists. Under that program one took the (third-year) internship in one of the army's major hospitals and was then assigned for one year back to one's university to finish the dissertation. For these two years of army-sponsored training one then owed three years of service as a clinical psychologist. The people in charge of this program hoped that most of those so trained would stay in the army and make it their career. In this I was to disappoint them.

My decision to enter that program turned out to be a good one. I served my internship at Walter Reed Army Hospital (now Medical Center) in Washington, D.C., where one of my supervisors was Captain Joseph V. Brady, who has long since shed both his uniform and his clinical psychology. Joe Brady's skeptical empiricism regarding the validity of projective tests may well have contributed to my own position on this matter. "Walter Reed," as the facility is known, was one of the few army installations that had a child guidance clinic for the families of military personnel. A rotation system enabled me to spend half of my internship year working with children, both in that clinic and on the pediatric service—an experience that was highly compatible with my old plan to become a child psychologist. Then came another chance encounter, this one in the locker room of the swimming pool at the officers' club.

A LOCKER-ROOM CONVERSATION.   I was at the point in changing from swimming trunks to uniform where second lieutenants and colonels are indistinguishable when another man, similarly attired, struck up a conversation with me. He asked what I was doing at Walter Reed, and when I told him that I was a psychology intern he identified himself as Colonel Zehrer, the head of all army psychologists, who had come from his downtown headquarters to take a swim. He wanted to know my university, and inquired about my interests. When I said "Yale" and "child psychology" he told me that in civilian life he had worked with children at an institution in Connecticut. "Get in touch with me when you finish your degree," he said as we put on our uniforms, his with silver eagles, mine with gold bars—for I had had to trade in my silver ones to get back into the army.

During the internship I gathered the data for my dissertation, which dealt with the effects of brain injury on tactual perception. I constructed a test for the quantitative assessment of tactile shape recognition, examined a normal control group, and then flew to four different army hospitals, where I obtained my brain-injured subjects—soldiers who had sustained bullet or shrapnel wounds at the Korean front. I was given access to their surgical records, so that I could see what part of the brain had been damaged—by today's standards, a sloppy way of localizing lesions. My results showed that those with parietal lesions were the most severely impaired—not too surprising, but publishable (Ross, 1954), and deemed worthy of a Ph.D.

Doctorate in hand, I was ready for my three years of indentured service, and I so notified my locker-room acquaintance from Walter Reed. That interview in the buff must have been as memorable to him as it had been to me, for he assigned me to the only other place in the United States where the army ran a child guidance clinic, Brooke Army Hospital (now Medical Center) in San Antonio, Texas. There were not very many psychologists or psychiatrists in the army who were interested in children. As a result, I immediately found myself appointed chief psychologist of the child guidance clinic. Looking at my vitae, someone once commented, "You have always been a chief, never an Indian." Well yes, but in San Antonio I was both chief and only psychologist in that clinic. Not unlike universities, the army is quick in giving out titles and slow in granting promotions.

RESEARCH, ARMY-STYLE.　　Toward the end of the Korean war, the two sides agreed to a massive exchange of prisoners, designated Big Switch. Someone in Washington came up with the idea of studying the effects on the personalities of our fighting men of having been a prisoner of war. The fact that there was no record of what their personalities had been like before they were imprisoned seemed not to matter. To implement this brilliant plan, every available clinical psychologist was flown to Korea under the highest priority.

I was one of these clinical psychologists, and on the way to Korea I had the heady experience of bumping colonels from overseas flights so that I could get to my destination without delay. Once there, we sat around for a week doing nothing until the first exchanges arrived. We were instructed to interview each of the men briefly to ascertain the circumstances of their being taken prisoner but not to ask about their prison experiences. That was to be left to specialists in debriefing, who were trying to identify those who had "collaborated with the communist enemy."

The exchanges were then placed on troopships that were to take them back to the United States. I was assigned to one of these ships with instructions to administer the Rorschach, specified cards from the TAT, and the Draw-a-Person test to a random sample of the men on board. I could not understand why I got so few and such banal responses and absolutely no responses to the red areas on the inkblot test. Later I learned that the debriefing interviews were continuing in another part of the ship, and I realized that the returnees had figured out that these interviews had to do with a search for traitors. I am sure that they suspected my mysterious tests of being part of this process.

The cubicle in which I did my testing was near the engine room; it was hot, smelly, and noisy. I suffered from seasickness, and under the best of circumstances my handwriting is barely legible; nevertheless the raw test protocols I thus produced were to be sent to Washington, D.C., by top secret courier as soon as I got ashore in Seattle. I can't believe that anybody could have used my "data" for anything. But maybe they were really just looking for "red" responses. Following orders, I put my notes into a big envelope, wrote "Top Secret" on it, and took it to the message center, where a clerk asked me whether I was cleared for top secret. "No," I said, and he grabbed the envelope out of my hand, shouting, "How did *you* get ahold of this?"

A REWARDING PUNISHMENT.　　Had I needed any reason for not making the army my career, that grotesque experience would have been high on the list. At the end of my second year of service, I received an official form that asked whether I would accept a

Regular Army commission to make the army my career. There was a place to check yes or no. I checked "no." That made the major who was head of my psychology unit furious. He accused me of unethical conduct and reported this opinion to APA's Division 7 (Developmental), to which I was applying for membership. They accepted me nevertheless, but that major was soon moved to Washington to become head of all army psychology. From that position he tried to punish me for what he saw as my disloyalty in checking "no" when I should have checked "yes." The punishment consisted of assigning me to be stationed in Europe when I had only 11 months of service left. This was meant as punishment because with an assignment of less than a year the army would not pay for the housing and travel of my dependents, forcing me to go alone. To avoid this, we paid for my family's travel ourselves. Once they were with me in Europe it was easy to persuade a local official to give us army housing, and the return trip the following year was at government expense.

By coincidence, and probably not part of the vengeful major's plan, my assignment in Europe was to the U.S. Army Hospital in Frankfurt am Main, where I had been born and where my fluent German came in handy. People have at times asked me what it was like to return to the German city where I had spent the first 17 years of my life. I think that they expect me to tell them about all sorts of strong emotions: Joy at having returned or sorrow about our losses; hatred against those responsible, or satisfaction at avenged wrongs; guilt about the destruction wrought by American bombers, or pity for those who had lost their homes. Somewhat to my surprise I experienced none of these, except for a feeling of numbness that I attributed to the many miles I had walked during the first week that I spent traveling all over town, visiting the graves of my grandparents, seeing a couple of my parents' friends who were still around, and looking at the places—mostly ruins—where I had lived and gone to school.

I suspected that this pilgrimage was my way of coping with whatever feelings I could not permit myself to experience. But then a lot of time had gone by between my leaving as a scared refugee boy of 17 and my return as a 34-year-old family man in the uniform of an officer in the U.S. Army.

I do not subscribe to a theory of collective guilt; individuals can do wrong, not all of the people who happen to share a nationality or religion. Thus, in that year in Germany, I would sometimes ask myself when I encountered a particularly unfriendly German in his 40s or 50s, "I wonder where *he* was and what he was doing 15 years ago," but I felt no animosity against the German people.

At any rate, by the time Ilse joined me three weeks after my own arrival, I had the need for walking out of my system and we thoroughly enjoyed my punitive tour of duty. With Judy and Pamela, who had been born while we were in San Antonio, we traveled all over Europe, using my weeks of accumulated leave and every long weekend. At the hospital I was again chief, of both the psychology section and of the child guidance clinic that I helped establish. This time, however, I also had a few Indians.

Despite the irritations and annoyances that are part of working in any large and therefore impersonal system such as the military, I have never regretted my decision to have the army underwrite my graduate education. My internship was a good learning experience, and the three years of clinical work that followed my doctorate laid a sound foundation for the rest of my career. Moreover, in view of the seniority I had accumulated in my prior years of service, the pay was better than it would have been in any civilian position a brand-new Ph.D. might have obtained.

The Child Guidance Years

New Haven

That my army pay had been more generous than that in any position I could find in civilian life was brought home to me when I began looking for a job after leaving the service in 1956. I contacted my old advisor at Yale, Seymour Sarason, who gave me two leads. One was the position of director of research at the E.R. Johnstone Training and Research Center in Bordentown, New Jersey, a state institution for retarded; the other was a job as chief (and only) psychologist at the Clifford W. Beers (child) Guidance Clinic in New Haven, Connecticut. I was interviewed at both places and had decided on the New Haven job by the time the people in Bordentown notified me that they were offering their position to someone else.

Once again everything turned out well. We bought a house, Ilse found a professional position that she enjoyed, and the children went to good schools. I received an appointment as assistant professor of psychology in the Evening College of what is now Southern Connecticut State College, where I taught courses in child development and intelligence testing. Moreover, Yale gave me an appointment as lecturer in return for my supervising some of their practicum students who were placed in our clinic. My clinical work consisted of the assessment and treatment of children, and in 1958 this experience qualified me to become a diplomate in clinical psychology of the American Board of Professional Psychology. Meanwhile I worked on the manuscript of my first book, *The Practice of Clinical Child Psychology,* which Grune & Stratton published in 1959.

THE FIRST BOOK.   The idea for my first book had come to me in 1955 while I was driving my sleeping family from San Antonio to New York City, whence I was to be flown to my army assignment in Germany. I have had academic aspirations ever since my college days, and recall a conversation with a young woman whom I was then dating. We were talking about my academic plans, when she made a disparaging comment about the limited income of college professors. I pointed out that one could supplement that income by writing textbooks and she skeptically replied, "Just like that?" "Yes, just like that—I'll show you," I thought; and though I had since married a far more supportive woman who has faith in my abilities, this silent vow remained with me through the years.

There was another, somewhat curious motivation for writing that first book. It had to do with my father-in-law. Ilse was born in Austria, where her father had been the music critic of Vienna's foremost daily newspaper. When I met him in New York, where he had immigrated, Alfons Wallis worked for a music publisher as an editor and arranger. He was the quintessential Central European intellectual. No aspect of culture, be it philosophy, history, literature, art, or music, was alien to him, and his conversations were sprinkled with relevant allusions to historical figures, ancient and modern. Compared to him, I saw myself and my parents as bourgeois philistines, and I felt a great need to have him see me as worthy of being his son-in-law. Writing a book should do it, I thought; and I think it did.

When the book appeared, "clinical child psychology" was an unfamiliar expression. I had been able to find only two articles in relatively obscure publications in which that term had been used. In the preface to that book I wrote, "It has been my conviction for some time that clinical child psychology is a distinct professional specialty," and I expressed the hope that this book would "contribute to the professional maturation of clinical child psychology." Looking at the field today, and seeing a journal with that term on its masthead, doctoral programs with that title, and announcements of position vacancies in that specialty, I feel safe in saying that my hope has been fulfilled. I like to think that I contributed to the founding of that specialty. The section on Clinical Child Psychology of APA's Division of Clinical Psychology seemed to share that impression when, in 1982, they gave me their Award for Distinguished Professional Contributions to the Service of Children.

CROSS-CULTURAL RESEARCH. During my three years in New Haven (1956 to 1959), I also became involved in my sole excursion into interdisciplinary research. Through the good offices of Seymour Sarason, I was contacted by Edward M. Bruner, then a member of Yale's Department of Anthropology, who wanted to conduct a field study on acculturation among a small ethnic group from a mountain village in Sumatra, some of whom had lately migrated to a large coastal city. In addition to the ethnographic material he and his wife were to gather, he also wanted to compare the personality characteristics of those in the traditional village with those in the city. My job was first to teach Bruner's wife how to administer the Rorschach and TAT and later to do blind interpretations of the responses, which she would translate and mail to me from Sumatra. The personality descriptions I produced in this unlikely manner coincided remarkably well with what the anthropologist couple said they knew about their subjects, and I performed better than chance in discriminating between the village and city people. Two publications resulted from that study (Ross, 1962; Ross & Bruner, 1963); but because our working styles were so incompatible that we eventually parted ways, I also learned from that experience never to enter into collaboration with someone with whose work habits I am not familiar.

Pittsburgh

The New Haven years had been pleasant enough. The staff of the clinic was collegial and compatible, the work not overwhelming, and although the psychiatrist-director was not overly stimulating, he generally let me decide what I wanted to do and how and when to do it. I don't know how long I would have stayed there had I not been offered the position of chief psychologist at the Pittsburgh Child Guidance Center in Pennsylvania.

The poverty-stricken New Haven clinic was housed in a former home; my office had once been a kitchen. The well-endowed Pittsburgh clinic, in contrast, was located in its own modern four-story building with elevator and central air conditioning; I was to have a corner office and a personal secretary. Whereas the New Haven staff, in addition to me, consisted of two social workers, one psychiatrist, and one secretary, Pittsburgh could boast of six social workers, four psychologists, three psychiatrists, and half a dozen secretaries, as well as residents, interns, and students in all three disciplines. It was a large pond, and I hopped into it with little hesitation, especially since the position carried with it an adjunct appointment as associate professor in the Psychology Department of the University of Pittsburgh.

The pond, unfortunately, soon became polluted by the arrival of a new psychiatrist-director. While the one who had brought me to Pittsburgh had been a bright, creative, relaxed, and rational individual who respected psychologists and psychology and believed in genuine teamwork among the three disciplines, his replacement was the exact opposite. An insecure, arbitrary, and petty autocrat, he insisted that the psychiatrists hold hegemony over all aspects of clinic operation and be in charge of everything having to do with treatment.

In those days, child guidance clinics employed the team approach to work with families. Theoretically, the psychologist did the testing, the psychiatrist the therapy with the child, and the social worker the counseling of the parent (read mother). In reality, because there was never enough psychiatric time available, the treatment of the child was handled by a psychologist, but—so it was decreed—always under the supervision of a psychiatrist. It was a demeaning state of affairs, to which I responded by withdrawing from treatment activities, concentrating instead on the supervision of the staff psychologists and interns, doing research, writing, and teaching at the university.

APA ACTIVITIES.   It was during those years that I became involved in the affairs of psychological organizations. I enjoyed these activities and invested a good deal of time in them; the fact that they often took me out of town and thus away from the clinic was an added bonus.

In 1961 I participated in the founding of the Section on Clinical Child Psychology of the Clinical Division of the APA, an event that I later described in "Clinical Child Psychology" (Ross, 1972a), a chapter in Wolman's *Manual of Child Psychopathology,* which also contains my chapter on "Behavior Therapy" (Ross, 1972b). The following year, 1962, found me on the committee that planned and organized the 1965 "Chicago Training Conference" (Hoch, Ross, & Winder, 1966), at which the concepts of professional schools of psychology and the Psy.D. degree received their first official discussion. In 1965 I was also appointed to the board of directors of the Joint Commission on Mental Health of Children, which labored mightily for four years, only to produce a report and recommendations that few read and none heeded. My reflections on that fiasco are recorded in *Clinical Child Psychology: Current Practices and Future Perspectives,* a volume edited by Williams and Gordon, to which I contributed a chapter with the imposing title, "Forecasting the Future and Four Years After the Forecast" (Ross, 1974a).

Conversion to Behavior Therapy [1]

As my 1959 book on clinical child psychology reflects, I approached my clinical work from a psychodynamic point of view. Assessment meant using projective methods to ascertain ego strength and to uncover conflicts and defenses. Treatment entailed the use of very permissive play therapy, through which the child was expected to express his or her problems so that I could provide interpretations that might lead to insight.

By about 1963 I had become increasingly skeptical about the efficacy of what I was doing for the children with whom I worked. More and more frequently, I felt that I was an overtrained, overqualified, overpaid baby sitter who kept the child occupied while my teammate, the social worker who was counseling the mother, was responsible for whatever it was that occasionally made the treatment seem effective. I say "seem" because we had neither a way to quantify change nor an objective record of the child's status before and after our intervention. Further, I say "occasionally" because it was only once in a while that we thought that the child's condition had improved. This was usually when the social worker had succeeded in persuading the mother to change the way she dealt with the child at home.

In 1963, I was invited to be the discussant in a symposium entitled "Clinical Aspects of Learning," which was to take place at the annual meeting of the American Orthopsychiatric Association, of which I was a member—in fact, a board member. "Ortho," as its members call the association, is an interdisciplinary organization of mental health professionals who shared the psychoanalytic orientation that, in those days, was pretty much the only game in town.

Unlike the usual hapless discussant, who is lucky to receive the papers to be presented at the symposium a day before the meeting, I received the contribution of one group of participants more than a month in advance. This gave me time to think about what I would say; and what I wanted to say after reading their paper was, "Oh, my god!" Here was a distinguished group of workers at a well-known children's clinic in Boston whose paper dealt with the difficulty reading-disabled boys often have in telling apart the lower-case letters *b, d, p,* and *q*. My colleagues from Boston were going to share with the convention the discovery that each of these four letters is composed of an oval adjacent to a vertical line that either stands erect or hangs down. They were going to remind their listeners that 6-year-old boys are anxious about things adjacent to ovals that either stand erect or hang down, and this they identified as the cause of little boys' letter reversal.

Now when you are a discussant on a symposium and have 20 minutes to fill, you can't just say, "Oh, my god" and sit down. Wondering what I could possibly say, I remembered that I had earned my Ph.D. at a time when Yale had been the fountainhead of learning theory. Here I was, a Yale-trained psychologist, being asked to discuss a paper that dealt with the psychological problems in learning to read. Surely,

---

[1] The following is a slightly modified part of the Invited Opening Address I delivered on 10/9/87 to the Eighth Annual Berkshire Conference on Behavior Analysis and Therapy, under the title "A Farewell to Freud."

I thought, there must be *something* I can say in my discussion that is based not on wild, metaphorical speculations, but on what psychologists know about learning. With that I went to the library and (without the help of a computer) searched *Psychological Abstracts* for references that dealt with the intersect of learning and psychological disorders. From this search emerged a discussion that was eventually published under the title "Learning Theory and Therapy with Children" (Ross, 1964). It was my first halting contribution to the literature of behavior therapy.

The literature I had set out to search was not very extensive in those days. When Kalish wrote his chapter on behavior therapy for Wolman's 1965 *Handbook of Clinical Psychology,* he could cite but half a dozen relevant papers. The earliest of these was the 1949 *Psychological Bulletin* article by Joseph Shoben entitled "Psychotherapy as a Problem in Learning Theory." A similar article, this one by Albert Bandura, was published 12 years later, in 1961. It also appeared in *Psychological Bulletin,* under the title "Psychotherapy as a Learning Process." Before that, there had been the 1958 book, *Psychotherapy by Reciprocal Inhibition,* by an unknown South African named Joseph Wolpe, and a 1959 article, "Learning Theory and Behavior Therapy," by the equally unknown Hans Jürgen Eysenck, who lived in England. Also in 1959, Stanley Rachman had reported on "The Treatment of Anxiety and Phobic Reactions by Systematic Desensitization Therapy."

I found all this very exciting; but most provocative and seminal in all this newly discovered literature was Chapter 24 of B. F. Skinner's 1953 *Science and Human Behavior.* Here was that Harvard psychologist, mention of whose name had made Neal Miller so uncomfortable in his learning seminar back in New Haven. Miller's parochialism notwithstanding, I am sure that my learning theory background from Yale enhanced my ability to understand and appreciate this new approach, which I greeted with much enthusiasm. Here were laboratory-derived psychological principles being applied to the kind of problems with which I, as a clinical psychologist, was supposed to be able to deal.

What I call my "conversion" from psychoanalytic to behavior therapy was almost instantaneous. Not unlike Saul of Tarsus on the road to Damascus, I had experienced a revelation. I had found the explanation of why a child's behavior improved when the mother had learned to change her parenting behavior. Moreover, I could now understand why the aggressive children I had attempted to treat had become ever more aggressive under my ministrations, which had consisted of permitting them—nay, encouraging them—to shoot, punch, kick, and stab the inflatable Bobo doll in my office. I realized that I had indeed been an overpaid baby sitter, and a bad one at that, but that I had been neither overqualified nor overtrained, but unqualified for what I was doing because I had been trained in what I now considered to be counterproductive methods.

At this point I began to retrain myself, without benefit of postdoctoral institutes or continuing education seminars, because those had not yet arrived on the scene. By studying the 1961 programmed text by Holland and Skinner, *The Analysis of Behavior,* I compensated for Yale's refusal to teach operant principles. Then I set out to read everything I could find on the behavioral approach to formulating and treating psychological problems. Soon there was much to read. The year 1965 saw not only the publication of the clinical and research volumes on behavior modification by Ullmann and Krasner (1965), but also the appearance of Eysenck and Rachman's *The Causes and Cures of Neuroses*. In 1969 Wolpe's *The Practice of Behavior Therapy* appeared, as did Bandura's *Principles of Behavior Modification.* The flood of publications that began then still shows no sign of abating. In this recitation of the early bibliography of behavior therapy that so impressed me, credit must also be given to a work that had appeared some 20 years before its time—Andrew Salter's *Conditioned Reflex Therapy* (1949).

My reeducation, however, was not limited to reading. By another of those coincidences that dot my career, there were at that time on the faculty of the University of Pittsburgh two clinical psychologists, Peter Lang and David Lazovik, who had conducted and published in 1963 the first controlled laboratory experiment on Wolpean desensitization. Some of their graduate students, such as Robert Hawkins and Carolyn Schroeder, were placed at the child guidance center for their internships, and they and I now began to apply to cases at our clinic the operant and respondent methods that I had been reading about, and that they had learned from Lazovik and Lang.

Behold, it worked! Children's behavior improved almost literally before our eyes, parents marveled at the miracles we wrought, and jealous psychiatrists asked to be taught our secrets. Here was an approach to treatment that not only made it possible to spell out exactly what we were doing and why, but that also permitted us to demonstrate constructive change in a very limited time. No more finger painting, marble rolling, block building, target shooting, and story telling. I find it difficult to communicate the excitement we experienced in those pioneering days. A fog had lifted, ending ten years of self-doubt and feeling like an imposter.

The University Years

The Midcareer Change

What remained of my relationship with the psychiatrist-director of the Pittsburgh Child Guidance Center came to an end in 1965 when that agency obtained the financial wherewithal to develop a research unit and he declared that the person to head it would have to be a psychiatrist. At that point I decided to get out of psychiatric settings and began looking for an academic position.

A WINDOW OF OPPORTUNITY.   It was a uniquely opportune time to contemplate such a move. Neither before nor since was it possible for a practicing clinician to transfer to a university career and to enter at a senior level. When people like Seymour Sarason were drafted from positions in such institutions as state schools for the retarded to found university clinical programs shortly after World War II, they had to start as assistant professors and climb the academic ladder.

In the late 1960s and early 70s the postwar "baby boom" had reached college age. To accommodate (and at times exploit) that large number of potential students, secretarial schools redefined themselves as colleges, teachers' colleges became liberal arts colleges, and liberal arts colleges expanded to become universities. This explosive growth in higher education brought with it a need for new faculty at every level of experience, and it was thus that departments of psychology looked to psychiatric clinics and hospitals to staff their newly established or expanding graduate programs in clinical psychology. All of this ended when the baby boom generation had passed through the pipeline, an economic recession set in, and the White House was occupied by Richard Nixon, who was not favorably disposed toward higher education. Now, as before these heady days, people contemplating an academic career must expect to enter at the bottom.

Between 1965 and 1967 I had considered a number of offers from universities that wanted me to join their faculties with the rank of professor. It helped that I had conducted research, authored a reasonable number of publications, and become visible through my organizational activities. Moreover, I had held the rank of professor, albeit in an adjunct status, at the University of Pittsburgh, where I had taught one course every semester.

GIVING CHANCE A HELPING HAND. In the state of New York, the explosion in higher education entailed the establishment of an entirely new system: the State University of New York (SUNY). One major university campus of that system was being developed near Stony Brook, a small village on Long Island. Located at the north shore, some 60 miles outside of New York City, this university, SUNY at Stony Brook, had just been the subject of a very positive two-article series in *Science*. Moreover, the founding chair of the Psychology Department, Harry Kalish, had authored the definitive chapter on behavior therapy for Benjamin Wolman's *Handbook of Clinical Psychology* (1965). Stony Brook sounded like an ideal place for a behavior therapist with family in New York City who liked to swim and wanted to get away from Pittsburgh. It was time for another coincidence, and since none seemed to materialize, I decided to give chance a helping hand.

My first attempt to make contact with Stony Brook was to seek out a member of the Pittsburgh faculty who had been a fellow graduate student of Harry Kalish's at the University of Iowa. I asked that man to write Kalish a letter on my behalf, but he replied, "Alan, there's nothing for you at Stony Brook," another memorable phrase that I store next to the ones about not buying at Gristede's and writing books "just like that."

My next opportunity for making contact with Stony Brook came through my service on the committee that was planning the Chicago Training Conference. This committee had decided that the conference participants would be divided into small workgroups, which would bring recommendations to plenary sessions for discussion and vote. Somehow I wound up on the subcommittee that was charged with deciding who was to be assigned to which workgroup. One of those invited was Leonard Krasner, who had just moved from Palo Alto to Stony Brook to develop its clinical program. Krasner and I were somehow assigned to the same workgroup so that we sat across the table from one another for five days and many evenings, helping to hammer out a model program for training clinical psychologists. This acquaintanceship resulted in my being invited to join the Stony Brook faculty, and we moved there in September 1967. Not once have either Ilse or I regretted that move, and I rarely have qualms about the subtle maneuvers that brought it to pass.

There is a story about a self-made millionaire who, when asked how it felt to be rich, replied, "I've been rich and I've been poor. Rich is better." I've been a practitioner in a community clinic and I've been a professor in academia. Academia is better. To me, there is no better life than the life of a college professor—especially when you don't have to sweat out promotions and tenure decisions but can start at the top, as I did. It is a life in which you can pretty well decide what you want to do and how you want to do it. Within broad limits, you control your own schedule. You can decide whether you want to work on your own or collaborate with someone else. You are surrounded by bright people in a stimulating environment and, through teaching and research, you are constantly enlarging your horizons. However, academic life is not for everyone. It calls for a great deal of intrinsic motivation and self-discipline. People who need a lot of structure in order to function, or who can't plan ahead and meet deadlines, do not succeed in the relaxed atmosphere of the college campus.

Stony Brook

Harry Kalish and Len Krasner had decided that clinical psychology at Stony Brook should be based on behavioral principles. The theories that graduate students would be expected to learn were the theories of respondent and operant learning; the therapy they would be taught would be behavior therapy; and the assessment procedures used would consist of objective tests and behavior observations. It was a revolutionary notion. One or two other clinical programs were teaching behavior therapy in addition to psychodynamic therapy, but nowhere was there a program that was explicitly and totally behavioral. Word of our approach spread quickly, and Stony Brook soon became known all over the world as the place to go if you wanted to learn behavior therapy. The graduate program, as well as the postdoctoral program we operated during the first eight years, attracted far more applicants than we could accommodate.

It was most rewarding to be a part of this exciting development. My own role was to help develop the child and family part of the program; and though I was never able to persuade my colleagues to establish a distinct specialty in clinical child psychology, the careers of many of our alumni reflect an interest in children.

RESEARCH. When working in a service-oriented community clinic, one usually has little time and less support for research; but while I was in Pittsburgh I had applied for and received grants, one from the National Institute of Mental Health and another from the National Science Foundation. They enabled me to carry out several investigations. One of these, conducted in collaboration with David Parton and Harvey Lacey, had resulted in the publication of a behavior checklist (Ross, Lacey, & Parton, 1965), which we had intended to use as a criterion measure in a projected study of treatment outcome. However, all three of us left that clinic for one reason or another before that study could get under way.

If one wishes to do research on a clinically relevant topic, one encounters a dilemma that needs to be resolved. The patient population and activities, such as treatment, are to be found in community clinics or hospitals, but these settings are rarely hospitable to investigators wishing to conduct controlled studies. The psychology department of a university is a far more hospitable environment. There, research is one of the activities that members of the faculty are expected to pursue, and students provide a source of motivated assistants. The typical department, however, has neither the patient population nor activities such as treatment on which clinical investigators want to focus their studies.

As a member of a psychology department faculty, I have tried to solve this dilemma in two different ways, and have found neither one completely satisfactory. One way is to go off campus and conduct research where the relevant subjects are. For a study on visual perception of deaf children that David Santogrossi, Ross Vasta, and I had planned, we bought a specially equipped laboratory trailer and parked it outside a school for the deaf, which had no suitable room for us. We connected the trailer to the house current and brought the children one by one to the trailer to be tested. When it rained or became cold, this meant helping the child into, out of, back into, and back out of hoods, coats, mittens, and boots. At another time the director of a Head Start Program very kindly let us use her storeroom so that Rita Wicks-Nelson and Rosemery Nelson could test subjects for a study on language acquisition. That storeroom, however, was so noisy that the children could not hear our questions, nor we their answers. The "real world" is rarely set up for scientific investigations that require equipment, space, and maybe even quiet.

The alternative to going where the subjects are is to bring the subjects to where the investigators are, on campus. This is done by opening a service facility on campus that can be used for both research and training. We did this at Stony Brook by establishing the Psychological Center, a mental health facility serving the off-campus community. Unfortunately, the triple functions of service, training, and research are largely incompatible. To render service and provide training one needs an all-purpose facility that is available to a wide variety of clients with a wide variety of problems. Most research projects, however, require a reasonably large number of fairly homogenous subjects with the same or similar problems. What to do?

In the 1970s, my students Rosemery Nelson and Julia Heiman and I wanted to test some hypotheses I had proposed in my 1976 *Psychological Aspects of Learning Disabilities and Reading Disorders.* I had grant support from the National Institute of Education, and all we needed was a group of children with reading difficulties; but no such children were coming to the Psychological Center at that time. Our solution was to hire a reading specialist and to establish a remedial reading program at the center, announcing its availability in the school districts surrounding the campus.

That solution, however, brought with it another problem, for when the research project ended and the grant expired we had to close the program. By this time, however, the community had learned that there was a remedial reading program on campus, and the referrals kept coming long after we had folded our tents and stolen away. The people who called had to be told that this service was no longer available. It was embarrassing to the center and disappointing to the referral sources we had cultivated. If this sort of thing is done repeatedly as different investigators want to use the service facility for their specialized projects, the facility soon loses the good will of the community.

With this in mind, I have alternated the site of my research projects between going into the community and bringing subjects to campus. The selective attention study with Carol Ford and William Pelham was carried out in the schools, while my ongoing project on personality variables in child-abusing mothers, in which Vivian Shaw Lamphear, Joseph Stets, Valerie Gaus-Binkley, and Karen Lieber have been or are involved, is being conducted on campus. Here again, it has been necessary to offer a service in the form of anger-control programs and child-rearing training in order to attract the necessary subject population.

TEACHING.   Just as I was moving to a full-time professorial position, universities throughout the country were experiencing an unprecedented period of unrest. College students and young faculty members were protesting the war in Vietnam, participating in the civil rights and women's liberation movements, experimenting with alternative lifestyles, and trying out various mind- and mood-altering drugs. Stony Brook was not spared. Shortly after my arrival there the county police conducted a politically motivated, early-morning drug raid on the dormitories, which outraged faculty and students alike and made headlines all over the country. People who had never heard of Stony Brook now greeted those who came from there with allusions to that raid. Especially during exam periods, classes were often disrupted by false fire alarms that required vacating the building. As was my custom in those days, when our classes were still small, I wanted to create a seating plan at the beginning of the term so that I could call the students by name; but one year several of the men in class protested, proclaiming that I had no right to make them always sit in the same seat.

As in the Chinese curse, we were living in exciting days, but my joy in teaching remained undiminished. I taught both graduate and undergraduate courses, and found that the less the students knew about the subject matter before they came to my course, the better I liked teaching them. Introductory Psychology has thus always been my favorite subject, followed closely by Psychological Disorders of Children, for which I wrote a textbook (1974b; 1980).

I continue to find teaching very rewarding. Twice our graduating psychology class has voted me "Professor of the Year," and in 1988 I received the University President's Award for Excellence in Teaching. Most rewarding of all, however, is when a stranger addresses me at a convention with the inevitable phrase, "Dr. Ross, you won't remember me, but. . ." This opening is usually followed by a reference to a class of mine in which that person had been enrolled and ends with how much he or she enjoyed that course. Sometimes such former students add that it was my course that made them decide to become a psychologist. Encounters like this always leave me with an intimation of intellectual immortality.

ORGANIZATIONAL AFFAIRS.   My years at Stony Brook have also been years during which I continued to be active in various professional organizations. Among the most stimulating and enjoyable of these involvements was my service on the board of trustees of the American Board of Professional Psychology (ABPP), during a time when a plethora of jobs and a dearth of qualified psychologists made trying to become a diplomate by taking that board's difficult examination something that relatively few considered worth their while. During these lean years the ABPP might well have ceased to exist had it not been for the fact that its president, the late Alfred J. Marrow, kept it afloat by providing a hefty subsidy from his own not inconsiderable financial resources. As a result, the ABPP was still alive when the job market tightened in the late 1970s, so that a job applicant with the board's diploma had an edge over those whose competence was not thus certified. With that, applications for admission to the ABPP exam increased, for holding the diploma had become desirable once again.

In 1972, Alfred Marrow, two other members of the ABPP board, and I established a subsidiary of ABPP, the National Academy of Professional Psychologists. The mission of that organization was to sponsor programs of continuing professional education for psychologists, a rather new concept at that time. To introduce it, I offered to spend part of my 1974 sabbatical leave visiting various state psychological associations and universities, promoting the academy and continuing professional education. Alfred Marrow was a trustee of the New School for Social Research, and through his influence and, I suspect, with his money, that university supported me during my sabbatical, while an anonymous patron of the academy paid for my travels. Wherever I went, people told me that continuing professional education was a great idea, but they demurred when it became available. It was a great idea—for the other person. We soon became aware that there would not be a market for continuing professional education until the various jurisdictions made it a condition of license renewal. In the 1970s, that time had not yet come.

Although the ABPP has not succeeded in promoting continuing education, we were instrumental in two other developments. One was that we laid the groundwork on which the APA was eventually to establish the Sponsor Approval System which approves organizations that sponsor programs of continuing education in psychology. The other, rarely recognized, contribution of the ABPP had to do with establishing an organization for the purpose of maintaining a list of psychologists qualified to provide assessment and treatment services to the public. As third-party payment for the services of psychologists became available, insurers often asked the APA for a list of its members who were qualified to render such services. For a number of reasons, the APA could not and would not provide such a list, and its leadership turned to the ABPP for help. Although the ABPP lacked the resources to manage that task, we did call a meeting of various interested parties. This meeting was held in Alfred Marrow's Fifth Avenue apartment in New York City, and it was there that the idea was spawned to create a new organization, charged with developing and maintaining a list of qualified practitioners. I had to leave that meeting early and, while driving home on the infamous Long Island Expressway, I came up with the cumbersome title for the organization we had been talking about: The National Register for Health Service Providers in Psychology. Upon arriving home, I called Marrow's apartment. The meeting was still in progress, and I transmitted my invention to the group through my friend, Carl Zimet, who was to become the first president of "The Register." I doubt that those who now have to struggle with that nine-word title look fondly upon my contribution.

Speaking of cumbersome titles, there was also the National Conference on Levels and Patterns of Professional Training in Psychology. This conference was held at Vail, Colorado and became known as the Vail Conference. Although I attended that meeting and had been on the steering committee that planned it, I take no credit for its title and do not want to be blamed for its product. Like its predecessor conference, which had been held in Chicago some ten years earlier, this one was called to deal with the marked changes that had been taking place in the professional environment; but there the similarity ends.

The Chicago Conference had been a response to the phenomenal postwar growth of psychology and particularly of clinical psychology in its various facets. That conference was attended by deans, department chairs, directors of clinical training, and heads of the psychological services at large and well-known institutions. They represented the establishment of psychology and, not too surprisingly, they voted to maintain in status quo the scientist-practitioner model, which a similar group had proclaimed at Boulder in 1949.

The first allusion that there might be other models for preparing clinical practitioners, such as the doctor of psychology (Psy.D.) program then being planned at the University of Illinois, was dispatched with the quasiempirical neutrality reflected in the following paragraphs from the conference proceedings (Hoch, Ross, & Winder, 1966):

It is recognized that other pilot or experimental programs in university psychology departments may be attempted. The experience with and the results of such programs will provide the only bases on which their effectiveness in producing clinical psychologists should be evaluated (p. 93).

The impetus for the Vail Conference came not so much from pressures within psychology as from the turmoil in American society, where such previously disenfranchised and underrepresented groups as Blacks, Hispanics, gays, and women were at last seeking their share of influence and power. The roster of those who were to attend that conference repeatedly prompted the question "Who's that?"; for unlike the list of participants in Chicago, it did not read like a Who's Who in American Psychology. It is thus not surprising that these conferees voted to open the professional preparation of psychologists not only to a greater variety of students, but also to a greater variety of levels and patterns of training. This included an explicit statement of support for practice-oriented programs leading to the Psy.D. degree, including programs in freestanding schools of psychology, not affiliated with universities or medical schools.

In those days I was still firmly convinced that the training of clinical psychologists should hew to the scientist-practitioner model. My 1970 President's Address to the Division of Clinical Psychology, seductively entitled "The Case of the Innocent Model," represented a vigorous defense of the Boulder model, and at Vail I resolutely voted against every motion designed to legitimize alternate routes into the field. Where do I stand today?

Reflections and Predictions

The Behavior Therapist as Scientist-Practitioner

The defense of the scientist-practitioner model of graduate training, which had been the substance of my President's Address to Division 12, was based on my conviction that the behavioral orientation presented the answer to the identity problems that plagued clinical psychology and that had occasioned the recurrent training conferences. I felt that to be scientist as well as practitioner, the clinical psychologist would have to hold an orientation that was as applicable in the laboratory as it was in the clinic. The behavioral approach appeared to be just such an orientation. It had served American psychology well in the laboratory; and behavior therapy based, as it then was, on laboratory research was proving itself in the clinic. A behaviorally trained clinical psychologist should thus be able to actualize the dream of Boulder: to move with ease between clinic and laboratory, carrying laboratory findings into the clinic and clinical problems into the laboratory. Conversely, I argued, the then-dominant psychodynamic orientation made this two-way traffic impossible, forcing clinical psychologists to approach their clinical work from one point of view and their laboratory work from another, with the result that few could be found who embodied the scientist-practitioner model.

I was able to hold fast to this point of view for many years, expressing it with conviction, and backed by data, in my 1981 text, *Child Behavior Therapy.* Clinical work with children, I still maintain, is best conducted from a behavioral point of view. The behavior of children is largely under environmental control, and their environment, in turn, is predominantly under the control of their parents and teachers. By influencing the environment you influence the child's behavior, making the principles of operant and respondent conditioning eminently useful for this purpose.

My colleagues who were working with adolescents and adults soon found themselves somewhat less enchanted with the Pavlovian and Skinnerian principles of the midtwentieth century. Much of the behavior of their clients seemed a function of private events. An unfortunate development ensued. Instead of trying to find out what modifications or extensions these principles might require or what untapped principles the psychological laboratory might have to offer that would meet the needs of clinical realities, they adopted approaches whose provenance bore a closer resemblance to the power of positive thinking, which the Rev. Norman Vincent Peale had promoted some 20 years earlier, than to the research conducted on the phenomena of social, developmental, experimental, cognitive, or personality psychology.

I want to define what I mean by behavior therapy, and can best do so by quoting from my Presidential Address to the Association for the Advancement of Behavior Therapy, as published in *Behavior Therapy* (1985):

> To me, behavior therapy is the empirically controlled application of the science of human behavior to the alleviation of psychological distress and the modification of maladaptive behavior. Note that this definition does not require behavior therapists to limit their treatment to systematic desensitization and

contingency management, as some traditionalists advocate. Neither, however, does it give therapists the license to include under the rubric of behavior therapy whatever intervention happens to strike their fancy, as is the wont of those who employ basically idiosyncratic treatment methods.

When, in line with my definition, behavior therapy is seen as the application of the science of human behavior, it cannot be a closed system, impervious to change. Like science itself, behavior therapy must be an open-ended, self-correcting, constantly growing enterprise. This it can remain only, however, if behavior therapists continue to relate their treatment methods to the contemporary knowledge derived from research in behavioral science (p. 196).

Addressing my fellow behavior therapists, I added the following sentence, which expresses the opinion I hold to this day:

It is from that point of view that I see our endeavor in default; in danger of ceasing to be the vibrant and challenging field it was when the women and men of my generation abandoned the archaic psychodynamic approach to participate in the advancement of behavior therapy (ibid.).

There are many former behavior therapists who attempt to cope with the inconvenient fact that not every problem they encounter in the clinic yields to the traditional methods of operant or respondent conditioning by invoking what they call "cognitive behavior therapy." Looking closely at what they do, it is neither cognitive nor behavior therapy, but a regression to an uncritical eclecticism that our pioneers fought so hard to exorcise. When I say that this development is not cognitive, I mean that it does not represent the application in the clinical setting of principles established in the cognitive learning laboratory, analogous to the earlier application of principles from the conditioning laboratory. Documentation and support for this assertion can be found in the paper just cited.

If cognitive behavior therapy were indeed the application of empirically derived laboratory principles, I would enthusiastically support it. As it is, the most charitable statement I can make about it is that the research being conducted in cognitive psychology is not yet at the point where it might provide clinicians with the tools they need for dealing with the problems they face.

THE CLINICAL BIND.   This leads me to what someone once called the "clinical bind." Psychologists as practicing clinicians are constantly faced with problems for which their science has not yet provided the answer. What are they to do? Admit their impotence by telling their clients that they don't know what to do? Tell them to come back when laboratory research is ready to provide the answer? Or proceed to treat their clients with whatever method looks promising?

The latter is the usual solution to the clinical bind, but that alone is not responsible clinical psychology. Since none of the other options is acceptable, responsible clinical psychologists must approach "whatever method looks promising" as the testing of a hypothesis; they must gather data to test that hypothesis and stand ready to discard the treatment method when this test shows that the method does not work.

This empirical approach had been the hallmark of behavior therapy. It entailed gathering objective, quantitative data before, during, and after therapy, and called for a follow-up evaluation to assess the maintenance of the behavior change. As far as I can ascertain, such an empirical approach is absent from the eclectic treatments that their practitioners refer to as cognitive behavior therapy, so that, whatever it might be, it is not the legitimate heir of behavior therapy. To my chagrin, I see that trend to an uncritical eclecticism even in the clinical psychology program of the institution that once was the fountainhead of behavior therapy—Stony Brook. This is one of the reasons that I ultimately chose to withdraw from active participation in that training program.

Behaviorism and Personality

I have decried the response of many of my fellow behavior therapists when they discovered the limitations of their method while working with the wide range of problems their adult clients bring them. Having had a somewhat analogous experience, I wish to report it and where it led me.

Twice a year, the clinical psychology faculty at Stony Brook discusses who shall teach what in the semester to follow. On such an occasion in 1980 I offered to teach our undergraduate course on personality, which up to that time had been labeled "Theories of Personality" and consisted of a recital of the 57 varieties of personality theory that are covered in Hall and Lindzey and its clones. I viewed it as a challenge to attempt to develop a personality course based not on the obsolete theories of dead theorists but on the contemporary science of psychology. Having been reasonably successful in bringing laboratory-derived psychology to bear on learning disabilities in my 1976 *Psychological Aspects of Learning Disabilities and Reading Disorders,* I saw no reason why it should not be possible to do the same with personality.

I set out to find a textbook that approached personality from a behavioral, or at least an empirical, point of view. Not too surprisingly, barring one rather unsatisfactory exception, there was no such thing. So I did what instructors do when they can't find a satisfactory text: I started to write my own. I began this project in 1981 and in the process, although less instantaneous than when I had moved from psychodynamic to behavior therapy, I underwent another conversion.

Let me relate where I was led by writing *Personality: The Scientific Study of Complex Human Behavior,* which was published in 1987.

Radical behaviorists among my friends ask me why I would want to write a book about personality, a construct which, like all others, they have long since eliminated from their vocabulary. My answer is that I am not now, nor have I ever been a radical behaviorist, and am thus not opposed to the constructs employed in the scientific study of personality. Both in my research and in my teaching of and writing about therapy (Ross, 1980, 1981), I have employed such mediating constructs as anger, attention, anxiety, expectancy, intelligence, and for that matter, learning, which I consider a mediating construct like all the rest.

Writing the personality text made it clear that there is simply no way of talking about the complex human behavior that people subsume under the term *personality* without resorting to these and other constructs, including those of the dispositional kind we refer to as *traits*. Moreover, as I immersed myself in the relevant research literature, partaking of another reeducation in the process, I came to appreciate that those who employ such constructs in their investigations of personality anchor them carefully in measurable and observable phenomena at the stimulus as well as at the response end in the best tradition of methodological behaviorism. These investigators have brought about a veritable renaissance in the field of personality, which had been lying dormant in the decades that were dominated by loose and abstract theorizing about such conceptualizations as ego strength, castration anxiety, superego guilt, inferiority complex, unconscious conflict, self-actualization, need and press, defense mechanisms, and the collective unconscious. Nowadays exciting progress is being made in tracing the sources of individual differences, predicting response dispositions, explicating person-perception and self-perception, outlining the parameters of affect, and discovering the variables of interpersonal attraction.

A fascinating fact emerges when one looks at the names of some of the investigators who have contributed to introducing and extending this new look in the field of personality. Albert Bandura, Arnold Buss, Donn Byrne, Paul Ekman, Norman Endler, Seymour Epstein, Carroll Izard, Walter Mischel, Rudolf Moos, Lawrence Pervin, Irwin Sarason, Janet Spence, Charles Spielberger, and Marvin Zuckerman: what do these people have in common? All of them had been trained as clinical psychologists in programs based on the scientist-practitioner model. From the same background have come such investigators as John Conger, David Elkind, John Flavell, and Norman Garmezy, who have contributed to bringing developmental psychology out of its motor-development-fixated, creeping and crawling stage to focus on cognitive, emotional, and social factors.

The Scientist-Practioner Model

There must be something right with a model of training that is capable of producing such innovative investigators as the outstanding psychologists just named. A similar list can be drawn up of men and women who were trained in line with that model and remained in and made scientific contributions to clinical psychology itself. Names like Allen Bergin, Leonard Eron, Benjamin Kleinmuntz, Peter Lang, Donald Meichenbaum, Barbara Melamed, Peter Nathan, Lee Secrest, Bonnie Strickland, and Hans Strupp come to mind. What, then, do I think about the Boulder model today?

I think that the scientist-practitioner model of training is in deep trouble. The principal source of the trouble can be found in the constructs that I so recently readmitted into my vocabulary. I offer the hypothesis that the traits, temperaments, values, and interests of people who are scientists are distinctly different from those of people who are practitioners. Scientists are fact-oriented, practitioners are people-oriented. Scientists seek general principles, practitioners try to understand the individual case. Scientists must be skeptical, practitioners must have faith in what they are doing. If even some of these assertions are correct, it would be most unlikely that there are enough individuals in whom the characteristics of the sicentist are combined with those of the practitioner to provide graduate students for the plethora of doctoral programs in clinical psychology now in existence.

I, and many others, long believed that the population from which our Boulder-model doctoral programs draw their graduate students can be viewed as a normal distribution, ranging from those interested in science to those interested in practice, where those interested in and suitable for both constitute the mode. It is my current view that we have been mistaken. I believe that we are dealing with two distributions, one representing the relatively small number of people with the characteristics required of the scientist, the other representing the far more numerous people with the characteristics required of the practitioner. These two distributions have a slight overlap, which accounts for the rare people who manage to combine the two characteristics and who are able to function as true scientist-practitioners, as do the clinical psychologists on the list presented earlier.

As long as there was no other route in psychology that led to clinical practice, scientist-practitioner programs had more than enough exceptionally bright applicants, all of whom, regardless of their actual career goal, stated in their applications that they were interested in doing research. Now there is another route for those whose aim is to enter clinical practice. No longer do they need to lie in their applications and dissemble in graduate school so as to convince a science-oriented faculty of their devotion to research. Now they can apply to one of the ever-increasing number of graduate programs that lead to a professional degree, typically the Psy.D. Why should those whose career goal is far removed from conducting research want to undergo the initiation exercises of quantitative and methodological courses, research requirements, and research-based doctoral dissertations?

If this analysis is correct, more and more practice-oriented students would apply to professional degree programs, while fewer and fewer applicants would seek the traditional scientist-practitioner preparation. I doubt that we can sustain very many doctoral programs with so few students, and this is why I say that the hyphenated program is in deep trouble. There will no doubt always be some students whose interests are in a combination of research and practice, but their number could probably be accommodated by three or four programs that continue to prepare their students along the lines of the scientist-practitioner model. The rest of psychology departments that now offer a scientist-practitioner program will have to choose between two alternatives in order to remain viable. One is to develop a practitioner track and to try competing with the Psy.D. programs; the other is to devote their efforts to training research investigators for the areas underlying clinical practice, such as experimental and developmental psychopathology. Either choice, in effect, means that they cease training clinical psychologists as we used to define them.

When I present this scenario to my colleagues at Stony Brook, trying to convince them to face that choice sooner rather than later, they inevitably respond with the assertion that one can't train scientists who will do research on clinical problems without giving them clinical training and experience. In answer I point to research in the biomedical fields, where investigators who hold the Ph.D. degree have for years been making trailblazing contributions without ever having received the clinical training that is required for the M.D. degree. Moreover, it is not uncommon in the biomedical field for individuals to obtain both the M.D. and the Ph.D. degree, sometimes in explicitly structured dual-degree programs, a model that psychology might profitably explore.

Clinical Psychology

Much has changed in clinical psychology since Gardner Murphy's dated information sent me to Yale and Seymour Sarason persuaded me to do my graduate work in that specialty. Not only has there been a phenomenal increase in the number of those who call themselves clinical psychologists, but the field has also spawned such new specialty areas as clinical child psychology, community psychology, clinical neuropsychology, pediatric psychology, and forensic psychology.

While undergoing these in-house changes, clinical psychology has also changed the face of American psychology as a whole. Early on, psychology departments had to change their internal structure if they wished to obtain financial support for their clinical training programs from the Veterans Administration and the National Institute of Mental Health. Where departments had once been unified and integrated, they became split into distinct program areas, each with a clearly identified body of students and a designated program head. Ironically, financial support from these governmental agencies has all but disappeared, but the structure they imposed continues to this day.

It was also for the sake of clinical psychology that psychology departments were obliged to consider accreditation and licensing requirements in their planning of academic programs and to invite representatives of the APA to review their faculty and course offerings. It was also clinical psychology and its need for fiscal support and regulatory control that created a schism within the American Psychological Association, changing it, as many assert and I believe, from a scientific society to a professional guild.

Finally, it was clinical psychology that wrought a substantial change in the public image of psychology. Once, the relatively few members of the public who cared about such things viewed psychology as an esoteric science, devoted to studying the behavior of cats, rats, and pigeons. Now almost everyone knows of psychology and, whether average citizen or incoming freshman, they equate it with *clinical* psychology. To them, a psychologist is a "shrink," frequently confused with a psychiatrist, who treats disturbed people. It often comes as a surprise to these members of the public to be told that (until now, at least) most psychologists are, in fact, not therapists but scientists who conduct research.

This list of changes should not be read as a list of grievances. Some of the changes, such as the growth of the field, are welcome correlates of the passage of time. Some, such as accreditation and licensing, were needed to prevent potential abuses, or to correct actual ones. Still others, such as those involving psychology's public image, are unfortunate, but probably unavoidable.

I am hardly in a position to complain, because in many of these changes I was an active, often enthusiastic participant. I was instrumental in bringing about the organizational change in the APA's Clinical Division that permitted the formation of sections and thus the founding of the first of these, the Section on Clinical Child Psychology, which I later chaired. I served on the APA's Committee on Accreditation, visiting many departments of psychology on its behalf to make sure that APA standards were being met. For two terms I sat as representative of the Clinical Division (Division 12) on the Council of the APA, looking out for the interests of clinical psychologists. I helped develop and later headed a large doctoral program in clinical psychology that produced some scientist-practitioners and a few scientists, as well as a large number of therapists, many of whom make their living in independent practice. Finally, I was for ten years a member of the New York State Board for Psychology, helping in the administration of its licensing examination. Thus, if I have complaints about organized psychology and the changes it has undergone, I must have complaints about my own contributions to these changes.

There is one crucial change, however, for which I will not accept blame, for I have consistently fought against it. This is the change in the image of clinical psychology brought about by the development of graduate programs that focus exclusively on the training of practitioners, the so-called professional programs. I refer to them as Psy.D. programs, although some of them are still permitted to award the Ph.D. degree, which is quite inappropriate because graduation from a technical school ought not to entitle one to receive the highest degree offered in course. Each year just one of these programs is able to turn out more people who call themselves clinical psychologists than all of the traditional scientist-practitioner programs combined. The overwhelming number of these practitioners is rapidly shaping the public image of clinical psychology into that of a profession almost entirely devoted to conducting psychotherapy, usually in the context of independent practice.

This poses a problem for me. I do not wish to be confused with the products of Psy.D. programs, no matter how good and legitimate they might be. I have therefore come to hesitate calling myself a clinical psychologist. When a lay person asks me about my profession I usually say that I am a college professor, and when that elicits, "What do you teach?" I say "Psychology." If my interlocutor then asks what courses I teach, I truthfully answer, "Introductory psychology and the personality course" because I am no longer involved in the training of clinicians. I thus avoid what has become an embarrassing and painful issue for me: the issue of my professional identity.

Integrity or Despair and Disgust?

Do I regret that I became a clinical psychologist, and would I do it over again? Despite my misgivings about the direction the field has taken, my answer is, "Of course I would do it over again, provided I could be assured that everything would again turn out as well as it has for me." I have (present tense!) a gratifyingly productive and enjoyable career that has enabled Ilse and me to live comfortably in pretty places and to lead a contented and happy family life. I could not have wished for better, and would not want to have had it any other way. I say all this despite the fact that I never enjoyed doing what most clinical psychologists spend most of their time doing—testing and therapy. I always preferred to lecture and write about clinical issues, to supervise others who were engaged in clinical work, to administer programs that offered or taught testing and therapy, and to do research on clinical problems. Administering and interpreting psychological tests and conducting therapy, whether psychodynamic or behavioral, bored me from the beginning, and I always found the other activities more stimulating, challenging, and rewarding.

There arises then another question: would I recommend a career in clinical psychology to a college student who comes to me for advice? Here my answer is a qualified "No," because I believe that the clinical psychology I knew has run its course and is being replaced by something that, but for the doctorate, is difficult to distinguish from clinical social work. To someone whose career objective is to be a psychotherapist, I suggest that he or she consider going to a graduate school of social work. I am convinced that for the treatment of behavior disorders and problems of living, clinical social workers are at least as well trained as graduates of clinical psychology programs. To young people who feel the need for a doctorate (and there exist certain realities that support that need), I reluctantly suggest that they explore Psy.D. programs that operate as an integral part of an established and accredited university, urging them to stay away from any program that is not so situated. For young people who wish to be able to treat the major affective or cognitive disorders and complex biopsychosocial problems, my advice is to prepare for the profession of psychiatry. I view the people who currently complete training in that field as far better equipped to deal with these problems than any of the other mental health professions, even if they should some day obtain the right to make hospital admissions and to prescribe medications.

Lastly, if someone's career objective is to conduct research on human behavior and its aberrations, I recommend the graduate study of psychology in one of the research-focused specialties of our field. Here I have in mind such areas as experimental psychopathology and neuropsychology, or one of the biological specialties such as neurobiology, biochemistry, or behavior genetics whence, I believe, answers to most of the important questions about psychopathology will be coming in the not-too-distant future.

This section is headed by the Eriksonian question appropriate for my phase of life. Do I have a sense of integrity, or am I experiencing despair and disgust? My answer, Erik Erikson's conceptualization notwithstanding, is "all of the above." I have an enormous sense of integrity about what I have done and continue to do, but when I look at the field of clinical psychology, and particularly at the products of freestanding professional schools that claim to prepare clinical psychologists in the absence of their own libraries and laboratories and with a largely part-time faculty, I am disgusted and therefore despair of the future of the field to which I have devoted the past 40 years of my life.

References

Bandura, A. (1961). Psychotherapy as a learning process. *Psychological Bulletin, 58,* 143–157.
Bandura, A. (1969). *Principles of behavior modification.* New York: Holt, Rinehart & Winston.

Boring, E. G. (1942). *Psychology for the fighting man*. Cambridge, MA: Harvard University Press.

Dollard, J., Auld, F., Jr., & White, A. M. (1953). *Steps in psychotherapy: Study of a case of sex-fear conflict*. New York: Macmillan.

Dollard, J. & Miller, N. E. (1950). *Personality and psychotherapy: An analysis in terms of learning, thinking, and culture*. New York: McGraw-Hill.

Eysenck, H. J. (1959). Learning theory and behavior therapy. *Journal of Mental Science, 105*, 61–75.

Eysenck, H. J. & Rachman, S. (1965). *The causes and cures of neurosis*. San Diego, CA: Elseveer.

Hoch, E. L., Ross, A. O., & Winder, E. L. (Eds.) (1966). *Professional preparation of clinical psychologists: Proceedings of the Chicago Conference*. Washington, DC: American Psychological Association.

Holland, J. G. & Skinner, B. F. (1961). *The analysis of behavior*. New York: Pergamon Press.

Hull, C. L. (1943). *Principles of behavior*. New York: Appleton-Century-Crofts.

Kalish, H. I. (1965). Behavior therapy. In Wolman, B. B. (Ed.), *Handbook of clinical psychology*. New York: Wiley.

Lang, P. J. & Lazovik, A. D. (1963). Experimental desensitization of a phobia. *Journal of Abnormal and Social Psychology, 66*, 519–525.

Rachman, S. (1959). The treatment of anxiety and phobic reactions by systematic desensitization therapy. *Journal of Abnormal and Social Psychology, 58*, 259–263.

Ross, A. O. (1954). Tactual perception of form by the brain-injured. *Journal of Abnormal and Social Psychology, 49*, 566–572.

Ross, A. O. (1959). *The practice of clinical child psychology*. New York: Grune & Stratton.

Ross, A. O. (1962). Ego identity and the social order: A psychosocial study of six Indonesians. *Psychological Monographs, 76*, 23. Whole #542.

Ross, A. O. (1964). Learning theory and therapy with children. *Psychotherapy: Theory, Research and Practice, 1*, 102–108.

Ross, A. O. (1971). The case of the innocent model—President's Address. *The Clinical Psychologist, 24(2)*, 2–6.

Ross, A. O. (1972a). Behavior therapy. In Wolman, B. B. (Ed.), *Manual of child psychopathology*. New York: McGraw-Hill.

Ross, A. O. (1972b). Clinical child psychology. In Wolman, B. B. (Ed.), *Manual of child psychopathology*. New York: McGraw-Hill.

Ross, A. O. (1974a). Forecasting the future and four years after the forecast. In Williams, G. J. & Gordon, S. (Eds.), *Clinical child psychology: Current practices and future perspectives*. New York: Behavioral Publications.

Ross, A. O. (1974b). *Psychological disorders of children: A behavioral approach to theory, research, and therapy*. New York: McGraw-Hill.

Ross, A. O. (1976). *Psychological aspects of learning disabilities and reading disorders*. New York: McGraw-Hill.

Ross, A. O. (1980). *Psychological disorders of children: A behavioral approach to theory, research, and therapy*, Second ed. New York: McGraw-Hill.

Ross, A. O. (1985). To form a more perfect union: It is time to stop standing still. *Behavior Therapy, 16*, 195–204.

Ross, A. O. (1987). *Personality: The scientific study of complex human behavior*. New York: Holt, Rinehart & Winston.

Ross, A. O. & Bruner, E. M. (1963). Family interaction at two levels of acculturation in Sumatra. *American Journal of Orthopsychiatry, 33*, 51–58.

Ross, A. O., Lacey, H. M., & Parton, D. A. (1965). The development of a behavior checklist for boys. *Child development, 36*, 1013–1027.

Ross, A. O., Murphy, G., & Schmeidler, G. R. (1952). The spontaneity factor in extrasensory perception. *Journal of the American Society for Psychical Research, 46*, 14–16.

Salter, A. (1949). *Conditioned reflex therapy*. New York: Farrar, Straus, & Giroux.

Shoben, E. J. (1949). Psychotherapy as a problem in learning theory. *Psychological Bulletin, 46*, 366–392.

Skinner, B. F. (1938). *Behavior of organisms*. New York: Appleton-Century-Crofts.

Skinner, B. F. (1953). *Science and human behavior*. New York: Macmillan.

Ullmann, L. P. & Krasner, L. (Eds.) (1965). *Case studies in behavior modification*. New York: Holt, Rinehart & Winston.

Wolman, B. B. (Ed.) (1965). *Handbook of clinical psychology*. New York: Wiley.

Wolpe, J. (1958). *Psychotherapy by reciprocal inhibition*. Palo Alto, CA: Stanford University Press.

Wolpe, J. (1969). *The practice of behavior therapy*. New York: Pergamon Press.

Edwin Shneidman, Ph.D.

Professor of Thanatology Emeritus
University of California, Los Angeles

◆

A Life in Death:
Notes of a Committed Suicidologist
An Epistolary Autobiography

Loomings

Would it not be appropriate—if one were given the enticing opportunity to do so—to begin with a candid portrait painted by a psychological Rembrandt, an artist who, in his own words, is "a veteran examiner of men," an acknowledged master of human assessment, and my own favorite psychologist? In a few brief paragraphs—with the strokes of his pen—he chides, flatters, exaggerates, exposes, embraces, exhorts, scolds, and, accurately describes—beautymarks, warts, and all. For the reader who does not know me on sight, it may be a useful one-way mirror, initiating the process of introduction. Here it is, in a letter—one of 170 he wrote to me over a 40-year period—by Henry A. Murray, a man admittedly given to occasional hyperbole.

December 30, 1966

Beloved Ed,

I was greatly disturbed by what I saw and heard of you in New York. In addition, I was stunned to see your Achilles heel for the first time (although I

---

always have a mind that every tragic hero has one). Now in retrospect, I recall previous intimations of essentially the same prideful sin against Nature. I am somewhat biased on this score, because of my experiences in the great outdoors, in athletics and physical adventure, in biology and surgery—all of which conspired to endow me with a profound veneration for life in all its manifestations— especially the wisdom of the body. Interrelated it seems to me are: your sleep- lessness, your absolutely unique conception of sleep as somehow comparable to suicide, your dashing off in the morning without breakfast, and your incessant restlessness of body, thought, wit, enterprise, and intention. And then your decision not to consider for a moment the possibility (I would say, the hardly disputable occurrence) of a rational and defensible suicide. And yet all the while you seem to be intent on over-expending and abusing the large reservoirs of energy that Nature has vouchsafed you, as if they were inexhaustible, as if your soaring ambition and indomitable will could triumph over the aging process which begins at conception. Actually you are racing toward the depletion of those priceless energies, or so it seems. In any event, you are unfortunately and miserably confronted by a diaphragmatic hernia, the severity of which I cannot, of course, appraise; and so I am in no position to urge you to do anything but find a highly-recommended doctor whom you like and trust, and don't let any pride or fears (in you) keep you from taking his advice. Personally I wouldn't trust him if he didn't insist on a complete rest for at least a fortnight. Granted that you were born with a rapid tempo of energy release, can do 5 times more than other persons in a day, have a brilliant and witty mind, and a loving kindness that is perpetually brimming over and much else beside, *still* there is a limit. Your being is so precious to me that it makes me sick at heart to witness your defeat in wisdom by a juvenile (in my scales) proudful determination to continue in perpetual motion.

Con Amore,
Harry

Was there ever a more affectionately scolding letter? I was then 48 and Harry— Henry A. Murray, M.D., Ph.D. (in biochemistry), psychoanalyst, Melville scholar, long-time director of the Harvard Psychological Clinic—was 73, exactly 25 years older than I, to the day. And if you think that at 48 I appeared in Harry's eyes as a willful and neurotic fellow, you should have seen me earlier.

In 1851, Herman Melville wrote to his friend Nathaniel Hawthorne that "Until I was twenty-five I had no development at all." That letter has given me great comfort. I am proud to be in Melville's company on any score, even as a case of arrested development.

At 30 I was not a very mature person. It is true that I was married and had a family, had been a captain in World War II, had earned a Ph.D. degree in psychology, and was employed at a neuropsychiatric hospital where I treated psychotic patients. On the surface this sounds like rather adult stuff. But it was equally (and perhaps more powerfully) true that I was not very psychologically developed and had relatively little acquaintance with my unconscious. That to me, now, betokens a kind of immaturity.

My wife Jeanne—the perfect spouse for me—was also fairly uncomplicated. She has straightforwardly loved me and accepted me, and I her, now for 45 years. And in my work also I was just about what I appeared to be: energetic, enthusiastic, straight-forward, sometimes delightful and funny, sometimes obnoxious and nasty; but even the furbelows and storms of my work-a-day behavior had a simple surface quality to them. There were no great adult Melvillean depths, no dark family secrets, no overt infantile traumas, no evidences of quick access to a rich unconscious. It seems obvious to me now that this pervasive surface quality was a conspicuous deficiency in my total psychological makeup.

Later in this piece I shall mention two publications, "Schizophrenia and the MAPS Test" (Shneidman, 1948), written when I was 30, and "Orientations Toward Death" (Shneidman, 1963b), written when I was 45. As I reread them now, it seems to me that it is not simply that the second was written by a person who was 15 years older, but by a different person altogether. In the second paper I was thinking differently and had another voice; as though, at last, I had begun to face some real problems in myself. I cannot claim then or now to have depth—*that* would be superficial—but I can say that I have tried to be more than a two-dimensional man and to admit that there are important dimensions to life other than the functionings of the conscious mind.

It was almost as though I did not start thinking anything that was worthwhile until age 30. I do not feel that way about myself now. What happened to me was quite simple. I found a master teacher who encouraged me to learn about others and about myself, and even more important, did not take away or threaten my own ideas, but stimulated them so that, on my own, I could enlarge them beyond what they would have been without his catalyzing encouragement.

Now, in my 70s, as I look back, it seems clear to me that there was one person who changed all that and enriched my life by enriching the texture of my perceptions and, by extension, the texture of my personality, and who was himself by far the most layered, contradictory, difficult, fascinating, embracing, exasperating, complicated, challenging person I have ever met outside the pages of a great novel. That person was Henry A. Murray.

But first I have to ask, why should one begin an autobiographical sketch with a portrait of another? A practical answer is that obviously every individual is indebted to others for major aspects of the self. My formative personality was made up of images and mirrors that I held up to myself of my parents, siblings, aunts and uncles, adolescent chums, high school teachers, wartime friends, and work colleagues.

As an undergraduate and for two years a graduate student at UCLA in the postdepression years from 1934 to 1940, I was living out time not knowing how to do those things that might help me with a future I simply could not see. (A few years later, the war changed my life.) At the university I drifted into psychology; to this day it is not clear to me why. There were stimulating teachers—notably Franklin Fearing and Joseph Gengerelli—but they were counterbalanced by two successive chairmen, Knight Dunlap and Roy Dorcus, who almost blighted whatever enthusiam for psychology I might have had. One book especially, J. F. Brown's *Psychology and the Social Order* (1937)—a brilliant, if flawed, amalgam of Freud, Marx, and Lewin—

used as a textbook in Professor Fearing's course, popped my eyes open in those otherwise dreary years. It belongs in a time capsule as representative of the intellectual enthusiasms and excesses of the 1930s. I liked it for both reasons.

For me, those two chairmen had an obvious anti-Semitic menace about them. One of them actually said to me, explicitly, that he could not encourage my applying to the doctoral program because he would not be able to place a Jew. I could hardly take that information home to my immigrant parents who were, so to speak, spending their own lives for their children as a kind of golden sacrificial bridge from a Czarist *shetl* to an American public university.

Among the professors whose classes I took but to whom I never spoke personally, I had two favorites: One was Carl Shelton Hubbell, professor of American literature, whose erudite and immaculately prepared and carefully spoken lectures I tried to take down verbatim. For this class I prepared a term paper on "Mark Twain and Religion," for which I read everything of Twain in print and reported everything he had said about any aspect of religion. Professor Hubbell honed my lifelong love of American poetry and prose and introduced me to Melville. Some years later, it pained me considerably to learn that this elegant man (who lectured in a black suit with his Phi Beta Kappa key hung on a large gold chain on his vest) had died in San Quentin prison, having been convicted of child molesting.

My other favorite professor was Dean (of Letters, Arts, and Science) Charles Henry Rieber, who, when I was a freshman, instilled in me an absolute fascination with the 64 inferences (not all of them valid) contained in each of the four basic (A, E, I, and O) Aristotelian statements. Much more important in my life, as we shall see, he also imparted a crystal-clear (19th-century) understanding of the fundamental importance of John Stuart Mill's canons of inductive inference, especially the Method of Difference. This idea became a habit of thought, so that ever after whenever I looked at almost anything I would automatically seek to compare it with something similar in all important ways but different in some one essential characteristic. Obviously, Mill's Method of Difference was in my head when I discovered the suicide notes in the Los Angeles County Coroner's office some years later, in 1949. The moment that I said to myself that these were "genuine" suicide notes, then the idea of generating a comparison group of nongenuine ("simulated") suicide notes came immediately to my mind. René Descartes and John Stuart Mill were my patron saints; Professor Gengerelli and Dean Rieber were their priests—and although I was a confirmed atheist, I was nonetheless a devout believer in the power of mind when it is focused by some comprehensive and commonsensical idea.

My admiration for Professor Gengerelli continued throughout my career. At my retirement party from the UCLA Neuropsychiatric Institute in June 1988—when he was in his late 80s—he told the following story about me. In 1936, when I was in my teens and an undergraduate at UCLA, and he was in his 30s, he returned an examination booklet to me (in a course on the history of psychology) on which he had written, "A distinguished paper. Your handwriting leaves something to be desired." He further related that, after class, I approached him and said, "Professor Gengerelli, about this comment that you have written, I can read the first few words, but I can't quite make out this last part." He still roars with laughter when he tells this story.

Of course, I dared exhibit this humorous impertinence only with a benign professor whose reactions I could count on to be understanding and to respond in the spirit of fun. I would never for an instant have considered making such a remark to Dunlap or Dorcus—nor would they ever have written such a generous comment in the first place. In those days Gengerelli would typically greet me by putting his face close to mine, squinting, and, with seemingly great seriousness, asking me, "Do you have any clear and distinct ideas?" He and I both knew that he was talking about doing the work of psychology with Cartesian precision of thought. I had taken a course on Descartes and, although I could not follow him to his conclusions, I reveled in reading about the dissection of his method of thought. In my mind, Gengerelli represented a dapper and cheerful Descartes come to life again.

Those two anti-Semitic professors, Dunlap and Dorcus, were also important to me in a roundabout way. I sensed that their psychology, which they ponderously propounded, was rather superficial; and my intuition told me that I need not believe their virulent disparagement of any theories relating to the study of the whole person, and especially to the unconscious, about which they were absolutely shrill. I decided that they were narrow-minded and could not hold out for me the prospect of a psychology that I was seeking. My syllogism went something like this: because I knew they were wrong in their anti-Semitism, I had good grounds to believe that they might be equally wrong in their oppositon to theoretical conceptions of psychology other than their own—although their pedantic textbooks and boring lectures were not very theoretical in the first place. I sought for wisdom elsewhere, in other books. Later, in the 1940s, Murray's *Explorations in Personality* (1938) changed my life and gave me a vision of what psychology—that glorious discipline—ought to be.

But in all fairness, I owe those two something. They taught me to be selective; to take the few things about them that were commendable—their diligent scholarship, their seriousness of purpose, their love of the university life—and incorporate these into my internal role model, while at the same time acknowledging to myself that the other aspects of them were negative models. This was, I believe, my first major conscious experience of having to reject large parts of a seemingly benign person in a position of undoubted authority—the kind of person I would ordinarily want to like—without feeling at all guilty about contravening such a person.

About that time I was reading Samuel Butler's *The Way of All Flesh*. In my internal struggle with those negatively tinged authorities at the university, I was encouraged and comforted by Butler's great book. It showed me that a son could disavow an inadequate or evil father-figure without necessarily being destroyed for such an independent act. The problem for me was not with my real father, whom I dearly loved and who loved me, but with those less-than-noble teachers, by whom I felt badly betrayed.

Apparently I needed a second father, and when I found Dr. Murray he had an important and pervasive effect on me. Why this was so requires some explaining.

Both my father and Dr. Murray were handsome, tall, and authoritative-looking. To me, all my life, my father represented rocklike stability and trustworthiness; Dr. Murray was the epitome of genteel society and wide-ranging learning. My father was without much formal education—he had been an art student in Czarist Russia—and was, rather unhappily, a merchant, constantly concerned with earning a livelihood for his family and almost always on the margin of debt. Dr. Murray was independently wealthy. He told me that while he was an undergraduate at Harvard, from 1911 to 1915, he was totally disdainful of the "greasy grinds" who were interested in grades. Later, during World War II, when he served as director of the operations to select agents for the Office of Strategic Services (OSS), he either forgot or advertently neglected to cash his monthly army paychecks. (I know this fact from James Grier Miller, who was then a captain and Colonel Murray's adjutant.) In sum, he was what every Jewish parent would want: a scholar, a physician, a biochemist, embryologist, psychoanalyst, Melville scholar, etc., etc.

Although the similarities between my father and Dr. Murray were sufficient to link them together in my conscious mind, the differences were enormous. That which was the obsessive focus of my *mother's* fantasies of grandeur—elevated social status, sufficient wealth, and towering educational and intellectual achievements—Dr. Murray casually possessed in reality. It was as though, in some unspoken subtle psychological way, she had directed me to become Dr. Murray's eager-to-please son. He had my father's frame, covered with my mother's fantasies. My older brother became my mother's son-the-doctor. With Dr. Murray, I was even better: I was her son-the-student, studying with "the-biggest-rabbi-in-the-whole-country." *That* would have come as quite a surprise to Henry Murray—although he surely must have sensed that I looked up to him as a father. And it is relevant for me to state that not one of these rather simple (and to me now rather obvious) insights ever occurred to me until after my last visit with Harry (on Nantucket, in August 1987, when he was 94 and I was 69).

I feel it as a palpable loss that I never had a chance to discuss these ideas with him. I have tried to imagine what his response would have been, but except for being certain that he would begin by vociferously protesting the element of implied flattery in this interpretation, I cannot formulate what his response would have been once he seriously put his clinical skills to this issue. All I know is that it would be something new to me, some fresh angle containing some absolutely unanticipated insight. What I can sense is the quality and color of his response—emotionally embracing and intellectually stimulating; what I cannot make out is the content of his answer that I yearn to know.

Somehow, in puzzling over this, I turn back to the image of my mother. She was, by nature, not an optimistic person, but her fantasies for herself and her children were filled with yearning; they were prideful; they were aspirational. Sometimes she behaved toward others as though her high goals had been achieved; as though she and her children, me especially, were above the fray of any everyday mercantile existence, as though we were some sort of great intellectuals, better than most other people. What saved me was that great equalizer that permits people of all social strata to meet at the same high intellectual level: *books*. In our home we had the public library list of "the great books." We independently, in my mother's mind at least (and in my own), created our own St. John's College and University of Chicago. The classical books were the great equalizer. If you knew Euclid, Shakespeare, Dostoevski, and Melville, you could, figuratively speaking, talk to anybody, even—to use my parent's language of that day—to Rockefeller. Or, in my case, even to Dr. Murray.

On my part it wasn't arrogance or cocksureness. It was the simple shock of recognizing that properly constructed English sentences floated just as well at Harvard as they did at UCLA and that you don't have to be a Brahmin New Englander to quote effectively from *Moby-Dick* at some apposite moment. *Moby-Dick*—an obsession of mine—reminds me of *the* most important book, beyond any question, in my life. It is the Ninth Edition of the *Encyclopedia Britannica.* Somehow, my parents had the perspicacity to buy it, along with a Victrola and records of Caruso and Geraldine Farrar, Mozart and Beethoven. (How did they know?) I was a sickly child and stayed home from school a great deal—although somehow my mother arranged to get me double-promoted four times in elementary school. (A bad mistake, which accounts in large part, for my social ineptitudes all through high school and college.) But among the happiest moments of my childhood were those spent alone at home (my parents working in their clothing store and my older brother and younger sister at school), in my parents' pleasant bedroom with its 1910 Grand Rapids mahogany furniture, all cozy in their bed—a great, white, billowy ship—listening to the phonograph and reading the *EB.* I think I learned over 50% of what I know today from the pages of the Ninth Edition of the *EB.* I am sure that accounts for my essentially 19th-century ideas about science. I muse that it could well be that my lifelong frenetic way of studying (or reading or writing) is a happy remnant of the fact that my earnest perusals of "The Geometry" and "Kant" were interrupted every several minutes by the necessity to leap out of my parents' bed either to change the record or to wind the Victrola. I believe that one reason that I so deeply love the intellectual life today is that initially I found my young mind's independence within the secure setting of an easeful bower.

The reader can easily imagine what it meant to me later, in my 50s, to be invited to contribute to the *EB,* and how pleased I am to see my own seven pages of printed text on "Suicide" (Shneidman, 1973c) in the 1973 edition of the set of books that once was my Testament, Koran, and Upanishads. It was as though, in this one respect at least, I had come full circle in my life and was, at last, grown up.

My genealogy is lost in the recesses of the pale of old Russia. By contrast, my wife has documents, including a poignant diary set in early America, tracing her ancestors from Worcester, England, in the 1700s. She is a true daughter of the American Revolution, whose great-grandparents settled the land in east-central Illinois, around Hoopeston, where she and both her parents had the same first-grade teacher. Of my father's family, amazingly, I know almost nothing. But recently I found a typed two-page piece about my maternal grandfather by my favorite uncle, Ernest, written in 1960, when he was in his 60s. It is entitled "Your Grandfather Samuel Zukin, A Portrait by His Son." Because I believe that it bears, albeit indirectly, so much on me—and because as I grow older I look increasingly like the pictures of my grandfather Samuel—I reproduced a few paragraphs here.

It is vain and shallow to be too proud of one's ancestors, nevertheless a knowledge of one's descent is a good thing. For instance, it is of value to know that your great grandfather was a rabbi. He was not just an ordinary rabbi of one synagogue, but a rabbi over a whole region in Russia. He travelled from town to town settling disputes and giving advice and sympathy.

(By a wild stretch of my imagination, it sounds vaguely like what I did for a time when I was at the National Institute of Mental Health, flying out to various places throughout the country—40 states in under three years—encouraging the besieged to keep up their faith in suicide prevention [and also encouraging grant applications and doing site visits], a kind of twentieth-century suicidological circuit-rider, consistent with my own distant heritage.)

The man I want to tell you about is your grandfather, my father, Samuel Zukin. I now picture him as a newly made American, getting his citizenship. He loved America and appreciated America in ways and intensity that many native-born Americans can scarcely understand, and he was very proud of his acquired citizenship. He really loved his new country.

My father was a born student. He was a Hebrew scholar in Europe, and discussed with men the meanings in the holy books and in the commentaries. He held to the essence in religion and not to the dogmas. It took great courage to send us kids to the government public schools and not to *cheder*. I went to school six days a week, Saturdays included. Father was after education for his children, and dogmas be hanged.

In New York, in his fifties, father read Shakespeare (in Yiddish), he studied algebra and geometry (in Yiddish) out of books in the public library.

I never heard my father talk ill about anyone. He never belittled anyone. He was extremely polite to people. He was kindly, gracious, patient and bore his burdens (and he had them) quietly. And he was tolerance itself.

Father believed in cleanliness. He worked as a presser of men's shirts, but he brushed his clothes and shined his shoes every morning before going to work.

Father was shy, thought a lot and said little. He liked people and just loved children. My memory of him is of a man with a faint smile and blinking eyes . . .

I'll just say a few words about your grandmother. My mother was beautiful, very feminine, kind, always giving of herself, self-sacrificing, very motherly, rather old-fashioned, rather unrealistic in facing the problems of life. She was a wonderful mother.

To this day I retain a distinct early kinesthetic and visual memory of my grandfather walking along the Pacific Palisades in Santa Monica with my little hand safely in his. (He died in January 1923, so I could not have been more than 4½ years old.) I can even see the spot; just north of the old iron cannon that points out over the carrousel on the Santa Monica pier. Of course I did not know the word *benignity* then, but that is the word that comes to mind as I think of that gentle, benign, mustached man with kindly eyes. Not much talk between us; we just waddle along contentedly, proud grandfather and happy gosling. (Shades of Konrad Lorenz!) Thereafter—imprinted as I must have been—when I found a grandfather-figure who quacked in just the right benign way, it seemed only natural for me to follow him, searching (and finding) intellectual and psychological rewards. For me now to posit a link between my ineffable infantile feelings toward Samuel Zukin and my enormously more complicated (and only partially explicatable) adult relationship with Henry Murray is not, in my opinion, a totally ridiculous idea.

Speaking of kinesthesis, one of my most treasured memories is the tactile memory of feeling my father's hand on my head. Occasionally at night, during my high school and some of my college years, when I was studying at my desk, my father, having returned from work at the store, would come into my room and place his hand lightly on my head and almost subliminally pat my head, like a gentle tremor of affection. To this day I can feel his hand on my curls, although I have long since been bald. Sometimes no words were spoken—after all, I was studying. Later, of course, I would go into another room, probably the kitchen, where he would be eating, join him and my mother, and we would talk. But that *feeling* of his having given me his parental blessing is very strong in me. What can parents give that is better than psychic transfusions of acceptance and support?

It would seem that, by definition, each life has its own unrepeatable sorrows and unrepeatable triumphs. For this reason, I believe that, within the setting and avowed purpose of this volume, *my* life—and, by extension, any individual's life—cannot serve as a guide or rutter for another person, even an aspiring young psychologist. The time and the *zeitgeist* in which my life occurred have gone; the nature of our profession has changed; my mentors and teachers were unique and irreplaceable; and the vacancies of opportunity that occurred to me at various times have been filled. A life is not a Baedeker; and neither is it necessarily a cautionary tale.

The simple fact is that I was sufficiently narcissistically delighted to be asked to be a participant in this volume that, in a series of introspective sessions at my electric typewriter, I have typed out a somewhat candid account of one sector of my life. It is neither a morality play nor underground theater. It is simply my report. Some may find my life somewhat dull, but for me it was indispensable—and, if given the opportunity, I would gladly live it again.

The last phrase—a direct borrowing from the prologue to Bertrand Russell's autobiography (1967)—has, to my mind, a specific latent message. It implies that I feel that my life was "a good enough life"; that I rather enjoyed it; that I got through it fairly well; further, that all along I *expected* to get through it relatively undamaged—in a word, that I am an optimist. I believe that optimism-pessimism is a basic dimension of human functioning. It is my observation that individuals who are dour, timid, nay-saying, lugubrious, and pessimistic participate, in part, in their own self-fulfilling prophesies and tend to come to sour endings to their unhappy lives. And I believe that the converse is true for people who are zestful, ebullient, enthusiastic yea-sayers—us optimists. I got this trait indirectly from my parents, who somehow gave their second son, a somewhat frail, often sickly, undersized, curiosity-filled, mildly hyperactive child—me—an ineffable sense of being special, someone to whom the really dire calamities would not occur, and if I behaved myself (as I almost always did) the "A's" of approbation would fill my report card of life.

It is much more relevant to note that my maternal grandmother died suddenly, in a subway in New York City, in February 1918. Her death plunged my mother (who was then carrying me in her belly—we were both in York, Pennsylvania) into a deep psychological and physiological depression, so that after I was born in May I was a bottle-fed and borderline failure-to-thrive child. It was probably the single best thing (next to conception) that ever happened to me, because my parents not only tried to keep me alive, but with the extra attention that that puny neonate and infant demanded made him feel—the opposite of the marasmic children described by René Spitz— charmed in some special way. Much later in my life I saw this phenomenon in a few individuals who had committed suicide (by setting themselves on fire, jumping from a high place, or shooting a bullet through the head) and had fortuitously survived, beating all odds, and thereafter—having made it through a life-threatening ordeal— felt curiously magical, totally unsuicidal, and (within realistic limits) somehow omnipotent. That describes one of my deepest core feelings about myself, given to me by my life-saving parents.

Having said all this, it may now surprise the reader for me to aver that I deeply believe that my adult lifelong interest (almost an obsession) with the *topic* of suicide is *not* an essential reflection of my innermost psychodynamics. (I have assumed that the editor's invitation for me to join this enterprise was based, in part at least, on the work I have done on suicide and suicide prevention.) But—as I shall detail later—I "got into" suicide quite accidentally, serendipitously as it were, by "discovering" some hundreds of suicide notes and intuitively recognizing their potential value for psychological science and, to be candid, for my own career in psychology.

At that time, in 1949, I was a VA clinical psychology trainee, and was keenly interested in thematic projective techniques. I thought Murray's Thematic Apperception Test the most ingenious and effective way of relatively quickly tapping an individual's governing psychodynamic themes. I had developed my own variation of the TAT, the Make-A-Picture-Story (MAPS) Test (Shneidman, 1947), and I was beginning to write *Thematic Test Analysis* (Shneidman, 1951)—in short, I had a keen interest in the use of "personal documents in psychological science" (Allport, 1942). For me there was a palpable voyeuristic attraction to other people's personal documents, their diaries, letters, and autobiographies. (Inexplicably, Allport did not mention the most personal of all documents, suicide notes).

The point is that suicide notes are personal documents, a legitimate part of psychological science, and I could not turn my back on them. I was not so much interested in the field of suicide as I was in giving expression to a basic aspect of my personality: the attractiveness of excitement, in this case, the excitement of intellectual pursuit. The psychodynamic chord that I believe was touched by my finding those suicide notes had much more to do with process than with content: the challenge of the chase; to wrest from the notes their latent secrets and to say something systematic about their writers. I truly believe that if I had come across a thousand schizophrenic diaries or a thousand homosexual autobiographies, I would have plunged into schizophrenia or homosexuality with equal zest—and would let anyone who wished make what he would of that. Actually, in the 1940s, suicide was a virgin area. Figuratively speaking, I felt like a cowpoke who, wandering home drunk one dark night, had stumbled and fallen into a pool of oil and was just sober enough to recognize its potential (in my case, purely intellectual) richness.

The autobiographical fact is that I have not really been concerned with death until rather recently (as any intellectually sensitive 70-year-old ought to be), and I very much doubt that I shall commit suicide because, among many other reasons, such an act might seriously tarnish my postself reputation as a suicidologist, which I have some wish to maintain. Of course, I am deeply concerned with local and global life-and-death issues—what thoughtful spouse, parent, grandparent, or citizen is not, especially in these uncertain and exciting days?

Spring: Pre-Suicidal Life

My six elementary school years are a pleasant blur of maternal teachers. I was the runt of the eighth-grade class. When I went to high school, I had just turned 12 and weighed 79 pounds. Life was pleasant: reading, listening to the classical music station (Mozart, Beethoven, and Tchaikovsky were constant themes in my life; I had a wide range of musical tastes); doing homework; and building an Eskimo kayak, which I suspended by a rope from a large limb of the backyard plum tree. I had to climb the plum tree in order to lower myself into the kayak so that I could read there, the perfect spot for intellectual adventure: *Two Years before the Mast* and *Moby-Dick* from a kayakian point of view!

Abraham Lincoln High School of Los Angeles was, in the early 1930s, I see now, a very interesting ethnographic site. The student body was made up mostly of the children of blue-collar Italian immigrants, with smatterings of Mexicans and North Europeans, a few Russians, and a handful of Jews (of which I was a small digit). Nowadays Lincoln Heights is largely Korean; in those days, we didn't know of Korea's existence. The faculty were all White, Anglo-Saxon, and Protestant, headed by the highly principled principal, Ethel Percy Andrus. After her retirement, Dr. Andrus founded the American Association of Retired Persons (AARP). In retrospect, she seems to have placed all of her high school students into two groups: the WASP students (a group into which I fell by default), who were given a no-nonsense four-year college preparatory course (Latin, science, mathematics, English), and all others, who were classified as "vocational" and were given either a domestic science course or shop training of one sort or another. The school, which was torn down after the 1934 earthquake, was beautifully situated on a hillside. It had a lively cultural life, including drama (with elaborate annual Shakespeare productions), a daily newspaper (*The Railsplitter*), and several science and language clubs. And there was Mr. Walter Potter, English teacher, linguist, musician—he taught himself Russian in order to introduce Shostakovich's quartets to America—socialist, and absolutely first-rate human being, who regularly invited some of us to his home, a few blocks away atop a hill in Holgate Square, where we discussed the right literature and left-wing politics. My children and I continued to visit this wonderful man well into his 90s. All in all, Lincoln High School is an integral part of my psyche.

I was an active little fellow in high school, into this and that activity, and a good student. I was editor of the school yearbook, the 1934 *Lincolnian*. As I reread my mid-Depression, exuberant, exhortational, puffed-up piece (written at 15) the puzzle to me is how in the world Ethel Percy Andrus let it be printed. Could it be—an unlikely event—that she did not see it beforehand? Or were there aspects of her character that I did not appreciate, such as the fact that she was a closet democrat? Here are two breathless paragraphs:

Editor's Foreword

The theme of the 1934 *Lincolnian* is the dawn of a new era of hope and enlightenment, in which the spirit of cooperation and service will triumph over greed and selfishness. The New Deal, wherein the time honored laissez faire policy was abandoned by the new leaders of the country showed the government stepping in to help regulate the predatory interests for the benefit of the people. . . .

It is the task of every member of this great republic to help build a better democracy, wherein poverty and wanton spiritual frustration will be unknown and a more abundant life will be the heritage of all.

Edwin Shneidman, Editor

Perhaps, unbeknownst to me, I was reflecting—from the incandescent, socially oriented atmosphere of my home—facets of the Depression-era proletarian style of prose that was then in the air. At that time, I felt a yearning for assimilation into the American mainstream much more than I felt a sense of alienation from it. What I experienced in my head in those years was a restless inquisitiveness, an impatience with Time, and a general anxiety about sorting out the (American) rules and then selecting which ones I wished to follow. What was absent in my life was terror, grinding poverty, violence, or tragedy—which are never beneficent, but which seem, in some sensitive people, to be a maturing and integrating force leading to self-understanding, emancipation, and growth. But I would much rather have read about Ernest Pontifex in *The Way of All Flesh* (1903) and Stephen Dedalus in *A Portrait of the Artist as a Young Man* (1916/1964) than have lived their lives.

I have some special thoughts about James Joyce and his alter ego, Stephen Dedalus. *A Portrait of the Artist* made a profound impression on me. It is written in Joyce's early, open, and completely available style and it presents his life's core dilemmas in an unforgettable way: to be a comfortable priest or an exiled artist; safe or free; at home or in exile; to belong to the Other or to the Self. I had never read those basic choices put in such a searing and electric way. Joyce's great book spoke to me; it articulated what I wanted to feel about myself.

If I blame my parents for anything, it is for their giving me a happy tepid home. They failed to provide me with something clear against which to revolt. There was no extreme dogmatism in our home; we were in the comfortable intellectual middle. Desperately, I tried to develop a passion for rebellion, but my parents did not provide me with a clear target, either in themselves or in some extreme institutional model against which to rebel.

I have lived safely in the middle. Even my falling deeply in love—the most exciting event of my life—lacked a profoundly dangerous quality; indeed, it had a traditional, romantic aura to it: young officer captures a beautiful wartime bride.

To the extent that I was hostile in my life, I was critical within my home, religion, work-place, profession, university, and country, but I was never independent enough to say (as Joyce did), *Non serviam.* I certainly wanted to have a great amount of independence, but I was not willing—nor did I see the need—to dwell apart or go into geographic or intellectual exile.

Thus my career has been that of an iconoclast *within* the temple. It did not occur to me to have the imagination to burn down the entirety of contemporary psychology—flawed in so many places—in order to build a better science in its place. I admire inordinately the radical imaginations of people like Galileo, Newton, Leibnitz, Darwin, Freud, Russell, Wittgenstein, and Henry Murray, but I do not have their passion for the intellectual destruction that is propaedeutic to asserting a radically new view—although I deeply wish that I did.

Thus I fault my parents for not providing me with the psychodynamics of a rebellious world-class hero, and for giving me, instead, a penchant for happiness, free of the great bifurcating dilemmas of the tortured creative mind. I believe that an important psychological mainspring for Joyce's genius was the omnipresent Catholic Church. The Church was the unmovable dogmatic rock that he could push off against. By contrast, in my life there were only sands of tolerance into which I could sink as easily as repel. They furnished no firm platform for clear counteraction or major rebellion. The result was no heroic dichotomies, no tragic bifurcations, no searing divorcements, no painful self-exilings, no great contra-objects against which to overreact and pit one's life. (At that time in my life, there were no Hitlers.) Just my loving parents and benign teachers. One simply cannot become a great thinker or writer on an uncracked foundation like that.

Again, reading saved me. The flawed innocence and bewildered purity of Billy Budd, for example, come about not because he was so handsome, but because he was illiterate (he could not "read" the most obvious interpersonal signs). No one who reads is dangerously innocent (he may be dangerous, but he is not innocent). And I would add now: no one who sees suicidal patients needs to be overconcerned with specious precision. In any event, in my 70s, looking back at myself at 15, I can see precursors of the *kind* of psychologist I would become: interested in understanding motivations and passions in beaten and flawed lives happily not my own. (I am not, of course, implying that I am not flawed.)

I believe that somehow clinical psychologists, with their sense of responsibility for the common man's economic and psychological needs, are more apt to come from liberal political backgrounds than otherwise. It bemuses me that, curiously enough, this attitude is more similar to the medieval feudal idea that the enjoyment of private advantage is inseparable from a sense of public responsibility than it is to either the ancient Roman or the modern conservative view (White, 1962, p. 31). In my mind, it is also an integral part of the Jewish tradition.

My first publication set a stamp on my professional life. I have mentioned that as a freshman at UCLA I had studied Mill's *System of Logic* and that the Method of Difference seemed to me to provide the intellectual lever that might help me pry out some of the secrets of psychological nature.

The setting of the experiment that led to my first publication was as follows. In 1941 I had received my M.A. at UCLA and was actively discouraged by an unfriendly chairman from seeking a Ph.D. degree. Coincidentally, the mayor of Los Angeles was recalled in a special election for having, among other acts, sold (or permitted to be sold) civil service examinations for municipal jobs, such as fireman and policeman. The entire civil service commission and staff was discharged, and examinations were held to recruit a fresh department. My memory is that most of the successful candidates were from UCLA. The director was in his late 20s; almost everyone else was younger. This was my first real job. I was a Civil Service Technician, helping to create multiple-choice questions and to conduct interviews and practical on-site examinations (when applicable) for a variety of city jobs—elevator operator, secretary, pile-driverman (in the harbor), motor sweeper operator. My job involved analyzing the work being done and then creating a sensible set of tests designed to select effective city emlployees. Our working place was the entire 22nd floor (the tower) of the city hall, which was then the tallest building in Los Angeles. I loved the work, and remember that as a very happy time.

I worked there for about a year and a half, then took an examination for personnel examiner for the city of San Diego. That was a move up, and I thought that perhaps I had found a career. Then came the bombing of Pearl Harbor, and I arranged to go into the Army Air Force, to join Major J. P. Guilford's Psychological Research Unit (selecting air crew) at nearby Santa Ana, with a promise of being sent to Officers Candidate School (OCS). I was inducted into the Santa Ana Army Air Force Base in March 1942 and was commissioned at the OCS in Miami Beach in October.

But back to my prewar work at the Los Angeles City Civil Service Commission. I had played a peripheral role in one of the large-scale clerks' examinations and had participated in some of the interviews. The ratings of the candidates were along such dimensions as appearance, alertness, congeniality, and an overall summary evaluation. The 15-to-20-minute interview was filled with questions. I puzzled as to how these clarified the situation or related to the overall judgments. It occurred to me that if we met the candidate, noted how he or she was dressed, talked, behaved, and responded to the examiners during the brief session—general deportment and demeanor—then the contents of the interview were irrelevant. We could talk about almost anything and come out with about the same results, including the same interrater reliabilities.

I proposed this idea and was frankly amazed when the director, Lyman Cozad (and, I assume, the commission), approved my scheme to recall 15 of the candidates (all of whom were already employed by the city) on the pretext that they needed to be reinterviewed. The second interview consisted of handing them the ten Rorschach ink-blot cards and simply asking them to tell what they saw. (None of the interviewers had any Rorschach test sophistication.) After the interview, each candidate was debriefed. Of course, only the first (legitimate) interview scores were used in the employment procedure.

What was most interesting to me was the finding that the two sets of (three each) interrater reliabilities—I was not an active rater in either set of interviews—were about the same, just as low and with just as wide a range. "Both boards behaved much the same in spite of the introduction of a drastically different method of interview" (Shneidman, 1943). Ratings were equally unreliable; content did not seem to matter much.

Equally as amazing as the fact that I was permitted to carry out this study as official city business was that there was not a single complaint from any of the experimental candidates. Nothing like this scheme could happen today: the commission would not approve it; some candidates would complain; and the city might be sued for a human rights violation. Actually, I would not do it again myself, but I think that the spirit of John Stuart Mill might be pleased with it.

In any event, this little study sold me on the possible applicability of the experimental method in real-life situations—later, clinical situations—and alerted me to the rather low agreements among experts of large segments of human behavior. That lesson was certainly reinforced by a study I did several years later with Kenneth B. Little, "Congruencies among Interpretations of Psychological Test and Anamnestic Data" (Shneidman & Little, 1959). This study showed that psychiatrists were capable of assigning radically different diagnostic labels to the same (mimeographed) cases after a ten-day interval. Some of my strong negative feelings about specious accuracy—which I now extend to the *Diagnostic and Statistical Manual* (any edition)—began to form in those days, based on my own experiences and studies.

As a result of this and other experiences, I became a keen believer in the opportunities for serious psychological science in the natural settings that exist all around us, if one but keeps one's eyes and ears open and one's wits lively. There are opportunities to do research and teaching and learning wherever a psychologist works.

My favorite example of this kind of natural, proactive psychological study is, not surprisingly, one of Henry Murray's bite-sized projects, a four-page paper (Murray & Wheeler, 1936) on the purported clairvoyance in dreams. The special merit of this study is that the dream-generated prophesies of the specific outcome in an unfolding real-life drama were all recorded *before* the actual facts of the matter became known; there was no opportunity, as is usually the case, for retrospective tailoring. This brief paper is practically definitive in its conciseness and clarity.

The sad background of the paper was the kidnapping of Charles Lindbergh's 20-month-old son in March 1932. On a train from New York to Boston, Murray overheard a conversation in which one woman said that she had had a dream the night before that revealed to her exactly where and how the baby was. A few days later, Murray published in a Boston newspaper a request for dreams relating to the kidnapping. The article was copied by other papers throughout the country, and within a short time over 1300 dreams were sent to the Harvard Psychological Clinic from all parts of the United States and Canada. Subsequently, the murdered baby's nude body was discovered in a shallow grave in some woods near a road. The kidnapper, Bruno Hauptmann, a German carpenter and exconvict, was convicted of the crime and eventually executed.

As for the 1300 dreams, Murray wrote,

> In only about five per cent of the cases did the baby appear to be dead [and] only four of the 1300 dreams contained the three items: death, burial in a grave, location among trees. . . . On the basis of pure chance one should expect a great many more dreams than were actually reported which combined the crucial items . . . [although] many of our correspondents claimed to have predicted some great events of the past: The World War, the Titanic disaster, and so forth. . . . The findings do not support the contention that distant events and dreams are causally related.

Simple, short, clear, conclusive.

Thinking of Harry's paper, I am reminded of another publication, this one by a member of my 1969 Death and Suicide class at Harvard (Moss, 1972). This paper also involved the use of a newspaper. This bright young student placed the following personal ad in *Boston-After-Dark,* a hippie, offbeat (and rather popular) publication: "M 21 studt gives self 3 wks before popping pills for suicide. If you know good reasons why I shouldn't please write Box D-673." Moss's sensitive analysis of the 169 letters he received within a fortnight constitutes an evocative contribution to suicidology.

I went through World War II more than unscathed. I was never sent overseas—I served as an Army Air Force Classification Officer in Texas and New Jersey. What I also remember from those years, 1942 through 1946, were the great friendships I made with two men in particular, both somewhat older than I. Harold Leuenberger had been a professor of psychology, and Bernard Davis had worked with Anna Rosenberg and FDR. They were mature, married men who adopted me and helped me—then a lonely, single, unworldly fellow—to grow up. Once when I was too shy to ask Jeanne (who was then the secretary to the inspector general of the Air Force Command where I was stationed) for a date, Bernie Davis, at my urgent request, went to her and said, "Captain Nemo would like to go out with you." When we got married, he put in an open order at Tiffany's for Wedgewood china for us.

During that period, as a young captain I became comfortable with command. Command changed my tone of voice and my attitude toward others. I spoke in a declarative tone, as though I were issuing orders, which I often was. It was a sense of easy authority, that later gave me the "right" to lecture and to make interpretations in therapy. Until then, I had assumed that I had no right to speak with authority. After that, whenever I felt competent, I was more relaxed about expressing authority. I was always appropriately deferential to designated superior rank, but I was not afraid of my father. I was free to act as I thought best. Still later, this sense of authority gave me permission to write books and articles for encyclopedias.

In my first posting as a brand-new second lieutenant I was assigned to be classification officer at Tarrant Field, a B-24 (four-engine heavy bomber) training base near Fort Worth. I reported to the commanding officer, Colonel Robert Stowell. He was an imposing man, well over 6 feet tall, large, a West Point graduate and a command pilot with a couple of rows of ribbons on his uniform. I was assigned an office, in which I found a box filled with hundreds of forms, one for each man on the base. Each form was a 9×12 cardboard sheet with information on both sides and small holes lining the four borders, which could be punched out to reflect typed-in information. The cards could then be grouped or sorted in any combination by use of a large sorting needle. This was the McBee sorting system, a primitive, preelectronic binary method— each hole was either punched out or it wasn't. In my first few days, among a dozen other chores, I made a set of 3×5 cards reflecting the civilian skills of all the men on the field that might conceivably come in handy: advertising, agriculture, architecture, art, and so on. I kept these cards in a small box on my desk.

A few weeks later my telephone rang. There was no mistaking Colonel Stowell's commanding voice: "Shneidman! I need an accountant and I want you to find me one by tomorrow!" "Sir," I said, "there are four men with accounting experience, two of them in the headquarters building. Their names are . . . " The line went dead. He had hung up. What in the world, I wondered nervously, had I done wrong?

In about two minutes I heard the patter of the feet of the colonel's black and white bulldog and then (to quote Melville) "reality outran apprehension"—Colonel Stowell stood upon the threshold. I immediately came to attention. He came into the room and said, somewhat menacingly, "How in the hell did you know that?" (He later told me that he thought that I had either memorized the records of a couple thousand men, or that I was bluffing!) I showed him the McBee cards and my 3×5 file. He then said, "Anything you want, you just let me know." I had been struggling with the ancient Underwood typewriter that had been issued to me. It was not rickety, just stubborn and recalcitrant. Emboldened, I said "Sir, I do need a new typewriter." As he turned to leave, he said gruffly, "Put your goddam needle through your goddam cards and find yourself a repairman!" On the spot he had taught me a memorable lesson about effective administration without increasing expenditures, and how to put a creative twist on a flawed petition—which is the basic paradigm of psychotherapy.

I, the lowest ranking officer on the field, became Colonel Stowell's drinking buddy. In the late afternoon he would have his chauffeur drive by my office in his GI-brown Ford sedan. The driver would honk the horn, I would grab my hat, beat it outside, salute the colonel, go around the car to the other door, climb in the back with him, and we would be driven to the officers' club, where we would roll dice for "depth bombs"—an unpalatable concoction made by dropping a small wineglassful of bourbon into a much larger glass of beer. The loser—that seemed to be my assigned role—had to chug-a-lug this brain-boggling potion. Two or three of those are quite a lot. I became a situational alcoholic—drunk most weeknights—for some months. This condition abruptly ended the day after Colonel Stowell flew off to North Africa, where he died in combat a few months later.

My wartime stories are tepid. Even though I was in uniform, I was, by sheer lot, stationed in the continental United States. Thus I lived the war vicariously, largely through the dramatic front-page battle maps of the *New York Times,* which, until the sudden victorious endings in both Europe and Japan, frightened me through and through, because I knew that an Axis victory would be the death of any exuberant form of life for me and people like me, if not of life itself.

When I was discharged from the service I briefly considered returning to my position in San Diego, but I was now eligible for the GI Bill, which provided free education. (I consider that bill to be one of the most farsighted pieces of legislation ever enacted.) I had returned to Los Angeles with my wife. For obvious reasons, I did not consider going to UCLA. I talked to Dean Clayton Loosli of the medical school at the University of Southern California (USC). That year the classes were standing empty. My impression is that the dean promised me admission if I would first take some additional premed courses, but just looking through my brother's copies of Gray's *Anatomy* and Maximoff and Bloom's *Histology* made me weary. I had been excited by the war years and felt too restless to memorize all that material, which was easy enough but just plain boring.

I believe that one nefarious consequence of war is that it excites people at a time of radically changed folkways and mores and thus renders almost every active participant, psychologically speaking and sometimes for a prolonged period after its ending, a displaced person. It is this sense of special excitement (and the extraordinary freedoms from usual restraints) that combat veterans seem to miss the most. Even I, having served in the safe haven of the domestic periphery, was unsettled by the excitement of the war and, after it, unwilling to return to my prewar routine. Also, psychodynamically speaking, I did not wish to compete with my brother directly, lest the issue of besting him become a problem. I had already crept up on him by skipping two years of school. My inner feeling has always been that in any enterprise he could easily make more money than I—an important criterion in my mother's eyes—but that I could, in the long run, do better than he in terms of intellectual values. However, I did not seek out direct confrontation, fearing not that I might lose but that I might win. The theme of sibling rivalry is a deep one in my life, and even now it is not sorted out. I feel that I am not essentially a competitor; I am a doer for my own sake. I would do it best or first to satisfy myself, never mind sibling-figures in the world. What motivates me are my own criteria, sometimes quite punishing ones.

In any event, in 1946 I went over to the USC main campus, talked to some people, J. P. Guilford among them, and was soon enrolled in the new postwar program in clinical psychology. One of my fellow students was Reuben Fine, the chess grandmaster. For a time, while Reuben was an undergraduate student in New York City, he earned money by playing all comers—I believe he said that it was in Times Square—simultaneously on several chessboards. If he won, his opponent paid; otherwise, he did. Over a few years, he must have played thousands of games. I once asked him if he lost many games. To this day I savor his reply, the answer of a true, self-confident champion. He said, "Why should I lose any?"

By far the most exciting thing about those two years was the concomitant internship in clinical psychology at the local Veterans Administration Mental Hygiene Clinic and Neuropsychiatric Hospital. The postwar VA clinical psychology training program, with its basic requirement of the Ph.D. degree for staff psychologists, played a major role in professionalizing psychology. The head of the national program was the brilliant young James Grier Miller, M.D., Ph.D., Harvard Junior Fellow, later a university president, author of the monumental *Living Systems* (Miller, 1978) and currently my occasional luncheon companion at UCLA. (I now know that Henry Murray was offered the job of head of the VA psychology program, but turned it down.)

Clinical psychology trainees were forced to live a kind of "schizophrenic" existence between the uptight nomothetic emphasis at the university and the necessarily clinical and idiographic atmosphere at the mental hospital and clinic. (More about those words, *nomothetic* and *idiographic,* later.) There were first-rate people on the VA psychology staff, regal Ruth Tolman and gentle Mortimer Meyer especially. Highlights for us trainees were the biweekly consultation visits of Bruno Klopfer, the benign wizard of projections. Bruno had a penchant for doing magical feats. Because he was so nearsighted, he seemed to smell out the typed protocols, like a terrier after some fugitive psyche. On one occasion, after reading the responses of a psychiatric patient to Rorschach Card III, he looked up over his glasses and innocently inquired, "And does this man also perhaps have cancer, yes?" And, of course, the patient did.

I learned several important lessons from Bruno, among them that while technically there is no such thing as intuition, there is, for all practical purposes, something that might be called an intuitive gift, consisting of exquisite sensitivity to dozens of tiny, almost subliminal clues. This isn't medieval magic, but rather focused and alert attention, quickness, rapid scanning, orientation as to place and circumstance, capacity to exploit any clues (without sharing the fact of that exploitation), risk-taking, derring-do, the courage to jump to hypotheses and to voice them, the stance of preferring to be hanged for a fool rather than for a coward—all the things that almost any extraordinary mortal can do, given the right circumstances and the right audience. The immodest fact is that even I, in time, could occasionally pull off such a caper and appear magical; but I knew that it was only very rapid calculation, including the calculated risk of being completely wrong, but of making a great impression when the arrow of thought hit the bulls-eye of known fact.

On the subject of intuition, I have been powerfully drawn to *both* Mill's reasoned induction (which constitutes the bulk of mental life) *and* Melville's dark intuition, side-by-side—the inner and the outer worlds coexisting and quick to be friendly with one another. Why not, in life, be both intellectual and romantic? View the world with both a critic's and a lover's eye? Be both—in response to Yeats's question—the dancer and the dance? Enjoy both clam and cod in one's bowl of life's chowder? (" 'But the chowder; clam or cod to-morrow for breakfast, men?' 'Both,' says I; 'and let's have a couple of smoked herring by way of variety.' " *Moby-Dick,* Ch. XV.) So, while trying always to be a "reasonable man," I would not, a priori, rule out the fructifying role of irrational love, paternal and filial devotion, transference and countertransference, patroitism, Beethoven, Melville, and "intuition." Of course, these generous boundaries do not include room for a square inch of silly ideas like phrenology, astrology, gematria, hagiology, palm reading, creationism, virgin birth, life after death, or tarot cards.

As much as I admired and loved Bruno—sentiments that grew over the years—even more exciting to me than the Rorschach blots was Murray's Thematic Apperception Test. From the beginning, the TAT was my favorite psychodiagnostic technique. It had to do with stories, narratives, threads, scenarios, plots, thema, scripts, imaginal productions—almost like short stories, and close to literature. If the Rorschach was a paradigm of the subject's perceptual styles, then the TAT was a paradise of the subject's psychodynamics, especially the interpersonal neuroses. The keys are in the thema.

From the very thorough way in which he interpreted Rorschach protocols, Bruno also taught me to attend to (and then to speak about) the subject's assets, strengths, and gifts, which are present in every record. The Rorschach technique pulls for pathology, and it is easy to tar anyone from the record, but it is an incomplete and tyro's report that does not also note the redressing strengths and coping capacities. Henry Murray once remarked that "One should never disparage a fellow human being in fewer than two thousand words." It was the same idea of not tarring a person with a simplistic, pejorative, highsounding, pseudomedical diagnostic label, such as schizophrenic reaction, paranoid type, or the current favorite, borderline personality disorder, as though a label could contain the complexities of a human personality.

One day, while I was administering the TAT, the idea occurred to me to separate the figures from the backgrounds and to permit the subject to chose among the figures, place them (in whatever combinations) on the background and *then* tell a story about the situation that the subject had in part created. That night I devised the Make-A-Picture-Story (MAPS) Test. I listed 21 backgrounds (living room, street, medical scene, bathroom, dream, bridge, bedroom, forest, cave, cemetery, and so on), and decided on the kinds of figures to include (adults, children, animals, legendary figures—67 in all). In the next few weeks, I had a student artist draw them for me. I quickly decided to make schizophrenic fantasy, using the MAPS Test, my dissertation topic. To this day, I believe that the MAPS Test is a powerful technique, and I occasionally find it enormously useful. To my regret, it has always been on the periphery of projective techniques and has never really caught on. The best single source of information about ways to interpret the MAPS Test is *Thematic Test Analysis* (Shneidman, 1951).

Although I could not have articulated it at the time, the MAPS Test was an effort to further the rapprochement between psychological science and clinical practice. The bibliography for "Schizophrenia and the MAPS Test" (Shneidman, 1948) does not list either Gordon Allport or Wilhelm Windelband, but in current terms, I was groping to combine a nomothetic approach of precise numbers—numbers of figures chosen, which figures chosen, how combined, and so on—with the necessarily imprecise (but obviously more relevant) idiographic approach of sensing the nuances in a spoken record, the intuitive "psychological criticism" of the protocol, as it were. (The terms *idiographic* and *nomothetic* are those of the German philosopher Wilhelm Windelband [1848–1915], who was introduced into American psychological thought in 1937 by Gordon Allport [1897–1967].) I touched on these themes in a quasihumorous way in a paper—my 1962 presidential address to the Society for Projective Techniques—entitled "Projections on a Triptych" (Shneidman, 1962). Today I believe that nomothetic (statistical, behavioral, cognitive) psychology has contributed a great deal to psychology; that it is certainly not the only legitimate psychology; and that it is often not the best or the most relevant psychology, especially if it lacks an idiographic (clinical) component.

During my internship at the southern California VA hospitals and clinics, I felt that if I were going to be an effective clinician, I needed to know, as a fundamental issue, whether or not psychotherapy with seriously demented persons really worked or was just hocum. I was a psychology intern at a VA neuropsychiatric hospital during the heyday of the unfortunate fad of prefrontal lobotomies, especially on hapless VA patients. I was reading books of a very different ilk: Rosen's *Direct Analysis,* Sechahaye's *Symbolic Realization* (or *The Autobiography of a Schizophrenic Girl*), and Fenichel's *The Psychoanalytic Theory of Neurosis* (1945) on the fulcrum power of transference. I went to the superintendent of the hospital, James Rankin, and arranged to do intensive psychotherapy with a patient who was scheduled for a lobotomy because of his hallucinations and violent behavior. The understanding was that the psychosurgery would be postponed as long as I did the therapy and as long as nothing really explosive occurred.

When I saw this 6-foot patient, he was in a separate room with a pile of mattresses (he had previously broken a bed), hallucinating that snakes were coming out from between the layers of the bedding. (This was a potentially dangerous situation for me, but I have always been motivated, often not prudently, by a strong counterphobic push). I saw him every day, promptly at a certain hour, for, as it turned out, almost two years. Even though I also had a spouse and young children, not to mention a hundred other responsibilities, large and small, I thought about this patient night and day.

Our typical session for the first couple of months can be described very briefly: he would sit and not say a single word, but at the end of the session, when I said that our time was up and that I would see him the next day, he would let loose a string of violent invective and often spit in my direction, aiming to soil me. But I was more stubborn than he; I met with him every day and stayed the full session. Then one day, right in the middle of the hour, seemingly out of the blue, with no preamble or clearing of the throat, he said, "In the Middle Ages there was a profession of evil men who would go from village to village, spot a bright child of a poor family, kidnap that child, break its bones, systematically deform it, teach it juggling and other tricks, and then sell it to some royal court as a jester or clown. My mother did that to my mind!" He talked constantly from then on, while I would occasionally interpose comments, interpretations (some quite direct, as Rosen or Sechahaye might have done), and even some parental suggestions.

Some months later he told me that my "bullshit interpretations" were totally off the mark, but what really got to him and swung him around to sanity and my sense of reality was that I came to see him every day, never abandoned him even on days of foul weather or his foul moods, and treated him seriously, with dignity, as though he were a person of merit. And he added that he came to believe that *I* was his personal rescuer. I cured him. He said so. And I do not believe for a minute that his change toward health was a spontaneous remission merely coincidental with my seeing him.

He was not lobotomized. He left the hospital, returned to the university, graduated, and became a teacher. The ostensibly irreversible psychosis (for which established medicine was going to slice up his living brain) had disappeared; he was a civilized citizen without obvious traces of insanity.

That experience gave me a permanent intense psychocentric bias, a belief that all individual cases, excluding those with palpable injury to the brain, were amenable to beneficent psychotherapeutic reversal or redress. The major shortcoming of the process is that it is grossly inefficient because it requires a therapist who is willing to pour almost unlimited amounts of time, energy, and concern into the rescue of one person. But the paradigm is clear; it can be done and, theoretically, what can be done for one person can be done for many. I had demonstrated to my own satisfaction that psychotherapy really works. I believe that firmly, even though I never again invested myself so deeply in a case. That experience (demonstrating, to my mind, the power of pertinacity, of the positive self-fulfilling prophecy, and of positive transference and countertransference) touched all of my subsequent efforts, and without any question greatly influenced my clinical work with and my attitudes toward both highly suicidal and dying patients, whom I saw as similar in their needs.

In 1948, I received my Ph.D. degree from the University of Southern California. I was working 39 hours a week in a veterans' counseling center, gathering dissertational data on a hundred subjects at the local VA neuropsychiatric hospital, married, with one child and another on the way, and eager to start a career in clinical psychology. In those two years I was too busy to develop a deep cathexis to USC; it was simply the place where, under the GI Bill, I got my Ph.D. as quickly as I could. A transfer was effected from trainee status to the regular payroll at the VA hospital. I condensed my dissertation on schizophrenia and the MAPS Test and sent it off, with a foreword by Bruno Klopfer, to *Genetic Psychology Monographs* (Shneidman, 1948). It looked then as though I might be paddling around for some time in the marshlands and quagmires—true to this day, in my opinion, mostly because of inadequate conceptualizations—of schizophrenia, or whatever those enigmatic behaviors will ultimately be called.

Events have a way of concatenating by accretion. The MAPS Test led to *Thematic Test Analysis*; and the editing of that book lead me to Henry A. Murray.

I delight in giving parties, especially intellectual parties. An example of an intellectual party would be an APA symposium or an emeritus luncheon group. "Would you please come and we'll discuss a case (details enclosed)" might be the gist of a typical invitation. The design is simple and the agenda straightforward: a comprehensive one-case study, preferably with extensive longitudinal data. That is essentially what *Thematic Test Analysis* is: a psychological party. The TAT and MAPS Test protocols of a 24-year-old man were the menu; Kenneth B. Little, Walter Joel, and I were the chefs; and the guest list was culled from the Debrett's lists of nobility in the world of projective thematic tests: Magda Arnold, Betty Aron, Leopold Bellak, Leonard Eron, Reuben Fine, Arthur Hartman, Robert Holt, Shirley Jessor, Walter Joel, Seymour Klebanoff, Sheldon Korchin, Jose Lasaga, Julian Rotter, Helen Sargent, David Shapiro, Percival Symonds, and Ralph K. White. The book focused on a single case using multiple assessors, each writing about the exact details of his or her way of doing things, including working notes, intuitions, tabulations, tentative inferences, and final comments; a cookbook not only of ingredients, but almost a motion picture of the process of how the stew is brewed.

That book received reviews that might turn the head of an ambitious young psychologist. (Thirty years later, another book of mine, *Voices of Death* (1980), was skewered and savaged in a grossly unfair review in the *New York Times,* with the immediate results that the publisher canceled the proposed promotion budget and the unhappy book, into which I had poured the anguish of diaries and letters of people who were on the verge of dying, itself suffered a rather quick death.) The review of *Thematic Test Analysis* in the *Journal of the American Medical Association* began, "This book represents what is probably the most intensive 'psychological dissection' ever performed on a human being." (I had used the phrase "psychological autopsy" in the book—a phrase to which later, as a suicidologist, I gave a more specific forensic meaning.)

As it turned out, I had even better luck relating to the foreword to the book. In 1950,

I had somewhat audaciously written to Dr. Murray and sent him the manuscript, requesting him to write the foreword. To my delight, he agreed, and some months later he sent me an absolutely marvelous foreword, the first line of which read, "Surely this book is an original, something unique in scientific literature, satisfying, in part, to curiosities which up to now psychologists have put aside as vain." I was ecstatic. To my amazement, Henry Stratton (of Grune & Stratton) refused to print it. On the telephone he asked me questions like, "An original *what?*" and I had to explain to him how an adjective can be used as a noun. He wanted the language "cleaned up."

Dr. Murray wrote to me,

> Sorry to say I found almost all the editor's changes objectionable. . . . It is not perversity, I believe, but a regard for the meaning I am trying to convey. Your editor at G&S needs a little gland therapy plus some schooling in the language. . . the piece must be reconstituted as I have indicated or no Foreword by Yours Cordially.

With a tone of bravado I did not really feel, I informed Mr. Stratton that I would legally interdict the publication of the book (then in galley proof) if he did not print the foreword exactly as Dr. Murray wanted it. It all got sorted out and there was an important—life-changing for me—consequence to this contretemps.

Seven years later, a special edition of the *Journal of Projective Techniques*—of which I was associate executive editor—was published honoring Murray. He invited me and some others to have dinner with him at Harvey's restaurant in Washington, D.C. Toward the end of the dinner, after sufficient bourbon all around, I told him that I had an additional favor to ask him: would he be willing to write a foreword to another book I was editing? I saw him stiffen, and he said, "Anything, old man"—his way of declining a request from an inferior—"What is it?" I said, "It's a foreword to a collection of forewords by Henry A. Murray." He went into a paroxysm of laughter, and when he recovered he said, "Oh, that's too good. Too perfect for words. You must come to Harvard!" The event did not actually happen for three years, but that is how it started.

Summer: Suicidology

The fulcrum moment of my suicidological life was not when I came across several hundred suicide notes in a coroner's vault while on an errand for the director of the VA hospital, but rather a few minutes later, in the instant when I had a glimmering that their vast potential value could be immeasurably increased if I did *not* read them, but rather compared them, in a controlled blind experiment, with simulated suicide notes that might be elicited from matched nonsuicidal persons. My old conceptual friend, John Stuart Mill's Method of Difference, came to my side and handed me a career.

With the feeling that two heads might be better than one, I called Norman

Farberow, who had recently (in 1949) completed a dissertation at UCLA on suicidal mental hospital patients, using the newly minted MAPS Test. For 17 years after that from 1949 until 1966 we worked together, with varying intensities and the normal furbelows of a constant relationship, until I went to the NIMH in Bethesda. During this time, we founded and co-directed the Los Angeles Suicide Prevention Center (LASPC), co-edited five books, and co-authored dozens of papers and book chapters. (The LASPC remained an autonomous unit until 1988, when it became part of the Family Service Agency of Los Angeles and, for all intents and purposes, disappeared. I decry that fact and am saddened by it.) It may very well be that the greatest contribution to the Los Angeles community of the LASPC over its 30-year life span was the training of large numbers of *general* mental health specialists, many of them volunteers, and the demonstration, with nationwide implications, that this kind of high-level training could be successful.

The LASPC was begun in a basement room at the Brentwood VA Neuropsychiatric Hospital, where Farberow and I were staff psychologists. Increasingly, we received permission to devote our time to the topic of suicide. We obtained additional suicide notes from the coroner's office, generated simulated suicide notes from fraternal groups and labor unions, analyzed the coded notes, and interviewed suicidal patients. Within a few years, we had worked out an understanding with the VA central office (and specifically with the medical director, Dr. William Middleton) whereby we could devote our full time to this project, with the sensible rationale that whatever we might learn would directly benefit VA patients.

The first public presentation of our work was at a meeting of the American Association for the Advancement of Science, held in Berkeley in 1954. That six-page paper, entitled "Clues to Suicide" (Shneidman & Farberow, 1956), reported on 32 each of committed, attempted, threatened, and non-suicidal subjects. (That is a rough categorization that I would now eschew; nowadays I would choose a continuum of "lethality".) The following year we published another short paper, "Some Comparisons between Genuine and Simulated Suicide Notes" (Shneidman & Farberow, 1957a), comparing 33 genuine and simulated notes written by Caucasian male young adults. We had quietly begun to investigate suicidal phenomena within the canons of scientific psychology. We had control groups, statistically decent numbers, blind analyses, and finite findings. Although we were enthusiastic about our labors, we were unaware of what impact these bite-sized studies might have.

By this time, our work had been noticed by Harold Hildreth, who had been chief of the nationwide VA clinical psychology program and was then at NIMH. He viewed the topic of suicide prevention as a major mental health area worthy of official support, and he appointed himself our unofficial sponsor. (Another of his adopted projects was Evelyn Hooker's pioneer study of male homosexuality—but more of that later.) I soon developed a special relationship with Hal and spent many hours with him, especially during the many times he came to Los Angeles. He was a fervent, almost evangelical, and sometimes tormented man.

Briefly stated, the administrative history of the LASPC goes something like this: We had three grants from the NIMH: (1) an initial three-year research grant, 1955 to 1958, for $5,200; (2) a five-year project grant, 1958 to 1963, which, in 1962, became

(3) a seven-year project grant, 1962 to 1969. The LASPC enjoyed an unprecedented period of 14 years of NIMH support; the total amount was over one and a half million dollars. (The grants were administered through the University of Southern California School of Medicine.) The project grants—heretofore undreamed-of combinations of different fiefdoms of NIMH, including training-research-demonstration-service—were entirely Hal Hildreth's doing, and represented a triumph of his dedication and perseverance.

In 1958, the LASPC began as a separate entity on the fourth floor of an abandoned TB hospital on the grounds of the Los Angeles County Hospital. (We took it because it was rent-free.) Robert E. Litman, a brilliant young psychoanalyst, was chief psychiatrist. The rest of the core staff consisted of Norman Tabachnick, Sam Heilig, David Klugman, Carl Wold, and Michael Peck. Bob Litman reminded me recently about our recruitment routine, which went something like this (the setting was a booth in Trader Vic's in Beverly Hills). Norm and I told Bob of our plans and aspirations and of the great opportunities at the new research-oriented suicide prevention center. After a while, Norman asked Bob if he'd like another drink. Before he could answer, I asked him if he would be our chief psychiatrist. When he said yes to Norman, I said, "Wonderful! We'll start on Monday." For 30 years at the LASPC, Robert Litman was a genius in his ability to create and maintain staff morale and to share his psychoanalytic orientation, leavened by extraordinary common sense and good humor.

Ground was broken for our own building, near downtown Los Angeles, on Columbus Day, October 12, 1962. Two young architects designed and built a no-nonsense two-story building near the corner of Pico Boulevard and Vermont Street, and we leased the building from them. The speakers on that glorious day included County Coroner Theodore J. Curphey, Dean Clayton Loosli, Councilman (later Congressman) Edward Roybal, and Hal Hildreth, representing the NIMH. My dear father, then almost 80, attended, and beamed throughout the ceremony.

The excitement of those early days at the LASPC is hard to describe. It was like sitting on the seat of a racing covered wagon, galloping into unknown territory, dust flying all around, with the reassuring anxious-and-friendly faces of fellow pioneers on all sides. The dangers were from ravines and flash floods and our judgment in choosing wrong trails. Every day seemed like a new high adventure.

I need to say something here about another important person in my life, Evelyn Hooker. Evelyn is 11 years older than I, tall and stately, clear and lucid, with a marvelous strong voice. Everyone agrees that she is an extraordinary and effective teacher; she has some special magic that draws people to her. In the early 1950s, she was teaching a psychology course at UCLA when some male students approached her after class and asked her to help them with their problem. What is that? she asked. They told her that they were homosexual. She said she knew nothing about that topic, but would try to help. That was the beginning of her special career.

Hal Hildreth's special mental health topic of interest (aside from suicide) was Evelyn's beginning study of male homosexuality. Eventually she did a monumental study (for one person) of 30 each of heterosexual and homosexual males who were functioning well in the community—not a hospitalized or patient population, on which practically all previous studies had been done. Eventually she received, for a few years, an NIMH Research Career Award to pursue her research.

Along with extensive interviews, Evelyn administered the Rorschach test, the TAT, and the MAPS Test to all 60 of her subjects. She asked Bruno Klopfer and Mortimer Meyer to interpret the Rorschachs and TATs—identity unrevealed, of course—and she asked me to come to her lovely home and blindly interpret the MAPS Test protocols. We began, tape recorder and all, sitting under an apricot tree in her garden, and we finished the 60 test records several months later, after the tree had bloomed and the fruit had been picked and eaten. The paradigmatic moment of this fascinating procedure came one day when I was interpreting the Bedroom scene of a MAPS Test record and saw that the subject had placed one nude male on top of another in the bed. I said, "I wish I could say that I see it all now, but I don't see a thing in terms of dynamics and certainly nothing in terms of pathology; this seems to be the record of an essentially normal man who happens to be homosexual."

Evelyn's response was to burst into laughter. But I choose to believe that I reenforced her now-famous major finding that the distributions of personality normalcy-aberrance for homosexual and heterosexual males are overlapping distributions, and not two immediately discernible distributions, as was previously believed.

My present deep relationship with Evelyn began early in 1957, not long after her husband, Edward Hooker, a distinguished Dryden scholar at UCLA, had died. He had died suddenly, in her presence, as he was about to walk their dog. Soon after his death I came unannounced to her rambling Bel Air home with a pinch-bottle of Haig-and-Haig. I let myself in and, after yelling for permission, I picked up two glasses from the kitchen and went into her bedroom. I poured us both some whiskey and we drank and she wept. Our friendship had quietly moved to a deeper level, where it has remained ever since. She is my dearest lifelong friend, and we have seen each other through many a rough spot.

One especially stimulating aspect of the LASCP was the invited Fellows, who represented a variety of social science disciplines. The selection of the Fellows was my special project, and I took a gleeful delight in surprising the SPC staff with their identity. They usually came for a year, and were supported out of the general grant. My goal was to create a university atmosphere, a think tank of suicide within the fructifying setting af a busy clinical center. Mere practice without thought is doomed to remain just that—practice without thought. There is nothing so professionally stimulating as theoretically oriented, critical but friendly minds commenting on one's day-to-day real-life clinical activities.

In 1967, I edited *Essays in Self Destruction,* which featured chapters by members of the SPC staff and by current and previous Fellows and other individuals who had been special guests at the center. Among the 24 chapters, some of my favorites include Henry Murray on the partial death of Herman Melville, Stephen Pepper on whether a philosophy can make one philosophical, Jacques Choron on death as a motive for philosophic thought, Talcott Parsons and Victor Lidz on death in American society, Harold Garfinkel on practical sociological reasoning in the work of the LASPC, Mamora Iga on Japanese adolescent suicide, Avery Weisman on self-destruction and sexual perversion, Robert Litman on Freud and suicide, Paul

Freidman on suicide among 93 New York policemen, 1934 and 1940, and Lawrence Kubie on multiple determinants of suicide. This mere listing cannot convey the potential of the ideas for the systematic study of suicide scattered in the contents of that jam-packed book.

For a while the LASPC was the standard in this country for service combined with training and research in suicide prevention. *Clues to Suicide* (1957b), with a spritely foreword by Karl Menninger, was the first book that Norman Farberow and I edited, and probably the one with the greatest impact. In a relatively short time, in the heady days of the 1950s and 1960s, the topic of suicide prevention had become a legitimate area for psychologists, psychiatrists, social workers, nurses, and health educators, and a genuine nationwide interest in the topic had begun.

In September 1961, I went on a year's leave from the Los Angeles Suicide Prevention Center to Harvard as a U.S. Public Health Service special research fellow. In May, Harry wrote me:

> Hallelujah! Hallelujah! Hallelujah! My cup of joy is full and runneth over. . . .
> The main event today is your grand decision to come to Harvard and the prospect of working out some new theories together. . . . If you will accept a niche in our domain you will find Erik Erikson and several other people whose ideas and researches are congenial to you. . . . P. S. Perhaps we should be more wary and not cheer too loudly at this point. As you know I am very difficult to get along with (at least *some* people have come to this conclusion), but my impression is that even a bastard can get along with you, and so the chances may not be so bad.

In that year I attached myself to Harry. I also had memorable contacts with the great logician Willard Van Orman Quine, who said to me "What you are doing is interesting, but it is not what I am interested in"; with Erik Erikson (I fumbled a chance to be his patient in psychotherapy, probably out of general apprehension and a neurotic sense of loyalty to Harry); Gordon Allport (whose proferred apple juice, as opposed to Harry's Sazerac, represented for me the paradigmatic difference between their two approaches to personality, one healthful but bland, the other more spirited and robust); Jerome Bruner, B. F. Skinner, David McClelland, I. A. Richards, Christiana Morgan, and dozens of other exciting intellects. In his dissertation about Murray and the Harvard Psychological Clinic, Triplet (1983) noted that as early as the late 1920s and early 1930s, "Murray brought to the Clinic luncheons such Harvard luminaries as the biochemist Lawrence J. Henderson, the philosopher Alfred North Whitehead, and the sociologist Talcott Parsons. There was also a standing invitation for any of Murray's literary, artistic, or intellectual friends to drop in whenever they happened to be in the Boston area. In this way, such people as Felix Frankfurter, Conrad Aiken, Katherine Cornell, Bertrand Russell, and Paul Robeson became frequent luncheon guests." Of course, this was before my time, but that aura of healthy diversity of views, of first-rate all-around enterprise, and of taken-for-granted civility of exchange was always Harry's way of conducting things.

Not long after I arrived in Cambridge, the regal Anne Roe, then professor of education at Harvard, and her husband, the renowned evolutionist George Gaylord

Simpson, invited us to a small dinner party—four couples, as I remember it. During drinks, Stanley Estes, a former member of the Harvard Psychological Clinic, took me aside and asked me, with obvious malicious pleasure, whether I was aware of the relationship between Harry (who was married to Josephine Murray) and Christiana Morgan. I was absolutely flabbergasted and shaken. I didn't believe him. He said, "Don't be a fool; ask Anne or G. G." I could see that he was telling a truth I didn't want to hear. I remember saying to him, "Get away from me. You are reptilian."

In the following days I evidently moped around the clinic, for Harry asked me one day whether something was wrong. Quite ingenuously, I asked him if what Estes had told me were true. He said, yes, of course, and was that a problem for me in working with him? I said that I would have to think about it. (I am appalled now by my naivete and my colossal moral superciliousness.) In a few days I told Harry that I was a fool, and that I had come to study with him and learn from him. In time, I came to know and to admire Christiana's special mystical qualities. All in all, that first stay at Harvard— when I was in my early 40s—was the most intellectually exciting year of my life.

At one time during that year I was propositioned by an attractive young woman, who offered to arrange an out-of-town assignation. When I mentioned this to Harry, he was very straightforward and unequivocal. He said; "Don't emulate me in this! It's not for you!" (How different from Jung's behavior with his wife and mistress.) In fact, I did not need Harry's verbal restraint; but his direct advice was marvelously reinforcing for me, and I appreciated his recognizing the real psychological differences between us, reflected in his wish to protect me from unnecessary travail.

In early 1963, after I returned from Harvard, Harry came through Los Angeles. Among other places, I took him to the forecourt of Grauman's Chinese Theater on Hollywood Boulevard, where he inspected, without comment, the handprints of the movie stars. We then drove up the hill to Yamashiro's restaruant, where we sat on a terrace, looked out over the city on a lovely afternoon, and talked, mostly about Melville and death.

Harry expatiated on various kinds of death: somatic death, psychic death, partial death, social death, death of the inner self and death of the outer self, being as good as dead, etc., etc. My interests were focused on the varieties of somatic deaths. (What was in my mind was a possible clarification and revision of the death certificate.) That afternoon, catalyzed by Harry's ideas, I developed the notion that all somatic deaths were intentioned, unintentioned, or—the most interesting category— subintentioned. Most of the ideas in my favorite theoretical paper, "Orientations Toward Death" (1963b), came from that afternoon's talkfest. I have lived off the nourishment of that day for almost 30 years.

For me, the notion of subintentioned death enlarged the conceptual base of the SPC, permitting us to include among our legitimate interests all sorts of indirect suicide, demeaned and truncated lives, self-defeating neuroses, obviously inimical behaviors, and even alcoholism and addiction.

The idea of subintentioned death tied in with another interest, the accurate certification of deaths. Many deaths are equivocal as to their mode. (The four traditional modes of death are natural, accidental, suicidal, and homicidal, which I had labelled, acronymically, the NASH categories of death.) Any uncertainty as to category usually devolves between accident and suicide. Dr. Theodore J. Curphey, Los Angeles County Chief Medical Examiner-Coroner, had heard me speak and invited us—myself, Norman Farberow, and Robert Litman—to meet with him to help him clarify cases of equivocal death. The key, of course, lies in the intention of the decedent vis-à-vis death. We developed a procedure of gently done systematic inquiries of survivors by trained behavioral scientist-clinicians, which I dubbed the "psychological autopsy." These inquires focused on clarifying this grey area (Litman, Curphey, Shneidman, Farberow, & Tabachnick, 1963; Curphey, 1967; Shneidman 1973a, 1977). Nowadays the psychological autopsy procedure, although not used as widely as it ought to be, is, on its practical merits, taken for granted as a useful adjunct to a coroner's activities. Occasionally one finds these merits over-stated in the heat of courtroom litigation.

Sometime during 1961, I was seated among the regulars at Harry's long oaken conference table at the Baleen, the Harvard Psychological Clinic. Knowing that Harry's 70th birthday was coming up in 1963, Jonathan Jenness and I hatched an idea, which we immediately took to Christiana Morgan, that a *festschrift* be prepared. There was a secret meeting with Erik Erikson, Robert White, Christiana, and a few others, at which it was decided to go ahead with the exciting project. Robert White would be the perfect editor.

I poured my heart and my mind into my chapter, "Orientations toward Death." A copy of *The Study of Lives* (White, 1963), with contributions by an honorable list of Harry's students, was presented to him on his 70th birthday, May 13, 1963. On May 15, I received a postcard of Dürer's *Knight, Death and the Devil*. The message read,

Dear Old Crony,
My birthday tenderloin of self-esteem was broiled to a turn by the coals of your generosity—your initiation of the enterprise that resulted in the intellectual plentitude I received yesterday at the last turn of my life. You are the key to it all &, in addition, your own brilliant paper! Hugs all around and grace to the end.
                                                                                        Harry

As a footnote, let me say that lest the reader conclude that all was unremitting peaches-and-cream between Harry and me (or, for that matter, between Harry and anyone who was close to him), two months after our conversation at Yamashiro's, in July 1963, I had misunderstood Harry's intentions in relation to a letter he had sent me about Justice Felix Frankfurter. In my prompt response I had indicated that *Harry* was *my* hero-figure. He had wanted to hear about Frankfurter and not about himself, and especially not about my affection for him. My reply ticked him off and he overreacted. I received a postcard of Blake's *The Minotour* on which, to my astonishment and disbelief, I read the following:

Dear Impossibility,
Gin & tonic to you for returning the paper so promptly, but *gin and arsenic* down your guts for conforming to my worst expectations, & stabbing me with the dastardly distortion of a benignantly simple intention. *Hero-Figure* my arse! Your delusional system has gone berserk, outside my range of confidence.
                                                                                   Bon Voyage.

I was flabbergasted, hurt, and angered. I had come too close to him too soon and he had, with a stroke, reestablished the "proper" psychological distance between us. It took us some time to work that one out and trim back to an even keel, and I never again saw anything with his distinctive handwriting on it without a momentary twinge of sharp apprehension.

His next letter read, in part,

Dear Magnanimous Ed:

I *did* mean what I said, but ¼ strength of what my words conveyed—that surplus was added for fun—not a great success as fun we must agree. O Misericordia!

While writing that piece about F. F. I was, of course, conscious of the embarrassing fact that I had said (1) that I was a friend of his and (2) that his needle pointed to men of true worth (therefore I am a man of true worth QED). But I did not see how I could deal with this without some even more embarrassing personal statements that would have the nasty odor of spurious modesty. . . .

I thought I would risk the possibility (preposterous but not too preposterous for your mind) that you would think: "Ah, yes HAM is Mr. Justice Holmes & I am little F. F., the hero-worshipper." But be simple for once: *F. F.* is the hero of that piece, and you're the hero of my heart. The rest is willful nonsense.

Salvos, H

In 1962, I returned from Harvard to the LASPC, refreshed, and with ideas and plans. Hal Hildreth continued to visit intermittently and to consult with Norman and me at the SPC and with Evelyn. One day in 1965, after several worrisome telephone calls about how things were going for him at the NIMH, he flew out to Los Angeles. I met his evening flight. He was a bit unsteady as he came off the airplane. We drove to his hotel, talked for two or three hours, and arranged to meet after he had slept. The next morning I called his room, but he did not answer. I went to his hotel, knocked on his door, and then asked a maid to let me into the room, telling her that I had left my key on the dresser. Hal was in bed, stone-cold. He had died during the night. It devolved entirely on me to take care of everything: telephone his wife, then notify several other key people, call the coroner, arrange for the disposition of the body (to a local medical school), see to the death certificate, and several important things besides. That day was perhaps the most miserable of my life.

In January 1966, Stanley Yolles, then director of the NIMH, invited me to consult there, specifically to make suggestions for a possible national program in suicide prevention. I spent a month at the NIMH, flying home every weekend, and in early February, having written a 36-page memorandum, "A Comprehensive NIMH Suicide Prevention Program," I had an exit interview with Dr. Yolles. The plan I came up with was a ten-point program organized around the concepts of prevention, intervention, and (my neologism) postvention. I felt that I had fulfilled the job and was ready to get back to Los Angeles, my family, my home, and the LASPC, when Yolles offered me a position. Of course, I turned it down. He then said, "All right, but you will never again have the opportunity to paint on a national canvas." That really got to me. But the coin that tipped the balance was my feeling that I needed to establish a suicidological identity entirely of my own, based on my own ideas. I asked Yolles for a few days, during which I discussed the matter with Jeanne and our four sons. We decided that, all in all, it was an offer I could not refuse. And that—to paraphrase Melville—is how I went awhaling.

At the NIMH, it seemed to me that there was a need for a national journal on suicide prevention. After a brief while I went directly to Stan Yolles with a mock-up copy of the first issue of the *Bulletin of Suicidology.* Yolles's response to the idea was positive, but he quibbled over the name. He said that "suicidology" was a neologism and, moreover, it was, etymologically speaking, a bastard word, combining a Latin root with a Greek suffix. I replied that every word is a neologism until it is used by a number of people, and, as for its being of mixed derivation, he was absolutely correct, as my friends in *sociology* had warned me. He answered "Touché," and signed the necessary approval form. That journal, co-edited with David Swenson, was published from 1968 to 1971, when I initiated *Suicide and Life-Threatening Behavior* as the official journal of the American Association of Suicidology. I edited *S& LTB* for 11 years, until 1982.

It is accurate to say that I kept myself busy at NIMH. In the less than three years I was there, I visited and encouraged suicide prevention activities and grants in 40 states. When I arrived at NIMH in 1966 there were three suicide prevention centers in the country; three years later there were over two hundred. Certainly, for a while, under Yolles (and Presidents Kennedy and Johnson), psychosocially oriented mental health programs took off and soared. It is a fact of political life that more conservative national administrations, as they touch and affect mental health programs, tend to be more biologically oriented—and in my opinion subtly more moralistic and more punitive—than do Democratic administrations.

Nowadays—for good or bad—knowledge follows funding. One major consequence of this fact is that we get more newspaper and television accounts about the biological side of mental health problems—alcoholism, suicide, obsessive neuroses, etc.; nevertheless, we should remain aware of the fact that much of the new information may just be a large-scale example of the Pygmalion phenomenon. Funding for the investigation of legitimate cultural, social, and psychodynamic aspects of human malaise would generate new findings (and give renewed emphasis) to those dimensions.

Of the dozens of grants and activities of the NIMH Center for the Study of Suicide Prevention from 1966 to 1969, two that especially pleased me were the training grant awarded to Seymour Perlin at Johns Hopkins University for fellowships in suicidology, and a small grant to William Henry at the University of Chicago to host a meeting, which I was to arrange. At that meeting in Chicago, on March 20, 1968, I believe that there was as much suicidological talent and experience as perhaps had ever come together in one place. The group consisted of philosopher Jacques Choron, statistician Louis I. Dublin, psychoanalyst Paul Friedman, educator Robert Havighurst, psychiatrist Lawrence Kubie, psychiatrist Karl A. Menninger, and (from England, having fled from Germany) psychiatrist Erwin Stengel, all then in their 70s or 80s.

That meeting was a kind of "reconvening" of the famous meeting in Freud's apartment in 1910 of Freud, Adler, Jung, Stekel, and Oppenheim. The 1910 meeting is reported in *On Suicide* (Friedman, 1967), which was my point of departure. In my comments at the 1968 meeting, I noted that the 1910 meeting was unusual in a number of ways, not the least of which was that it was the occasion of the first enunciation, by Wilhelm Stekel, of the psychoanalytic formulation that the yearning for death is the mirrored wish for the death of another, or hostility turned around toward the self—what I called murder in the 180th degree.

In any event, by the end of the day—with the feeling that the time had come for a national organization for suicide prevention—we had started the American Association of Suicidology (AAS). I was blessed with the special help of Avery Weisman, whose counsel was indispensable. Of course, I conferred with Henry Murray. At my request, Calvin Frederick, who was then working with me at NIMH, prepared a constitution and a set of bylaws patterned more or less after those of the multi-disciplinary American Orthopsychiatric Association. By the end of that day, in our minds at least, the AAS was a reality. One year later, at our second meeting, in New York City, I found myself president. Happily, the organization soon had a life (and travails) of its own. If the association were to have a motto, it would be "Research, Training, Service." *On the Nature of Suicide* (1969a), which I edited, reflects the contents of the 1968 meeting—and, in an entirely indirect way, illustrates some of the advantages of "federal power."

I was at NIMH, living in Chevy Chase, Maryland, from 1966 to early 1969. I had planned to stay until July, but in December 1968, Robert Rosenthal, a professor at Harvard who had been my trainee at the Brentwood VA Hospital called to ask if I would return to Harvard as visiting professor for the winter 1969 semester. This invitation came about because Robert White was retiring a semester early. He asked me what I wanted to teach, and after a moment's thought I replied, "Death and Suicide." And so I returned to Harvard for five months. An added gift of the magi was the opportunity to work, as a thanatologist-clinician, with Avery Weisman, America's wisest thanatologist, on the wards of Massachusetts General Hospital. Mornings at the MGH with Avery; afternoons at the Baleen with Murray teaching Death and Suicide to two hundred life-oriented Harvard undergraduates; meeting every class right through the Harvard student strikes. (I later edited a book, *Death and the College Student* [1972], about that class.) Long talks at Harry's house. Heaven.

Of course, I hoped to stay at Harvard. On May 30, 1969, I was invited to attend a special faculty session in Longfellow Hall on Appian Way. There were ten other people there—nine high-ranking professors and a dean. We stood around talking. After a while, clinging to my glass of sherry, it seemed to me that I was being passed from person to person and being asked a series of questions on other than purely social topics, questions relating to the conduct of a psychology department and to my thoughts about an optimal program in clinical psychology. I finally tumbled to the fact that this was an employment interview, for a position I had not known about and had not sought—but no doubt would have taken. And I failed it. There were many reasons why they did not want me, but I am sure that the main one was that to each person I had praised Harry and his work, and it was apparent that they definitely were not looking for a Murray clone—not that I would have qualified. I had been loyal, if not prudent. Part of Harry's letter of August 5, 1969 (to me, back in Los Angeles) reads,

> I was disheartened to hear the names of those chosen to pick the new professor of clinical psychology. [Leon] Eisenberg is the only one whose judgment I have any reason to respect in his area. I gather that they didn't think you fitted the requirements they had in mind and were put off by your general point of view as expressed in the interview. Also, they failed to appreciate Bob Holt. So far they have no hero.

A marvelous event occurred during that time at Harvard: Harry married Caroline (Nina) Fish. Jeanne and I were invited to the afternoon reception in their garden. Nina was 49; Harry, 76. Nina, a psychologist by profession, is a wholesome, vivacious, effervescent woman. It was my extreme good fortune that she liked me. And so my visits to "22"—Harry's and Nina's gracious home—continued after Harry's death in June 1988. Nina and I remain the best of friends. I also continue to enjoy a warm and cordial relationship with Harry's daughter, Josephine Lee Murray, a pediatrician who is greatly concerned with peace and the environment.

After Harvard, I went to Palo Alto. Like everyone else who has been there, I can report that my year at the Center for Advanced Study of the Behavioral Sciences was a marvelous one. During my year there I edited *Aspects of Depression* (1969b, with Magno Ortega) and *The Psychology of Suicide* (1970, with Norman Farberow and Robert Litman), and found time to read and even to think. And there was time enough to do an empirical research study.

I went down the hill from the center to see Robert Sears, then dean emeritus and executor of the Terman Study. The Terman Study of 1528 bright children in California was begun in 1921, with the aim of determining what kind of children they were and what kind of adults they would become. The unforeseen results changed forever our views of gifted children and introduced profound changes throughout pedagogy. Knowing of my interest, Professor Sears provided me with a list of some 20 suicidal deaths. The list included five suicides, all by gunshot, of men around 55 years of age. It was arranged by Robert Sears for me to examine the complete records, from 1921 onward, of 30 men, up to age 50 with the last several years of their lives deleted. I would not know whether they were dead or alive, and if dead, how they had died. The flaw in the study was that I knew there were five suicides; it would, of course, have been better if I had not known how many suicidal deaths there were in the group. In any event, I studied those 30 cases for several months, drew up a Meyerian (from Adolph Meyer, 20th-century American psychiatrist) life chart for each subject, and made all sorts of internal ratings and judgments. Then I wrote a memorandum to Sears, rating each subject from 1 to 30 in terms of the probability of that person's having committed suicide.

There were, to my mind, three especially interesting findings from that study:

1. It is possible, beyond chance, to predict suicide at age 55 from a detailed study of a life history. I picked four of the suicides in the first five, and all five in the first six. The early notion that we had at the LASPC that there are clues or prodromal markers to suicide is true if one takes into account the entire life span.

2. These markers or prodromata are not seen especially early in life, but they were evident, with this group of subjects, in early adulthood, specifically by age 30. For this group of bright males the important decade seemed to be from age 20 to 30, after they had finished school, the age when a person of this educational class ordinarily has to find a spouse and begin or establish a career. It was during their 20s that the patterns of these men's lives began subtly to diverge.

3. The role of the spouse was, literally, vital. Simply put, a competitive spouse—not so much overtly hostile as almost sibling rivalrous—could be lethal.

All this, with the supporting information, is published in "Perturbation and Lethality as Precursors of Suicide in a Gifted Group" in the first issue of *Suicide and Life-Threatening Behavior* (Shneidman, 1971).

Of course, I believe in the primary place of psychodynamics, the unconscious mental aspects, in suicide; they are central. But I also believe that the cognitive, mentational, or syllogistic styles—the individual's *logical* patterns, which cannot be separated from his psychodynamic constellations—are also an integral part of any suicidal scenario. In 1957, I wrote about *catalogic*—that is, ways of thinking that destroy the logician (Shneidman, 1957b). This paper was followed, through the years, with analyses of the logical styles of such self-destructive minds as that of a 23-year-old suicidal woman (1969c) who wrote a suicide note and then shot herself; Joseph Conrad (1979b), who as a young man put a (nonfatal) bullet through his chest; Cesare Pavese (1982a), the Italian poet, novelist, and translator of Melville, who sedated himself to death; and a paper on the seemingly innocuous adverbial conjuction "therefore," as in "On 'Therefore I Must Kill Myself' " (1982b). But, by a curious turn, the work on logical styles for which I received the most attention was on nonsuicidal *political* figures, which I used initially just by way of illustration.

My 1948 dissertation on schizophrenic fantasy had set me to thinking about language. Kasanin's 1946 monograph on language and thought in schizophrenia, especially von Domarus's chapter on schizophrenic logic, continued to buzz in my ear. And then, during the VA and SPC years, three books opened a new world to me: Edward Sapir's *Selected Writings in Language, Culture and Personality* (1949), edited by David Mandelbaum; Benjamin Lee Whorf's *Language, Thought and Reality* (1956), edited by John B. Carroll (that was the basic book); and Hajime Nakamura's monumental *The Ways of Thinking of Eastern Peoples* (1960), which I discovered in the United Nations bookstore. Later, I came across Nicholas Rescher's slim monograph, *Temporal Modalities in Arabic Logic* (1967).

The essence of the linguistic idea that so intrigued me, now commonly referred to as the Sapir-Whorf hypotheses, is that "all higher levels of thinking are dependent on language; and that the structure of the language one habitually uses influences the manner in which one understands his environment. The picture of the universe shifts from tongue to tongue" (Stuart Chase, foreword to Carroll's book of Whorf). We speak with our brain, but we think through our tongue. Language is archetypal and reflects our earliest memories.

I reasoned that if individuals of different language groups think (that is, perceive the world) differently—Indo-European (English, French, German, Latin), Hopi, Maya, Eskimo, Chinese, and so on—then why can this not be said for different individuals within the same language group, between schizophrenics (whatever that is) and nonschizophrenics, between Mr. Jones and Ms. Smith, between you and me? Indeed, why not?

And so I developed a logic of my own. The logic started with the premise that there are no intrinsic errors in logic, only idiosyncrasies. (I had noted that every suicide made "logical sense" to the person who committed it, given his premises and idiosyncratic ways of reasoning.) My task was not to criticize but to understand. My logic schema had four parts:

1. *Idio-logic.* The idio-logic consists of 27 aspects of reasoning and 35 cognitive maneuvers. (Examples of aspects of reasoning are irrelevant conclusion, argumentum ad hominem, equivocation, isolated predicate, and contradiction. Examples of cognitive maneuvers are to be irrelevant, to repeat, to allege but not substantiate, to deny without warrant, to digress, and to attack. Any text, spoken or written, might be analyzed in these terms. In all this work, Peter Tripodes informed me, guided me, wrote for me—he was indispensable.

2. *Contra-logic.* Contra-logic is the individual's private epistemological and metaphysical view of the world that might be reasonably inferred from his idio-logical patterns. Contra-logic is our reconstruction of an individual's private, usually unarticulated notions of casuality and purpose that make his idio-logic seem errorless to him. Contra-logic serves to contravene or "explain" the individual's idio-logic. In the same sense that every person has an idio-logical structure that can be explicated, there is for each individual a complementary contra-logical position that can be inferred. Understanding this position answers the question, How must he be thinking in order to make what he did or said seem reasonable to him? This information can help us to understand our opponents, our spouses, and our children as well as our patients.

3. *Psycho-logic.* Psycho-logic answers the question, What kind of person would he have to be, in terms of his mentational psychological traits (such as flexible-rigid, spontaneous-inhibited, combinatory-atomistic, conforming-iconoclastic)—in order to have the view of the world that he does (contra-logic) as manifested in his ways of thinking (idio-logic)? The psycho-logic represents the more-or-less mentational aspects of personality, which color all of the personality.

4. *Pedago-logic.* Pedago-logic addresses the question of how best to teach or instruct or communicate with—or conversely, to confuse, circumvent, or mislead— the individual, given his logical idiosyncrasies. If one understands a person's logical system, one can interact with him more effectively, whether that person is a patient, student, military recruit, spouse, child, boss or enemy. In relation to bosses, it is easy to see that one would want to use very different styles to brief one's boss if he were President Kennedy, Johnson, Eisenhower, Nixon, Ford, Carter, Reagan, or Bush. Although not totally inspiring, this list makes the point of the usefulness of different pedago-logics for different folks—different textbooks on the same subject for different kinds of minds.

Out of my thinking on this subject came a series of publications (Shneidman, 1959, 1960, 1963a, 1966, 1969c, 1982a, 1986). I would like to speak briefly of two of these pieces.

In 1962, the television industry and the APA sponsored a national contest; the winning papers were presented in *Television and Human Behavior* (May & Arons, 1963). My paper, "The Logic of Politics" (1963a), was a logical analysis, in terms of the ideas outlined above, of the verbatim text of two of the 1960 Kennedy-Nixon debates. For each of the men, I indicated percentages (added to 100) of 32 idio-syncracies of logic, summarized their idio-logical patterns, characterized their contra-logical positions, and wrote about their psycho-logical mentational traits.

The conclusions were lengthy and technical, but the essence was that Kennedy came through as a "doer," even though he might impulsively do some "wrong" things, while Nixon came through as a man who might "deliberately" do wrong things, but with careful attention to detail.

As a result, I developed some ideas about the biopsychological foundations of thinking, including logic. To me, among the most interesting facts about us human beings are that we speak and write to one another, and that only the tiniest number of us are hermits; that is to say, we are essentially social and communicating creatures. With a few inductive leaps, this leads me to believe in an *interpersonal* concept of mentation.

I am not convinced that the paradigm of "thinking" is isolated man, Descartes syllogizing alone by the fireplace. I believe that all of Aristotelian (and Schoolman) deductive logic is a fascinating mind-game, but that it is psychologically irrelevant. It makes more sense to me to believe that what we have always considered to be man's unique achievement, private and introspective thought (the reality of which I do not question for an instant) is, in fact, a complicated set of social and evolutionary acts of adaptation embedded in an active environment.

For me, this means that the essence of thought, and the motivation for all thought, can be contained in a set of "cognitive maneuvers" (Shneidman, 1960, 1963a, 1966, 1969c), by means of which an individual shapes himself, his environment, and the inner contents of his mind. Phenomenologically speaking, these cognitive maneuvers consist of rather simple gambits. They include to elaborate a point, to branch out or explicate, to use an example, to deduce from the preceding, to synthesize or summarize, to make a distinction, to obscure or equivocate, to paraphrase, to repeat, to be irrelevant, to allege but not substantiate, to deny or reject, to accept conditionally, to take issue, to digress, to initiate discontinuities, to move toward specificity, to move toward generalities, to contradict, to attack, and so on. Most interior monologues have an ultimate *dyadic* purpose. Of course, man can think in isolation, but abstract thinking is functional (in the Darwinian sense) because it relates to ways of communicating, debating, influencing, placating, dominating, and, ultimately, to ways of surviving—and its basic elements are neither syllogisms nor inductions, but these elementary maneuvers of cognition. We mentate in order to stay alive.

Harry wrote to me (January 18, 1965) about my mentational logics, "I have a hunch that this is *very* important—it *must* be. . . . I would look first for relative frequencies in each variable in different classes of the population—Supreme Court, advertising, etc. . . . In short, it looks to me as if you had broken entirely new ground, & provided a basis for 50 years of research. . . ."

These researches had at least one interesting consequence. In 1965, I was flown to the U.S. Naval Ordnance Testing Station (NOTS) at China Lake, a site in the California desert that occupies a piece of real estate about the size of the state of Rhode Island. At China Lake, I met with the scientific director. My task was to do a psychological analysis of two world leaders, Macmillan and Khrushchev. That seemed reasonable enough, and I bent to the task. A few days later, someone—I don't remember who it was—gave me some text and asked me to do a mentational analysis, especially of the person's "pedago-logics—how to instruct that person and most particularly, how to circumvent him." I was not told who it was, but I gathered that it was the NOTS's principal opponent, an admiral in the Pentagon. It took me less than a moment to realize that I was in over my head, playing with the big boys, and that I would be killed in the cross-fire. A few hours later I declared that I had urgent personal business in Los Angeles and requested to be flown home the next morning.

I dropped the logic—although I received inquiries about it from Poland, Bulgaria, and Czechoslovakia (!) for about 20 years, when I picked it up again and expanded it in new directions in a chapter combining two of my deepest interests, logic and Melville (Shneidman, 1986).

I did not return to the LASPC from the NIMH-Harvard-Stanford. Louis J. (Jolly) West saw to that. At the NIMH there were presentations by chiefs and directors three times a year to the NIMH Council, the institute's outside advisory or overseeing group. Dr. West was then chairman of the Department of Psychiatry at the University of Oklahoma and a member of the council. As chief of the suicide prevention center at NIMH, I periodically presented my charts and my 10-minute spiel before this august group. For my part, I did it in good fun. I knew that I was doing a more than adequate job, and when I arrived I knew that I would be leaving in three years. I certainly was not trying to hold on to a federal position. (That, and my being a psychologist, the only non-M.D. at that level and thus not legally eligible for the director's job, gave me a special advantage at the institute.) One day, after a council meeting, Jolly invited me to lunch. Over sandwiches, he asked me how I would like to be a professor in his department. I told him that I was enormously impressed by him, but that I just wasn't the type of fellow who belonged in Oklahoma. He asked me if I could keep a secret; he was the new chairman of psychiatry at UCLA and did I care to join him *there*. I said, "In that case, I'll buy you lunch." Out of his pocket, so to speak, he gave me a tenured FTE (full time employment) professorship—no application, no review, no search committee, no free lunches. That is his marvelous idiosyncratic style. Of course there was hell to pay, but the flack was directed against him, not me. So that is how I returned, in September 1970, to my alma mater as a professor in the medical school. When I graduated in 1938, who could have predicted that?

Many times later I reflected that it was Hal Hildreth who had advocated a national suicide prevention program at NIMH; that it was evident that he was not going to be offered the position of heading it; and that, considering the relationship between us, I could never have taken the post as chief of the suicide prevention program at NIMH if he were there. Death in life, filled with paradoxes and sardonic twists. He was 55 years old, and seemed worn by life, when he died. In 1967, at NIMH, I dedicated the product of the LASPC, *Essays in Self Destruction,* "To the Memory of Harold M. Hildreth, Devoted Godfather to the Scientific and Humanitarian Study of Self-Destruction in Man."

Autumn: Thanatology

The year 1973 was an especially good time for me. I had settled in as professor of medical psychology at the UCLA Neuropsychiatric Institute; I was teaching a popular undergraduate course on death and suicide (a course that I eventually taught for over 20 years); I had an interesting thanatological clinical (no fee) practice of suicidal or dying UCLA personnel—hospital patients, professors, students, and staff who were referred to me; I was consulting twice a month at the Brentwood VA Hospital; and I was studying and writing. In that year my article on suicide appeared in the *Encyclopedia Britannica* (1973c); I wrote and had published in *Psychiatry* a mildly heretical piece entitled "Suicide Notes Reconsidered" (1973b), in which I radically reversed the stance I had propounded since 1949 about the potential usefulness of suicide notes for the understanding of suicide; and *Deaths of Man* (1973a) was published and, to the publisher's amazement, was nominated for a National Book Award.

Who does not thrill to receive nice surprises in the mail, like an invitation to speak *ex cathedra*, in the *Encyclopedia Britannica*, on one's professional topic? That was my pleasure in 1971, a year after I arrived at UCLA. I examined the articles on suicide in the previous editions of the *EB* and determined to write an essay without a single table or chart of dreary and not too illuminating statistics, unlike all the past pieces. I sent the editors a rather longer essay than they had requested, but they printed every word. However, when the *EB* published a thoroughgoing revision a few years later, I was not invited to contribute again.

In February 1973, Harry wrote me a letter, one paragraph of which was about my *EB* article. I knew my own unhappiness with that piece: it did not contain new theory, and it was not truly encyclopedic; rather, it was iconoclastic. The *EB* was hardly the arena for me to press my disdain of unreliable nomothetic data. Nevertheless, Harry wrote,

> Your encyclopedia article is masterful—a wonderfully condensed, coherent and sophisticated survey of the whole conglomerate of today's knowledge of suicide that exists—handsomely written to a marked extent in your own terminology. I couldn't help thinking that this was possibly the timely moment to consider a shift of focus for a renaissance of spirit and mind after lying fallow for a season.

I knew Harry well enough to put aside the exaggerated praise and to know that the real meat of that paragraph—his intended message—lay in the criticism implied in the second sentence: that I was temporarily burnt out on the topic of suicide and that I ought to take a vacation from it, to consider a shift of focus, and to think new thoughts on some related topics for a while. And so, on the strength of Harry's advice in that one sentence, I decided to shift at least for a few years, from suicidal patients (who were dying, so to speak, of their own accord) to patients who were dying unwillingly, and their survivors. I became more active on the wards of the UCLA Center for Health Sciences, to which the NPI is attached, as a clinical thanatologist, trying to help dying persons die better and survivors survive better—better, that is, than if a clinical thanatologist had not helped them.

There was also a shift in my mind. I started to think almost exclusively about the dying process; but still, in the back of my mind, I was looking for anything that might throw light on why physically healthy people wanted to end their lives. It was obvious that both groups of patients were in great pain. The key lay in the difference in the *kind* of pain or the *source* of pain. Pain that comes from one's soma is received and viewed (and tolerated) in ways that are different from "psychological" pain—the pains related to affect and frustrated psychological needs. There is no question that my experiences with dying people enlarged and changed my views about suicide. In any event, within a few months I asked my estimable chairman, Jolly West, if I might change my title to reflect my activities and interests. In due time (in 1975) my university title was changed and I was officially designated the first-ever Professor of Thanatology. I continued to see dying patients in the UCLA Center for Health Sciences, and later wrote about some of them in *Voices of Death* (1980).

Working intensively with dying patients is quite different from therapy with suicidal people, or with the usual psychotherapy patient. On occasion, as I walked toward the hospital room of such a patient, I would think that I would rather take a beating than face the next hour with that benighted and beleaguered fellow human being. I somewhat feared the work; and yet for several years I was drawn to it, perhaps counterphobically. (I find that nowadays I can live happily with it.)

During that period, I was seated one day beside a dying woman who was lying in a hospital bed with the vulgar tubes and needles in her. I had seen her on many successive days, but had really not looked around the room, a private UCLA hospital room of a type with which I was very familiar. But on that day I looked up from her face to the opposite wall and I absolutely froze. I shuddered. For there on the wall was a pleasant Renoir print with its frame screwed into the wall a tiny bit askew. I suddenly remembered that this was the very room in which some months before I had been a prisoner, lying in that bed thinking that I was dying. That turned out to be a transient episode of something that healed completely. But in that moment I reflected that her fate was my fate. It was not like someone else's schizophrenia, or an addiction that *I* would never have; it was *mortality,* and I had it too. That, for openers, is why the countertransference is radically different in thanatological practice, and it helps explain everyone's (and especially physicians') skittishness with the dying process.

In 1979 I spent part of an academic leave in Stockholm at the Karolinska Hospital, working with the dear and gifted thanatologist-physician Loma Feigenberg. While I was there I sat in on several of his sessions with dying patients and, by his arrangement, for several weeks I treated a Swedish woman who was dying of cancer and who spoke in English for my benefit. In the long northern summer evenings, sitting on the lawn of his suburban home, he and I discussed and clarified for each other the important details that specifically characterize thanatological care. (Dr. Feigenberg died in 1988.)

Our article, "Clinical Thanatology and Psychotherapy: Some Reflections on Caring for the Dying Person" (1979a), makes the following points:

1. The goals are different, more finite, more concerned with comfort, less concerned with addictions or characterological patterns.
2. The rules are different, and one can move with more celerity and elicit a deeper and more dependent transference.
3. The therapist is much more flexible than in ordinary psychotherapy, in that there are history taking, just plain talk, communicative silences, and anxiety-reducing reassurance.
4. The focus is on benign intervention in the form of interpretations, suggestions, advice (when asked for), and practical interventions on the ward.
5. Meeting with spouse and children, and acting as the patient's ombudsman in a variety of ways, is appropriate.
6. There is a subtle abandonment of working toward total psychoanalytic grace or complete "working through," and it is recognized by both parties that the process may end, psychologically speaking, intestate.
7. The dying person sets the pace; in a sense, the disease is in charge, and different levels of candor can be equally therapeutic if they lead to increased comfort.
8. Some denial will always be present, either as a constant process or intermittently, as the patient (and sometimes the therapist) "knows," forgets, or outright denies certain lugubrious facts.
9. The role of transference is paramount, the place of countertransference is very important, and a good external support system is a necessity. Nor should a therapist see intensively more than two or three dying persons at a time.
10. The doctors and the nurses (especially) are an integral part of the private dyadic therapy, and while details of the patient's life should not be related, the general day-to-day flow of the sessions should be shared and professional staff should be made to feel that they too are part of thanato-therapy.
11. The survivors are the victims and postventive work—sessions with the spouse, for example—should begin well before the death of the patient.

In his work, Dr. Feigenberg emphasized the unique nature of the existential confrontation between the dying patient and the not-dying-at-that-time therapist; the alterations in the perception of time in the thanatological scene; the likelihood of intense transference and the special responsibilities of the therapist; the role of flexibility in the therapist; the importance of empathy, beyond identification and befriending to true caring; and the special ambience of the dying scene, with both its general declination of energy and its unexpected explosions of a variety of painful emotions: rebellion, aggression, grief, fear, submission, withdrawal, capitulation, terror. The presence of terror can be taken for granted, and its existence should be acknowledged and countered by words and touch.

Back at UCLA, I continued to see oncological patients. Working with death and dying is constantly sobering, sometimes sharply abrasive. One continually needs an outside support system for personal sanctuary and replenishment—I simply cannot see how I could have done this work without my matchless wife and the haven she provided for me at home. But the self-evident rewards of working with dying people are enormous: the opportunity to help; the opportunity to suffer and to grow; and the rare opportunity sometimes to come close to the deepest mysteries of life: love, our distant roots, our immediate and inevitable future, and our capacity to survive travail.

For me, part of the excitement of working with dying people was discovering the ways in which the integrity of the interaction, the depth of the transference, the intensity of the countertransference, and the discipline required by both parties in the dying scene are radically different clinically from those found in any other interpersonal relationship, whether ordinary talk or usual psychotherapy. I have viewed each dying person with whom I have worked intensively as a vicarious rehearsal for a different kind of scenerio for my own dying, and I puzzle how I will choose among them when my own turn comes. If I were to ask me how I liked my professional thanatological work over the past 20 years I might, in an unguarded moment, blurt out that I had hated it, but I would quickly add that I would not have wanted to do anything different for the world. If, in fact, I was relatively socially retarded as an adolescent and as a young adult, then my experiences with dying persons have sobered me up sufficiently, so that now, in Melville's words (*Moby-Dick*, Ch. 1), "Not ignoring what is good, I am quick to perceive a horror, and could still be social with it."

I see absolutely no brownie points in pain; I see catabolism as the enemy; but I aspire to be as *graceful* as possible in the overall manner of my dying, and I know that the key to this goal lies in what Murray and Otto Rank called "willing the obligatory." And, to me, that is *all* that dying is. I would not demean myself by adding supernatural or religious (they are synonymous in my book) meanings to this perfectly natural event—in any case, an event not for me, but for my unhappy survivors.

In 1983, I had an opportunity to extend the range of my clinical experiences. I was invited to spend three months as visiting professor of thanatology at the Soroka Medical Center of the Ben Gurion University of the Negev at Beer Sheva, in the middle of the Sinai desert. This was not my first visit to Israel, but it was my most extensive. Dr. Abraham Halmosh was my genial host; I was on his psychiatric ward almost every day. An international array of psychiatrists—Jews from around the world imploding in Israel—soon became my indelible friends. I also visited with Dr. David Davidson, previously at Johns Hopkins, at his hospital at Ashqelon, north of Gaza. And at the invitation of Colonel Ron Levy, who later visited me at UCLA, I addressed a group of mental health officers of the Israeli Defense Forces at Tel Hasamir. Beer Sheva was the one genuine, albeit brief, frontier experience of my life. A more startling contrast to the leisurely ambience and low level of tension of Stockholm, the site of my previous academic leave, could hardly be imagined.

At UCLA, I continued to be interested in the topic of suicide. In fact, I never left that topic. I wanted to know more about unintentioned death (say, from cancer) in order to know more about suicide. (The topic of death of course is superordinate to the topic of suicide.) And there was a "kind" of suicidal person who interested me especially: those few individuals who had committed suicide and had fortuitously survived. My countertransference feelings to them were more than ordinarily intense. I thought they were magical in some special way (and so they were). They had "done it" and survived—a kind of medieval trial by fire, almost as though they had gone across the River Styx with Charon and had come back. (This has nothing to do with the so-called—and to my mind banal—pseudoscientific "near-death" experiences.)

One of my most interesting patients was a young woman who had poured a gallon of gasoline over herself in her small sedan and lighted a match. Another was a young woman who ingested several barbiturate capsules and had her stomach pumped. Then, when her husband overtly rejected her, she jumped from a high balcony. And a third was a young man who, intending to shoot his brains out, placed a shotgun under his chin, pulled the trigger, and blew his face off. I reproduce the following three excerpts verbatim from tapes and written records, to give the reader a vivid notion of how a suicidological practice actually sounds.

Immolator: I remember sitting in the car and it was sort of like a blank in my mind. I felt very calm. I felt a kind of hush over my body. That everything was going to be O.K. And I remember then pouring the gasoline first over the front seat and of course over myself to a great extent. Even then no thoughts went through my head at all of the pain that it was going to entail, the misery, the hurt, any of that. I guess I didn't think that burns would really hurt, but none of that went through my head, it just felt good. It was the first time, in fact, that I had felt at peace, that I wasn't hurting inside. And for once it seemed like I had taken care of my problems and that my pain would just go away. It was not going to exist anymore, especially my mental pain. And I remember very slowly striking the match and at that moment the fumes ignited, just a tremendous explosion.

Jumper: I was so desperate, I felt, my God, I can't face this thing. Everything was like a terrible whirlpool of confusion. And I thought to myself, there's only one thing to do, I just have to lose consciousness. That's the only way to get away from it. The only way to lose consciousness, I thought, was to jump off something good and high. I just figured I had to get outside. I just slipped out. No one saw me. And I got to the other building by walking across the catwalk thing, sure that someone would see me, you know, out of all those windows. The whole building is made of glass. And I just walked around until I found this open stairway. And as soon as I saw it, I just made a beeline right up to it. And then I got to the fifth floor and everything just got very dark all of a sudden, and all I could see was this balcony. Everything around it just blacked out. It was just like a circle. That was all I could see, just the balcony. I climbed over it and I just let go. I was so desperate.

Shooter: There was no peace to be found. I had done all I could and was still sinking. I sat many hours seeking answers and all there was was a silent wind and no answers. The answer was in my head. It was all clear now. Die. The next day a friend of mine offered to sell me a shot gun. I bought it. My first thought was what a mess this is going to make. The next day I began to say goodbye to people. Not actually saying it but expressing it silently. I didn't sleep. The dreams were reality and reality dreams. One by one I turned off my outside channels to the world. My mind became locked on my target. My thoughts were: Soon it will all be over. I would obtain the peace I had so longed for. Those around me were as shadow, apparition, but I was not actually conscious of them, only aware of myself and my plight. Death swallowed me long before I pulled the trigger. I was locked within myself. There comes a time when all things cease to shine, when the rays of hope are lost. I placed the gun under my chin. Then I remember a tremendous explosion of lights like fireworks consumed within a brilliant radiance. Thus did the pain become glorious, becoming an army rallied to the side of death to help destroy my life which I could feel leaving my body with each rushing surge of blood. I was engulfed in total darkness.

These quotations tell us about the inside of suicide better than any professional can; they describe, poetically and from the gut, the pain, the perturbation, the desperation, the ambivalence, the constriction—all the primitive elements of the basic suicidal drama. The raw material of my work has always been what my patients have told me.

Just as I was trying to wrestle with suicide—that is, with the question "Why suicide?"—I was continuously puzzling over suicide notes. My initial response on finding the large number of suicide notes in 1949 was one of somewhat exaggerated enthusiasm. (Harry called me an "arch enthusiast.") Suicide notes were, I averred (to myself and to the profession) much as dreams were to Freud; they were the royal road to the deepest reasons for (and thus the understanding of) suicidal phenomena. But after almost a quarter-century of earnest effort, on my part and on the part of others, "the golden haven was not found." I was woefully unhappy with what the study of suicide notes had yielded. One day, while in the shower, I admitted a secret to myself: many suicide notes are dull; they are banal; they communicate very little because very little is communicated. And then the idea hit me: Suicide notes could not be full and explanatory documents because they were, by their very nature, written in a period of constricted thinking. Indeed, if one could write a full, explanatory, psychodynamically lucid document, one would not have to commit suicide. I had been a fool all along, looking for eloquence from a partial mute.

So I sat down and within a week wrote "Suicide Notes Reconsidered" (1973b), sent it off to *Psychiatry,* and saw it in print within a few months. I still like the enthusiasm and fervor of the language of that piece, but I now disagree with most of its content. I see it now as an interesting example of what Hegel called the antithesis, jumping, in my case precipitously, to the opposite of one's original position or thesis. Thesis: Suicide notes are magical. Antithesis: Suicide notes are worthless. Of course, I was not ultimately happy with that position either.

I sent a copy to my old, favorite professor, Joseph Gengerelli, to which he responded with characteristic bubbling generosity:

May 1, 1974

Dear Ed,

Thanks for the learned and beautifully written paper on suicide notes. I read it with interest, especially since it was consonant with the conclusions I had reached from such nonsystematic thinking as I had done on the subject. The contents of suicide notes, I surmised, would be as varied and particularistic as the domain of human personality and motivation. There's one thing surely common to them all: dissatisfaction with the Status Quo.

Ginger

The clue to it all lay before my eyes when I did a year-long study of suicide among the gifted in 1969 and 1970 at the Center for Advanced Study on the Stanford campus. A few years later, when I was writing *Voices of Death* (1980), did I follow up that study and write to various counties in California to obtain the suicide notes of half a dozen Terman Study subjects. Only then, when I placed the notes *within the context of the life,* did they become "alive." Practically every word resonated to some aspect of the style, or the penchant for special frustration, or unity thema within *that* individual's life history. Here is the Hegelian synthesis: suicide notes are, by themselves, neither everything nor nothing; but, placed within the life of which they are very much a part, they can be very illuminating and useful documents.

Voices of Death is a book built around personal documents, letters, diaries, and suicide notes, and about my patients at UCLA. It is about people who killed themselves, people who died unwillingly by invasion of a lethal disease, and people who were murdered by sadistic fiends. Of course, I had had hundreds of suicide notes and some diaries in my files for years, but the book started when a student gave me some material that he had obtained from Oswiecim (Auschwitz). These documents had been found in the 1960s, buried in cans and jars near the gas chambers and ovens. This resolve to write about those materials was further strengthened when Eugene Loebl (a former Czechoslovakian government official who had been imprisoned by the Soviets for 11 years and later came to America, where he became a professor) gave me a set of Vladimir Clementis's letters[1]. (Clementis had been minister of foreign affairs for Czechoslovakia in 1948. He had written the letters in a Soviet prison before he was hanged in 1952, at the end of the anti-Semitic Slansky trials.)

I also had letters from Jewish and non-Jewish German citizens, written just before they were executed by the Nazis. There were moments while I was writing *Voices of Death* when I wept; and I found some documents so powerful and private that I left them out of the book. But the book was also about the heroism of "ordinary" victims of cancer, and about the desperation of "ordinary" self-destruction. In my mind, that

---

[1] I first met Loebl in Regina Ryan's Central Park West apartment. Regina arranges all my book contracts. She also taught me to write more straightforward sentences. Once she sent me a page of my typescript that contained some extremely long Melville-like sentences and another (blank) sheet of paper on which she had touched a pencil point several times. Her accompanying note said, "Here are a dozen periods. Please distribute them judiciously through your page of text."

book is my realistic addendum to Gordon Allport's heuristic monograph on "The Use of Personal Documents in Psychological Science" (1942).

I could not seem to escape the lure of editing books, even though I enjoy writing them infinitely more. While at UCLA, at the invitation of my stalwart friend and colleague Milton Greenblatt, I edited *Suicidology: Contemporary Developments* (1976b), and in the same year a collection of contemporary essays on death, *Death: Current Perspectives,* (1976c), which went into two more editions, in 1980 and 1984 and, with Gordon Strauss, is scheduled for a fourth edition.

In 1981, an edited selection of my pieces on suicide was published, *Suicide Thoughts and Reflections* (1981a). In addition, I rather enjoyed editing 44 issues of *Suicide and Life-Threatening Behavior,* from its inception in 1971 to 1982, when Ronald Maris, a sociologist, became editor.

And so my work went along at UCLA. I was happy, as I have been most of my life; meteorologically speaking, there were no sustained dark clouds in my skies in the almost 20 years I was at UCLA. This was due to my penchant for independent work, and to my chairman, Jolly West, who, as far as I was concerned, provided a perfect environment for my academic and clinical labors. In 1973, Jolly tried to initiate a comprehensive Center for the Study of Violence, but it was doomed when then-Governor Ronald Reagan *endorsed* it in one of his state-of-the-state messages—the kiss of death. One consequence of this situation was that Jolly suddenly had an embarrassment of personnel riches, specifically Nancy Allen, a health educator whom I had previously invited to be on the NIMH CSSP committee in Bethesda. Jolly then transferred Nancy to me with my enthuiastic permission. For several years, my entire "staff" of the officially designated UCLA Laboratory for the Study of Life-Threatening Behavior has consisted of me, Nancy, and an administrative assistant-secretary. What I have loved about the laboratory is its isolation and our congeniality. Nancy and Evelyn Hooker remain my two best friends.

I seem to be defining myself (or at least describing myself) largely in terms of publications. That seems both accurate and appropriate. There are four more books of which I wish to speak, two of them by other people; one my favorite edited book; and one a book I wrote.

It pleases me enormously to have played a catalytic role in Antoon Leenaars's *Suicide Notes* (1988), for which I contributed a foreword (Shneidman, 1988). I once began to do a book along these lines, but I quickly perceived that Leenaars could get it done with more dispatch than I could; and besides, he could more effectively and gracefully than I summarize the suicidological work of Adler, Binswanger, Freud, Jung, Kelley, Menninger, Murray, Shneidman, Sullivan, and Zilboorg.

Another such project is Jack Kamerman's ongoing work with the survivors of the 93 New York City policemen who committed suicide in the years 1934 to 1940. I took the first manuscript about this project directly from Paul Friedman's hands (in his Park Avenue apartment) and published it in *Essays in Self-Destruction* (1967b). Friedman had obtained those data from Gregory Zilboorg; years later I gave them to Kamerman, who plans to do the monumental job of obtaining all the requisite permissions from the NYPD, the protection associations, and so on, and then to interview the surviving widows, the children, and perhaps the grandchildren to investigate the sequelae of suicide. My ambition is to write a foreword to this work, *Legacy of Suicide.* I now see all this information as relating to generativity; that is, to give to the next generation what one sees ought to be done but cannot do oneself. I can honestly say that I now derive as much pleasure from Leenaars's and Kamerman's work as if it were my own.

My favorite edited book was, by far, the most difficult publishing enterprise of my life. The problem, though, enormously complex, was very simple to identify. The problem was Henry Murray.

As early as 1969, I had yearned to prepare a comprehensive one-volume collection of Murray's published writing, and I had discussed this idea with him more than once, especially when I was at Harvard during the 1969 winter term. On subsequent short visits I pursued this topic.

About the projected "Murray Reader," Harry was ambivalent, indecisive, and plainly resistant to the idea of his earlier writings being reprinted without his having the opportunity to revise them—which, realistically, was not possible. On the other hand, I wanted to present his unavailable nonpareil works to a new generation of readers. To my intense discomfort, I found myself somewhat in the position of a firm grown son saying to an older revered parent, I am intent upon giving you this gift because I believe it is best all around; best for you, and, primarily, best for all the others who might share it. Although I seem to have been obdurate in this project, I can report that—for reasons quite different from Harry's—I too was very ambivalent. I asked myself, Why create this unnecessary tension? Over the span of 11 years, Harry's letters to me reflected his mental backing and filling on this topic.

June 23, 1973

Today your latest plan arrived, embarrassing me still further with thoughts of the amount of time you have spent on this project—this huge effort to rescue me from oblivion. Except for the welcome deletion of several second-rate papers, I find quite a few features—I regret to say—which are somewhat discomforting to my eccentric palate. . . . Please put the whole matter aside until you have heard from me again. . . . The scientific papers (personology &c) are mostly "old hat" as they stand. If I am capable of improving them, why not do so? If I die within a year or so, you may publish whatever you choose.

July 1, 1973

Why has my stomach turned sour on the plan for the Reader as recently set forth? Hard to say. Being a psychologist of sorts, the book must float or sink according to the worth or worthlessness of the section on personology. As the section stands it consists of a series of quite repetitive approximations, more or less, with numerous variations, up to the Encyclopedia article—an article which, in condensed *unintelligible* form, contains 80 percent of what I have to say. I think it would take me several months to expand the Encyclopedia article, & weave in parts of the earlier short articles. Nothing less would be good enough to publish. . . . Forgive me if you can.

Six years later, during a visit in 1979, I asked him directly if I had his approval to pursue this project. His words were, "A green light."

When the enterprise finally had Harry's ambivalent approval, it seemed such a heavy responsibility for me to assume singly that I immediately asked four former students of his (and friends of mine) to assist me by constituting themselves an informal committee to help make the final selections and to edit my interstitial materials. Fortunately, they all lived in California, and so we—Gardner Lindzey, Donald MacKinnon, Nevitt Sanford, Brewster Smith, and I—met in April 1979 at the Center for Advanced Study in the Behavioral Sciences, of which Lindzey was director. We subsequently corresponded several times on major and detailed issues.

Harry was, of course, ex officio chairman of the group. No item was included or excluded without his knowledge and approval. The title of the volume was his selection. The seventh member of the committee was Nina Murray and it is no exaggeration to say that her efforts were invaluable. She was the *sine qua non* of the book—without her constantly maintaining Harry's begrudging and nominal approval, it could not have been done. She once whispered to me, "You just leave him to me." Harry wanted to rewrite his printed essays—which, realistically, he never could have done. I just wanted to reprint a selection of the already printed gems.

September 8, 1979
A moratorium (a year's postponement) would... allow me time to supply that which is now conspicuously lacking here and there in the papers, and rectify the most glaring flaws—errors, confusions, cliches galore, &c &c .... And you wisely predict that if you don't get *some* such collection of papers from me *now*, when conditions are favorable, I may labor over the business of correcting and reconstructing them, and *never* finish before I die.

July 13, 1980
Sorry to delay the parade of the press even by a minute or two. .... James Joyce, as you know, spent about 14 years excising and rewriting the parts of his *Ulysses.* I counted over 30 corrections he made on page 1 of the printer's proof....

January 28, 1981
Some months ago—as you were told no doubt—Corona[2] sent me a few sheets to be filled out as part of the charge of the light or heavy advertising brigade. I would have perjured myself for your sake, but I honestly couldn't think of a soul who could be advantaged by scanning the pages of that omnibus. I dread the coming event, with you so innocent and tender, open to the teeth of abusive criticism. .... When you had a Mss for publication, Harpers paid you 25 grand (as I remember); when I had a Mss in 1937 I paid Oxford 1 grand. That's the

---

[1] Harry was referring to Corona Machemer, editor at Harper and Row. I had hand-carried the manuscript to Harper and Row (on the tangentially sentimental ground that Harper and Brothers had been the American publishers of *Moby-Dick* in 1851), and I had persuaded Corona to look at it. She took it home, read it, and fell in love with Harry's elegant prose. Without her uncommon perspicacity, enthusiasm, and support—all unknown to Harry—there probably never would have been a published book. When she finally met Harry, after the book was published, she was as nervous as a schoolgirl and he was as gracious as a lord.

difference—You're Grander. That's it! Now no more teasing. Just heard from the Bowlbys (in London). They want to stay with us from April 1 to 5. Does that conflict with the Big Book Boosting Bash? I'm ready—Yes, to be forgiven.

Toward the end of his life, Harry seemed to have softened his bred-in-the-bone position about the appropriateness of receiving praise or of praising oneself. In 1979, when he was 87, on the occasion of the dedication of the Henry A. Murray Center for the Study of Lives at Radcliffe College, Harry began his remarks something like this: I'll tell you what is wrong with receiving praise, compliments, kudos, awards, honors, approbation. There simply isn't enough of them!"

But unfortunately, after it had been agreed to publish the book, another item for disputation developed. There was talk of having a party for Harry at the Radcliffe Center, in April 1981, to celebrate the publication of the book. Harry focused the reservoir of his negative feelings about the entire project on that event. In early February, he canceled the event at Radcliffe, because, as he wrote to me, he felt that it might be seen as an occasion "for commercial gain"—although by whom it was not clear. By me? Rather put out, I wrote to him on February 8, "If there were any imputation that the goal [of commercial gain] was any part of my motivation then I would be deeply wounded and offended." In his response, he directed this arrow toward Harper and Row, unable to leave it without sarcastic, pointed, and nasty digs. I was reminded of something Nevitt Sanford had said about his student years at Harvard in the 1930s: "I knew that money was important in New England, the evidence being that it was never talked about." (Sanford, 1978; Triplet, 1983).

February 12, 1981

Scrumptious friend:

Of course I did not attribute a mercenary motive to you!! I found *myself* thinking about the time and thought that the two good angels, Corona and (name has gone for a moment) had spent to get *Endeavors* successfully delivered. How nice for them if Harper were to make 100 bucks on the book! I might help to bring that about mightn't I? Appear on television, wow the audience, and sign copies at a cocktail party? I would be willing to do all this for them at the next APA meeting, but not within the immaculate precincts of Radcliffe. Did you ever read about how that 33-year-old agitator in Jerusalem drove the money-changers out of the Temple? Can you see Lincoln selling packaged copies of that speech he gave? or was it an address in Pennsylvania?

I realize that Harry was deeply distressed that he did not have the creative energy in his late 80s to rewrite and update his personological theory, and that his irritation with himself came out in part as irritation toward me. I also believe that the only thing he could latch onto to criticize was Harper and Row's routine advertising of the book. To Harry this was commercial; and commerce (to second-generation wealth) is crass. My motivation was to present him a gift of his own essays and to make the inaccessible Murray material available to a new generation of readers. There was no way, really, to please him in this, and possibly the whole project would have been best left undone. The sad fact is that within half a dozen years of publication the book was out of print. For the record, I never came near recouping the out-of-pocket permission-to-reprint fees, but more than once I suffered Harry's jibes about the vast amounts of royalties I must be making from the book.

Nina Murray later told me that Harry placed a copy of *Endeavors* upright on his desk in his second-floor study and that as he gazed at it, his eyes had the patina of tears. And Rollo May told me that in the last few months of Harry's life, he pointed to *Endeavors* and said to Rollo, "It was certainly good of Ed to do that." That comment was one of the great rewards of my life.

Endeavors in Psychology: Selections from the Personology of Henry A. Murray (Shneidman, 1981b) consists of 27 of Harry's papers and chapters from other books. They are about himself (two autobiographical pieces), personology theory (the heart of the book), psychology, psychoanalysis, Melville, the devil, science and religion, and a plan for world peace. All in all, I believe it is the best single book, next to *Explorations in Personality,* that young psychologists can read to get their bearings and to understand the true nature and purpose of the study of *clinical* psychology. For that reason, in spite of everything, I am glad that I did it.

After all that, it is easy to imagine why I trumpet the joys of writing a book all by oneself. Books are like one's children; one loves all of them. But if they are like children, they are peculiar in at least one way: all of my books have had short deliveries but extremely long gestation periods. In *Deaths of Man,* (1973a) I spoke of "a twenty years interest (obsession?)," and in *Voices of Death* (1980) I wrote that "I had been working at this book for the past 30 years." I think that it is accurate to say that *Definition of Suicide* (1985a) had its beginnings as early as 1956.

The development of the book, as I now reconstruct it, went something like this:

1. The idea that there might be tip-offs, premonitory signs, *clues* to suicide ("Clues to Suicide," 1956).
2. The idea that there might be fables and *facts* about suicide ("How to Prevent Suicide," 1967).
3. The idea that there might be a few ubiquitous, measurable dimensions directly relevant to suicide—specifically, perturbation and lethality ("Perturbation and Lethality as Precursors of Suicide in a Gifted Group," 1971).
4. The idea that there might be some *aphoristic truths* about suicide ("Aphorisms about Suicide and Some Implications for Psychotherapy," 1984a).
5. The idea that there might be a finite number of *psychological commonalities* that are present in all suicides (*Definition of Suicide,* 1985a).
6. The idea that a *theoretical model* might be developed that could relate suicidology to the wider body of academic psychology—the general topics of perception, memory, discomfort, stimulus effectiveness, and so on ("A Psychological Approach to Suicide," 1987).

I began *Definition of Suicide* with the goal that if I could not write something truly original, I could at least do something that was clearly different. My first task was to clear the underbrush. I decided that I would lean on the suicidological giants, Freud and Durkheim, as little as possible; that I would eschew the dreary demographic facts, and try to cut across sex, age, race; that I would ignore the obfuscating psychiatric categories of schizophrenia, depression, borderline states, assuming that 100% of individuals who committed suicide were, in one way or another, significantly perturbed; and, finally, that I would try to come to the topic of suicide from non-suicidal theoretical directions.

Definition of Suicide propounded ten common characteristics of suicide:

1. The common purpose (to seek a solution).
2. The common goal (cessation of consciousness).
3. The common stimulus (intolerable psychological pain).
4. The common stressor (frustrated psychological needs).
5. The common emotions (hopelessness-helplessness).
6. The common cognitive state (ambivalence).
7. The common perceptual state (constriction).
8. The common action (egression).
9. The common interpersonal action (communication of intention).
10. The common consistency (with lifelong coping patterns).

These common characteristics—essentially a *motivational* theory of suicide—apply, by definition, to male and female, to adolescent and octogenarian, and to all racial and ethnic groups. With *anyone* who is highly suicidal the plan of action is the same. Redress *that* person's psychological pain, by reducing that person's perturbation in terms of that person's frustrated psychological needs, and the *raison d'être* of that suicidal push will be dissolved and the impulse to commit suicide will be lowered.

Psychological pain can concatenate so that it seems to have a life of its own. When that life-of-pain dominates the life of a person, we generally call that situation "depression." Depression means that there is a great quantity and a great intensity of psychological pain. The individual is benumbed with psychic pain. The sun ceases to shine; every day, every hour is like (in Melville's felicitous phrase) "a damp, drizzly November in my soul." The key words are intolerable, unbearable, unendurable pain, without the vision of succor or hope of relief. Suicidal perturbation is psychological pain run amok, out of control; it is sometimes, in its depths, too much pain to commit suicide. (This accounts for the fact that many suicides occur when the acutely dysphoric peson begins to make some improvement, with the return of a modicum of energy.) The most targeted treatment of suicide is still the reduction of pain—optimally in a safe environment that provides sanctuary—and not necessarily a focus on depression itself. Psychological pain is best understood in terms of frustrated or thwarted psychological needs, precisely the kind outlined and explicated by Murray in Chapter 3 of *Explorations in Personality* (1938).

My treasured friend Robert Litman points out that by "pain" I do not mean so much the mere existence of psychological pain as I do the unwillingness of that person to endure it. (We all know that pain is the common lot of human beings; pain is inevitable, "suffering" is optional.) Litman wrote to me, "People commit suicide because they cannot accept their pain, because the pain does not fit into their concept of themselves, to their sense of self or identity." In my own defense I would say that I have always implied this, specifically when I wrote about "psychological pain idiosyncratically defined." The pain we are talking about in suicide (such as the pain of shame, guilt, powerlessness, disgust, pride, the inability to acccept the world) are not only psychological—in the mind—they are also metapsychological; that is, stressful affective states or frustrated psychological needs are viewed (obviously in the mind) as unacceptable, intolerable, beyond the limits, too much to live with. The person has a skewed concept of the relationship between life and pain and is unwilling to bear the pain. There are two keys to the suicidal drama: the perception of enormous psychological pain, and the unwillingness (inability) to bear it. But I believe that Litman and I have been agreeing all along, just saying it slightly differently.

In their remarkably understanding critique of *Definition of Suicide* in *Contemporary Psychology,* Karl Slaikeu and Robert Moats (1986) made this warranted criticism:

> Researchers will want more steps toward theory building as a guide for future research. This shortfall is unfortunate because this book clearly has all the requisite ingredients for a model that might inspire meaningful research. To elaborate, the author's ten characteristics of suicide would readily be cast into a framework that would allow data on a range of intrapsychic variables (thoughts, feelings and bodily sensations), as well as relational aspects (interpersonal) and overt behavior, including a range of situational stressors.

Of course, they were right. And so, when I was invited to give the APA Master Lecture later that year (1986), I developed and presented a *cubic* model of suicide, in which the three faces of the cube are labeled Pain, Perturbation (made up of constriction and a penchant for action), and Press. In the cube there is one suicidal cubelet where the maximum Pain, Perturbation, and (negative) Press come together.

The practical implication is obvious: get the person out of the suicidal cubelet—reduce the pain, and/or lower the perturbation, and/or mollify the negative press in both the inner and outer environments. The theoretical implications of the cubic model address Slaikeu and Moats's criticism of my previous omission. Here, I believe, is a schema that will permit the stitching of suicidology into the body of academic psychology. We can do experiments, and we can review previously published studies in all the traditional areas of experimental clinical and social psychology that legitimately can be related to the wide meaning of pain, perturbation, and press. These topics include perceptual styles, attention and concentration, memory, styles of thought, restraint and impulsiveness, reactions to stress, and so on. Obviously, as a topic, suicide is subordinate to psychology and should, in my opinion, find its home among (and within) practically all of the chapters of a contemporary textbook of general psychology.

The casual reader is apt to miss the secret agenda of *Definition of Suicide.* It does not lie in the section on suicide, but rather in the prolegomena, those three chapters on Stephen Pepper's root philosophical metaphors (Pepper, 1942), Henry A. Murray's overarching personological theory (Murray, 1938), and James G. Miller's explication of living systems (Miller, 1978). For me this is the most interesting part of the book: nonsuicidal theory with great potential for yielding fresh insights into human self-destruction. In a sense, this interest reflects my search for the explanation of inimical behavior and failure (obviously, in different degrees) in my patients, my parents, my children, my colleagues, my fellow citizens in the world, and myself. What I like especially about Pepper, Murray, and Miller is that they play a fundamental role in explaining the orderliness of life. Each of their great works is a search for under-standing, with the hope that those efforts will provide some answers to troubling questions. For me the question is, What are the explanations of self-destruction by cells, by organs, by groups, by societies, by civilizations, and especially by individual human beings? I remain convinced that, in our time, the best explanation of human self-destruction will be consonant with explanations of self-destruction below and above man, essentially in systems theory terminology, with terms like entropy, eccentricity, selfishness (as in the "selfish gene"), thwarted biological and social and psychological needs, and the unbearable "noise" of pain. I wish that I could articulate better what I feel on the threshold of understanding.

Being at the UCLA Neuropsychiatric Institute for 20 years in a medical setting had its price, especially in the lack of access to graduate students and dissertation projects. But it also had its benefits: the constant availability of patients and the clinical ambience that fostered thinking in terms of therapeutic (but definitely not, in my case, medical) modes. It is my observation that physicians, including psychiatrists, know little more than ordinary folks about human self-destruction. Their "trained incapacities" (Veblen's term) lead them to change "suicide" into affective disorders (mostly depression) and other pigeonhole categories in the pseudo-accurate *Diagnostic and Statistical Manual* (DSM); in other words, to biologicize unhappiness and dysphoria. But that is not what my kind of clinical psychologists do, and, I am convinced that that kind of reductionism is not the answer to *suicide* (as opposed, say, to some depressions). Being suicidal is more appropriately conceptualized as a state of mind than a condition of brain. (Of course, "mind" is a function of brain, but changes of mind may be concomitants or causes rather than effects of electro-chemical changes in the brain organ.) The fact that I have saved the lives of some suicidal persons by addressing their minds directly, without chemically or electrically changing their brains, demonstrates, to my mind, the vital soundness of this view.

Perennials: Melville and Murray

If from time to time Harry feigned being a trifle confused between his own identity and Melville's, little wonder that I occasionally fantasized about one of them when I was really thinking about the other. Harry delighted in the similarities between himself and Melville, and he played at them. In "Bartleby and I" (1966, 1981), he wrote: "My identification with Melville is facilitated by the approximation of our initials, HAM and HM: . . . I have only to delete the middle A, which stands for the Old Adam of original sin at the center of my nature." And once, in 1962, when I was arranging for an examination for candidates for the American Board of Professional Psychologists in Boston, Harry returned a schedule-form that I had sent him signed "Herman Alexander Melville." And then there is this paragraph, which to my mind is a perfect description of Murray's personological theory and of his *Explorations in Personality*:

But still more extraordinary and portentous were the penetration and scope, the sheer audacity of the author's imagination. Here was a man who did not fly away with his surprising fantasies to some unbelievable dreamland pale or florid, shunning the stubborn objects and gritty facts, the prosaic routines and practicalities of everyday existence. Here was a man, who, on the contrary, chose these very things as vessels for his procreative powers. . . . Here was a man who could describe the appearance, the concrete matter-of-factness, and the utility of each of those natural objects, implements, and tools with the fidelity of a scientist, and while doing this explore it as a conceivable repository of some aspects of the human drama; then, by an imaginative *tour de force,* deliver a vital essence, some humorous or profound idea, coalescing with its embodiment. But still more. Differing from the symbolists of our time, here was a man who offered us essences and meanings which did not level or depreciate the objects of his contemplation. On the contrary, this loving man exalted all creatures by ascribing to them "high qualities, though dark" and weaving around them "tragic graces." Here, in short, was a man with the mythmaking powers of a Blake, a hive of significant associations who was capable of reuniting what science had put asunder—pure perception and relevant emotion—and doing it in an exultant way that was acceptable to scepticism.

Of course, that is Henry Murray's description of Herman Melville; it is from Harry's essay on *Moby-Dick,* "In Nomine Diaboli," an essay that forever changed the permissible limits of serious Melville scholarship in America. But the point is, Harry could have been describing himself, as when he once quoted from Melville in order to describe Melville (and, in so doing, summarized his own life): "In his Being, was not this man 'a wonder, a grandeur, and a woe'?"

How does this relate to me? It relates, through the path of empathy, to my vicarious and inner life, and how the life of my imagination has, willy-nilly, become an integral part of my total personality, reflecting not only experiences that I have felt with my own eager eyes and racing heart, but also experiences that I have known and felt at a remove—hearing about them, or reading them in vivid personal documents; one as real an experience as the other, but only one set of them part of my actual anamnestic record. I have lived only my own life, but you cannot understand me at all if you do not believe that the lives and writings of Melville and Murray (and others) are an integral part of my personality.

In April 1967, while I was in Bethesda at the NIMH, Harry wrote me a wrenching letter, straight from his broken heart.

Beloved Ed,
    In desolation I must tell you that my soul's joy, Christiana—who had a special fondness for you—was drowned in two feet of water as she was going for her usual morning swim off a solitary coral beach on the Caribbean island of St. John. She had had occasional heart attacks with fainting and falling (though never in water). But at this time—after three beautific weeks together in that balmy climate—she seemed to be at the top of her possible healthfulness and radiance, and looking forward to our being married in May. When I found her

about ten minutes later, she was beyond the power of my protracted efforts to resuscitate her. I don't want to distress you with my grief, but you should know the reason why I shall never be the same again, though cleaving as ever and forever to our precious friendship. It will be awhile before I have gained enough control for you to see me without intense discomfort. But you will visit me, won't you? in due course at your first opportunity. Around May 20th when everything is in bloom, I have the last rite to perform at the Tower on the river in Newbury, as she wished it, strewing her ashes on the good earth—"all to the furrow, nothing to the grave." [3]

Let me know your program for the Spring and give me news of your health, your work, and your family.

Intimately
Harry

My interest in the relationship between Harry and Christiana has recently been refueled by his leaving to me, in an almost deathbed wish, over three hundred letters written between them during the years of the war (1944 to 1947), when Harry was in Washington or overseas in England and China with the OSS. Only after reading these intensely personal documents and perusing Jung's *Visions Seminars* (1976) (mostly about Christiana) do I have a glimmering of the important although indirect, intellectual role that Christiana played in what appeared to me, at the beginning, to be entirely Harry's superhuman range of interests, from the ordinary to the most imaginal and symbolic.

As though they were writing a universal masterpiece over a sustained span of almost 40 years, Harry and Christiana jointly focused their considerable creative energies on their private goal of forging their own unique Proposition, a perfect union of minds, mutual love, and sex. They were married, but not to each other. They lived a dual existence, one in their private world, often in a secluded tower by a coastal river in northern Masschusetts or on an isolated island in the Caribbean (where their lives were dominated by Jung, Melville, and their own quest for synergy); and the other, in the public society of upper-class, straitlaced, unforgiving New England society. That they carried it off as long and as well as they did (until one of them dissolved into alcoholism and an untimely death) is nothing less than a grand triumph of the Human Will guided by the Romantic Spirit. Their hundreds of unexampled letters to each other are one of the world's great treasure troves of intimate personal documents.

Just as Harry was crucial in shaping the inner psychological dimensions of my life, so Christiana—whom I knew only slightly in person but whom I have come to know rather well through Harry's talk to me and then through her hundreds of letters to Harry—played an important, albeit indirect, role in my life. For me, she is the prototypical dark woman—the one I never had known in my personal life, the one I perhaps sought but did not really want to find.

---

[3] From "The Poet's Testament," in *The Complete Works of George Santayana.* Lewisburg, PA: Bucknell University Press, 1979.

In a letter to Christiana (March 5, 1946), in which he was discussing his thoughts about his forthcoming introduction to Melville's *Pierre,* Harry wrote,

> HM's description of "That Face"—the Dark Beautiful Tragic Face—*exactly* corresponds with my own experiences before I had read anything in this vein. The Romantics of the 30s & 40s (& 20s of course) had numerous dark mournful heroines, but I don't ever remember reading of a compulsive preoccupation with such a face (as mine was & Pierre's). Also why Tragic? (Think, today in America it has no general appeal—not a single tragic pin-up girl!) . . . .

Christiana is Harry's Isabel Banford, in Melville's *Pierre,* as opposed to Pierre's fiancée Lucy Tartan; she is Harry's French lieutenant's woman. She is the woman of mystery, she is an artist, she is Excitement, the excitement that makes life dramatically interesting and intense. She creates great turbulence for herself and others, the kind of perturbation that is said to be an essential ingredient in the creation of great literature.

I had a sense of longing for the excitement of the darkness and mystery that Christiana represented. I feel that I have lived that scenario, vicariously, following their lives (especially in the letters that he left to me), and was spared the destructive ordeal of experiencing it myself. That is why I am endlessly fascinated by the relationship of Harry and Christiana—a wish to understand another's life through the window of epistolary art.

The best preface to *Moby-Dick* is Viola Meynell's 3-page introduction in the 1923 Oxford University Press World's Classics edition (Nina Murray gave me Harry's rebound copy, 3×5 inches, which he had carried for years in his pocket.) Viola Meynell wrote, "Herman Melville has here endowed human nature with writing that I believe to be absolutely unsurpassed. To read it and absorb it is the crown of one's reading life." I believe that.

The best introduction to *Pierre* is Harry's 90-page essay (in the Hendrik's House edition, 1929). It is the most thorough, scholarly, psychodynamically insightful literary piece that I know. It is one of the best clinical reports ever written. And it is a very eerie experience for me to read it, for there I am, reading Henry Murray (with his mistress and his wife on his mind) writing about Herman Melville (who had the lascivious Fayaway and his prim wife, Elizabeth, on *his* mind), writing about Pierre (who was struggling with the vapid Lucy Tartan and the tantalizingly illicit Isabel Banford on *his* mind).

I see myself now as an interesting combination of intellectual adventurism and moral restraint. This combination stems from my parents' basic oxymoronic admonition to me as a little boy: be smart; be good. (Brain, 100%; gonads, 0%.) Better advice might have been: be bright; be civilized; be natural. In any event, the mantle they threw over me was both a loose-fitting gymnast's outfit that permitted considerable freedom for the restlessness of my mind, and at the same time, a close-fitting tailored suit, especially below the waist, that imposed restraint on urges of libido. The world may have lost a fine novelist in that process. (My consolation: there is a plethora of novelists, but not many suicidologists.) But the tasks of the novelist and of the suicidologist are quite similar: they both study lives, although novelists are not so hampered in the range of permissible styles of language.

The suppression of an active participation in the dark side of life led me to a vicarious interest in it—to a deep interest in fiction, in biography, and in clinical psychology. I believe that this has been an adequate substitute for the lack of the experiences themselves, so that I seem to have emerged, generally speaking, safe but sufficiently experienced, and not scarred in any incapacitating way. I am sure that my parents would have preferred it that way—and everything considered, so do I.

So the pull to Melville (starting with the lascivious Fayaway in *Typee*) and attraction to Murray (with his brilliant need-oriented explanation of the unconscious) proved to be irresistible. No American psychologist—there is not even a close second—has the elegance of thought and expression of Henry Murray. But Melville, with the advantage of dealing in fiction, can be even more immediate and exciting. For me, no one uses language and thought like Melville. He is Beethoven and Mahler, and sometimes, on sufficiently infrequent occasions to make it interesting, when he wants to be, just for the hell of it, he can be Chopin or even Paganini. When I read him at night I have to make an effort to put him down at some point or I will be up all night. *Moby-Dick* should be read aloud like the Old and New Testaments and other great fictional epics.

I have written four pieces about Melville:

1. A psychological autopsy of Captain Ahab in "Orientations toward Death" for Harry's *festschrift* (1963b).
2. "The Deaths of Herman Melville," a paper that I truly believe almost pleased Harry, presented at the 1967 Melville Society meeting at Williams College (1968).
3. "Some Psychological Reflections on the Death of Malcolm Melville" (1976a), a psychological autopsy of Melville's son that Harry attended at UCLA.
4. More recently, a combination of my interest in logic and in Melville, "Melville's Cognitive Style: The Logic of *Moby-Dick*" in *A Companion to Melville Studies* (1986), in which I discussed Melville's deductive gambits in that great book.

A fifth item, "The Diary" (1983), relates my finding in a California mountain town and then losing a priceless 1852 segment of Melville's diary—a report that does not adhere entirely to known fact.

Melville has been the vehicle through which I have tried to think through my evolving ideas about suicide, the psychological autopsy, subintentioned death, post-vention, inimical behaviors, the cruical role of psychological pain, and appropriate death—all the ideas that have infused my professional work. Melville is my one real hobby; reading him and thinking about his life and works is one of my principal recreational pastimes. I am not sure that I would have wanted to know Melville personally, but there is something in me that makes me feel that I cannot know enough about him or read him often enough to sate my appetite for more.

In regard to *my* topic, suicide, Melville is right on the mark. From the very beginning of *Moby-Dick*—the stunning first paragraph—the subject matter is made crystal clear. This book is about suicide. Not overt suicide, but indirect suicide, substitutes-for-suicide, partial death, and especially subintentioned death. Listen!

Call me Ishmael. Some years ago—never mind how long precisely—having little or no money in my purse, and nothing particular to interest me on shore, I thought I would sail about a little and see the watery part of the world. It is a way I have of driving off the spleen, and regulating the circulation. Whenever I find myself growing grim about the mouth; whenever it is a damp, drizzly November in my soul; whenever I find myself involuntarily pausing before coffin ware-houses, and bringing up the rear of every funeral I meet; and especially whenever my hypos get such an upper hand of me, that it requires a strong moral principle to prevent me from deliberately stepping into the street, and methodically knocking people's hats off—then, I account it high time to get to sea as soon as I can. This is my substitute for pistol and ball. With a philosophical flourish Cato throws himself upon his sword; I quietly take to the ship.

And Melville says it again, in Chapter 112, "The Blacksmith," when he describes the utterly destructive alcoholism of the blacksmith Perth, and indicates that burying oneself in endless voyages at sea, a kind of living death, is indeed a viable, although unhappy, alternative to overt suicide.

Death seems the only desirable sequel for a career like this; but Death is only a launching into the region of the strange Untried; it is but the first salutation to the possibilities of the immense Remote, the Wild, the Watery, the Unshored; therefore, to the death-longing eyes of such men, who still have left in them some interior compunctions against suicide does the all-contributed and all-receptive ocean alluringly spread forth his whole plain of unimaginable, taking terrors, and wonderful, new-life adventures; and from the hearts of infinite Pacifics, the thousand mermaids sing to them—"Come hither, brokenhearted; here is another life without the guilt of intermediate death; here are wonders supernatural, without dying for them, Come hither! bury thyself in a life which, to your now equally abhorred and abhorring, landed world, is more oblivious than death.

The missing keystone to the intellectual arch that I was trying to erect for my conceptual suicidal edifice was provided for me by Harry in *Explorations*. The key to suicide is *pain*, psychological pain, as idiosyncratically defined by that particular sufferer. Murray wrote, "Suicide does not have *adaptive* (survival) value but it does have *adjustive* value for the organism. Suicide is *functional* because it abolishes painful tensions." (Murray, 1938). And in another place (1967), speaking of suicidal events, he wrote, "Their intention is no more than an urgently felt necessity to stop unbearable anguish, that is, to obtain relief by interrupting the stream of suffering... for what is suicide... but an action to interrupt or put an end to intolerable affects?" There, in a sentence, lie the keys: reduce the pain (the intolerable anguish); *and*, the way in which the pain can be effectively reduced is by identifying and addressing the hurting affective (emotional) states and the frustrated psychological needs that exacerbate the sense of pain. It took me the better part of a book (Shneidman, 1985b) to try to sort these matters out. Like Melville, I wish to explore the mystery of man's death-bound plight, to which all good and evil are related—there being an obvious underlying relationship between behavior and the threat of its cessation.

I last saw Harry in August 1987, in Nina's big house on Nantucket. Nina was waiting in the car to take me to the airport, and I went to say goodbye to him in his ship-cabin-sized bedroom on the first floor—he could not then make it up the steep stairs—and when I turned to go I heard him whisper, "I love you." I had won what I had set out to earn.

Harry died at home on June 23, 1988, aged 95. There was a small private burial at Mt. Auburn Cemetery, and a few months later there was a public memorial occasion in the Memorial Church in Harvard Yard. Nina asked me to be one of the four speakers, along with Professors Daniel Aaron and Howard Gardner and President Matina Horner of Radcliffe College. What could I say about Harry in a few minutes to a mourning crowd? That *I* loved him? That he was the center of *my* intellectual life? I needed a mollifying neutral ground to escape the sin of bathos and to avoid focusing on my sense of loss. Melville provided the perfect "middle term" between Harry and me and permitted me, within the limits of controllable emotion, to state, in Melville's own "bold and nervous lofty language," some of my inner thoughts and feelings appropriate to the occasion.

Borrowing Melville's words about certain New England sea captains (*Moby-Dick*, Ch. 16, "The Ship"), I described Harry:

> So that there are instances . . . of men, who . . . strangely blend . . . a thousand bold dashes of character, not unworthy a Scandanavian sea-king, or a poetical Pagan Roman. And when these things unite in a man of greatly superior natural force, with a globular brain and a ponderous heart; who has also . . . been led to think untraditionally and independently . . . , and thereby chiefly, but with some help from accidental advantages, to learn a bold and nervous lofty language— that man makes one in a whole nation's census—a mighty pageant creature formed for noble tragedies.

One key idea for Harry was that life was—in the special way he defined the word— a "spiritual" pilgrimage, focused on the search for essential truths. And truths could be presented not only in carefully chosen words, but in artistically rendered objects, in wood or stone, in music or paint, or in relationships themselves, just as the search for truth itself could be touched by beauty, converting the very process of the search into Art. As Melville wrote in a poem entitled "Art":

> In placid hours well-pleased we dream
> Of many a brave unbodied scheme.
> But form to bend, pulsed life create—
> What unlike things must meet and mate:
> A flame to melt—a wind to freeze;
> Sad patience—joyous energies;
> Humility—yet pride and scorn;
> Instinct and study; love and hate;
> Audacity—reverence. These must mate,
> And fuse with Jacob's mystic heart,
> To wrestle with the angel—Art.

Thus it can be truly said that in his way of living, Harry was a supreme artist; and if we view his life as a vast, almost century-long panorama, we see that he created a living montage of intense and complex beauty. It was the brilliance and the beauty of the process of his being that, for many of us, made knowing him the apogee of our lives. Melville's "Monody" is my own:

> To have known him, to have loved him
> After loneless long;
> And then to be estranged from life,
> And neither in the wrong;
> And now for death to set his seal—
> Ease me, a little ease, my song!

Indian Summer: Life-Span Studies

In the Indian summer of my own life I am truly astounded at, and grateful for, the way in which events seem to anticipate themselves. For example, I initiated a weekly emeritus luncheon group some years before I became emeritus myself. In the past several years the more-or-less regular members of this group have included Benjamin Aaron (law), Irving Bernstein (political science), Bruno Bettelheim (psychology),[4] Lester Breslow (public health), Paul Desmarais (music), John Espey (English), Milton Greenblatt (psychiatry), Alma Hawkins (dance), Hilda Kuper (anthropology), Leo Kuper (sociology), Judd Marmor (psychiatry), James G. Miller (psychiatry and systems theory), Frederick Redlich (psychiatry), Jean Sanville (social welfare and psychoanalysis), Joel Shor (psychology, psychoanalysis), Harry Wasserman (social welfare), the late Lynn White (medieval studies), and John Young (theater arts). That luncheon-and-good-talk event is the highlight of my week.

During my stay at UCLA, the people with whom I have enjoyed the warmest relationships—in addition to my chairman, Jolly West—are Milton Greenblatt, former commissioner of mental health for the Commonwealth of Massachusetts, and Fritz Redlich, former dean of the Yale Medical School. In significant part, they were the reasons that I wished to start a luncheon discussion group.

Another more weighty example, of how events anticipate themselves is that in 1969, when I was 51 and a Fellow at the Center for Advanced Study in the Behavioral Sciences, I arranged with Robert Sears, of Stanford, to study suicide among the Terman Study population (Shneidman, 1971, 1984b, 1989). In 1981, as an indirect consequence of those earlier studies, I began a quite different project directly involving some 35 Terman Study men, so that my present work with septuagenarian men comes, with some psychodynamic convenience, during my own septuagenarian

---

[4] Bruno Bettelheim died on March 13, 1990. He committed suicide using a plastic bag. Bruno's death distressed me and thousands of others a great deal.

years. Planning? Timing? None of those. Happy and fortuitous coincidence is the answer—unless the reasons lie deeper in my unconscious than I am able to plumb.

The present study of the Terman septuagenarians—very much in process as I write this—has two aspirations. The first is to study the changes in vocabulary (language and thought) of a group of 35 men as they move through their seventh decade. This goal addresses the question of what changes occur in natural thought, as evidenced in ordinary conversation, from the late 60s through the 80s. This is a study in developmental psychology of nonaberrant subjects of a rather underreported population, 70-year-olds. What I have attempted to do with the indispensable help of an electronic word processor is to generate total word counts and concordances of biannual interviews, since 1981, of 35 septuagenarian and octogenarian Terman Study subjects, focusing on year-by-year changes in terms of several categories, such as health, family, occupation, and leisure (Sears, 1977). Some preliminary results of this study were reported in "The Indian Summer of Life" (1989).

The second goal of the study is to collate, for half a dozen subjects, the interview data that I have gathered over the last several years with the vast amounts of information available from around 1921 on these same subjects, on file at the Terman Study offices at Stanford, and to write extended biographies of these half-dozen lives. The purpose here would be to look for consistencies and changes from childhood to over age 80. In this project I look forward to the assistance of my young colleague Gordon Strauss, a Stanford alumnus who is now a psychiatrist at UCLA.

Already, the Indian Summer of Life study has opened my eyes to some new outlooks. I now no longer view the human life course as simply a linear set of progressions—infancy, babyhood, childhood, adolescence, young adulthood, middle-age, senior, oldster, very old age—as the Greek (Hippocrates, Solon)-medieval-Shakespearean-Eriksonian view of life would have it; life as a fixed series of stages (Sears, 1986). Rather, I tend to conceptualize human life more as a cyclical process. This cyclical view of life is certainly consistent with Freudian thought, although Melville said it earlier (in 1851, six years before Freud was born). In *Moby-Dick* (Ch. 114, "The Gilder"), Melville wrote of life's progress in this stunning way:

> The mingled, mingling threads of life are woven by warp and woof: calms crossed by storms, a storm for every calm. There is no steady unretracing progress in this life; we do not advance through fixed gradations . . . . But once gone through, we trace the round again; and are infants, boys, men and Ifs eternally.

In that same passage, Melville wrote that the final secrets of our lives lie in our graves, and we must go there to learn them; in contemporary words that means that the psychodynamic cyclings of life are not over until the last breath is drawn.

I see no reason why, in our conceptual imagination, we cannot have both: the Hippocratean-medieval-Shakespearean-Eriksonian rooms or stages of life arranged around a Melvillean-Freudian spiral ramp—like the spiraling architecture of the Guggenheim Museum—repeated over and over. In considering any individual life, say of Rembrandt, this would amount to a series of portraits at different chronological ages but at similar points of the compass of his life, painted at different "elevations" in the spiral. Such an arrangement would involve one Rembrandt depicted and portrayed several different times. I call this the multiple *helictical* view of human life (Shneidman, 1989).

This helictical quality is certainly true of my life. I have touched the same neurotic compass-points over and over in the spiraling unfolding of my life, and have repeated the "same old mistakes" (and, conversely, achieved the "same" minor successes) in every decade of my life—although the spacing of these events has not been that regular.

If it is true that I shall die more or less as I have lived, then it is more powerfully true that I shall live on as I have lived in the past, with a more or less consistent personality, albeit amenable to occasional radical changes. My life has been a spiral, a complicated helix, touching over and over certain particular headings of my idiosyncratic psychodynamic compass.

My recent years at UCLA were additionally enlivened by two almost yearlong special guests: Fr. Matthias O'Connnor, a Dominican priest, who came out of a closed society to study secular self-destruction with me; and Dr. Yoshitomo Takahashi of Yamanashi Medical College, a Fulbright Scholar from Japan. Dr. Takahashi is a diligent and productive young psychiatrist-suicidologist, from whom I expect important contributions (long after I am gone) in his native land.

In accounts of this sort it is customary to cite a few offices held and awards received. Mostly in the 1960s, I was president of two APA divisions, Clinical and Public Service, and received their awards for distinguished contributions. Twice I served on the APA Council of Representatives and twice on the board of directors of the American Board of Examiners in Professional Psychology. My highest honor was to be given an APA Award for Distinguished Professional Contributions to Public Service.

I also especially prize the "name" awards that I have been given, names that are an integral part of my own intellectual history: the Bruno Klopfer Award from the Society for Projective Techniques, the Harold M. Hildreth Award from the APA Division of Psychologists in Public Service, and the Louis I. Dublin Award from the American Association of Suicidology. Perhaps most gratifying of all is the fact that an annual young contributor's award is given by the AAS in my name. It seems that I—needful, covetous, childlike—have become an official father-figure. I am not comfortable with that role and probably never will be. Although I love being a professor, I would much prefer to be the special student of some extraordinary teacher—some great guru, rabbi, sage, elder, mentor, father, grandfather, secular divinity, who would teach me for Knowledge's sake and protect me for my own sake. Harry came as close to that as I could find on earth; and there have been several "good enough" runners-up to make me feel worthwhile and treasured.

Award ceremonies have often been psychologically laden occasions for me. Once, at a convention, I was giving an invited "APA Conversation Hour," sitting in the center of a room filled with listeners who were seated and standing all around me. Some minutes into the hour Harry came into the room. Of course, many people immediately offered him their chairs, but he imperiously stretched himself out full-length on the floor right in front of me, as I continued to talk. Then, a few minutes later, Evelyn Hooker appeared at the door, descried Harry, let out a cry of greeting, came hurriedly into the room, tripped, and fell right on Harry, into his arms on the floor, amidst much general laughter. I remember saying, as an audible aside in the middle of a sentence, that I didn't at all mind witnessing the primal scene, but that I rather objected to it while I was lecturing. At that time I thought that a rather witty remark, but I now believe that there was much more, in my unconscious mind, than mere humor, relating to my deep need to remain a child-student. Even at the moment when I was lecturing as an expert, I preferred not to be the parent, but the child, watching and learning the secrets of life from my elders and betters.

On this same general topic of attainments, as a minor footnote, I am cited (for "suicidology") in the new *Oxford English Dictionary*. I reflect that that tiny item is perhaps my most certain lien (beyond the infinitely more important one of my biological descendants) on some generations beyond my death. My postself lies hidden in the microscopic print of the *OED*.

Macroscopically, one special feature that perhaps makes me somewhat different from most clinical psychologists (and from most people in the world, for that matter) is—to quote a 1989 letter to me from Jerome Bruner—that I have made "the claim that a rich contemplation of death and dying make that much richer a participation in life and living." I have lived a richer life in death, happily and productively, proud to be called a suicidologist and thanatologist. Living in a fertile and beneficent valley even at the base of Mt. Thanatos can be good, as long as it lasts. But that is all that one can realistically say of anything, no matter how dearly treasured. I do not at all agree with Ernest Becker's *Denial of Death*—in my mind the most flawed book ever to win a Pulitzer Prize—that all of man's works are stimulated by his fear and omnipresent concern with death. It is quite another matter to believe, as I do, that one's knowledge that the circus will end (and also taking special pleasure in the exitings, the egressions, and the climaxes of the performances) can, if one has the right attitude, enhance one's enjoyment of the moment, and all the moments, past and future, related to it. This is the attitude with which I have tried to live, looking excitedly at life, albeit with thanatological eyes, and thereby enhancing it in the process. If my life has a "lesson," that is it. But I know that—like the Magic Theater in *Steppenwolf*—it is "not for everybody."

In a sense, I have always written as if I were dying. All my writing, from the very beginning, long before I knew anything about thanatology, has had this death-laden cast. It goes with my sense of impatience, informed by knowledge of my own finiteness. I have not been especially depressed about it; just mindful. Melville's haunting line from *Pierre* is apposite here: "Oh, what quenchless feud is this, that Time hath with the sons of Men!" That, and Francis Bacon's "He that hath wife and children hath given hostages to Fortune" (from his essay "Of Marriage and Single Life") are, to me, among the most illuminating sentences in the English language, all the more powerful because of their undeniable truth. The ongoing life-and-death debate in my head takes the form of a tension between my constantly wanting to know (learning) and continuously wanting to write (achievement and service) on the one hand, and on the other hand, wanting to use my finite time for creature comforts and sentient gratifications—knowing that, in the end, neither matters too much, because aspirations, no matter how lofty, are always embedded in the humble conditions of real, ordinary life. This latter feeling is especially true for me in the seventh decade of my life.

A few "personal" details: My Jeanne has been the perfect partner for me, truly facilitating my work and elevating the level of joy in my life. We have four marvelous and interesting sons, all grown: a dentist and three physicians. To date, we have four lovely grandchildren who—in that I eschew intergalactic space—are my personal lien on intercentennial time.

A few words about me as a patient are in order. As I write this, now in my 70s, I am in rather good health—so far, no cancer, strokes, or heart attacks—but I have, in fact, been hospitalized over the last 30 years in some of the finer medical centers in the country: Massachusetts General Hospital, Lankenau Hospital in Philadelphia, Stanford Hospital, St. John's in Los Angeles, the Jules Stein Eye Center, and the UCLA Center for Health Sciences.

I once did a little experiment by putting together the nurses' notes about me written during my various hospitalizations. Roughly speaking, two kinds of psychological pictures emerged: I am perceived as civil, cooperative, cheerful, even charming, *or* as a regular SOB, a real pain in the neck. The difference, so far as I can figure it out, devolved not on how sick (close to death) I actually was, but rather on my degree of fright or terror at the time. The more anxious I was—about possible loss of sight (it did not happen), or loss of control (but not about loss of life)—the more difficult, surly, and demanding I behaved as a patient. At other times (as when my oldest son, David, came into an intensive care unit, checked my flagging vital signs, and actually saved my life), when I did not sense any danger, I was, at least from the nurses' point of view, a pussycat.

I predict that I shall die—if I die of an illness in a hospital—pretty much the way I have responded to failure, threat, stress, duress, or sense of degradation previously in my life. I believe that this consistency is true of almost everyone. After all, dying is an integral part of living; unless sedated or unconscious, one is usually very much alive as one is dying.

In 1973, 15 years before his death in 1988 at the age of 95, Harry wrote to me,

> As for death, I have felt prepared for 40 years or more to take the obligatory cessation of cherished activity, but I do hope for as much time as possible to give back to the world what the world has given to me—i.e., to pay back a greater proportion of my enormous debt than I have so far proved capable. I take this to be commonplace for a man of 80.

In my early 70s—feeling rather young and spritely and almost without any pressing sense of being aged or doomed (denial?), although I have been in a discernible mild depression since Harry's death—I share his sentiments about my enormous debts to my "patrons" in the world, to my parents, teachers, mentors, spouse, children, dear friends, and friendly acquaintances. But I want to find out for myself if such thoughts are, indeed, commonplace for a man of 80. And then, if they are (and if I have the brains to do it)—I'll renegotiate.

Considering that I am, in my own mind at least, an almost totally nonmystical person, there have been, nonetheless, four mysteries—intrigues, puzzlements, perplexities—that have fascinated me all my life. The first one relates to the mysterious power of *words.* I believe, with Bruno Schultz (1988)—echoed by Eva Hoffman in her *Lost in Translation* (1989)—that "language is man's metaphysical organ"; that *words* are preliminary to myth and philosophy; that the great artifact of any literate civilization is its dictionary; that etymology contains values and goals; that words are precious things and should be carefully used; that books are miracles; and that the library is a sacred place.

The second mystery relates to the mystical power of *ideas.* It is endlessly intriguing to me that the brain—which is, after all, just a vast bunch of cells—is an organ that *thinks.* The brain secretes ideas the way sebaceous glands produce sweat. Ideas have to do with work; and as I love ideas, so I love the joy of work. The notion of a thinking organ—of mere cells producing ideas, feelings, sentiments, passions, musical phrases, introspections—somehow transforming molecular biochemical energy into thought and language is, in my mind, one of the most impressive things in the world.

Third, there is the pleasure-giving occurrence of *relationships,* in which one separate organism, through words and ideas, can form deep and meaningful sentimental attachments to another separate creature, and experience profound feelings of affection, fealty, and pleasure in the other's company. In my own life I think immediately of Harry and then of Evelyn Hooker and Nancy Allen, Mamoru and Marye Iga, and hundreds of pleasant and joy-giving fellow creatures who have defined my life and my very personality.

And then, best of all, there is the mystical power of *love,* the ineffable—beyond the power of words and ideas, and transcending even the joy of relationships—mystical power that I feel with Jeanne and with our children and grandchildren, and that I felt for my parents. With Jeanne, with whom I actually spend a relatively small fraction of each day's cycle, I feel an almost physical identity. We love each other. We think alike in basic ways. We often anticipate each other's thoughts. We have gone to a strange city and inadvertently separated without making the necessary plans to meet later that day, and then magically have come together at the same place and the same moment as though by the most careful and explicit prearrangement. I write these lines, in my university office, all by myself; no one is here and the building is very quiet, and yet, if I stop to think about it, I feel that I am actually part of her and she part of me. This has been so all my adult life. The mystical power of love is the apogee and summation of the mystical power of words, ideas, and relationships. That is why I feel that I was the luckiest mortal conceived sometime in the autumn of 1917 in York, Pennsylvania, in the front bedroom of the small frame house at 918 King Street.

References

Allport, G. (1942). *The use of personal documents in psychological science.* New York: Social Science Research Council.
Brown, J. F. (1937). *Psychology and the social order.* New York: McGraw-Hill.

Butler, S. (1903). *The way of all flesh*.

Curphey, T. J. (1967). The forensic pathologist and the multidisciplinary approach to death. In Shneidman, E. S. (Ed.), *Essays in self-destruction*. New York: Science House.

Encyclopaedia Britannica, Ninth Ed. (1884). Philadelphia: J. M. Stoddart.

Fenichel, O. (1945). *The psychoanalytic theory of neurosis*. New York: Norton.

Friedman, P. (1967). (Ed.) *On suicide*. New York: International Universities Press.

Hoffman, E. (1989). *Lost in translation*. New York: Dutton.

Joyce, J. (1916/1964). *A portrait of the artist as a young man*. New York: Viking.

Jung, C. G. (1976). *Visions seminars*. Zurich: Spring Publishing Co.

Kasanin, J. S. (Ed.) (1944/1964). *Language and thought in schizophrenia*. New York: Norton.

Leenaars, A. (1988). *Suicide notes*. New York: Behavioral Sciences Press.

Litman, R. E., Curphey, T. J., Shneidman, E. S., Farberow, N. L., & Tabachnick, N. D. (1963). Investigations of equivocal suicides. *Journal of the American Medical Association*, 184, 924–929.

May, M. & Arons, L. (Eds.) (1963). *Television and human behavior*. New York: Appleton-Century-Crofts.

Melville, H. (1851). *Moby-Dick*.

Meynell, V. (1923). *Introduction to Melville's Moby-Dick*. London: Oxford University Press.

Mill, J. S. (1843). *System of logic*.

Miller, J. G. (1978). *Living systems*. New York: McGraw-Hill.

Moss, L. (1972). Help wanted: A limited study of responses to one person's cry for help. In Shneidman, E. (Ed.), *Death and the college student*. New York: Behavioral Publications.

Murray, H. A. (1938). *Explorations in personality*. New York: Oxford University Press.

Murray, H. A. (1966). "Bartleby and I." In Vincent, H. P. (Ed.), *Bartleby the Scrivener*. Kent, OH: Kent State University Press. Reprinted (1981) in *Endeavors in psychology*. New York: Harper & Row.

Murray, H. A. (1967). Dead to the world: The passions of Herman Melville. In Shneidman, E. S. (Ed.), *Essays in self-destruction*. New York: Science House. Reprinted in Shneidman, E. S. (Ed.) (1981), *Endeavors in psychology: Selections from the personology of Henry A. Murray*. New York: Harper & Row.

Murray, H. A. & Wheeler, D. R. (1936). A note on the clairvoyance of dreams. *Journal of Psychology, 3*, 309–313.

Nakamura, H. (1960). *The ways of thinking of Eastern peoples*. New York: Japanese National Commission for UNESCO.

Pepper, S. (1942/1967). *World hypotheses*. Berkeley and Los Angeles: University of California Press.

Rescher, N. (1967). *Temporal modalities in Arabic logic*. New York: The Humanities Press.

Russell, B. (1967). *The autobiography of Bertrand Russell*. Boston: Little, Brown.

Sanford, N. (1978). *Reminiscences and celebrations: Explorations in personality, forty years later*. APA Symposium, Toronto, August 31.

Sapir, E. (1949). *Selected writings in language, culture and personality*. Berkeley and Los Angeles: University of California Press.

Shneidman, E. (1943). The experimental study of the appraisal interview. *Journal of Applied Psychology*, 27, 186–205.

Shneidman, E. (1947). *The Make-A-Picture-Story (MAPS Test)*. New York: Psychological Corporation.

Shneidman, E. (1948). Schizophrenia and the MAPS Test. *Genetic Psychology Monographs, 38,* 145–223.

Shneidman, E. (1951). (Ed.) *Thematic test analysis.* New York: Grune & Stratton.

Shneidman, E. (1956). (With Farberow, N.) Clues to suicide. *Public Health Reports, 71,* 109–114.

Shneidman, E. (1957a). (With Farberow, N.) Some comparisons between genuine and simulated suicide notes. *Journal of General Psychology, 56,* 251–256.

Shneidman, E. (1957b). (Ed., with Farberow, N.) *Clues to suicide.* New York: McGraw-Hill.

Shneidman, E. (1959). (With Little, K. B.) Congruencies among interpretations of psychological tests and anamnestic data. *Psychological Monographs, 73,* 1–42.

Shneidman, E. (1960). Psycho-Logic: A personality approach to patterns of thinking. In Kagan, J. & Leser, G. (Eds.), *Current issues in thematic apperceptive fantasy.* Springfield, IL: Charles C Thomas.

Shneidman, E. (1962). Projections on a triptych; or a hagiology for our time. *Journal of Projective Techniques, 26,* 379-387.

Shneidman, E. (1963a). The logic of politics. In May, M. & Arons, L. (Eds.), *Television and human behavior.* New York: Appleton-Century-Crofts.

Shneidman, E. (1963b). Orientations towards death: A vital aspect of the study of lives. In White, R. W. (Ed.), *The study of lives.* New York: Atherton.

Shneidman, E. (1963c). (With Litman, R. E., Curphey, T. J., Farberow, N. L., & Tabachnick, N. D.) Investigations of equivocal suicides. *Journal of the American Medical Association, 184,* 924–929.

Shneidman, E. (1966). (With Tripodes, Peter). *The logics of communication: A manual for analysis.* China Lake, CA: U.S. Naval Ordinance Test Station.

Shneidman, E. (1967a). Description of the NIMH Center for Studies of Suicide Prevention. *Bulletin of Suicidology, 1,* 2–7.

Shneidman, E. (1967b). (Ed.) *Essays in self-destruction.* New York: Science House/Jason Aronson.

Shneidman, E. (1968). The deaths of Herman Melville. In Vincent, H. P. (Ed.), *Melville and Hawthorne in the Berkshires.* Kent, OH: Kent State University Press.

Shneidman, E. (1969a). (Ed.) *On the nature of suicide.* San Francisco: Jossey-Bass.

Shneidman, E. (1969b). Suicide, lethality and the psychological autopsy. In Shneidman, E. & Ortega, M. (Eds.), *Aspects of depression.* Boston: Little, Brown.

Shneidman, E. (1969c). Logical Content Analysis. In Gerbner, G. et al. (Eds.), *The analysis of communication content.* New York: Wiley.

Shneidman, E. (1970). (Ed., with Farberow, N. L. & Litman, R. E.) *The psychology of suicide.* New York: Science House.

Shneidman, E. (1971). Perturbation and lethality as precursors of suicide in a gifted group. *Suicide and Life-Threatening Behavior, 1,* 23–45.

Shneidman, E. (1972). (Ed.) *Death and the college student.* New York: Behavioral Publications.

Shneidman, E. (1973a). *Deaths of man.* New York: Quadrangle/New York Times.

Shneidman, E. (1973b). Suicide notes reconsidered. *Psychiatry, 36,* 379–395.

Shneidman, E. (1973c). Suicide. In *Encyclopaedia Britannica.* Chicago: William Benton.

Shneidman, E. (1975). Postvention: The care of the bereaved. In Pasnau, R. O. (Ed.), *Consultation-liaison psychiatry.* New York: Grune & Stratton.

Shneidman, E. (1976a). Some psychological reflections on the death of Malcolm Melville. *Suicide and Life-Threatening Behavior, 6,* 231–242.

Shneidman, E. (1976b). (Ed.) *Suicidology: Contemporary developments.* New York: Grune & Stratton.

Shneidman, E. (1976c). (Ed.) *Death: Current perspectives.* Palo Alto, CA: Mayfield.

Shneidman, E. (1977). The psychological autopsy. In Gottschalk, L. I. et al. (Eds.), *Guide to the investigation and reporting of drug abuse deaths.* Washington, D.C.: U.S. Government Printing Office.

Shneidman, E. (1979a). (With Feigenberg, L.) Clinical thanatology and psychotherapy: Some reflections on caring for the dying person. *Omega, 10,* 1–8.

Shneidman, E. (1979b). Risk writing: Special notes about Cesare Pavese and Joseph Conrad. *Journal of the American Academy of Psychoanalysis, 7,* 575–592.

Shneidman, E. (1980). *Voices of death.* New York: Harper & Row.

Shneidman, E. (1981a). (Ed.) *Suicide thoughts and reflections, 1960–1980.* New York: Human Sciences Press.

Shneidman, E. (1981b). (Ed.) *Endeavors in psychology: Selections from the personology of Henry A. Murray.* New York: Harper & Row.

Shneidman, E. (1982a). The suicidal logic of Cesare Pavese. *Journal of the American Academy of Psychoanalysis, 10,* 547–563.

Shneidman, E. (1982b). On "Therefore I must kill myself." *Suicide and Life-Threatening Behavior, 12,* 52–55.

Shneidman, E. (1983). The diary. *Melville Society Extracts* (May).

Shneidman, E. (1984a). Aphorisms of suicide and some implications for psychotherapy. *American Journal of Psychotherapy, 38,* 319–328.

Shneidman, E. (1984b). Personality and "success" among a selected group of lawyers. *Journal of Personality Assessment, 48,* 609–616.

Shneidman, E. (1985a). *Definition of suicide.* New York: Wiley.

Shneidman, E. (1985b). Some psychological reflections on Herman Melville. *Melville Society Extracts, 64,* 7–9.

Shneidman, E. (1986). Melville's cognitive style: The logic of *Moby-Dick.* In Bryant, J. (Ed.), *A companion to Melville Studies.* Westport, CT: Greenwood Press.

Shneidman, E. (1987). A psychological approach to suicide. In VandenBos, G. R. & Bryant, B. K. (Eds.), *Cataclysms, crises and catastrophes: Psychology in action.* Washington, DC: American Psychological Association.

Shneidman, E. (1988). Foreword to Antoon Leenaars's *Suicide notes.* New York: Behavioral Sciences Press.

Shneidman, E. (1989). The Indian summer of life: A preliminary report of septuagenarians. *American Psychologist, 44,* 684–694.

Schultz, B. (1988). *Letters and drawings of Bruno Schultz.* Ficowski, J. (Ed.); Arndt, W. & Nelson, V. (Trans). New York: Harper & Row. (Also see review by John Updike, *The New York Review of Books*, October 30, 1988.)

Sears, E. (1986). *The ages of man: Medieval interpretations of the life cycle.* Princeton, NJ: Princeton University Press.

Sears, R. S. (1977). Sources of life satisfaction of the Terman gifted men. *American Psychologist, 32,* 119–128.

Slaikeu, K. A. & Moats, R. W. (1986). A multidimensional view of suicide. *Contemporary Psychology, 31,* 574–575.

Triplet, R. G. (1983). Henry A. Murray and the Harvard Psychological Clinic, 1926-1938: A struggle to expand the disciplinary boundaries of academic psychology. Unpublished dissertation, University of New Hampshire. Ann Arbor, MI: University Microfilms International.

von Domarus, E. (1944/1964). The specific laws of logic in schizophrenia. In Kasanin, J. S. (Ed.), *Language and thought in schizophrenia*. New York: Norton.

White, L. (1962). *Medieval technology and social change*. New York: Oxford University Press.

White, R. W. (1963). (Ed.) *The study of lives*. New York: Atherton Press.

Whorf, B. L. (1956). *Language, thought and reality*. New York: Wiley.

Hans H. Strupp, Ph.D.

Distinguished Professor of Psychology
Vanderbilt University, Nashville, Tennessee

◆

Reflections on My Career in Clinical Psychology

I appreciate Dr. Walker's invitation to reflect on my scientific and professional career—how I came to be the clinical psychologist I am. A scientist's basic tenets and lived beliefs do not spring full-blown from the brow of Zeus; instead, they are deeply anchored in one's biography. At least in part, they are, as Freud discovered, attempts to master basic problems of one's childhood to find solutions to fundamental existential questions. Surely, no one can sustain a long-term interest in a topic of science without a deep personal commitment. One's choice of subject matter, research problems, and investigative techniques, as well as one's philosophy of science, must be personally meaningful in a deep sense. Of course, that too, is not the whole story. Nothing in human living ever is, and so I suspect that no scientist can fully explain what fuels or inspires his or her beliefs over the years.

A field like psychotherapy, which is perhaps more closely linked to personal concerns than many others, particularly invites speculation concerning an author's motives. This is even more true in the case of someone whose major aim in life has been to investigate, research, and above all understand the process of psychological change.

Early Life

I was born on August 25, 1921, the first child of a middle-class Jewish family in Frankfurt am Main, in West Germany. I share this birthplace with the city's most famous son, Johann Wolfgang von Goethe, as well as the sign of the zodiac (Virgo). I have always admired Goethe.

My mother who, like my father, came from a family with six children, had emigrated from Strassburg after World War I. The reason for the move, I have been told, was the fact that her three brothers had fought on the German side, which precluded their opting for France when Alsace-Lorraine was ceded in 1918. My father hailed from a small village in Bavaria (Mittelsinn in Unterfranken). My grandfather, a deeply religious man, had been the local teacher and ritual slaughterer. After his retirement he moved to Frankfurt, where he lived until his death in 1933. My grandmother had died in 1924, and a maiden aunt kept house for my grandfather. My father had been trained as a tailor. Following his military service during World War I he settled in Frankfurt, where he married my mother in 1920. (Her sister had previously married one of my father's brothers.) He became the branch manager of a haberdashery store. The firm had been founded—or, better, transplanted—by two maternal uncles and other relatives who constituted the board of directors. The firm eventually had about 30 stores throughout Germany, but went bankrupt in the early thirties.

I gathered that my father had been somewhat of a "poor relative" who was given a fairly responsible job that included signature privileges (*procura*). Both parents had only a modest education, and no relative on either side had ever attended a university, perhaps not even a high school. My parents occupied a comfortable apartment in one of the better areas of town.

My father, like his, was a religiously observant man. He performed the daily ritual of laying *tefilin* and attended the synagogue at least on the high holidays. On Sunday it was his custom to visit his parents, and I frequently accompanied him on these visits. My mother acquiesced in the religious observances, although she came from a family that laid little stress on such matters.

The idyll of my early childhood—if that's what it was—was rudely broken by the birth of a younger brother, in 1925. Werner, according to reports and snapshots, was a sunny and contented child, in contrast to his older brother, whose visage and bearing were usually sullen and somewhat morose. Perhaps for this reason he seemed to be preferred by my parents, which presumably deepened my sense of having been dethroned. At any rate, I remember very few "good times" from my childhood. The sense of being displaced, deprived, and disadvantaged was combined with other unhappy childhood experiences, of which I will say more presently.

Perhaps because I was inquisitive and bright, my father conceived the idea that I should study to become a rabbi; however, he was not destined to determine my career choice. In the midtwenties he was already experiencing recurring attacks of pleurisy, which left him in an increasingly debilitated state. A few years later, his illness worsened and cancer was diagnosed. He became increasingly weak and bedridden. In 1930, October 28 to be precise, he died. Some time before this fateful event, my brother and I had been sent to live with relatives in the city, and I was not told of his death until after the funeral. Thus he left me without saying goodbye or pronouncing the traditional blessing. I can still identify the spot on the street, near my uncle's house, where my uncle stopped the car to tell me about my new status as an orphan.

That same day my uncle and I visited the rabbi, who impressed on me that I was now the head of the family and had to look out for my mother. These well-meant words had unfortunate consequences. My mother, who was only 38, had to struggle with her loss and was probably clinically depressed for some time. I felt responsible, but at the age of 9 obviously was in no position to help her or function as the head of the household. Ever since, depression in people close to me, particularly in women, has imbued me with a deep sense of incompetence and powerlessness. I don't recall anyone being concerned with my own feelings of loss. It was somehow assumed that children had no feelings.

Another unfortunate consequence was the fact that my grandfather and a parental uncle decreed that, for an entire year, I should attend the synagogue daily and recite the prayer of mourning (Kaddish). It was the custom for bereaved men to stand in front of the congregation and recite the prayer, which occurred toward the end of the service. Naturally, I was the only child among the men. Particularly on the high holidays, when the synagogue was filled, I experienced my status as shameful and demeaning, since it occasioned being noticed by the congregants, some of whom had known my father and expressed curiosity about the little boy. I was entrusted to the custodian (*shames*), who was supposed to look out for me during the services. I felt hurt by having this assignment thrust on me, and almost reflexively opposed it. In vain. I rebelled similarly when, after my grandfather's death in 1933, I was forced, against my vigorous protests, to attend his funeral. After all, I had to represent my deceased father.

This may be the place to comment on the status of children in Germany, perhaps especially in middle-class Jewish families. Children were essentially considered nonpersons who had no rights and presumably no feelings—certainly no feelings that needed to be listened to or taken seriously. A child's prime duty was to give no offense and, above all, to obey. These requirements were also emphasized in the elementary school and in the high school I attended. I feared my teachers, all of whom were male; some were indeed brutal and sadistic. Major techniques of discipline were shaming, ridiculing, and the "silent treatment" (giving no response), as well as physical beatings.

All of these disciplinary methods were used in my family. I remember several times being taken to the bathroom by my father, beaten, and then locked up for some time. These instances were usually the consequence of misbehavior at the dinner table— proper behavior at mealtimes seemed particularly important! I was then banned from the table for at least one meal and had to eat in the kitchen with the full-time maid. I must have developed a certain expertise in provoking my father (which apparently was easy enough to do, since he was somewhat of a house tyrant). My misbehavior also brought special attention, which I probably did not get any other way.

Among more pleasant memories were our frequent Sunday hikes in the nearby mountains (Taunus). But here, too, I remember being punished for blowing bubbles with a straw at an outdoor restaurant.

Much later I resonated strongly to the sentiments expressed by Kafka in his *Letter to My Father.* My edition of this slim volume has the German original on one side and an English translation on facing pages. Although I eventually mastered the English language, I always found Kafka's description of the father-son relationship in the German original much more powerful and searing. In my experience, no other language lends itself so readily to hostility, disparagement, and venom as does German. The English translation struck me as a pale replica of the profound affect evoked by the German original. Kafka of course was a master craftsman in expressing the anger, shame, hatred, resentment, and rage that characterized his feelings toward his father.

As I discovered much later, I developed strong oedipal feelings and fantasies and was always close—too close—to my mother. Although she had some business experience (she took over one of the family stores after the firm's bankruptcy), our forced emigration to the United States and the necessity of accepting menial jobs as "companion" to an elderly lady and housekeeper in a physician's home demoralized her deeply. She became overly dependent, particularly on her sons, for whom she later kept house, insisting that it was their obligation to take care of their ailing parent (she had become somewhat of a hypochondriac), even at the expense of advancing their own education and careers.

For complex reasons, I became deeply imbued with my mother's philosophy of life. Applied to me, this meant holding down a full-time job and furthering my education at night. In the process, I had to pass up opportunities to accelerate my college education and subsequently felt prevented from pursuing full-time graduate study. (An opportunity to do graduate work presented itself when, in 1945, after graduating from college summa cum laude, I was offered admission and a modest stipend by the Massachusetts Institute of Technology, where Kurt Lewin had just inaugurated his Research Center for Group Dynamics.) It took great effort and many hours of therapy for me to come to terms with these early experiences. A social worker at the Jewish Social Service in Washington, D.C., which supplied some of the secondhand furniture that allowed us to carry out my mother's plan for a *ménage à trois* (in 1941), expressed grave reservations about the wisdom of the proposed arrangement; but I did not adequately grasp her concerns.

But let me return to my life in Germany. Without my realizing it, my father's premature death must have propelled me into a period of profound mourning, manifested in a massive social withdrawal. I increasingly spent my free time alone and separated myself from my peers during class intermissions. A few years later, when I acquired a bicycle, I rode into the woods to nurse my feelings of sadness, whose meaning and significance I did not realize.

I was an excellent student and earned good grades in most subjects, except for gymnastics, drawing, and music. School was moderately satisfying, except for fairly constant anxiety, particularly during examinations.

I had a number of physical illnesses, particularly bouts of tonsillitis, which occurred about once a month. As a consequence of my bad tonsils, I came down with scarlet fever. I spent six weeks in isolation at the Jewish hospital, after which my mother and the doctors decreed that the tonsils had to be removed. The tonsillectomy, accomplished at about age 13, was preceded by a deathly fear of surgery. The experience itself was something of a nightmare that seemed to justify my apprehensions.

The Nazi Period and Emigration

Another blow to my self-esteem was occasioned by the Nazi revolution, which got underway early in 1933. Thereafter the 6 or so Jewish boys in a class of over 40 were increasingly shunned by teachers and fellow students. Aryan students joined the Hitler Youth, often appearing at school in uniform; teachers had to join the Nazi party. By 1937, it had become abundantly clear that public schools had become untenable for Jewish children. I might have transferred to a Jewish school, but for some reason this was not considered to be a viable option. The idea that emigration was inevitable also gained ground, with the result that Jewish families decided to have their children gain competence in a vocation one might be able to transplant, such as acquiring manual skill, or second best, gaining business experience. Since I showed little talent for the former, it was decided to send me as an apprentice to a Jewish firm that manufactured costume jewelry, where I might gain office skills. Since the firm exported its wares to England and Scandinavian countries, I had a chance to translate correspondence with English-speaking clients. This job lasted until our emigration in 1939. Once a week I was required to attend a vocational school that had special classes for Jewish students. This training in office routines and bookkeeping proved handy when I started looking for a job in the United States.

Following the *Kristallnacht*[1] in November 1938, even those Jews who viewed the Nazi government as a transient phenomenon became convinced that emigration was the only sensible solution for those who had the opportunity. As the minor son of a widow who for American immigration purposes came under the French "quota" (since my mother's birthplace was Strasbourg, now in France), we obtained a visa fairly promptly, consequent upon one of my mother's brothers establishing an affidavit that would guarantee our support in the United States, should it become necessary. My mother had to liquidate her store, and whatever money was left fell victim to the confiscatory taxes that had been imposed on Jews for "fleeing the Reich." Thus when we arrived in New York in June 1939, each family member had $10 with which to start a new life.

As I discovered much later, I greatly missed paternal guidance and support. However, there were two men who in a limited way met my needs. The first was the principal of a high school who had been forced into early retirement because his wife was Jewish. He gave me private lessons in English and Spanish (there was a possibility

---

[1] The assassination of an attaché at the German embassy in Paris by an embittered Polish Jew was used by the Nazis as a pretext to set fire to synagogues throughout Germany, smash windows of Jewish stores (hence the euphemism "crystal night"), and arrest many Jewish men, who were then incarcerated in concentration camps for extended periods.

that we might emigrate to a country in South America), and he also taught me, as a bonus, something about art history and architecture. I greatly valued these lessons, and have never forgotten an automobile trip on which he invited me and my younger brother. He eventually emigrated to Colombia, and I took pains to find his address. We corresponded a bit, but then lost track of each other. We corresponded about such topics as philosophy and *Weltanschauung*. I was interested at the time in Nietzsche and his elitist philosophy. I also read Otto Weininger, a contemporary of Freud, who wrote tracts on sex and character. The father of a friend of mine whom I occasionally visited in New York, a psychiatrist, half seriously forbade me to bring such books to his house. Weininger, a radical but fairly obscure philosopher, eventually committed suicide. The first psychiatrist I consulted in 1945 in Washington, D.C., bore the same last name. My choice had not been accidental.

The second male figure to whom I became attached was a pediatrician whom I saw in his apartment, after hours, which intensified the meaningfulness of our encounters. Around age 13, probably related to pubertal struggles, I had developed a fairly severe case of bronchial asthma. (As a small child I had been afflicted by eczema.) Medications had proved more or less unsuccessful. The pediatrician treated me with intravenous injections of calcium, to which, miraculously, I responded very well. Later I learned that calcium had been shown to be quite useless in treating asthma. I probably responded more positively to his interest and attention than to the injections.

New York and Washington, D.C.

Soon after we had settled in New York City, where my brother and I shared a room in the home of another immigrant family, I found a job in the office of an automobile upholstery wholesaler, to whom the father of a friend had referred me. Jobs, it should be noted, were difficult to find, since the United States was still at the tail end of the Great Depression. Thus to find a job that paid the munificent sum of $11 a week was an achievement. Within a year I was making $17 a week, and was offered a job paying $20 a week at the Washington, D.C. subsidiary of the firm. I accepted and moved to Washington, which became my home for 17 years.

After arriving in New York City I gained admission to the "evening session" of the College of the City of New York as a "nonmatriculated student," as non-New Yorkers were called, and started to take a few courses at $4.50 per credit hour. Among others, I took an advanced German course on Faust, American government, and English for foreigners. Slowly my ear began to get used to American English. Walter Reis, a fellow refugee, who became a psychiatrist and psychoanalyst, was taking courses in psychology, and he invited me to a class in which the instructor showed a movie on metrazol shock, a gruesome experience. The professor was Isidor Chein, who later became well known as a social psychologist.

Walter Reis also introduced me to Freud's writings. Although it took me many years to gain an adequate understanding of Freud's work, I believe that his insights have more profoundly influenced me than those of any other author. (Freud has remained one of my great heroes, the other being Mozart.) In those days, however, and at least for another 20 years, psychoanalysis, particularly the practice of psychoanalytic psychotherapy, was considered largely a medical prerogative, and thus as a non-M.D. I felt more than a twinge of guilt for even showing an interest in this "forbidden" territory.

My brief stay at City College was terminated by the move to Washington, where I enrolled as an evening student at George Washington University. Eventually I earned B.A., M.A., and Ph.D. degrees from that institution, all by part-time study.

My initial fascination with philosophy (nurtured at George Washington University by the late Professor Christopher Browne Garnett, Jr.) presently gave way to the study of psychology—a more "practical" endeavor—which I found only moderately absorbing. Abnormal psychology, to which Professor Thelma Hunt introduced me, was another matter, although the prevailing emphasis was too "organic" for my liking. A true inspiration, however, was the training program offered by the Washington School of Psychiatry and writings of its leader, Harry Stack Sullivan (of whom I caught only glimpses, but whose influence was profound). Memorable teachers at the school were Frieda Fromm-Reichmann, Otto A. Will, Jr., Clara Thompson, Cora DuBois, Ernest Schachtel, Leon Salzman, and Alfred Stanton. For a number of years after I graduated from the school in 1952 (receiving a quaintly named "Certificate in Applied Psychiatry for Psychologists") I probably would have been called a "Sullivanian," although Freud's influence reasserted itself later.

I can best explain the development of my ideas by reference to the vagaries of my academic training, which, to say the least, was anything but standard. Although I gradually developed a strong allegiance to clinical psychology, I was not formally trained as a clinical psychologist; in fact, my entry into the field was through the "back door." Second, although I received extensive training in psychoanalytic psychotherapy and have practiced it for almost 30 years, I have never felt comfortable with the term "analyst," and have never called myself one.[2] Third, although I left the

---

[2] My relationship to psychoanalysis has remained thoroughly ambivalent. My first analysis, which lasted six years, was with a young psychiatric resident who before going into private practice was studying at the Washington School of Psychiatry, where he was supervised. He was a fairly orthodox Freudian in most respects. Therapy with him proved quite helpful. My second analysis was with a psychiatrist who later became a training analyst. This therapy lasted three and a half years and was terminated at the analyst's initiative. In retrospect, this was a damaging experience, which took prolonged effort to undo. As I learned later, this man was generally disliked for his arrogance and pompousness by the psychologists who were his colleagues at the university where he practiced. It also dawned on me eventually that he apparently had little use for me as a person. However, I was not able to recognize this while the therapy was in progress, which speaks to my unresolved dependence on the man. He later became embroiled in a scandal involving overprescription of drugs and sexual abuse of women patients. Additional therapy in later years has been both helpful and rewarding. Much of what I have learned about psychotherapy derives from these personal exeriences.

I remain firmly convinced that psychoanalytic ideas have done more to advance our understanding of the psyche than any other theory, and I remain loyal to Freud's great discoveries, particularly those centering around transference, which I consider the heart of psychotherapy. On the other hand, my relationship with organized psychoanalysis has remained a painful chapter in my life. I have not forgotten the rudeness with which my application for formal psychoanalytic training was rejected by one of the "official" institutes of the American Psychoanalytic Association, although, in retrospect, it was probably more salutary for my professional development not to be permitted to "merge." From the perspective of free scientific inquiry, organized psychoanalysis has been one of the great deterrents to progress—indeed, it can be described as an unmitigated disaster. Furthermore, Freud's great ... the unholy alliance between psychoanalysis and medicine have unfortunately been fully borne ... e is becoming evident again in the 1980s, with the attempted "remedicalization" of psychotherapy.

medical setting after having held a professorship in a department of psychiatry for nine years, my research interests and clinical commitments (training and professional practice) are in many ways better represented by psychiatry than by academic psychology. Indeed, for many years my research was—and perhaps still is—better known in psychiatric circles than in clinical psychology. My major reason for leaving the medical school was my growing unwillingness to tolerate the second-class status accorded to clinical psychologists. In brief, I consider myself a hybrid in the fields of clinical psychology, psychiatry, and psychoanalysis, feeling most at home in clinical psychology.

Entry into Psychotherapy Research

The Ph.D. degree that I received in 1954 was in social psychology, although I had chosen as the topic of my dissertation an empirical study of psychotherapists' techniques. I will sketch the stimulus for this study later in this essay. Because George Washington University did not have a clinical psychology program at the time, one's major field of study had to be in one of the "established" areas. My dissertation committee, under chairmanship of Professor Curtis E. Tuthill, was notably generous and broadminded to sanction a study that grew out of my own interests, regardless of "area." By that time I had taken almost every graduate course the Department of Psychology had to offer, from test construction to factor analysis, survey research, experimental psychology, phsysiological psychology, endocrinology, and, of course, abnormal/clinical psychology.

In 1949, I obtained my first position as a psychologist; I was an "aviation psychologist" with the Department of the Air Force. Thus my first experience as a full-time researcher was in the area known as "personnel psychology." I felt that my academic training had equipped me with a good appreciation for empirical research and a respect for data and for the methods of science. I had also acquired reasonable competence in research design, hypothesis testing, and statistical analysis. These skills were further developed over a six-year period that included a year with the Adjutant General's Office of the Department of the Army. Howard J. Hausman and Dorothy E. Green were good role models and friends. I also learned a thing or two about scientific writing from my immediate superior, Luigi Petrullo, a highly critical but constructive taskmaster.

I mention these facts to document the antecedents of my training as a researcher. Although I developed a love for "doing science," for framing questions and attempting to obtain meaningful answers, I must confess that the problems the governmental agencies sought to elucidate—for example, constructing and validating oral proficiency examinations for B-29 aircraft mechanics, studying attitudes of mechanics toward their crew chiefs and the effects of these attitudes on the crew's productivity, and identifying malingerers from test responses—did not exactly make my imagination soar. However, as I said, I led a dual existence, because I was taking night courses at the Washington School of Psychiatry and was undergoing psychoanalysis. I also arranged for training as a therapist, under supervision. The psychoanalytic and psychiatric subject matter vitally interested me, and I began to wonder how one might apply the methods of science to the fascinating problems in that domain.[3]

The practical difficulties were formidable. There were few experts one could consult; my alma mater did not have a program in clinical psychology, and it was not feasible to go elsewhere; there was a meager research literature on psychotherapy (which presently became my overweening area of interest); and I had no clear idea of how one might undertake research along these lines, particularly in the absence of a suitable position and money. The situation, I might note, did not substantially improve after I had obtained my Ph.D. degree and had published three papers based on my dissertation (Strupp, 1955a, 1955b, 1955c). The earliest of these (Strupp, 1955a) was greeted enthusiastically by Lawrence Shaffer, then the editor of the *Journal of Consulting Psychology,* who selected it as the lead article. I still had no acceptable credentials as a clinical psychologist or a clinical researcher, as departmental chairmen and senior colleagues around the country to whom I sent my vita were quick to point out. My file of rejection letters grew to a thickness of about 3 inches.

One never knows precisely how ideas germinate, but I recall the impact of a study by E. Lakin Phillips, one of my professors at George Washington University (Phillips & Agnew, 1953). He had constructed a multiple-choice questionnaire, which he administered to a sample of psychotherapists. Each item represented a statement a patient had made early in therapy, followed by several response choices, one of which was a client-centered one. Phillips hypothesized that the client-centered response would be chosen with greater frequency than others. I suspect that the cards had been stacked somewhat in favor of client-centered therapy, to which Phillips at that time subscribed. At any rate, the results supported his hypothesis. I began to wonder what might happen—always the beginning of research!—if therapists were given free rein to respond to a collection of patient statements. Thus the methodology of my dissertation was born: I assembled a collection of presumably representative statements that had been made by patients early in therapy and presented them individually (on cards) to therapists in Washington, D.C.[4] Their task was simply to

---

[3] I cannot let the opportunity pass without recording a serendipitous event, which fully fits Bandura's (1982) observation that often a person's career is determined by quite fortuitous happenings. Pedestrian as the government projects seemed, they resulted in voluminous data, which several of my colleagues used for their doctoral dissertations. (They too were part-time students who earned their doctorates while working for a living.) I had similar plans and would have acted on them had it not been for an order issued by then Secretary of Defense Charles Wilson (of "What's good for General Motors is good for the country" fame), which forbade the use of government data in dissertation research. Quite unwittingly, Wilson did me a great favor, because the edict forced me to do something on my own, even though it was considerably more arduous and difficult.

[4] In retrospect, it took a certain amount of audacity (*chutzpah?*) to telephone practicing therapists (mostly medical analysts) and ask whether they would agree to be interviewed for an hour or two by an unknown researcher who was interested in studying psychotherapeutic techniques. I am still amazed that most consented, and when I visited them they were gracious and gave generously of their time. I wound up with an *n* of 50, augmented by a number of psychologists and social workers who were affiliated with the outpatient clinic of the Veterans Administration.

read the statement and tell me what, if anything, they might say to the patient. A minimum of contextual information was given. In addition, I collected various items of information from each respondent—professional affiliation, theoretical orientation, length of experience in psychotherapy, whether he or she had undergone personal analysis, and the like. The responses to the structured task were then quantified by the Bales (1950) system of interaction process analysis, and were related statistically to background variables.

The design was not exactly elegant, the experimental situation was artificial, and the study was clearly deficient in other respects as well; however, I was breaking ground in an area into which few researchers had ventured. Fiedler's (1953) studies had recently appeared, and they were justifiably heralded as innovative and creative. The excitement in this area of research is difficult to capture 30 years later, after literally thousands of studies in psychotherapy have appeared in print.

This may be the time for a brief excursus on the place of psychotherapy in academic departments of psychology in the early 1950s. As I have hinted, psychotherapy was predominately a medical specialty, and psychotherapy research was virtually nonexistent. Departments of psychology, even if they had APA-accredited clinical programs, taught "counseling psychology," but not psychotherapy as such. To practice clinical psychology meant almost exclusively to engage in diagnostic testing. Projective tests, particularly the Rorschach, were held in high esteem, and the writings of Bruno Klopfer, Samuel Beck, David Rapaport, Ernest Schachtel, Roy Schafer, and Robert Holt had significant impact on the training of graduate students. David Rapaport was one of the psychologists who concerned himself seriously with psychoanalytic theory, not only with reference to psychological testing. However, as his obituary some years later noted, he was not fully accepted by either organized psychology or psychoanalysis.

In short, psychotherapy—and particularly psychotherapy based on psychoanalytic principles—was not readily accessible to graduate students in academic departments of psychology. Counseling that became wedded to psychotherapy was best represented by the teachings of Carl Rogers, who became very influential in the early 1950s. Rogers's important work, *Client-Centered Psychotherapy* (dubbed "poor man's psychoanalysis" by *Time* magazine), had been published in 1951. From the standpoint of psychotherapy research, the publication of a collection of studies under Rogers's direction (Rogers & Dymond, 1954) was of even greater importance. This was undoubtedly the first set of systematic studies of psychotherapy; it was truly a pioneer effort and a tribute to Rogers's leadership. It established that psychotherapy was a legitimate area of scientific inquiry; that psychologists were entitled to learn, teach, and practice psychotherapy; and that they were uniquely qualified to research it.

In subsequent years I have repeatedly pointed out to graduate students that while psychiatrists and other mental health professionals may practice psychotherapy as competently as clinical psychologists, only clinical psychologists usually have the requisite expertise to conduct systematic research. In psychology's great urge to achieve parity in the field of practice, the profession has often undervalued and even depreciated the research training provided by academic departments of psychology.

Although never a Rogerian, and in later years an outspoken critic of Rogers's *Weltanschauung* as an educational philosophy (Strupp, 1976), I have always respected his contributions to the scientific study of psychotherapy—a commitment that he eventually seemed to disavow. Against the background of Freud and Sullivan, client-centered therapy also impressed me as a pallid approach that largely missed or ignored the depth dimension in human suffering and unhappiness. This limited perspective was perpetuated in the training of psychology students, who gained their primary clinical experience in counseling centers and remained relatively untouched by the broad spectrum of psychopathology found in the "real" world.

Let me briefly recapitulate the strands that shaped my early career as a psychotherapist and researcher of psychotherapy:

1. From the German-Jewish tradition, I acquired an appreciation for ideas, the liberal tradition, philosophy, music, and literature, all of which combined with romantic yearnings and youthful *Sturm und Drang*.
2. From Sigmund Freud and the neo-Freudians (notably Harry Stack Sullivan), I acquired an abiding preoccupation with the vicissitudes of the psyche—how to conceptualize "problems in living" and resolve them via psychotherapy. No problem has intrigued me more than the fundamental one of how psychological change is brought about.
3. From academic psychology, I acquired great admiration and respect for empirical research based on hard data (here, I came to feel, the field of psychoanalysis and its practitioners had much to learn.)
4. From the circumstances of my life, I acquired a strong drive to learn, understand, achieve, and persist in the face of adversity.
5. Finally, but perhaps most importantly, having benefited immensely from personal therapy, I became convinced that, at least under particular circumstances, psychotherapy has a great deal to offer. To be sure, it cannot work miracles; but, for many people, what are the alternatives?

I empathize with young psychologists who today are struggling to find positions commensurate with their training and ambitions. It was equally difficult 30 years ago. That may be small consolation to contemporary job seekers, but perhaps I have a lesson to offer: If you are intent upon pursuing a goal, don't give up easily! I am a firm believer in persistence, and am often reminded of a quotation that is etched in my mind. It goes something like this: "Bright ideas are plentiful in science, but there are relatively few people who have the persistence to do the hard work of following one of them through."

Becoming a Psychotherapy Researcher

As I noted, my doctoral dissertation was a success and attracted a certain amount of attention. Nonetheless, I was still trying to find a clinical research position that would allow me to pursue my newfound interest. Since I was unable to get appointed to an existing position, it eventually dawned on me that perhaps I might be able to create my own.

In this spirit, I wrote a letter to Dr. Winfred Overholser, who was superintendent of Saint Elizabeth's Hospital in Washingon, D.C., and chairman of the Department of Psychiatry at the George Washington University School of Medicine. I described my doctoral research and wondered whether he might be willing to co-sponsor an application for a research grant. This would permit me, I explained, to leave my government position and work full-time as a psychotherapy researcher. I also indicated the possible next steps in the research—to expand the sample of therapists, to create more realistic stimulus situations (perhaps on film), to develop a system for quantifying therapists' communications, and the like. The proposal apparently appealed to Dr. Overholser, and he turned it over to one of his younger colleagues, a psychiatrist named Leon Yochelson. Dr. Yochelson got in touch we me, and we began to discuss an application for a research grant to the National Institute of Mental Health, which had recently come into existence. If the grant was approved, George Washington University would provide space and facilities, but no academic appointment. That seemed good enough for the time being, and we decided to proceed.

I then received a second stroke of luck: the application was assigned for review to Dr. Jerome D. Frank of Johns Hopkins University—one of the most distinguished psychotherapy researchers of our time, and one of the finest people I ever encountered. I shall always be grateful to him for launching my career. He conducted a "site visit" by asking me to come to Baltimore, since there was no site to visit in Washington, D.C. Apparently he was favorably impressed, and the grant was duly approved and funded for a period of three years, with an annual budget in the $15,000 range. My starting salary was $7500 a year. It was rare for psychologists to do "real" psychotherapy research in those days (as opposed to research on "counseling"), and so one of the members of the review panel telephoned Dr. Overholser (as he told me later) to inquire about the personal and professional qualifications of the fledging applicant. The purpose of the call was to make sure that there would be no embarrassment to the field of psychiatry. Dr. Overholser gave the necessary assurances, but as a safeguard it was stipulated that a psychiatrist would consult with me on a weekly basis.[5]

---

[5] On one occasion, circa 1956, I had secured permission from Dr. Franz Alexander, that remarkably open-minded analyst, to speak about my research and to collect data from the members of the Chicago Institute of Psychoanalysis after one of their weekly luncheon meetings. Dr. Gerhard Piers, then a senior member of the institute, greeted me, saying somewhat archly, "So, you've come to pick our brains." Few investigators at that time had had the audacity to study what analysts "do", this was equated with invading the privacy of their consulting rooms. Like Dr. Piers, I was aware of (one of) the meanings of the enterprise. When the time came for the analysts to view my experimental film, about a dozen complied with the experimental task of writing down their responses. However, several showed overt anger, and one or two wrote letters documenting their displeasure at what they regarded as a highly artificial and meaningless assignment. Admittedly, the experimental task was contrived, but, as I discovered, it was far from meaningless. As a matter of fact, it revealed a great deal about the respondents and their approach to psychotherapy. Was their anger a response to what they experienced as an invasion of their privacy?

Thus it came about that in 1955 I became a full-time psychotherapy researcher. Dr. Overholser assigned me an office in the Chaplains' Department of Saint Elizabeth's Hospital—it was actually the office of the part-time rabbi—and I was "in business." The grant provided modest support for a research assistant, a job that was admirably filled by Rebecca Rieger, a young psychologist who joined me on a part-time basis. I soon discovered that full-time research can be a rather lonely existence, but that mattered little, because I now had the opportunity I had been praying for.

For two and a half years I worked as hard as I have ever worked to carry out an expanded study of therapists' techniques, using an analogue situation that consisted of a film of an initial psychiatric interview. The film had been produced by the Veterans Administration, under the direction of Dr. Jacob Finesinger, for training purposes, and I adapted it by inserting titles at 27 strategic places ("What Would You Do?"). During each 30-second pause, respondents were requested to write down what they would say to the patient. I collected extensive data from psychiatrists, psychologists, and social workers in Washington, D.C., Baltimore, New York, and Chicago. The results of the work were published in a series of journal articles (Strupp, 1958a, 1958b, 1958c), and eventually in book form (Strupp, 1960a). In addition, I developed a system of process analysis (Strupp, 1957c), which I also applied to published interviews (Strupp, 1957a, 1957b).

The research was well received,[6] and in 1957 I was able to choose between two desirable academic positions. The first was a lecturer's appointment at Harvard University (time-limited and with an uncertain future); the second was a position as director of Psychological Services, with the rank of associate professor in the Departments of Psychiatry and Psychology, at the University of North Carolina (UNC) at Chapel Hill (a five-year appointment that might result in promotion and tenure). For various reasons, partly related to growing family responsibilities, Chapel Hill won out. I later learned that Harvard had been miffed, because "no one, but no one, ever turns down Harvard!" I stayed in Chapel Hill for nine years and sometimes wonder what my career would have been like had I gone to Harvard.

Let me say a few words about my family, of whom I am enormously proud. In 1951, I married Lottie Metzger, a German refugee, who was also my second cousin. Our children, Karen, Barbara, and John, were born in 1954, 1955, and 1958. Karen earned her Ph.D. degree in clinical psychology at the University of North Carolina at Chapel Hill and is now in full-time practice in Houston. Barbara, a biopsychologist, received her Ph.D. degree from Cornell University, and is married to David Levitsky, a professor of psychology at Cornell. John, our youngest, holds an M.D. degree from the University of Tennessee, and is married to Dana Morris. He is an oncologist in private practice. They have one child, Emily, born in 1988.

---

[6] In 1958, this research received Honorable Mention from the Hofheimer Prize Committee of the American Psychiatric Association. The prize itself was awarded that year to James Olds for his research on the pleasure centers in the brain.

The Chapel Hill Years

The period 1957 to 1966 contributed a great deal to my professional growth, although in many respects those were stormy years. When I joined the Department of Psychiatry as director of Psychological Services, I knew precious little about clinical psychology in a medical school and even less about administration. Earl Baughman, then director of clinical psychology training at UNC, who had been instrumental in recruiting me, became a friend and a staunch ally, and my psychologist colleagues in psychiatry were likewise helpful supporters.

Soon after my arrival, the faculty of the Department of Psychiatry voted that psychologists were not to practice psychotherapy except for research, and then only under psychiatric supervision. The ensuing controversy was eventually resolved in our favor, but the incident conveys something of the prevailing turmoil, with which I did not feel adequate to deal.

As a sidelight on historical developments, it may be appropriate to comment on the role and status of clinical psychologists in a medical setting, circa 1960. The Department of Psychiatry at UNC was a major training center for psychiatrists, and probably a fairly representative one. It was chaired, as was then the custom, by a trained psychoanalyst, Dr. George C. Ham, who also had extensive interests in research, training, and patient care. Each year the department admitted about ten psychiatric residents, who received training in adult inpatient and outpatient care, as well as in outpatient child psychiatry, consultation, and student health. To a much lesser extent, they concerned themselves with research. UNC and Duke also administered a psychoanalytic training program, which operated under the aegis of the Washington (D.C.) Psychoanalytic Institute. It was prestigious for residents to be admitted to psychoanalytic training (this usually occurred during their second or third year of residency). Some members of the psychiatric faculty also functioned as teachers of psychoanalysis, and in a few cases as training analysts. No psychologists had ever been admitted to psychoanalytic training, and those who tried (myself included) were unceremoniously rejected, with no reasons given.

Clinical psychologists held academic appointments in the medical school, but in this hierarchically organized setting they enjoyed fewer privileges than did the medically trained faculty. For one thing, they were excluded from private practice (psychiatrists typically doubled their academic salaries in this manner); for another, they did not attend departmental faculty meetings (which were open only to psychiatrists); and they did not benefit from other privileges (such as insurance, travel to scientific meetings, and so on). Accordingly, the most junior psychiatrist had an income equal to that of the most senior psychologist. Psychiatric social workers, occupational therapists, nurses, and other "ancillary" professionals ranked even lower in the hierarchy.

To "do" psychotherapy was a privilege jealously guarded by psychiatrists, although clinical psychologists gradually gained entry. The "proper" functions of the psychologist were psychodiagnosis (which held a certain prestige) and research. In the latter capacity, they often served as junior authors. For the department to appoint as director of psychological services a psychologist who specialized in research on psychotherapy was somewhat unorthodox. With the passage of time, even greater liberalization occurred. A decade later, psychologists had achieved higher status, although hardly parity. Psychologists throughout the state attempted to get a licensing law enacted, but the move was typically opposed by the medical profession (in fairness, it should be noted, also by some prominent psychologists, who felt that such legislation would abridge their academic freedom). At the time, only a few states had such statutes on the books. Private practice, either within or outside of the medical setting, was nonexistent. All of this, of course, was destined to change within a relatively short time. Indeed, clinical psychology has come a long way!

At diagnostic case conferences, which served an excellent teaching function, it was the rule for a psychiatrist to preside, although the psychologist's contribution was typically valued and respectfully received. I learned a great deal about patients and their problems in this setting, unequaled by any other experience. It was possible for psychologists to receive supervision from more experienced psychiatrists and psychoanalysts, and the latter often collaborated in clinical research. The department also engaged in basic research, where psychologists attained considerable recognition. The same was true of community psychology, which gradually gained a foothold. Money for research and training was fairly readily available in the "golden sixties."

The psychology staff in the Department of Psychiatry grew from a small nucleus of 4 in 1957 to perhaps 12 or 15 about ten years later. In the academic Department of Psychology, we trained practicum students who worked toward their doctorates in clinical psychology and presently obtained approval from the American Psychological Association for internship training. The clinical duties of staff psychologists initially entailed work on the major services, adult inpatient and outpatient as well as outpatient child psychiatry. In due course, these activities expanded to include other departments in the medical school. Thus a modest beginning was made in health psychology and behavioral medicine. Psychologists in the Department of Psychiatry also participated on a limited basis in formal teaching and supervision of psychiatric residents and medical students.

I must not fail to mention that clinical psychologists who held faculty positions in the Department of Psychiatry had joint appointments in the academic Department of Psychology. As already indicated, this allowed us to teach and supervise graduate students as well as to serve on dissertation committees. It would be inaccurate to say that relations between the two psychologist groups were altogether harmonious, but on the whole a spirit of collaboration prevailed.

Among my early students were Marty Wallach (who tragically died of Hodgkin's disease) and Ron Fox. Both became valuable collaborators in my research, which I was able to continue despite many competing responsibilities. Joan Williams Jenkins and Ken Lessler also became team members. Research support from NIMH continued for some years but then ceased. The most significant research during that period, a retrospective study of former patients (Strupp, Fox & Lessler, 1969), was completed with a minimum of external support.

In 1961, having passed the examination of the American Board of Professional Psychology, I achieved diplomate status in clinical psychology, and in 1962 I became a full professor. Other honors that came my way included an invitation to participate in the First Conference on Research in Psychotherapy, held in Washington D.C., in 1958 (Rubinstein & Parloff, 1959); chairmanship of the Second Conference on Research in Psychotherapy, held in Chapel Hill in 1961 (Strupp & Luborsky, 1962); the Helen Sargent Memorial Prize of the Menninger Foundation; the Lasker address at Michael Reese Hospital in Chicago; and an invitation to participate in the 70th birthday celebration of Franz Alexander, held in Los Angeles in 1963.

In 1966 I accepted a professorial appointment in the Department of Psychology at Vanderbilt University in Nashville, Tennessee, which has been my home ever since. For nine years (1967 to 1976) I served as director of clinical psychology training, and eventually became the senior faculty member in clinical psychology. I also discovered that an academic department of psychology is a better place for a clinical psychologist than a department of psychiatry in a medical school.

The Vanderbilt Years

I was 45 when I came to Vanderbilt University. Our two teenage daughters attended public school, where they soon made friends. Our son was 8 years old. Lottie accepted a part-time position as research assistant at the Vanderbilt Psychological and Counseling Center. After holding several other positions, she became the full-time administrator of the Vanderbilt Institute for Public Policy Studies, an assignment she still holds. I felt accepted by my new colleagues but had no external research support, graduate students, or research assistants. In short, I was largely on my own.

This situation soon changed. For one thing, the position of director of clinical training brought about greater contact with faculty colleagues and students. Soon I also acquired several graduate students, whose work I supervised. The teaching load was moderate, and the administrative duties, while not devoid of frustrations, were stimulating. Psychotherapy research continued to fascinate me, and although I wished to stay in that area, I wasn't clear what projects to tackle next.

In 1966, the Third Conference on Research in Psychotherapy was held in Chicago; as the organizer of the second conference I was, of course, invited. I have no particular memory of this conference, perhaps because it failed to break much new ground. In the following years it became clear that the National Institute of Mental Health was no longer interested in supporting research conferences. This decision provided the stimulus for the founding of the Society for Psychotherapy Research (SPR), which has become the foremost international forum for researchers in this area. In the 20 years of its existence, SPR has grown and prospered. It now has more than 1,000 members, includes a European branch, and continues to hold annual meetings, which researchers attend at their own expense (in contrast to the three invitational conferences sponsored by NIMH).

An early organizational meeting of the society was held in Highland Park, Illinois, a suburb of Chicago. Fewer than 20 people attended. Ken Howard, David Orlinsky, Sol Garfield, Allen Bergin, and I were among the prime movers. I have never missed an annual meeting. In 1971 to 1972 I served as president of SPR, and in 1986 I received SPR's Distinguished Career Contribution Award, a recognition I value more than any other.

Another development that had a decisive influence on my career occurred in 1968. Joseph Matarazzo, one of the planners of the Chicago research conference, took the initiative, together with a small group of prominent researchers, in charting the future of psychotherapy research. He was also able to enlist the interest and support of the National Institute of Mental Health, and notably that of A. Hussain Tuma. The immediate plan was to conduct a thorough review of research accomplishments to date, then to explore the frontiers, and ultimately, if it appeared promising, to make recommendations for coordinated or collaborative studies that might significantly advance the state of knowledge.

It was decided to appoint two knowledgeable and committed researchers to spearhead this venture. The choice fell on Allen E. Bergin, then a professor at Teachers College of Columbia University (a client-centered and behavioral researcher) and me (representing the psychodynamic orientation). We did not know each other but, as Joe later told the story, he reasoned that since he got along well with each of us individually, the two of us would also hit it off. This was a serendipitous judgment, because Allen and I not only collaborated effectively but became good friends and have remained so over the years.

Having applied for and received a research grant from NIMH, our first task was to conduct a careful review of the literature, a job that was accomplished with a minimum of delay. Our sponsors, and a group of colleagues who had been asked to comment on our work, seemed pleased. In 1969, two issues of the *International Journal of Psychiatry* were devoted to the review and commentaries. We were now ready for the next phase, which consisted of intensive interviews with some 35 researchers, therapists, theoreticians, methodologists—in short, a sample of prominent people who might help to assess the current status of psychotherapy research and assist in peering into the future. How might the field best be advanced? Did collaborative studies seem promising? What kinds of research might be most fruitful? Was it possible, in Joe Matarazzo's memorable phrase, to "kick the *Zeitgeist*?"

Allen Bergin and I traveled a fair amount, interviewed experts jointly and at times separately, wrote up our interviews, had lengthy discussions, and exchanged memoranda, letters, and drafts. The yield of our work was eventually published as *Changing Frontiers in the Science of Psychotherapy* (Bergin & Strupp, 1972). We outlined a number of promising studies, but reached the conclusion that large-scale collaborative studies did not seem feasible at the time. Only a few years later the National Institute of Mental Health, under the directorship of Gerald Klerman, initiated a large-scale collaborative study on the treatment of depression, which still stands as perhaps the largest and most ambitious study of its kind.

Toward the end of our collaborative efforts, Allen Bergin decided that he did not wish to pursue any of the studies we had sketched, and our formal collaboration came to an end. For myself, I did want to pursue one of the projects that had intrigued me. I wanted to shed further light on a central and controversial issue, namely the relative effects on outcome of so-called "specific" (technique) and "nonspecific" (interpersonal relationship) factors. Was it possible to sort out empirically whether and to what extent technical factors contributed to therapeutic outcomes, as opposed to the "common factors" operating in any good human relationship? Thus the foundation was laid for what eventually became the Vanderbilt I study. Before being formally initiated, it was preceded by pilot work and refinements in the design. Martin T. Orne, a highly respected and sophisticated researcher and methodologist, was most helpful in advising me on the grant application, which was approved in 1976.

By this time I had completed a project on role induction of psychotherapy (Strupp & Bloxom, 1973); had made a foray into the area of negative effects in psychotherapy (Strupp, Hadley, & Gomes-Schwartz, 1977); had made a brief excursion into psychophysiology, with the able assistance of three graduate students, William Ray, Robert Levenson, and Steven Manuck; had acquired outstanding research assistants and collaborators, first Anne Bloxom, who was followed by Suzanne Hadley and Stephanie O'Malley; and had become the mentor of a number of exceptionally fine graduate students who were vitally interested in psychotherapy research. Prominent members of this group were Grady Blackwood, Dianna Hartley, and Beverly Gomes-Schwartz, who were followed by equally able ones, as well as by Fellows who entered my postdoctoral research training program, which began around 1980. Thus a productive research group gradually came into being. I have always been extremely proud of these young colleagues and their contributions; I have also derived much satisfaction from the reputation I gained as a trainer of psychotherapy researchers and from my ability to assist them in furthering their careers. The Vanderbilt research team now numbers 10 or 12 people, whose individual projects and team efforts are the backbone of our research.

The Vanderbilt I Study

Using a control-group design, my collaborators and I sought to explore the hypothesis that, with a reasonably specific patient population (in this case, male college students suffering from moderately severe anxiety, depression, and social withdrawal), the technical expertise of professional therapists would yield superior therapeutic results when compared to the activities of untrained (in psychotherapy) college professors. We reasoned that professional therapists and carefully selected college professors would provide comparable therapeutic "climates" (analogous to Rogers's "facilitative conditions"); therefore, systematic differences in outcome favoring professional therapists would constitute evidence for the unique importance of technical factors. The therapy was time-limited (up to 25 hours), and techniques were allowed to vary freely. The professional therapists, who had no special expertise in time-limited therapy, were either psychoanalytic or client-centered/humanistic in their theoretical orientation.

The major results of the study are well-known: we replicated the common finding that some form of psychotherapy is better than no treatment, but it seemed to make little difference who administered it. In retrospect, and in the light of more recent advances in research, neither the conceptualization nor the experimental design was felicitous. Had we stopped with the traditional group comparisons which, on the basis of subsequent reanalyses of the data, were judged particularly inadequate, we would have learned very little. However, in contrast to most studies previously undertaken, we had made careful assessments of patients at intake, termination, and follow-up; we had collected assessments from multiple perspectives—patient, therapist, and evaluating clinician (Strupp & Hadley, 1977); and, most important, we had complete sound recordings of every therapy hour and videotapes of selected ones.

With this auspicious constellation of factors, we carried out a sizable number of studies that explored in detail and depth the vagaries and vicissitudes of the patient-therapist interaction in individual cases. Particularly fruitful were comparisons between high and low changers treated by the same therapist. To aid these explorations, we developed several new methodological tools, notably the Vanderbilt Psychotherapy Process Scale (VPPS) and the Vanderbilt Negative Indicators Scale (VNIS), which were used in assessing salient aspects of the therapist's and the patient's behavior as well as their interaction. By deliberately weaving between the quantitative measures and the clinical data, we sought to advance our understanding of both. Now, to the highlights:

1. Neither professional therapists nor college professors were notably effective in treating patients with more pervasive personality problems (whose suitability for time-limited therapy emerged as questionable in our retrospective assessments). On the other hand, professional therapists were most effective with patients showing the following characteristics: high motivation for psychotherapy; ability to form a good therapeutic relationship (working alliance) early in treatment; and relative absence of long-standing maladaptive patterns of relating. The latter were defined by such qualities as pronounced hostility, pervasive mistrust, negativism, inflexibility, and antisocial or asocial tendencies.

The foregoing is not meant to imply that professional therapists were most effective with the least disturbed patients. Rather, these therapists were particularly effective with patients whose personality resources and capacity for collaboration allowed them to take maximal advantage of the kind of relationship and traditional techniques proffered by the therapists. These findings were in general agreement with the literature (Luborsky, Chandler, Auerbach, Cohen, & Bachrach, 1971; Kernberg, Bernstein, Coyne, Appelbaum, Horwitz, & Voth, 1972).

2. The quality of the therapeutic relationship, established early in the interaction, proved to be an important predictor of outcome in this time-limited context. In particular, therapy tended to be successful if by the third session the patient felt accepted, understood, and liked by his or her therapist (Waterhouse & Strupp, 1984). Conversely, premature termination or failure tended to result if these conditions were not met early in treatment. In addition, we obtained preliminary evidence that reasonably accurate predictions of process and outcome can be made from initial interviews, specifically in terms of judgments relating to the patient's motivation for therapy (Keithly, Samples, & Strupp, 1980) and quality of interpersonal relationships (Moras & Strupp, 1982). Stated differently, we found no

evidence that an initially negative or highly ambivalent patient-therapist relationship was significantly modified in the course of therapy under study. Furthermore, the patient's perceptions of the therapeutic relationship were found to remain fairly stable thoughout therapy and to the follow-up period.

3. The quality of the therapeutic relationship appeared to depend heavily on the patient's ability to relate comfortably and productively to the therapist in the context of a traditional therapeutic framework. This capacity, in turn, seemed to be a function of the patient's personality resources and suitability for time-limited therapy (point 1). In short, there was compelling evidence that the quality of the patient-therapist relationship was significantly, although not entirely, determined by patient variables.

4. Professional therapists gave little evidence of adapting their therapeutic approach or techniques to the specific characteristics and needs of individual patients. Instead, the kind of relationship they offered and the techniques they employed were relatively invariant. Similarly, therapists did not tailor their techniques in specific ways to the resolution of "target symptoms," and they did not seem to formulate specific therapeutic goals of their own that were then systematically pursued in therapy.

5. Professional psychotherapists, in general, had little success in confronting or resolving the marked negative reactions characteristic of the more difficult patients. Instead, they tended to react negatively and countertherapeutically to a patient's hostility, mistrust, inflexibility, and pervasive resistances, thereby perhaps reinforcing the patient's poor self-image and related difficulties. The result of such interactions tended to be (a) negative attitudes on the part of the patient toward the therapist and therapy; (b) premature termination; and/or (c) a poor therapeutic outcome (that is, no change or negative change).

Although not intended to examine whether lay therapists might be as effective as professional therapists, the study has frequently been cited as "proof" of the null hypothesis, namely that college professors can be as effective as professional therapists. In the charged political climate surrounding psychotherapy in the 1970s and 1980s, we were accused by the critics of psychotherapy of disbelieving our own findings. The critics, for their part, also ignored the special circumstances of the study—relatively well-functioning patients; careful selection of lay therapists on the basis of their kindliness, understanding, and warmth; and the surveillance of the college professors by the project's professional staff, which stood ready to intervene in an emergency. It is also possible that there was a particular affinity between college professors as therapists and college students as patients. Their common interests tended to provide topics for discussion that otherwise might have been absent. At best, one can conclude that, *under special circumstances,* college professors can be effective therapists, which is different from the inference that professional training is unnecessary or expendable.

Interlude: My Relationship with Clinical Psychology

Having been involved, as part of my professional career, in training clinical psychologists as scientist-practitioners, I became increasingly disquieted, in the late

1960s and early 1970s, by developments that I identified as an "erosion of excellence" (Strupp, 1975). I perceived an influx of anti-intellectualism, antiscientism, and irrationalism that was also prevalent in other sectors of our society. In various guises, camouflaged and intertwined with social, professional, and political issues (notably the war in Vietnam and the student unrest), this trend became salient in various phases of academic and professional training, with what I saw as potentially disastrous results.

As president of the APA Division of Clinical Psychology (1974 to 1975), I wrote several editorials and devoted my presidential address (Strupp, 1976) to these problems. I concluded the presidential address as follows:

It is undeniably true that as soon as reason and rationality are brought to bear on the immediacy of human experience, one deprives it of something valuable and at times of its beauty. Thus, one may interfere with a fuller understanding of the other person. In studying and understanding a process in which one participates, one becomes an observer who stands apart. The pleasure (and also the pain) of participation is intrinsically different from that of observation. A certain unbridgeable loneliness is inherent in the observer role, the intellectual pleasures that derive from conceptualizing, formulating, reflecting, and organizing one's observations are on a different plane from those that derive from abandoning oneself to the here and now. This is the ancient difference between the Apollonian and Dionysian ways of life, the schism between reason and emotion, between mind and body that characterizes the soul of Western man.

It is the alienation in modern society that the irrationalists in clinical psychology attempt to heal. In essence, however, their proposed solution counsels the rejection of reason, which they have previously identified as the spoiler of pleasure, joy, and human relatedness. The solution is as one-sided and destructive as the rationalist position against which they inveigh. One of the unique beauties of being a psychotherapist in the twentieth century is the opportunity for oscillation between observation and participation, between taking part and standing back, between feeling and thinking, between (controlled) abandonment and study. It is this process of oscillation, the unique human ability to resonate, identify, and therapeutically respond to the unconscious themes in the patient's experience, that the irrationalists ignore, deny, and reject. As one devotee of sensitivity training told Kurt Back (1972), when he expressed the investigator's concern with assessment technique: "Do not try to prove things; give yourself a chance to live the experience" (p. 15). The message is clear: Do not try to understand why a psychotherapeutic technique works under particular circumstances, but not under others; live the experience! The message also mirrors the profound contemporary disillusionment with science by government and the public.

In clinical psychology this position is expressed by the growing criticism of "traditionalism" in doctoral training and blind veneration of the "innovative." In this attack, psychoanalysis becomes the target as much as behavior modification with virtue lying on the side of what contemporaneously passes for humanism. In this charade, anyone who advocates study and scientific inquiry is perceived as an enemy of all that is good, open, spontaneous, authentic, beautiful, and enjoyable in human experience. The innovators see only the restrictions in clinical training, restrictions that are seen as being imposed by the academic establishment and ultimately by society. Thus learning, study, and disciplined inquiry are viewed as straightjackets in which the emotions and the senses become imprisoned. If we could only be honest and open with each other, our social problems would disappear! If we could but introduce joy into our training programs, how much more creative would our students become! "This optimistic view," notes Back, "amounts to a denial that there is a tragedy within man which arises from the fact that, at some point, social needs and human needs are contradictory, the good of the individual and of the group cannot always be identical, and then one of them has to give" (p. 235).

To translate this lesson to the training and practice of psychotherapy, the therapist's personal development, valuable though it is, cannot be the ultimate goal of a profession that proclaims its commitment to the advancement of knowledge and service to humankind. Depression, schizophrenia, neurotic problems, and other difficulties in living that patients bring to the psychotherapist are not only, although they are in part, the outcome of an oppressive environment; nor do they melt in the transient atmosphere of a weekend encounter or a Gestalt workshop. Skills and expertise are typically acquired by a combination of hard work and solid commitment. Work can and should be fun; unfortunately, often it is not. On a mundane level, this is what many of our graduate students rebel against, with powerful support from those committed to "innovation," "celebration," and "self-empowerment." The field, clearly, must reassert the values that have served us well in advancing our understanding of the perennial mysteries of the human soul. Contrary to Carl Rogers, I see less danger in ignoring the "dark" side of human experience—it is receiving very adequate attention in our time—than in substituting meditation for learning and sentimentality for the study of people.

America's involvement in the war in Vietnam and the student unrest have passed, and clinical psychology has undergone important developments, the increasing professionalization of the field being a prime example. Students also realized that in a competitive society one needs a solid foundation of clinical skills. Concomitantly, there occurred a renewed interest in and commitment to professional training and knowledge, if not research. The human potential movement and humanistic psychology declined and, with them, client-centered psychotherapy. The latter was superseded by the "cognitive revolution," as exemplified by various amalgamations of cognitive and behavioral forms of psychotherapy. Somewhat surprisingly, we are witnessing a renewed interest in psychotherapy based on psychodynamic principles, reflected in part by the rise of self-psychology within psychoanalysis and by renewed efforts to develop treatments for affective and personality disorders. The growing professionalization of clinical psychology has also given rise to renewed conflicts with psychiatry, a battle that is likely to lead to further struggles and confrontations. Whatever the outcome, clinical psychology has clearly established itself as one of the major mental health professions. It is gradually achieving parity in a marketplace that is increasingly being controlled by insurance companies and other "third parties."

The Vanderbilt II Study

In the Vanderbilt I project, we demonstrated that the performance of therapists representing a wide range of experience levels varied considerably across patients. Specifically, they often performed poorly with patients who manifested hostile and negative behaviors commonly associated with a variety of personality disorders. Microanalyses of cases by the same therapist with contrasting outcomes uncovered high levels of negative interpersonal processes in the poor-outcome cases that remained unrecognized by the therapists. Examples of such interactions included interpretations made in a blaming manner of "supportive" messages that included elements of implied criticism (Henry, Schacht, & Strupp, 1986; Strupp, 1980a, b, c, d).

After Vanderbilt I, several years of exploratory work led to the design of the Vanderbilt II study. This investigation was designed to focus on the manner in which specialized training might improve the quality of the patient-therapist relationship and the therapeutic process, especially with interpersonally difficult patients. To this end, pilot work included development and field testing of a manual for time-limited-dynamic psychotherapy (TLDP : Strupp & Binder, 1984). In the main study, 16 experienced therapists (8 clinical psychologists and 8 psychiatrists) each treated 5 carefully selected patients (2 before, 1 during, and 2 after 12 months of supervised TLDP training), resulting in a total n of 80. Therapy was limited to a maximum of 25 sessions, and multiple measures of initial patient status, therapy process, adherence to TLDP principles, therapist personality, and outcome were obtained from the various perspectives of patient, therapist, and independent evaluators as appropriate. All therapy sessions were sound recorded, and selected ones were videotaped. The resulting data bank represents one of the largest archives of its kind anywhere. Data analysis has been in progress since 1987, and will continue for a considerable time.

Several major conclusions have emerged so far. They are, of course, subject to refinement and modification as further analyses are undertaken.

1. Therapists can be trained to meet technical adherence criteria in a manual-guided training program in psychodynamic-interpersonal psychotherapy. This result echoes similar findings by others (Luborsky, McLellan, Woody, O'Brien, & Auerbach, 1985; Rounsaville, O'Malley, Foley, & Weissman, 1988).

2. TLDP training as conducted in the Vanderbilt II study can enhance treatment outcomes, but the relationship is far more complex than had previously been assumed, due to a number of complicating factors that need to be addressed in further research. It suffices to note that manual-guided therapy, taught by means of traditional training methods, did not result in the "therapist variable" actually being specified or controlled to the extent hoped for.

3. When novices in a given approach apply technical interventions, they may do so in a forced, mechanical manner that may have deleterious effects on the therapeutic process, even though the process may meet technical adherence criteria. Furthermore, less skillful application of technical interventions may actually increase patients' resistance and inhibitory processes, which may be particularly problematic in time-limited therapy. We must seriously consider the likelihood that more specific and more focused therapeutic approaches may actually create certain types of problematic process. Further analyses of the process are necessary to reach a better understanding of what happens when therapists attempt to apply new techniques and to determine whether improved training can avert the observed problems.

4. The effects of training cannot be adequately understood without concurrent examination of the personal qualities of the therapist-trainees, such as their own interpersonal histories. These qualities appear to interact with technical adherence, yielding complex process and outcome relationships.

5. Our central finding continues to be that experienced therapists often engage in countertherapeutic interpersonal processes with difficult patients, and traditional modes of instruction do not seem to rectify this problem (though they may have other benefits). Put simply, the absence of "poor process" does not ensure good outcomes, but the presence of certain types of poor process is almost always linked to adverse or inconclusive outcomes. This conclusion is consistent with an emerging body of empirical evidence pointing to the fact that even though dynamic approaches remain the principal theoretical approach to individual psychotherapy, interventions are often performed in ways that may not promote optimal therapeutic process.

Overall, these data strongly suggest that the meaningfulness of our research will be enhanced if we can acquire a deeper understanding of exactly what happens in the therapeutic process when therapists attempt to apply particular therapeutic techniques. There is clearly no "straight-line function" between technical training and adherence on one hand and uniformly improved therapeutic process and efficacy on the other. The analyses of group trends indicate that technical adherence, interpersonal process, and patient and therapist characteristics interact in complex ways to shape treatment outcomes. In order to extract the fullest possible meanings directly relevant to treatment efficacy and future training programs, it is now necessary to search for and describe groups of dyads sharing common process and outcome features. Future analyses will address these questions by examining specific technical events and task-situations across contrasting sessions, cases, and groups. Results will then be incorporated into an improved training program for therapists.

The analyses currently in progress or planned for the next several years require the application of complex technical procedures and rating instruments, such as the Vanderbilt Psychotherapy Process Scale (VPPS), the Vanderbilt Negative Indicators Scale (VNIS), and Benjamin's Structural Analysis of Social Behavior (SASB), all of which have proved of great value. Several doctoral dissertations have been completed (Henry, 1986; Flasher, 1986; Talley, 1988), and others are in progress.

Before concluding this section, I wish to underscore again the theme that has emerged from a number of studies, dating back to my earliest research efforts in the 1950s. I am referring to the importance of *negative complementarity*. In simplest terms, psychotherapy patients—particularly "difficult" ones, such as borderline patients or individuals with other personality disorders—have the uncanny ability to evoke in their therapists attitudes and emotional reactions that frequently give rise to therapist communications (interpretations) that are experienced by the patient as critical, pejorative, or demeaning. These interpretations may engender a vicious cycle between patient and therapist. The ubiquitous tendency for patients to engage in interpersonal processes that result in negative responses from the therapist is central to the problem they experience in their interpersonal relations outside of therapy. Indeed, it may be said that this tendency, which is roughly identical with negative transference, is the core of their "illness." Although therapists are enjoined by their training to desist from involvement in the patient's neurotic maneuvers, it is exceedingly difficult—and at times impossible—to do so. A therapist who wishes to form a productive working relationship with a patient—a *sine qua non* for dynamically oriented psychotherapy as well as for psychoanaylsis—can avoid negative complementarity only with great difficulty. Although traditional training has focused on the potentially deleterious effects of the therapist's "countertransference," the problem is far more pervasive and potentially more serious than has generally been recognized.

Having demonstrated the adverse effects of negative complementarity, it will now be necessary to develop improved techniques for alerting therapists-in-training to potential pitfalls and to incorporate these "lessons" into improved training programs. To this end, ways and means must be found to complement traditional training methods, such as reading, lectures, supervision, and personal analysis, with modern instructional technology, such as videodiscs. My colleagues Tom Schacht, Bill Henry, Steven Butler, and Jeffrey Binder and I plan to construct a "developmental psychology of expertise" that will place the training of psychotherapists on a sounder and more efficient footing. One of the distinctive features of this approach is its basis in empirical research, as opposed to armchair theorizing or unguided clinical observation, valuable though the latter may be. In this way we hope to make research findings directly relevant to clinical practice, a prospect we find exciting and challenging. When brought to fruition, this approach may lead to forms of psychotherapeutic training and practice that are superior to anything that exists today.

As we have confirmed time and again, therapeutic success is importantly determined by characteristics and qualities of the patient, such as motivation, severity of the problems brought to therapy, and ability to form a productive working relationship with a therapist. In short-term therapy, in particular, the outcome appears to be determined by the quality of the therapeutic alliance established early in therapy (often by the third session). If the process contains distinctive elements of negative complementarity, the chances for a good outcome are sharply diminished. The patient's difficulties along these lines may be analogous to crippling conditions that may at times be virtually impossible to overcome. Therapists, to be sure, are not magicians; but technical expertise, combined with impressive personality resources, can go a great distance. Whatever the final verdict about therapeutic success or failure may turn out to be, the limits surely have not been reached.

My Credo

Finally, I would like to turn to a discussion of "lived beliefs," insights, and principles that have guided my research and practice of psychotherapy over the past 35 years.

1. I have never wavered in my conviction that truly excellent therapists, a relatively rare breed, share important elements with the artist; that is, the practice of psychotherapy involves a fair amount of creativity and intuition. At the same time, I continue to believe that psychotherapy has the potential to become a scientific discipline. [7] Important aspects of therapeutic enterprise, such as criteria for patient selection, assessments of outcome, and technique, are to some extent susceptible to scientific examination. Furthermore, if the field is to advance, it must rely increasingly on empirical research and resist authoritarian and doctrinaire pronouncements, which have remained rampant. Thus the impressive growth of empirical research in psychotherapy over the last 30 years has been very pleasing to me, and I take pride in having played a part in these developments. In short, I have held fast to the belief that empirical research, while presenting seemingly insuperable difficulties, remains psychotherapy's best hope. The cogency of this belief has gained added support in the 1980s, when psychotherapy's credibility has been challenged as never before.

2. For psychotherapy research to be truly meaningful, it must influence therapeutic praxis. Psychotherapy research at its best should be "action research" in Kurt Lewin's sense (Marrow, 1969). In other words, research should lead to modifications in practice, which should then be subjected to further investigative scrutiny. This goal has been difficult to achieve, and there has remained a great gulf between researchers (who, in earlier years, were often far removed from clinical practice) and clinicians. The latter, if not openly disdainful of research, have been at least indifferent, claiming—with a fair amount of justification—that the bulk of research findings are of little utility to the practicing therapist. The problem of how research can influence clinical practice has engaged my interest for many years (Strupp, 1960b), and my investigations since the early 1970s have led to the development of a specialized training program for therapists in the Vanderbilt II study. On the whole, however, therapists are still learning a great deal more from the clinical experience of their preceptors, and from clinical writings in general, than from the research literature. This may remain true for many years to come.

---

[7] Like great painters and composers, psychotherapists—it seems to me—are not born but made. To be sure, native talent is a prerequisite in all instances (I am sure that the struggle with and mastery of personal problems in living heighten many therapists' sensitivity and abiding interest in therapeutic work), but study, prolonged training, and careful supervision are essential. They provide the skills and the "specific factors" that are woven into the therapist's stance and that guide his or her communications at every stage of therapy. I discovered early in my research that the skilled therapist's communications tend to be sparing, concise, empathic, and "alive." Because the therapist's skills—like the artist's—are subtle, they are difficult to document and even more difficult to dissect. Indeed, I have become increasingly convinced that attempts to separate "specific" (technique) from "nonspecific" (interpersonal) factors are doomed to failure, for the reasons just mentioned (Butler & Strupp, 1986).

This is no argument against research, which, in my opinion, has influenced the *zeitgeist* of therapeutic practice in many ways—for example, by fostering a generally critical attitude; by insisting that claims for the effectiveness of particular techniques be subjected to scientific scrutiny; by curtailing the flights of theoretical fancy to which the field has been prone from its inception; by searching for common therapeutic principles in all approaches; by studying the relationships between theory and practice; and by building bridges between psychotherapy and other relevant scientific disciplines, such as cybernetics, systems theory, cognitive psychology, social psychology, and others. The cogency of these observations is dramatically illustrated when one looks at certain therapeutic schools (sects?) that over the years have practiced in "splendid isolation."

3. Almost at the beginning of my career, I became strongly impressed by the idea that psychotherapy is not a medical treatment and that medical analogies are both erroneous and detrimental to scientific progress. In part, I took my cues from Freud, who characterized psychoanalysis relatively early as a form of "after-education" (Freud, 1917, p.449), thus laying the groundwork for viewing psychotherapy as a learning process. Toward the end of his life, he made the point more forcefully by stating that psychoanalysis is part of psychology and is essentially unrelated to medical practice. In my time, Franz Alexander (1958) pursued the notion of psychotherapy as a form of learning, together with Dollard and Miller (1950), who attempted to translate psychoanalytic terms into learning theory. For many years, these thrusts failed to gather momentum. However, a change is now occurring as part of a trend to search for common factors in all forms of psychotherapy, as well as part of the movement toward "rapprochement" (Goldfried, 1982). Far from being simply a semantic nicety, the question of whether to regard psychotherapy as medical treatment or as a learning process has far-reaching implications. The most important of these implications are:

a. If therapy is primarily regarded as treatment in the medical sense, one tends to focus on the study of techniques and to ask what kind of treatment might be best for what kind of patient. One is also led to identify technical operations as the "specific" factors in psychotherapy, as opposed to so-called "nonspecific" or interpersonal factors that are inherent in any "good" human relationship (see the earlier discussion of the Vanderbilt I study). I have since adopted the position that the controversy surrounding specific and nonspecific factors in psychotherapy has been a pseudo issue par excellence, in the sense that it is impossible, by means of our prevalent investigative models, to assign "portions of the variance" to one set of factors or another. This is true particularly if outcomes of therapy conducted over relatively short periods of time become the decisive criteria.

b. The next implication is closely related to the preceding one. The conception of psychotherapy as "treatment" leads to a one-directional as opposed to a dyadic or systems view. According to the former, psychotherapy is "administered" by an impersonal technician to a passive patient, who responds to the treatment as one would a drug. The techniques of psychotherapy thus become analogous to active pharmacological ingredients, whereas nonspecific aspects are akin to "placebo effects." The opposing view emphasizes the transactions between patient and therapist throughout therapy and regards the participants as engaged in a dynamic process to which cybernetic feedback principles apply at every stage.

The former view, in my judgment, perpetuates an obsolescent conceptualization that will predictably lead researchers into a blind alley. Among the flagrant errors of this position is that it views therapists as interchangeable units, thus falling prey to one of the "uniformity myths" in psychotherapy, identified years ago by Kiesler (1966). The second position, on the other hand, is in keeping with a slowly emerging trend in the behavioral sciences that highlights interpersonal and systems notions (Anchin & Kiesler, 1982). Above all, this approach is guided by the credo that in order to understand the basic problem in psychotherapy research—how personality and behavior change is achieved—one must study the therapeutic process; that is, the transactions between two human beings who send verbal and nonverbal messages to each other and who react to each other's communications in particular ways. Thus the contributions of the therapist become as crucial as those of the patient. By the same token, such traditional concepts as transference and countertransference (which originated in unidirectional thinking) must be redefined and understood in systems terms. This means, *inter alia,* that the relationship between patient and therapist is always "real" (as well as transferential), and that there is always a subtle mixture of "transference" and "countertransference" phenomena. This complicates the task of the researcher, particularly since in our standard statistical models we continue to cherish (unidirectional) "main effects." Nonetheless, I am convinced that the future lies with the dynamic-interactional model.[8]

The rudiments for the preceding views can be found in my early research (Strupp, 1958c). It will be recalled that I studied therapists' responses to a film of an initial psychiatric interview. In this study, the therapists were asked to assume that they were interviewing the filmed patient, who was rather hostile, angry, negativistic, and demanding. To my surprise, viewers very rapidly formed strong, sometimes passionate attitudes toward the patient, which appeared to be out of keeping with the facts that there was no "real" contact between viewer and patient and that the experimental

---

[8] As a result of powerful political trends, the "treatment model" has gained new currency in recent years. Among these trends are vigorous attempts at the "remedicalization" of psychotherapy and the government's insistence on hard research evidence concerning psychotherapy's safety and efficacy as a precondition for recognizing it as a health care technology. Accordingly, stress has been placed on clinical trials research as a means for answering these questions. For the reasons just stated, I consider these regressive steps, because they will predictably deter meaningful research progress. I also doubt that strong main effects of particular treatment modalities can be demonstrated, precisely because dyadic relationship variables create "noise" in the statistical analyses, thereby weakening possible conclusions about the effects of treatment. Finally, as I have argued elsewhere (Strupp, 1986), the basic issues relating to psychotherapy's credibility are only in part scientific. Thus even if we had many more refined studies than currently exist, the legislators' and policy makers' reservations about psychotherapy's value would not be diminished. The reason I believe this to be the case is that the fundamental issues are less scientific than they are ideological. Thus, in the current climate of opinion, it is an understandable ploy to send psychotherapists and researchers on long-term expeditions in search of "scientific evidence." This is not to argue against more and better research, but to highlight society's pervasive ambivalence toward psychotherapy.

situation, being contrived, had no "action consequences" for the viewer. Specifically, I found that in numerous instances, respondents reacted with counteranger to the patient's expressions of affect, and, perhaps more important, that these reactions were clearly reflected in their diagnostic and prognostic judgments. I wondered what might have happened if the patient had entered therapy with one of the respondents who effectively rejected him after having observed his interview behavior for only a few minutes. I extrapolated that a therapist's negative reactions might fuel the patient's anger, thus leading to greater anger on the therapist's part and to an eventual therapeutic impasse or a prolonged, hostile, and dependent relationship. Conversely, a benign cycle might be created if the therapist were able to view the patient's behavior as an expression of the "illness" for which he desired professional help.

Interestingly, therapists who had undergone personal therapy appeared to be less prone to negative reactions, or at least they gave them less direct expression. Personal analysis, I concluded, seemed to produce a certain distance between the therapists' immediate emotional reactions and their immediate expression, in terms both of responses to the interview and of the viewers' clinical practice, but, as far as I can tell, it has had little impact. I did not vigorously pursue the problem either, until, in a series of studies (Strupp, 1980a, 1980b, 1980c, 1980d), I adduced more convincing evidence of the phenomenon through analyses of the therapeutic process in actual cases. So did my student Bill Henry (1986), in his doctoral dissertation (see also the Vanderbilt II project discussed earlier).

4. Having been an avid student of Freud's writings and the psychoanalytic literature, I early formed the conviction that transference was one of Freud's most revolutionary and creative discoveries. Unfortunately, it remained shrouded in his instinct theory and other formulations that in part continue to obscure the brilliance of his insights. Not only did Freud discover the universal human tendency to "transfer" unresolved interpersonal difficulties from the past to the present, where they tend to be enacted with significant others, he also came to the highly original conclusion that "transference" (I use quotation marks to highlight the older practice of viewing the process in static or reified terms) was an integral part of the patient's "illness." Indeed, it *was* his or her illness; hence the term "transference neurosis." As if all of this were not enough, Freud was able to forge a unique therapeutic instrument that, under favorable circumstances, permitted modification and amelioration of these transference tendencies.

The role Freud created for the therapist had the following essential ingredients:

a. The therapist adopts, as consistently and as steadfastly as humanly possible, the role of a mature adult (which, one hopes, is largely veridical!), thus serving as a model for emulation and identification ("mentor and guide").

b. The therapist assumes an asocial role—that is, he or she refrains from playing the roles the patient unwittingly assigns to the professional helper.

c. The therapist seeks to understand the meanings of the transference tendencies as they are being enacted with the therapist and significant others in the patient's life.

d. The therapist shares this understanding with the patient at appropriate times and in appropriate terms.

These operations often have the effect of helping the patient to master traumas and conflicts carried forward from the past and to modify his or her behavior with significant others. Finally, the therapist's operations are informed by Freud's powerful insights into the role played by primitive fantasies, distorted beliefs, sexual and aggressive impulses, and the universal experience of having been a child who views the world from the perspective of childhood.

While these formulations are thrice familiar (which does not detract from their great significance), their implications for research have yet to be adequately realized. What I mean is this: transference in a strict sense refers to the transactions between patient and therapist in the here and now, and, more specifically, to the manner in which past wishes, fantasies, beliefs, and so forth "come alive" and obtrude upon the adult-adult relationship that ostensibly governs the therapeutic relationship. Accordingly, transference refers to an exquisitely empirical set of phenomena that can be studied objectively.[9]

For example, one might examine the therapeutic contexts in which certain interventions are conducive to the modification of transference tendencies, or, conversely, when interventions fail to achieve the desired objective, the extent to which therapeutic learning bears fruit in the patient's "real life," and a host of related questions. Of equally great importance would be studies directed at the therapist's reactions and responses to transference reenactments (I recommend that we abandon altogether the antiquated term "countertransference"). In short, Freud laid the groundwork for studying and putting to therapeutic use the dynamic interactions between patient and therapist. He went a considerable distance in this endeavor, but clearly he was a child of his time. Thus it remained for later generations to pursue and expand his rich legacy. This task is being carried forward by a cadre of clinicians, researchers, and thinkers who have recast, refined, and built upon Freud's seminal ideas.

Among the unique features of the transference model, whose importance remains insufficiently appreciated, is its firm commitment to the goal of maturity, autonomy, and individuation. Not only does the model embody these values as a philosophy of psychotherapy, it also represents an instrumentality for realizing—or at least approximating—them. Stated differently, the transference model offers a pragmatic solution to a troublesome paradox: since a fundamental but unstated goal of every patient who enters psychotherapy is to seek gratification of his or her wishes for dependency, how can a human relationship that overtly or covertly provides such gratification be used to wean the person who craves it?

Whether recognized or not, I take it for granted that any contact, and particularly any prolonged contact, between a help-seeker and a professional helper allows the former to live out deep-seated wishes for love, support, acceptance, and succor that have their origins in early childhood. Thus every therapeutic experience represents in

---

[9] Whenever I have made this point to nonpsychoanalytic therapists (especially behavior therapists), they express surprise, because their background has apparently taught them to lump transference with metapsychological concepts, such as death instinct, that are far removed from observational data.

part a nurturing experience that in certain respects makes up for early deficits and traumas. With intensive and prolonged patient-therapist contact, the danger of perpetuating the patient's dependency is heightened. (Here is a major reason why termination is such a crucially important aspect of therapy.) Analytic psychotherapy deals with this problem by subjecting the transactions between patient and therapist— including, most importantly, the nature of the relationship itself—to careful scrutiny. In other forms of psychotherapy, the patient-therapist relationship generally does not receive the same degree of careful scrutiny. This is not to attribute unique effectiveness to the analytic appraoch, but to highlight the fact that, unlike any other approach, it seeks to help the patient overcome his or her childhood wishes and needs, instead of capitalizing on the pervasive human tendency to search for magical helpers.

I have always felt that the bulk of studies devoted to therapy outcomes have paid insufficient attention to increments in patients' autonomy, independence, and personal maturity. A greater sense of mastery, which is a regular feature of good therapy outcomes (Strupp, Fox, & Lessler, 1969), is probably a concomitant of these changes, which are admittedly quite elusive. Nonetheless, to me they are among the most valuable gains a person can derive from psychotherapy. Stated differently, I believe that the kinds of problems for which psychotherapy has its greatest potential are those that can be seen as deriving from personal immaturities corresponding to developmental arrests. In general terms, psychotherapy has a much better chance of alleviating symptoms and character traits that manifest themselves as inhibitions and constrictions in personality functioning than it does of modifying those that are usually characterized as (antisocial) "acting out." In other words, psychotherapy is much better suited to problems involving overcontrol than to those involving under-control. Yet another way of putting the matter is to state that, other things being equal, it is easier to mitigate an overly severe superego than to reconstruct or strengthen a deficient one.

5. In keeping with the foregoing, I remain convinced, on the basis of both cumulative research evidence and my clinical experience, that under appropriate circumstances psychotherapy has a great deal to offer. Such circumstances prevail when the "right" patient meets the "right" therapist (Paul Meehl once estimated the probability of this occurrence as .04).

Let me be more specific: for psychotherapy (notably those forms based on psycho-analytic principles) to have a reasonable chance of success, we need patients who meet fairly stringent criteria that are often spoken of as "ego strength" or "ego resources." These include such variables as the ability to stand back and critically examine one's feelings, cognitions, fantasies, and actions (that is, a certain ability to be introspective); willingness and commitment to work collaboratively with a professional person over a more or less extended period of time (which means, in part, tolerating inconveniences and frustrations, making some financial sacrifice, and facing troublesome and conflictual patterns of thinking, feeling, and acting); evidence of reasonable maturity, which includes demonstrated ability to assume adult responsibilities, (such as holding a job, maintaining enduring and reasonably stable adult relationships, and showing ability to persist in achieving personal and vocational goals); and reasonable impulse control (such as the absence of pronounced antisocial or self-destructive "acting out"). In short, the person must be sufficiently uncomfortable (anxious, depressed, and so on) to desire change strongly (be "motivated for therapy"), and must also possess a set of qualities that constitute a reasonably solid foundation on which therapy can build. When these preconditions are not met or are only partially met, which is typically the case, psychotherapy faces an uphill battle.

The general public has shown a marked reluctance to accept these limitations, with the result that psychotherapists are often accused of selecting individuals who seemingly need therapy the least while rejecting truly incapacitated persons, such as those suffering from psychoses or chronic personality disorders. There is a certain amount of truth to this allegation, which brings both therapists and the public face to face with psychotherapy's unquestioned limitations. The situation, however, is not intrinsically different from comparable ones regularly encountered in medicine or education. For example, a particular medical treatment may be highly effective with a patient who is young, resilient, and cooperative, whereas it may be much less effective or even ineffective with a patient who is elderly or suffering from complicating conditions; if the condition has done irreversible damage to tissue and bones; or if the patient fails to comply with the prescribed regimen. In education, students are most likely to succeed if they are intelligent, highly motivated, and have a history of educational achievements. No one blames the teacher for failing to teach calculus to students whose IQ is 90. In psychotherapy alone, it seems, therapists are expected to shoulder the blame for limits set by nature. In part, this appears to be the result of people's fantasies of omnipotence (whose recurrent counterpart is the therapists' alleged impotence), as well as a fair amount of "overselling"—a charge to which the mental health professions must indeed plead guilty. An important goal for future research is to spell out with increased precision what psychotherapy can do well, what it might be able to do with difficulty, and what it cannot do at all.

A final comment on patients' qualifications: psychotherapy, as I view it, is basically a human relationship that is intended to correct the adverse consequences of earlier relationships. Therefore, in order for therapy to be effective, a patient must have a history of sufficiently rewarding and satisfying relationships in the past. The memories of such experiences and their aftermath, which are reflected in the qualifications previously mentioned (that is, in successful socialization), allow the patient to become engaged in and to profit from another human relationship (in this case, with the therapist). Where there have been very severe problems with earlier interpersonal experiences (as occur, for example, in the cases of psychopaths and other individuals suffering from impulse disorders), the obstacles to the formation of a productive and satisfying therapeutic alliance are formidable, if not insuperable.

What is a "right" therapist? The therapist, above all, must supply a good model for identification. He or she must be a reasonably mature person, one who is capable of considerable empathy (since understanding another person's inner world is a prime task), and one who is willing to make a genuine commitment to a particular patient's growth and development. The therapist must care and communicate this caring through his or her attitudes and actions. Following Freud, one may assume (perhaps overoptimistically) that the therapist is a person of considerable integrity who takes his or her personal professional responsibilities seriously. Other personal qualities that I consider important include respect for the autonomy of another person; marked patience (the counterpart of "pushing" the patient); the ability to accept human limitations (the opposite of perfectionism and omnipotence); and a sense of humor. The quality of humor seems particularly important when the going gets rough, as it often does. Last but not least, a certain detachment, which I would like to call unflappability, also impresses me as an important therapist quality.

As mentioned previously, I believe that, within limits, therapists are made, not born. Accordingly, I would like to see therapists who think, question, examine the empirical evidence, and are self-critical. More specifically, the therapist should have extensive experience in playing the asocial role (called by Sullivan "participant observation"). That is, the therapist must participate as a partial co-actor in the plots, scripts, or scenarios that the patient unwittingly enacts; yet he or she must be capable of desisting from enmeshment. Instead, the therapist must identify the nature of these scenarios, call them to the patient's attention, and raise questions about their adaptive value and general utility. This must be done with skill, tact, respect, and concern for the patient's vulnerability and deficient self-esteem. As part of this activity, the therapist must draw on significant clinical experience, including both personal therapy and supervised work.

In 1958 (Strupp, 1958c), I characterized the therapist's contribution in terms that I still consider cogent:

> The therapist's contribution to the treatment process (may be conceived as) a dual one: it is personal and technical. His personal attributes (maturity, warmth, acceptance, etc.) enable him to create the kind of interpersonal relationship in which constructive personality change can take place; his knowledge of psychodynamic principles and techniques permits him, in and through his relationship, to initiate the kinds of emotional unlearning and learning experiences that are considered necessary to the alleviation or resolution of neurotic conflicts. The latter would be impossible without the former; the former, by itself, would never be sufficient (p. 66).

6. The last point in this sketchy list relates to the belief that there are many ways in which one person can have a beneficial influence on another. (There are equally many ways for the influence to be detrimental; see Strupp, Hadley, & Gomes-Schwartz, 1977.) Just as many neurotic symptoms and personality trends are not produced by a single experience or trauma, amelioration—I am reluctant to speak of "cure," which I believe occurs only in the rarest instances—cannot be traced to a single intervention or set of interventions. The mental life of human beings is far too complex for that! To me, this position has the following implications:

a. It is naive to assume that there are specific techniques or operations, such as systematic desensitization, interpretations, or cognitive restructuring, that are uniquely effective.

b. It is equally unrealistic to think of the therapeutic influence as being restricted to one or another technique. In other words, the therapeutic influence is made up of multiple facets, it is always produced and importantly defined by the quality of the relationship between the participants, and there appears to be no effective way of separating techniques from relationship factors via research; the two are inseparably intertwined (Butler & Strupp, 1986). Human beings always react cognitively and affectively to the message as well as to the interpersonal context in which it is encoded.

c. Because symptoms and problems in living are generally part of an interpersonal context, it makes sense to assess therapeutic outcomes in terms of changes that occur in that interpersonal context. Thus outcomes are, or should be seen as, multidimensional.

d. Seemingly divergent therapeutic approaches probably share a good many common elements that overshadow (in terms of their measurable effects) whatever singular characteristics may appear to differentiate them. I emphatically do not take this to mean that "anything goes" in psychotherapy, or that a highly trained therapist is interchangeable with any well-meaning person. Even in the face of contradictory evidence (to which I have unwittingly contributed; see Strupp & Hadley, 1979), I firmly believe that when the appropriate refinements in research are made, we shall find that a well-trained and sophisticated therapist is at a marked advantage over a layperson. To be sure, I do not expect this to be demonstrated by crude outcome measurements in short-term psychotherapy.

e. Because any form of psychotherapy is made up of highly complex and interdigitated operations, it seems essentially futile to run "horse races" between two or more broadly differentiable approaches. The outcomes of such comparisons are almost certain to be weak and inconclusive. (The bulk of the available research evidence generally supports this position; see Smith, Glass & Miller, 1980.)

f. Group comparisons of the kind made in the typical psychotherapy outcome study provide only a very limited amount of information. For psychotherapy research to advance, we must invest major energies in the intensive study of individual dyads. For example, careful process studies designed to examine why one therapist works productively with one patient while failing with a seemingly comparable one might prove extremely illuminating (Strupp, 1980a, 1980b, 1980c, 1980d). Concerted efforts must be made to link process with outcome, as exemplified by the Vanderbilt studies.

Needless to say, as in any science, much remains to be learned. However, as I ponder the developments in psychotherapy research over the last 35 years, I think it is fair to say that the field has come along way. Equally important, despite challenges on various fronts—including prominently, sharply diminished governmental research support—the future looks promising. In another 30 years, no doubt with the aid of computer technology, we will know a great deal more about the principles underlying psychological change. To have played a part in this evolution is one of my greatest satisfactions.

References

Alexander, F. (1958). Unexplored areas in psychoanalytic theory and treatment. *Behavioral Science, 3,* 293–316.

Anchin, J. C. & Kiesler, D. J. (Eds.) (1982). *Handbook of interpersonal psychotherapy.* New York: Pergamon Press.

Back, K. (1972). *Beyond words: The story of sensitivity training and the encounter movement.* New York: Russell Sage Foundation.

Bales, R. F. (1950). *Interaction process analysis.* Cambridge, MA: Addison-Wesley.

Bandura, A. (1982). Self-efficacy mechanism in human agency. *American Psychologist, 37,* 122–147.

Bergin, A. E. & Strupp, H. H. (1972). *Changing frontiers in the science of psychotherapy.* Chicago: Aldine-Atherton.

Butler, S. F. & Strupp, H. H. (1986). "Specific" and "nonspecific" factors in psychotherapy: A problematic paradigm for psychotherapy research. *Psychotherapy, 23,* 30–40.

Dollard, J. & Miller, N. (1950). *Personality and psychotherapy: An analysis in terms of learning, thinking, and culture.* New York: McGraw-Hill.

Flasher, L. (1986). *Negative factors in short-term psychotherapy: Focus on therapist-interventions.* Unpublished doctoral thesis, Vanderbilt University.

Fiedler, F. E. (1953). Quantitative studies on the role of therapists' feelings toward their patients. In Mowrer, O. H. (Ed.), *Psychotherapy: Theory and research.* New York: Ronald Press.

Freud, S. (1917). Analytic therapy. In *The standard edition of the complete psychological works of Sigmund Freud,* Vol. 16. Strachey, J. Ed. and Trans. London: Hogarth Press, 1963.

Goldfried, M. R. (Ed.) (1982). *Converging themes in psychotherapy.* New York: Springer.

Henry, W. P. (1986). *Interpersonal process in psychotherapy.* Unpublished doctoral thesis, Vanderbilt University.

Henry, W. P., Schacht, T. E., & Strupp, H. H. (1986). Structural analysis of social behavior: Application to a study of interpersonal process in differential psychotherapeutic outcome. *Journal of Consulting and Clinical Psychology, 54,* 27–31.

Keithly, L. J., Samples, S. J., & Strupp, H. H. (1980). Patient motivation as a predictor of process and outcome in psychotherapy. *Psychotherapy and Psychosomatics, 33,* 87–97.

Kernberg, O. F., Bernstein, E. D., Coyne, L., Appelbaum, A., Horowitz, L., & Voth, H. (1972). Psychotherapy and psychoanalysis: Final report of the Menninger Foundation's psychotherapy research project. *Bulletin of the Menninger Clinic, 36,* 1–276.

Kiesler, D. J. (1966). Some myths of psychotherapy research and the search for a paradigm. *Psychological Bulletin, 65,* 110–136.

Luborsky, L. M., Chandler, A. H., Auerbach, J., Cohen, J., & Bachrach, H. M. (1971). Factors influencing the outcome of psychotherapy: A review of the quantitative research. *Psychological Bulletin, 75,* 145–185.

Luborsky, L. M., McLellan, A. T., Woody, G. E., O'Brien, C. P., & Auerbach, A. (1985). Therapists' success and its determinants. *Archives of General Psychiatry, 42,* 602–611.

Marrow, A. J. (Ed.) (1969). *The practical theorist: The life and work of Kurt Lewin.* New York: Basic Books.

Moras, K. & Strupp, H. H. (1982). Pre-therapy interpersonal relations, a patient's alliance, and outcome in brief therapy. *Archives of General Psychiatry, 39,* 405–409.

Phillips, E. L. & Agnew, J. W. (1953). A study of Rogers' "reflection" hypothesis. *Journal of Clinical Psychology, 9,* 281–284.

Rogers, C. R. (1951). *Client-centered therapy.* Boston: Houghton Mifflin.

Rogers, C. R. & Dymond, R. F. (Eds.) (1954). *Psychotherapy and personality change.* Chicago: University of Chicago Press.

Rounsaville, B. J., O'Malley, S., Foley, S., & Weissman, M. N. (1988). The role of manual-guided training in the conduct and efficacy of interpersonal psychotherapy for depression. *Journal of Consulting and Clinical Psychology, 56,* 681–688.

Rubinstein, E. A. & Parloff, M. B. (1959). *Research in psychotherapy: Proceedings of a conference.* Washington, D.C.: American Psychological Association, April 9–12, 1958.

Smith, M. L., Glass, G. V., & Miller, T. I. (1980). *The benefits of psychotherapy.* Baltimore: Johns Hopkins University Press.

Strupp, H. H. (1955a). An objective comparison of Rogerian psychoanalytic techniques. *Journal of Consulting Psychology, 19,* 1–7.

Strupp, H. H. (1955b). Psychotherapeutic technique, professional affiliation and experience level. *Journal of Consulting Psychology, 19,* 97–102.

Strupp, H. H. (1955c). The effect of the psychotherapist's personal analysis upon his techniques. *Journal of Consulting Psychology, 19,* 197–204.

Strupp, H. H. (1957a). A multidimensional system for analyzing psychotherapeutic techniques. *Psychiatry, 20,* 293–306.

Strupp, H. H. (1957b). A multidimensional comparison of therapist activity in analytic and client-centered therapy. *Journal of Consulting Psychology, 21,* 301–308.

Strupp, H. H. (1957c). A multidimensional analysis of techniques in brief psychotherapy. *Psychiatry, 20,* 387–397.

Strupp, H. H. (1958a). The psychotherapist's contribution to the treatment process: An experimental investigation. *Behavioral Science, 3,* 34–67.

Strupp, H. H. (1958b). The performance of psychiatrists and psychologists in a therapeutic interview. *Journal of Clinical Psychology, 14,* 219–226.

Strupp, H. H. (1958c). The performance of psychoanalytic and client-centered therapists in an initial interview. *Journal of Consulting Psychology, 22,* 265–274.

Strupp, H. H. (1960a). *Psychotherapists in action: Explorations of the therapist's contribution to the treatment process.* New York: Grune & Stratton.

Strupp, H. H. (1960b). Some comments on the future of research in psychotherapy. *Behavioral Science, 5,* 60–71.

Strupp, H. H. (1975). Training the complete clinician. *The Clinical Psychologist, 28(4),* 2–3.

Strupp, H. H. (1976). Clinical psychology, irrationalism, and the erosion of excellence. *American Psychologist, 31,* 561–571.

Strupp, H. H. (1980a). Success and failure in time-limited psychotherapy: A systematic comparison of two cases (Comparison 1). *Archives of General Psychiatry, 37,* 595–603.

Strupp, H. H. (1980b). Success and failure in time-limited psychotherapy: A systematic comparison of two cases (Comparison 2). *Archives of General Psychiatry, 37,* 708–716.

Strupp, H. H. (1980c). Success and failure in time-limited psychotherapy: With special reference to the performance of a lay counselor (Comparison 3). *Archives of General Psychiatry, 37,* 831–841.

Strupp, H. H. (1980d). Success and failure in time-limited psychotherapy: Further evidence (Comparison 4). *Archives of General Psychiatry, 37,* 947–954.

Strupp, H. H. (1986). The nonspecific hypothesis of therapeutic effectiveness: A current assessment. *American Journal of Orthopsychiatry, 56,* 513–520.

Strupp, H. H. & Binder J. L. (1984). *Psychotherapy in a new key: A guide to time-limited dynamic psychotherapy.* New York: Basic Books.

Strupp, H. H. & Bloxom, A. L. (1975). Preparing lower-class patients for group psychotherapy: Development and evaluation of a role induction film. *Journal of Consulting and Clinical Psychology, 41,* 373–384.

Strupp, H. H., Fox, R. E., & Lessler, K. (1969). *Patients view their psychotherapy.* Baltimore: Johns Hopkins University Press.

Strupp, H. H. & Hadley, S. W. (1977). A tripartite model of mental health and therapeutic outcomes: With special reference to negative effects in psychotherapy. *American Psychologist, 32,* 187–196.

Strupp, H. H., Hadley, S. W., & Gomes-Schwartz, B. (1977). *Psychotherapy for better or worse: An analysis of the problem of negative effects.* New York: Jason Aronson.

Strupp, H. H. & Hadley, S. W. (1979). Specific versus nonspecific factors in psychotherapy: A controlled study of outcome. *Archives of General Psychiatry, 36,* 1125–1136.

Strupp, H. H. & Luborsky, L. (1962). *Research in psychotherapy,* Vol. 2. Washington, DC: American Psychological Association.

Talley, P. F. (1988). *Matchmaking in psychotherapy: Patient-therapist dimensions and their impact on process and outcome.* Unpublished doctoral thesis, Vanderbilt University.

Waterhouse, G. J. & Strupp, H. H. (1984). The patient-therapist relationship: Research from the psychodynamic perspective. *Clinical Psychology Review, 4,* 77–92.